Indigenous Peoples' Status in the International Legal System

MATTIAS ÅHRÉN

OXFORD
UNIVERSITY PRESS

OXFORD
UNIVERSITY PRESS

Great Clarendon Street, Oxford, OX2 6DP,
United Kingdom

Oxford University Press is a department of the University of Oxford.
It furthers the University's objective of excellence in research, scholarship,
and education by publishing worldwide. Oxford is a registered trade mark of
Oxford University Press in the UK and in certain other countries

First Edition published in 2016

Impression: 3

Published in the United States of America by Oxford University Press
198 Madison Avenue, New York, NY 10016, United States of America

British Library Cataloguing in Publication Data
Data available

Library of Congress Control Number: 2015960807

ISBN 978–0–19–877819–6

Printed and bound by
CPI Group (UK) Ltd, Croydon, CR0 4YY

INDIGENOUS PEOPLES' STATUS IN THE INTERNATIONAL LEGAL SYSTEM

Acknowledgements

The origin of this book is a doctoral dissertation defended at UiT-The Arctic University of Norway, in October 2010 titled 'The Saami Traditional Dress & Beauty Pageants: Indigenous Peoples' Rights of Ownership and Self-Determination over their Cultures'. This book largely maintains the doctoral dissertation's general conclusions as to the content and scope of the most central features of the international human rights system, as it pertains to indigenous peoples. The work does, however, substantially elaborate on these findings, at the same time as it omits the detailed analysis as to what rights indigenous peoples possess over their collective creativity.

The supervisor for the doctoral dissertation was Professor Martin Scheinin. Many of the ideas and arguments in this book have been developed as a result of discussions with and advices given by him, not only in his capacity as supervisor, but also as a mentor, colleague, and friend.

I am also grateful towards the opponents at my dissertation defence, Professor Maglosia Fitzmaurize, and, in particular, Professor S James Anaya. It was Jim who advised me to transform the dissertation into a textbook format. Together with Martin, Jim is the main inspiration behind the lines of argument in this book.

My gratitude also goes to Jacob R Adams, for providing invaluable assistance on how to improve the language in the book, and for suggestions on how to strengthen and clarify some of the arguments presented.

Among others whose thoughts and ideas have inspired me, I would like to particularly mention Lars-Anders Baer, Patricia Borraz, Leif Dunfjeld, Lola Garcia Alix, Svein Ole Granefjell, John B Henriksen, Professor Ole Henrik Magga, Professor Susann Funderud Skogvang, Anders Åhrén, and Ingwar Åhrén.

This book is dedicated to indigenous leaders and representatives around the world. Without their tireless efforts, the law this book analyses and presents would not have emerged. It is also dedicated to the reindeer herders of *Sápmi*, for having established the borders of *Sápmi*, and for having defended them ever since.

Table of Contents

PART II.
INDIGENOUS PEOPLES' LEGAL STATUS AND THE RIGHT TO SELF-DETERMINATION

List of Abbreviations

ACHR	American Convention on Human Rights
ADRDM	American Declaration of the Rights and Duties of Man
AfCHPR	African Charter on Human and Peoples' Right
AfCommHPR	African Commission on Human and Peoples' Rights
AGS	African Group of States
CBD	Convention on Biological Diversity
CCPR	International Covenant on Civil and Political Rights
CERD Committee	Committee on the Elimination of All Forms of Racial Discrimination
CERD Convention	International Convention on the Elimination of All Forms of Racial Discrimination
CESC	Committee on Economic, Social and Cultural Rights
CESCR	International Covenant on Economic, Social and Cultural Rights
Commission HR	Commission on Human Rights
CRC	Convention on the Rights of the Child
CSCE	Conference on Security and Cooperation in Europe
EC	European Community
ECHR	European Convention for the Protection of Human Rights and Fundamental Freedoms
ECJ	European Court of Justice
ECommHR	European Commission on Human Rights
ECOSOC	Economic and Social Council
ECtHR	European Court of Human Rights
EFCPNM	European Framework Convention for the Protection of National Minorities
EMRIP	Expert Mechanism on the Rights of Indigenous Peoples
EU	European Union
FAO	UN Food and Agriculture Organization
HRC	Human Rights Committee
HR Council	Human Rights Council
IACHR	Inter-American Court on Human Rights
IACommHR	Inter-American Commission on Human Rights
ICJ	International Court of Justice
ILA	International Law Association
ILC	International Law Commission
ILO	International Labour Organization
ILO 107	International Labour Organization's Convention No 107 Concerning the Protection and Integration of Indigenous and Other Tribal and Semi-Tribal Populations in Independent Countries
ILO 169	International Labour Organization's Convention No 169 Concerning Indigenous and Tribal Peoples in Independent Countries

Minority Declaration	United Nations Declaration on the Rights of Persons Belonging to National or Ethnic, Religious and Linguistic Minorities
OAS	Organization of American States
OSCE	Organization for Security and Cooperation in Europe
PCIJ	Permanent Court of International Justice
Permanent Forum	United Nations Permanent Forum on Indigenous Issues
Sub-Commission	Sub-Commission on Prevention of Discrimination and Protection of Minorities/Sub-Commission on the Promotion and Protection of Human Rights
UDHR	Universal Declaration on Human Rights
UN	United Nations
UNDRIP	United Nations Declaration on the Rights of Indigenous Peoples
UNESCO	United Nations Economic, Social and Cultural Organization
UNGA	United Nations General Assembly
UNWGM	United Nations Working Group on Minorities
VCLT	Vienna Convention on the Law of Treaties
WGDD	Working Group on the Draft Declaration on the Rights of Indigenous Peoples
WGIP	UN Working Group on Indigenous Populations
WIPO	World Intellectual Property Organization

1
Introduction

1.1 The Premise and the Outline of This Book

This book aspires to outline the nature of indigenous peoples' rights under the contemporary international legal system in a concise and straightforward manner. The underlying premise of the book is that to understand indigenous rights properly, one only needs to know the answer to two questions: What is meant by (i) 'peoples', and (ii) 'equality', under international law? The answer to the first question is important mainly because it explains to what extent indigenous peoples are beneficiaries of the right to self-determination. From a correct understanding of equality follows, inter alia, what property rights indigenous peoples possess over lands and natural resources traditionally used.

The chapters of the book can be divided into three blocks. Following this introductory chapter, the first block consists of Chapters 2–4. This block sets the stage for the subsequent analyses of contemporary international norms relevant to indigenous peoples' rights. It does so by outlining and analyzing some underlying principles and theories that are important in order to properly understand what rights indigenous peoples possess under international law.

Chapter 2 outlines what position classical international law and philosophy took towards indigenous peoples' capacity to hold sovereign (i.e. political) as well as private (i.e. proprietary) rights over territories and natural resources. Many of the keystones that underpinned classical international law still constitute fundamental building blocks in the international legal system today. Yet other norms that formed part of classical international law may no longer be valid law today but may nonetheless continue to exercise influence over state and human behaviour. Consequently, should one be able to properly understand contemporary international law on indigenous peoples' rights, it is important to grasp at least the basic contours of the classical international legal system.

In this context, it is highlighted that for the sake of simplicity the book refers to indigenous populations and groups as 'indigenous peoples' from the very outset, i.e. also when discussing time-periods where no international legal order in any real sense of the term existed. One could argue that this is incorrect in the sense that in international law, the term 'peoples' have legal connotations, so technically speaking, from an international legal point of view, there can be no indigenous (or other) peoples before law to that effect exist. But again, the term is taken throughout so as not to overcomplicate matters.

Chapter 3 describes contemporary political philosophy theories. Historically political thought has undoubtedly impacted on international law, and may still do so today. To the extent such is the case, a basic knowledge of relevant philosophical theories are necessary if one wants to be correctly informed about the content and scope of indigenous peoples' rights.

The final chapter of the first block of the book, Chapter 4, articulates international law on international legal sources. Obviously, knowledge of what are relevant international legal sources, as well as their relative status, is paramount to any analysis of what rights indigenous peoples hold under international law. That is particularly so since many of the sources to which we look for the content and scope of indigenous rights are so called 'soft law' sources. Consequently, the question as to whether 'soft law' is in fact law at all is cardinal for the present purposes. For similar reasons, it is relevant to be informed about the extent to which international treaty provisions have the capacity to evolve and take on new understandings. This might be particularly important since United Nations (UN) treaty body jurisprudence is another category of legal sources of significant relevance to the indigenous rights discourse. Treaty bodies not only interpret the respective treaties they have been established to monitor, they also, through their jurisprudence, have the capacity to progress the understandings of treaty provisions.

Mindful of the conclusions drawn in the first block of the book, blocks two and three proceed to analyze contemporary international norms relevant to indigenous peoples' rights. The second block consists of Chapters 5 and 6. Chapter 5 surveys indigenous peoples' legal status under international law. More precisely, the chapter explains how contemporary international law has come to recognize indigenous peoples as peoples for international legal purposes, whereby they are beneficiaries of rights as such, including the most prominent of peoples' rights, that of self-determination. Subsequently, Chapter 6 examines what is the content and scope of the right to self-determination when applied not to aggregate populations of states, but to sub-segments thereof, such as indigenous peoples.

The third block of the book consists of Chapters 7, 8, and 9. This block turns our attention to the interrelated rights of equality (or non-discrimination) and property. Chapter 7 articulates the conventional understanding of the right to non-discrimination, and then contrasts it with the contemporary understanding of that right. Subsequently, Chapter 8 analyzes how the understanding of the right to equality directly impacts on indigenous communities' right to have property rights acknowledged over territories traditionally used. Finally, Chapter 9 surveys the more precise content and scope of indigenous communities' property rights over lands and natural resources.

A final Chapter 10 summarizes the conclusions of the book.

1.2 Relation to Previous Works

The conclusions in this book are, in addition to being based on primary international legal sources, guided by previous works in the field. James Anaya's

Indigenous Peoples in International Law[1] comprehensively articulates what rights indigenous peoples possess under the contemporary international legal system. Writings by legal scholars such as Alexandra Xanthaki, and, in particular, Martin Scheinin, have also fed into the work.

Certain scholars have been particularly helpful with regard to the conclusions made in particular parts of the book. The first part of the work on the status of indigenous peoples in the classical international legal system draws from (in addition to James Anaya's writings) Antony Anghie's *Imperialism, Sovereignty and the Making of International Law*,[2] among others. The chapters of the book that address indigenous property rights over lands and natural resources have in particular benefitted from Jérémie Gilbert's *Indigenous Peoples' Land Rights under International Law*.[3]

A clear ambition of my book is to explain where indigenous rights fit in the international legal system in general. As to the outline of the basic principles of international law, my work in particular relies on works by scholars such as Ian Brownlie, Antonio Cassese, and James Crawford. Specific attention is given to what relevance norms for international law making have to the indigenous rights discourse. Here, my book draws heavily from Martti Koskenniemi's *From Apology to Utopia*.[4] As indicated, my work also examines what influences classical and more recent schools within political philosophy may have exercised on the indigenous rights discourse, where the writings of Will Kymlicka have been especially helpful.

Other scholars that are frequently referred to, and thus have contributed to this book, include Philip Alston, Alan Boyle, Joshua Castellino, Christine Chinkin, Hurst Hannum, Benedict Kingsbury, David Lea, Nathan Lerner, Timo Makkonen, David Raic, Paul Reuter, Dinah Shelton, Patrick Thornberry, James Tully, Jeremy Waldron, Steven Wheatley, and Iris M Young.

By drawing from acknowledged scholars' works on classical international law, the properties of the international legal system in general, international law-making, political philosophy, and on the contemporary indigenous rights regime, this book presents one coherent theory on the principal rights indigenous peoples possess under international law. This work explains the international legal system—as it pertains to indigenous peoples—in a simple and straightforward manner. It makes it easy for legal scholars, those that practice law, diplomats, students, and others to understand what indigenous peoples' rights are really about, at their core. This is the principal manner in which my book, in my view, compliments previous works within the field.

[1] S James Anaya, *Indigenous Peoples in International Law* (2nd edn., Oxford University Press, 2004).

[2] Antony Anghie, *Imperialism, Sovereignty and the Making of International Law* (Cambridge University Press, 2004).

[3] Jérémie Gilbert, *Indigenous Peoples' Land Rights Under International Law: From Victims to Actors* (Transnational Publishers, 2006).

[4] Martti Koskenniemi, *From Apology to Utopia—The Structure of International Legal Argument* (Cambridge University Press, 2005).

PART I

HISTORICAL BACKGROUND AND UNDERLYING PRINCIPLES AND THEORIES RELEVANT TO THE INDIGENOUS RIGHTS DISCOURSE

2

Classical International Law and Early Philosophy Theory on Peoples' Rights

2.1 Introduction

A basic understanding of the history of the international legal system, as well as of the interplay between law and philosophy at the time, is imperative to properly grasp contemporary international law on indigenous peoples' rights. That is so for two interrelated reasons.

First, any analysis of what rights indigenous peoples possess as collectives today is intrinsically linked to how international law has conventionally understood the concept of 'peoples'. The historical understanding of this concept is important because, as this chapter explains, the contemporary international legal system adopted classical international law's perception of states and peoples. Hence, classical international law assists us in understanding contemporary international law's position on peoples' rights, or, at least, what this position has been until very recently.

Second, the states that took form in Europe following the Peace of Westphalia in 1648 sent vessels to explore other continents. This brought Europe into increased contact with peoples there, including indigenous peoples. To 'legally justify' the taking of indigenous peoples' territories and natural resources, European legal scholars developed certain doctrines, doctrines that have continued to exercise influence over international law for centuries.[1]

That said, the aspiration of this chapter is not to comprehensively outline classical international law's position on peoples' rights. Neither does it aim to provide a full account of the philosophical theories that emerged in tandem with the early international legal system, theories that exercised considerable influence over the

[1] Classical international law's position towards indigenous peoples and their rights, as outlined in this chapter, has been articulated in various ways in previous works such as S James Anaya's, *Indigenous Peoples in International Law* (2nd edn., Oxford University Press, 2004), from which this book draws. This might lead some to question the need for repetition. Still, even if the presentation here is not necessarily entirely novel, it may add certain elements to previous descriptions of the historical background to the contemporary indigenous rights discourse. Moreover, as this chapter further elaborates, a basic knowledge of this historical background is imperative to grasp fully the contours of contemporary indigenous rights. This warrants that certain space is devoted to what position classical international law took on indigenous peoples and their rights also in this work, although some of the explanations might be repetitive.

law. For present purposes, it is sufficient to provide a general outline of the basic features of classical international law, and of the theories that underpinned it.

2.2 The Period Prior to the Peace of Westphalia

Ideas and philosophies that were legal in character, albeit blended with theology, emerged in Europe during the Renaissance era. Theology aspired to establish the content of a divine order of affairs. Simultaneously, other scholars embarked on defining a natural legal order that was perceived to pre-exist human society, and which was intrinsically linked with the rest of God's creation.[2] This school, that professes that there exists a law given by nature—or God—which is independent of any norms created by humans, is commonly referred to as the natural law school.[3] To Renaissance legal scholars such as Francisco de Vitoria (1486–1547), issues pertaining to realms and nations were irrelevant to the question as to what rights people ultimately possess under the law. These rights can, and should, be deduced from nature/God—de Vitoria and other legal scholars of the era maintained—irrespective of the will and power of the realm.[4]

As mentioned, during the Renaissance, European explorers intensified the exploration of other continents, thereby increasingly bringing Europe into contact with overseas populations. Thus, at this point European scholars had both started to develop legal theories and witnessed 'the world increase'. Against this backdrop, it was only natural that these scholars commenced developing theories as to what laws should govern Europe's relationship with populations on other continents. In doing so, the early European legal scholars took the position that indigenous peoples' societal structures constituted distinct polities that possessed political rights under international law.

For instance, de Vitoria—surely the most influential legal scholar of his era[5]—developed a natural law theory that professed that the indigenous peoples of the Americas held autonomous rights handed down to them by God which the European realms were obligated to respect. Based on this basic premise, de Vitoria crafted an elaborate system of rules that aimed to regulate European encounters and relationships with indigenous societies.[6] He held that indigenous peoples'

[2] Alexander Orakhelashvili, *The Interpretation of Acts and Rules in Public International Law* (Oxford University Press, 2008) 61–62; Martti Koskenniemi, *From Apology to Utopia—The Structure of International Legal Argument* (Cambridge University Press, 2005) 95.

[3] Natural law has been defined as rules and principles deducible from nature, reason, or ideas of justice. Natural law is therefore norms given to man by a 'power' above human—sovereign—law-makers. Natural law thus has authority irrespective of the will of earthly law-makers. See Orakhelashvili, *The Interpretation of Acts and Rules* (n 2) 60–1.

[4] Koskenniemi, *From Apology to Utopia* (n 2) 95–101.

[5] Antony Anghie, *Imperialism, Sovereignty and the Making of International Law* (Cambridge University Press, 2004) 13–14; Andrew Fitzmaurice, 'Discovery, Conquest, and Occupation of Territory', in Bardo Fassbender and Anne Peters (eds.), *The Oxford Handbook of the History of International Law* (2012) 2.

[6] Anghie, *Imperialism* (n 5) 30; Koskenniemi, *From Apology to Utopia* (n 2) 100–01; James Crawford, *The Creation of States in International Law* (2nd edn., Clarendon Press, 2006) 263–64.

autonomous rights extended to both public and private affairs. As a consequence, according to de Vitoria, European explorers and sovereigns could only appropriate indigenous lands if they followed procedures prescribed by law. Further, he posited, indigenous peoples' status as distinct legal and political entities should be respected. That said, de Vitoria's theory added that unlike the European realms, indigenous peoples were not full sovereigns. He introduced the concept of 'just war' which a European realm was entitled to wage on an indigenous people that failed to meet certain interests of the realm. Indigenous peoples were for instance obliged to allow European realms free passage into their territories. They also had to share the wealth of their lands. If these criteria were not met, a realm was entitled to wage just war against the indigenous people. It should also be noted that de Vitoria did refer to 'the Indians' in North America as 'barbarians'.[7]

Francisco de Vitoria exercised considerable influence over Hugo Grotius (1583–1645), generally held as the most prominent among the founding fathers of international law.[8] As de Vitoria before him, Grotius held that indigenous peoples' societies constitute polities with rights under international law. Grotius further agreed with de Vitoria when rejecting that the European realms could claim rights over indigenous peoples' territories through 'discovery' alone. He maintained that discovery doctrines apply only to things genuinely belonging to no one.[9]

In sum, early international legal theories acknowledged indigenous peoples as international legal subjects, with rights as such. This recognition was reflected in the fact that during this era, the European realms entered into treaties and other political agreements with indigenous peoples. These treaties were considered to have full international legal status.[10] That said, indigenous peoples' legal status was not necessarily completely on par with that of the European realms. Only the European model of political and social organization—characterized by exclusive territorial domain and hierarchical, centralized, authority—qualified as nations proper.[11]

[7] See Jérémie Gilbert, *Indigenous Peoples' Land Rights Under International Law: From Victims to Actors* (Transnational Publishers, 2006) 9–11; Anghie, *Imperialism* (n 5) 52–60; Fitzmaurice, 'Discovery, Conquest, and Occupation of Territory' (n 5) 2, 5; Liliana Obregón Tarazona, 'The Civilized and the Uncivilized', in Bardo Fassbender and Anne Peters (eds.), *The Oxford Handbook of the History of International Law* (2012) 2, 7. It might be added that although de Vitoria held that *in principle* just war could be waged against indigenous peoples, this is not to say that his view was that the Spanish had waged a just war when they conquered the Americas, as is sometimes claimed. See Fitzmaurice, 'Discovery, Conquest, and Occupation of Territory' (n 5) 5.

[8] Hersch Lauterpacht, 'The Grotian Tradition in International Law' [1946] *British Year Book of International Law*, 23, reprinted in Malcolm Evans and Patrick Capps (eds.), *International Law* (Vol I) (Ashgate Publishing, 2009); Anghie, *Imperialism* (n 5) 13–14; Fitzmaurice, 'Discovery, Conquest, and Occupation of Territory' (n 5) 5.

[9] See Anaya, *Indigenous Peoples in International Law* (n 1) 19; Fitzmaurice, 'Discovery, Conquest, and Occupation of Territory' (n 5) 5; Gilbert, *Indigenous Peoples' Land Rights* (n 7) 12. As with de Vitoria, Grotious also questioned whether the Spanish in fact had acted within the boundaries of just war when they conquered the Americas. See Fitzmaurice, 'Discovery, Conquest, and Occupation of Territory' (n 5) 5.

[10] Paul McHugh, *Aboriginal Societies and the Common Law: A History of Sovereignty, Status and Self-Determination* (Oxford University Press, 2004) 98–108.

[11] Anghie, *Imperialism* (n 5) 52–53.

Most indigenous peoples' societies were, viewed through a European lens, organized in less stringent structures. In other words, it was not the fact that indigenous societies were indigenous that disqualified most of them from the status of nationhood in the mind of the European law-makers. Rather, it was their perceived loose societal structure that failed to meet the European idea of a nation. This distinction allowed Grotius, as de Vitoria before him, to infer that 'just cause' entitled the European realms to claim rights over indigenous peoples' territories through 'just war'.[12]

2.3 The Period between the Peace of Westphalia and the League of Nations

2.3.1 States, state sovereignty, and classical international law's understanding of 'peoples'

Although structures with state-similar features had previously existed in Europe, it is largely agreed that the embryo to the contemporary state and law of nations surfaced in tandem in Europe following the end of the 30-Year War in 1648, replacing a feudal order.[13] The Peace of Westphalia cemented the realm of the kingdoms in Europe, and offered the idea of certain stability in the relations between the 'nations' of the region. At Westphalia, European sovereigns agreed that order was to be guaranteed by the sovereigns themselves. Implicit in this notion was that the right of the sovereigns to provide order was inherent. The 'state', for international legal purposes, had seen the light.[14]

Simultaneously, classical liberal theories emerged in Europe, breaking with the natural law ideals that had until that point dominated philosophical thought. Liberal thinkers gradually abandoned the idea that there exists a legal order given by nature or God that pre-exists human polities and law-makers.[15] According to Thomas Hobbes, a leading scholar of the era, natural law ideas are merely a set of

[12] Gilbert, *Indigenous Peoples' Land Rights* (n 7) 12–13.

[13] Ibid., 22; Gerry Simpson, 'International Law in Diplomatic History', in James Crawford and Martti Koskenniemi (eds.), *International Law* (Cambridge University Press, 2012) 30; Antonio Cassese, *International Law* (2nd edn., Oxford University Press, 2005) 23–24; William Kurt Barth, '"Cultural Rights": A Necessary Corrective to the Nation State', in Francesco Francioni and Martin Scheinin (eds.), *Cultural Human Rights* (Martinus Nijhoff Publishers, 2008) 85.

[14] Federico Lenzerini, 'Sovereignty Revisited: International Law and Parallel Sovereignty of Indigenous Peoples' [2006] *Texas International Law Journal*, Vol 42 157; David Raic, *Statehood and the Law of Self-Determination* (Kluwer Law International, 2002) 20–21; Koskenniemi, *From Apology to Utopia* (n 2) 94; Wayne Hudson, 'Fables of Sovereignty', in Trudy Jacobsen, Charles Sampford, and Ramesh Thakur (eds.), *Re-envisioning Sovereignty—The End of Westphalia?* (Ashgate Publishing, 2008) 28; Paul Keal, 'Indigenous Sovereignty', in ibid., 315.

[15] See Koskenniemi, *From Apology to Utopia* (n 2) 75–82, 94, 107–08. The succinct outline of the history of international law presented here must necessarily oversimplify matters somewhat. It should be noted that early liberals did not immediately denounce the existence of a divine or natural order of affairs. Rather, they initially assumed that natural laws were of a very general nature. They consequently doubted that these laws would be readily translated into practical circumstances. Further, to the extent natural laws could be discerned, liberals gradually came to presume that such laws were in

subjective preferences and speculations in disguise of a general idea of justice. Hobbes submitted that '[g]ood and evil are not objective or unchanging qualities of things but the subjective description of the apparently beneficial or harmful effect of things.'[16]

As an alternative to natural law, liberal philosophers and legal scholars such as Samuel Pufendorf (1632–1694) suggested that social order should be based on the subjective consent of individuals. They submitted that respect for individual decisions results in a societal order that represents the will and interests of each individual in the best possible way. Therefore, everyone must reasonably agree to such a system. The founding fathers of liberal political theory imagined a social contract. Social contract theories assume that a number of individuals have freely come together to form a polity because they share a common culture and have a joint desire to live together. However, not only had these groups of individuals consented to come together to form a distinct society, they had also, according to classical liberalism, agreed that this society should be governed by a sovereign. The group of men had done so, it was submitted, because a sovereign was paramount to social order and only social order could prevent violence and save individuals from constant fear. In other words, the duty to obey the sovereign was based on self-interest. Hence, according to classical liberal theory, each individual has the right to agree to her or his personal preferences. But importantly, once these preferences are in place and can be ascertained, the sovereign has the right to enforce such norms. They can no longer be challenged by the individual based on subsequent changed will.[17]

Conventional liberalism uncritically accepted the aggregate populations of the European realms—or states—as such groups of men that had willingly and deliberately come together to form polities through social contracts. This assumption did, however, square badly with the reality on the ground. The European realms—and as a consequence the European 'peoples'—were not products of anything close to social contracts. Rather, military power determined territorial control. Territories defined by the wage of war and military might became states. As a

conformity with state practice. Consequently, liberals abolished the quest to identify a natural order of affairs. As they presumed that state action represents natural law, it was not necessary to independently deduce a law of nature from other 'sources'. In other words, natural law theories prevailed as theories, but gradually lost relevance to the practical understanding of international law. See Martti Koskenniemi, *The Gentle Civilizer of Nations The Rise and Fall of International Law 1870 1960* (Cambridge University Press, 2002) 92–96, 100; Koskenniemi, *From Apology to Utopia* (n 2) 108, 130–31.

[16] Hobbes is cited from Koskenniemi, *From Apology to Utopia* (n 2) 79–80.

[17] Classical liberal philosophers such as Hobbes, Locke, Kant, and Rousseau and legal scholars such as Pufendorf all used the notion of a fictitious social contract to justify their respective theories of justice. See Bardo Fassbender, 'The United Nations Charter As Constitution of the International Community' [1998] *Columbia Journal of Transnational Law* 36, reprinted in Evans and Capps (eds.), *International Law* (n 8) 559; Will Kymlicka, *Contemporary Political Philosophy: An Introduction* (Oxford University Press, 2002) 61; Vernon Van Dyke, 'The Individual, the State, and Ethnic Communities in Political Theory', in Will Kymlicka (ed.), *The Rights of Minority Cultures* (Oxford University Press, 1995) 34; Koskenniemi, *From Apology to Utopia* (n 2) 81–82 and 113; Martti Koskenniemi, 'International Law in the World of Ideas', in James Crawford and Martti Koskenniem (eds.), *International Law* (Cambridge University Press, 2012) 52.

quote of Charles Tilly, restated by Gerry Simpson, aptly puts it, 'War made the state, and the state made war.'[18] Correspondingly, the populations of the states—thus defined—became 'peoples',[19] irrespective of whether the state, and hence the 'people', were made up of several groups with different ethnic and/or cultural backgrounds. In other words, liberalism provided a theory that professed that states created through force are *the* international legal subjects and legitimized these international legal subjects' (i.e. the states') sovereign right to rule. The opposite side of that coin was that peoples—in the meaning groups of men with common ethnic and/or cultural backgrounds—had no place in international law. In conclusion International law came to define peoples solely in terms of aggregate populations of states.

The theories coined during this era were not confined to apply only to the relationship between the individual and the state. Based on the theory articulated above on the relationship between the state and the individual, liberal legal scholars proceeded to formulate theories pertaining to intra-state relationships. It is telling that Emmerich de Vattel (1714–1767), surely the most influential international legal scholar of the time, viewed states as super-individuals.[20] As sovereigns, states were perceived to be free in a manner comparable to individuals. Consequently, states too were only bound by norms they had consented to. The will of the sovereign—and only the will of the sovereign—created law, liberal scholars professed. Since all states were sovereign, no state had the right to impose norms on the other.[21] But at the same time, similar to the norms that applied to individuals, once a state had consented to be bound by a norm, the state could no longer opt out of the norm due to a subsequent change of preferences. A 'law of nations' replaced natural law.[22]

Obviously, the notion of state sovereignty, which had now become the constitutional principle of international law, squares badly with natural law theories. By definition natural law is a normative code that pre-dates the sovereign and which the sovereign has no power to change or nullify. In contrast, the new legal order submitted that only laws originating from the sovereigns are normative.[23] For natural reasons, the new legal order that the liberal scholars professed was an instant hit with the sovereigns. This understanding of international law not only established the state as the international legal subject. It also identified state action as law.[24] The interest of the realms and liberal theory formed a perfect match. The sovereigns wanted to fortify their sovereignty and to be bound only by norms of their own liking. Liberal scholars advocated that this interest was indeed matched by the constitutional principle of international law.

[18] Simpson, 'International Law in Diplomatic History' (n 13) 31.

[19] Anaya, *Indigenous Peoples in International Law* (n 1) 19–22.

[20] See Koskenniemi, *From Apology to Utopia* (n 2) 113; also Gilbert, *Indigenous Peoples' Land Rights* (n 7) 22.

[21] Lauterpacht, 'The Grotian Tradition' (n 8) 29; Koskenniemi, *From Apology to Utopia* (n 2) 115–21.

[22] Anghie, *Imperialism* (n 5) 42–43.

[23] Koskenniemi, *From Apology to Utopia* (n 2) 115–21, 224.

[24] Ibid., 120.

In sum, the theory of justice that took form in Europe in the wake of the Peace of Westphalia, and that would become entrenched during the following centuries, not only rests on the idea that states pre-date the law and that the aggregate populations of states constitute 'peoples'; it presupposes it.[25] These basic building blocks of this international legal system follow indirectly from the principal assumptions (i) that groups of individuals have—prior to the formulation of any theory of justice—come together and through social contracts formed polities and accepted to be governed by a sovereign, and (ii) that the geographical boundaries that define the polity to which the liberal theory applies (i.e. the state) have been established prior to any theory of justice. The state as *the* subject of international law could no longer be challenged. It had become self-evident that the world was naturally divided into states and that these states possessed rights precisely by the virtue of being states. As Gerry Simpson puts it, the Peace of Westphalia 'has come to represent . . . a point of inauguration for modern international law and for the modern state . . . '.[26]

The articulated international legal theory had no view as to what societal structures amounted to a state. The formation of a new state 'was a matter of fact, not of law'.[27] In other words, the 'existing states' determined what other polities constituted states. Vattel's theory on sovereignty fundamentally rejected the idea that polities not organized as European realms could be sovereigns. Consequently, indigenous peoples' societies could not qualify as states. The European powers—and thus international law, since the practice and views of the European powers *was* international law—viewed indigenous peoples' societies as uncivilized, meaning insufficiently similar to themselves.[28] Not only did indigenous peoples' societies that clearly differed from that of the Europeans, such as nomadic tribes, fail to qualify as sovereigns, stationary indigenous societies were also regarded as uncivilized. They could not qualify as sovereign states or other polities, as they were not organized on the European state model. Rather, according to the Europeans, these societies were 'organized primarily by tribal and kinship ties, [with] decentralized political structures . . . [and] have enjoyed shared or overlapping spheres of territorial control'.[29]

International law's understanding of states, peoples, and sovereignty as outlined above got entrenched during the centuries that followed.[30] In the 1800s,

[25] Joseph Carens, 'Aliens and Citizens: The Case for Open Borders', in Kymlicka (ed.), *The Rights of Minority Cultures* (n 17) 341–42.

[26] Simpson, 'International Law in Diplomatic History' (n 13) 30.

[27] Crawford, *The Creation of States* (n 6) 10–14.

[28] Emmerich de Vattel, *The Law of Nations* (1758).

[29] See Anaya, *Indigenous Peoples in International Law* (n 1) 22. Consequently, territories outside Europe were awarded status as states only if the European powers deemed them sufficiently 'civilized', or in other words, sufficiently 'European like'. Examples of such polities that with time became accepted as states were the United States, the Ottoman Empire, China, Afghanistan, Bukhara, Burma, Ceylon, Japan, Korea, Siam, Brunei, and the Mogul and Maratha Empires of India. See Crawford, *The Creation of States* (n 6) 14 and 260–61; Anghie, *Imperialism* (n 5) 58; Cassese, *International Law* (n 13) 25–31.

[30] Anghie, *Imperialism* (n 5) 33 and 43; Koskenniemi, *From Apology to Utopia* (n 2) 122–23, 132, and 141–43.

international lawyers were viewed as scientists. That is not to say that their task was to formulate theories about the content of a law handled down to man by nature or God. Rather, the international lawyer should identify the law through study of sovereign, i.e. state, practice. Law, it was held, could be objectively understood by analyzing states' developments through history. State practice was perceived as an inevitable historic development towards the highest possible degree of freedom, and as such reflective of objective law.[31] Unsurprisingly, these studies concluded that the European powers were the most developed states. As a consequence, international law, legal scholars argued, must be based on European cultural processes, processes of civilization in contrast to other cultures that were deemed half-civilized or even savage. In the minds of the scholars of the era, norms proclaimed by the European sovereigns reflected the most developed and, as a consequence, correct law.[32]

The conclusion that the practices of the most 'developed' nations mirrored objective law allowed lawyers to legally distinguish between civilized and non-civilized societies. Only when having reached the required facet of civilization could societal structures enter the international legal community.[33] Sovereignty was thus essentially a European feature.[34] Through colonization, the rest of the world was integrated into an international legal system that was essentially European. The 'civilized' European nations determined what constituted international law. They could therefore unilaterally decide their legal relationship with populations in the rest of the world, including with indigenous peoples,[35] who naturally were considered non-civilized societies. Consequently, breaking with the teachings of Francisco de Vitoria and Hugo Grotius, international law held that, generally speaking, indigenous peoples do not constitute international legal subjects.[36] That said, certain indigenous peoples were continuously recognized as nations.[37]

As seen, the social contract theories that were embedded in classical liberalism awarded the sovereign the right to establish and enforce norms that its individual subjects had no right to challenge. As they had entered into a social contract, the

[31] Anghie, *Imperialism* (n 5) 43; Koskenniemi, *From Apology to Utopia* (n 2) 122–23, 141–43.

[32] Koskenniemi, *From Apology to Utopia*, (n 2) 144–47, 153–54, 232; *The Gentle Civilizer of Nations* (n 15) 51, 72–73; Anghie, *Imperialism* (n 5) 40–41, 48–49, 61–62.

[33] Gerry Simpson, 'Two Liberalisms' [2001] *European Journal of International Law* 12, reprinted in Evans and Capps (eds.), *International Law* (n 8) 544–48; Koskenniemi, *The Gentle Civilizer of Nations* (n 15) 73–75, 135.

[34] Koskenniemi, *The Gentle Civilizer of Nations* (n 15) 127–28.

[35] Koskenniemi, *From Apology to Utopia* (n 2) 144–47, 153, 232; Anghie, *Imperialism* (n 5) 32–33, 53–61, 98–99.

[36] Koskenniemi, *The Gentle Civilizer of Nations* (n 15) 113–15, 126; Crawford, *The Creation of States* (n 6) 29.

[37] See e.g. the United States Supreme Court's ruling in *Cherokee Nation v Georgia* 30 US 1 (1831) and *Worcester v Georgia* 31 US 6 Pet 515 (1832) where the Supreme Court held that 'the Indian nations had always been considered as distinct, independent political communities, retaining their original natural rights as the undisputed possessors of the soil from time immemorial . . . '. Another example was the Maori Confederation in New Zealand. Hawaii and Tonga also acquired early status as nations under international law. See Crawford, *The Creation of States* (n 6) 260–63.

subjects were obliged to abide by the norms the sovereign proclaimed. Liberalism is, however, a school of thought that at its core professes the freedom of the individual. Against this backdrop, it was only natural that classical liberal scholars developed the first human rights ideas in Europe. With time, the individual's rights and freedoms vis-à-vis the state became an integral part of liberalism.[38] That said, for a considerable time human rights theories by and large remained precisely theories. Classical international law did not, generally speaking, embrace human rights norms, although rights such as those of personal freedom, civil liberty, commerce, property, and freedom of conscience were to some extent acknowledged at times.[39] Still, a coherent and comprehensive human rights system would only emerge much later.[40] In addition, and arguably more important for the present purposes, the human rights ideas that were developed in the centuries that followed the Peace of Westphalia proclaimed human rights of the individual only. Classical liberal theory did not consider group rights.[41] The state–individual dichotomy was deeply entrenched in, and integral to, classical liberalism.

In sum, the state emerged in Europe in the aftermath of the Peace of Westphalia. The legal theories that surfaced simultaneously and were entrenched during the centuries that followed took the state for granted as *the* international legal subject. It was presumed that a 'people' equals the aggregate population of the territory of the sovereign, i.e. the state, for international legal purposes. Further, the dominating philosophical theory of the era gradually held it self-evident that no law can pre-exist the sovereign because the sovereign is the sole creator of law. International law became synonymous with the will and action of the sovereigns. 'Savage' indigenous peoples could not be state-forming polities, and hence lacked legal personality. In addition, the early human rights ideas by-passed indigenous societies, as human rights were perceived to pertain only to relationships between the individual and the state. Groups has no place in an international legal system to which the state–individual dichotomy was integral.

[38] Asbjørn Eide, 'Economic, Social and Cultural Rights as Human Rights', in Asbjørn Eide, Catarina Krause, and Allan Rosas (eds.), *Economic, Social and Cultural Rights—A Textbook* (2nd edn., Martinus Nijhoff Publishers, 2001) 12–13.

[39] Koskenniemi, *The Gentle Civilizer of Nations* (n 15) 55.

[40] See Cassese, *International Law* (n 13) 143. In absence of a comprehensive coherent system of human rights, a number of human rights treaties, particularly on freedom of religion, were entered into in the time-period between the Peace of Westphalia and the creation of the League of Nations. However, these treaty provisions were haphazard, incoherent, and often not adhered to in practice. See Nathan Lerner, *Group Rights and Discrimination in International Law* (2nd edn., Martinus Nijhoff Publishers, 2003) 7–8. Also, certain practices such as slavery were with time considered illegal. Still, it was only with the adoption of the human rights instruments after the creation of the United Nations that human rights genuinely became part of the international legal system.

[41] Darlene M Johnston, 'Native Rights as Collective Rights: A Question of Group Self-Preservation', in Kymlicka (ed.), *The Rights of Minority Cultures* (n.17) 185; Nathan Glazer, 'Individual Rights against Group Rights', in ibid., 126; Susanna Mancini and Bruno De Witte, 'Language Rights and Cultural Rights; A European Perspective', in Francesco Francioni and Martin Scheinin (eds.), *Cultural Human Rights* (Martinus Nijhoff Publishers, 2008) 251.

2.3.2 Post-Westphalian international law's position on indigenous peoples' traditional territories—the *terra nullius* doctrine

As seen, post-Westphalian international law broke with the notion that indigenous peoples are polities with rights. Simultaneously, European powers developed an interest in natural resources situated in indigenous peoples' traditional territories. These two factors together contributed to the emergence of an international legal doctrine which holds that although indigenous peoples' territories are clearly literally populated, such territories are nonetheless uninhabited, from an international legal perspective. As a consequence, the European realms were legally entitled to place such territories under their hegemony and control.

In fact, international law not only supported the colonization of indigenous territories, it largely emerged for the precise purpose of facilitating European imperialism.[42] As Martti Koskenniemi, referring to Anghie, puts it, 'the non-European world appeared to Europe predominantly as an object of colonisation, evangelisation and civilisation'.[43] International law of the era defined indigenous peoples' lands as territories over which no one exercised political control. Therefore the European powers were free to occupy such lands. The outlined theory is commonly referred to as the *terra nullius* doctrine.[44] That said, colonizing powers did not explicitly invoke the *terra nullius* doctrine in all indigenous areas. Sometimes, other theories and systems were used or referred to in order to justify the taking of indigenous peoples' territories. One example is the *encomienda* system used by the Spaniards and Portuguese when occupying Latin America, which granted the conquerors rights over land areas as well as to the labour of the Indians. In yet other areas, no references were made to any specific theory or doctrine in order to explain why the taking of indigenous territories were legal.[45] Nevertheless, irrespective of whether the *terra nullius* doctrine was explicitly invoked or not, the effects on indigenous peoples and their territories were essentially the same.

[42] See Kymlicka, 'Beyond the Indigenous/Minority Dichotomy?', in Stephen Allen and Alexandra Xanthaki (eds.), *Reflections on the UN Declaration on the Rights of Indigenous Peoples* (Hart Publishing, 2011) 183, with references. For similar observations, see Jérémie Gilbert and Cathal Doyle, 'A New Dawn over the Land: Shedding Light on Collective Ownership and Consent', in ibid. 292–93; James Crawford and Martti Koskenniemi, *International Law* (Cambridge University Press, 2012) 15; Simpson, 'International Law in Diplomatic History' (n 13) 27.

[43] Koskenniemi, 'International Law in the World of Ideas' (n 17) 54.

[44] As indicated, *terra nullius* literally means 'empty territory'. But in the described context, the term has been employed to refer to a territory that is *not necessarily literally speaking uninhabited*, but which those empowered to make the law define as such for *political and legal* purposes. See Gilbert, *Indigenous Peoples' Land Rights* (n 7) 26–27. That said, one should note that although *terra nullius* is the term most often used to describe a territory deemed to be legally and politically speaking uninhabited irrespective of the fact that it is populated, this might be a somewhat inaccurate use of the term. Andrew Fitzmaurice points out that when first used in a legal context, the term *terra nullius* was employed to describe territories with no or very little population, most often in the Polar Regions. By contrast, the term *territorium nullius* was used in the context of the 1885 Berlin Conference, where the European powers met in order to divide populated territories in Africa among themselves, to refer to territories that were legally speaking uninhabited, alththough not factually so. See Fitzmaurice, 'Discovery, Conquest, and Occupation of Territory' (n 5) 9–11. Nevertheless, since *terra nullius* is the term most often used in this context, the book will stick to this terminology too.

[45] Gilbert, *Indigenous Peoples' Land Rights* (n 7) 6–9.

The *terra nullius* doctrine consists of two elements: the first relates to the political status of populations, the second to their capacity to establish private rights over land. As to the first element, as seen, the international legal system of the time only recognized states as international legal subjects. In order to hold sovereign rights over their traditional territories, indigenous peoples' societies therefore needed to qualify as states. This they failed to do, as the European realms—and as a consequence international law—defined indigenous peoples' societies as uncivilized, as opposed to the civilized European states. Or to put it differently, the European realms viewed indigenous peoples' societies as insufficiently similar to their own, and only those endowed with civilization were recognized as proper subjects of international law. Thus, those deemed, measured against the European standard, to stand outside civilization were also left outside the international legal system. By excluding those 'uncivilized', only the civilized nations were allowed to participate in the international legal project.[46] In short, the European realms invoked the notion of state sovereignty and the positive law of the sovereign to declare that uncivilized indigenous peoples by the very nature of their societies could hold no sovereign, or political, rights over their territories.[47]

As to the second element, the *terra nullius* doctrine professes that in order to establish *private rights* over lands and natural resources, a population must improve on or add value to the land. Accordingly, invoking the *terra nullius* doctrine, the European realms denied indigenous peoples private rights over lands and natural resources as well, because indigenous peoples, it was asserted, had failed to sufficiently improve on the land when measured against European standards. In other words, indigenous peoples' land utilization was not sufficiently similar to European agrarian practices. British philosopher John Locke (1632–1704) is often referred to as the founding father of this line of thought. He held that uncultivated land could not constitute property. According to Locke, man must improve on land to establish property rights thereto—the land must be transformed into valuable and productive property. Property rights over land were perceived to occur as a result of definitive occupation, in other words as a result of occupation by means of

[46] Frédéric Mégret, 'International Law as Law', in James Crawford and Martti Koskenniemi (eds.), *International Law* (Cambridge University Press, 2012) 65; Gilbert, *Indigenous Peoples' Land Rights* (n 7) 22–23; Obregón Tarazona, 'The Civilized and the Uncivilized' (n 7) 2.

[47] Lassa Oppenheim, *International Law: A Treatise* (2nd edn., Longmans, Green & Co, 1905) 292; Koskenniemi, *The Gentle Civilizer of Nations* (n 15) Ch 2; Cassese, *International Law* (n 13) 28; Hurst Hannum, *Autonomy, Sovereignty, and Self-Determination: The Accommodation of Conflicting Rights* (Revised edn., University of Pennsylvania Press, 1996) 93; Crawford, *The Creation of States* (n 6) 263–67; Patrick Macklem, 'Indigenous Recognition in International Law: Theoretical Observations', in *Michigan Journal of International Law* [2008] Vol 30 1 184; Anghie, *Imperialism* (n 5) 34; *McHugh, Aboriginal Societies and the Common Law* (n 10) 98–108; Joshua Castellino, 'Conceptual Difficulties and the Right to Indigenous Self-Determination', in Ghanea and Xanthaki (eds.), *Minorities, Peoples and Self-Determination—Essays in Honour of Patrick Thornberry* (Martinus Nijhoff Publishers, 2005) 69; 'Territorial Integrity and the "Right" to Self-Determination: An Examination of the Conceptual Tools' [2008] *Brooks Law Journal of International Law*, Vol 33:2 522, 529–31; 'The Right to Land, International Law & Indigenous Peoples', in Joshua Castellino and Niamh Walsh (eds.), *International Law and Indigenous Peoples* (Martinus Nijhoff Publisher, 2005) 92–101; Tarazona, 'The Civilized and the Uncivilized' (n 7) 2, 7, 9–10; Gilbert, *Indigenous Peoples' Land Rights* (n 7) 23–25.

(European style) agriculture.[48] The legal scholar Emmerich de Vattel shared Locke's view. He held that under international law, indigenous peoples' way of using land could not amount to 'a real and lawful taking of possession'.[49] Again, international law gave the European realms the prerogative to take this position. As sovereign states, with them vested the exclusive right to decide what constitutes international law.

In sum, classical international law professed *first* that only states could possess sovereign—or political—rights over territory. The European powers—as sovereign law-makers—decided that indigenous peoples' societies were too uncivilized, measured against their own standards, to qualify as states. As a consequence, indigenous peoples could hold no political rights over land. *Second*, indigenous peoples had not sufficiently cultivated their lands, again measured against European standards. Therefore, they had failed to establish private rights over such lands as well. In other words, international law of the era professed a dynamic of difference to justify that the European colonizers were legally entitled both to place indigenous peoples' territories under their realm of sovereignty, and to declare that indigenous peoples held no private rights over such territories either.[50] Figuratively speaking, one could say that international law of the era viewed indigenous peoples as mere ghosts in their own landscapes.[51]

A final observation shall be offered at this stage. The *terra nullius* doctrine demonstrates, albeit in a problematic manner, that when analyzing what rights that attach to a land area, one should distinguish between sovereign and property rights. Sovereignty is governmental authority over a territory. Property rights involve rights in relation to property, including land, that arise under and are regulated by domestic law. The distinction is critical, not least in an indigenous rights context. The fact that a polity 'acquires' sovereignty, and hence sovereign rights, over an indigenous people's territory does not in itself result in acquisition of property rights over the same land. Rather, establishment of property rights requires enactment of domestic law to that effect.[52] The book will return to the cardinal importance of this distinction to the indigenous rights discourse, in particular in Chapter 8.

48 See John Locke, *Two Treatises of Government* (1689). See also James Tully, *Strange Multiplicity: Constitutionalism in an Age of Diversity* (Cambridge University Press, 1995) 72; Tarazona, 'The Civilized and the Uncivilized' (n 7) 2, 7; Fitzmaurice, 'Discovery, Conquest, and Occupation of Territory' (n 5) 8; Gilbert, *Indigenous Peoples' Land Rights* (n 7) 24–26.

49 Vattel is cited from Peter Fitzpatrick, 'Terminal Legality: Imperalism and the (De)composition of Law', in Diane Elisabeth Kirkby and Catharine Coleborne (eds.), *Law, History Colonialism, The Reach of Empire* (Manchester University Press, 2001) 14. See also Fitzmaurice, 'Discovery, Conquest, and Occupation of Territory' (n 5) 3.

50 Antony Anghie, 'Finding the Peripheries: Sovereignty and Colonialism in Nineteenth-Century International Law' [1999] *Harvard International Law Journal* 40 24–28.

51 See Andrew Huff, 'Indigenous Land Rights and the New Self-Determination' [2005] 16 *Colo J Int'l Envtil L Pol'y* 295, 298. For similar lines of thought, see further Anaya, *Indigenous Peoples in International Law* (n 1) 22–23; Crawford, *The Creation of States* (n 6) 263–67; Anghie, *Imperialism* (n 5) 30, 34; Mattias Åhrén, *The Saami Traditional Dress & Beauty Pageants: Indigenous Peoples' Rights of Ownership and Self-Determination over their Cultures* (Doctoral Dissertation delivered at Tromsö University, November 2010) 28–29.

52 Kent McNeil, 'Judicial Treatment of Indigenous Land Rights in the Common Law World', in John V Cioffi and Peer Zumbansen (eds.), *Indigenous Peoples and the Law: Compartive and Critical Perspectives* (Hart Publishing, 2009) 3.

2.3.3 The rule of *uti possidetis*

As seen European powers invoked the *terra nullius* doctrine to claim sovereignty over indigenous peoples' traditional territories. When the former colonies started to gain independence in certain parts of the world, the newly formed states invoked another theory—*uti possidetis*—to justify continued colonization of indigenous peoples' territories.

The *uti possidetis* theory professed that the former colonies were entitled to rely on the previous colonizers' 'just wars' against indigenous peoples to legitimize that the borders drawn by the colonizer should be maintained, also following independence. As a consequence, the fact that the previous colony had now gained independence and had become a state made little difference to indigenous peoples. For them, this only implied a change in ruler. The new state had the same borders as the former colony, and indigenous peoples continuously enjoyed no rights over their traditional territories. For instance, when Latin America gradually gained independence in the eighteenth and nineteenth centuries and new states were formed there, these states invoked the rule of *uti possidetis* and claimed that the borders drawn by the Europeans, rather than the natural borders between the first inhabitants of the continent, should determine what political entities existed in Latin America.[53] The *uti possidetis* rule was later invoked also when the present day African states gained independence—and so too in Asia, although perhaps to a lesser degree.

2.4 The League of Nations Epoch

2.4.1 International law on rights of peoples and minorities during the League of Nations epoch

The early 20th Century witnessed the first trembling steps towards genuine democracy in some countries. The genesis of democratic governance did not, however, impact on international law's understanding of 'peoples'. Democracy theory has no opinion on what are the peoples—the *demos*—that are entitled to democratic governance. As classical liberalism, democracy theory takes for granted the polity to which the theory applies. In other words, democracy theory uncritically accepts that states, or perhaps more precisely, the aggregate populations of states, are the politics within which democracy is to be exercised.

In an attempt to avoid further global conflicts after the end of World War I, states came together and formed the first world organization—the League of Nations. Under the auspices of the League, states set out to codify and structure, but also to some extent reshape, the patchwork of post-Westphalian international legal norms. The aim was to craft the first comprehensive and coherent international legal system.[54] Doing so, the League of Nations entrenched the basic premise of international law. The League era affirmed classical international law's position that

[53] Gilbert, *Indigenous Peoples' Land Rights* (n 7) 21, 36.
[54] Anghie, *Imperialism* (n 5) 123–25.

international norms emerge only as a result of state consent, as is well illustrated by the Permanent Court of International Justice's (PCIJ) ruling in the *Lotus Case* (1927). Here, the Court inferred that '[i]nternational law governs relations between independent States. The rules of law binding upon States therefore emanate from their own free will as expressed in conventions or by usages generally as expressing principles of law . . .'.[55] At the same time, however, the League of Nations epoch sought to break with classical liberalism's position that statehood is a matter of fact and not law.[56] The League attempted to objectively define what polities constitute states. The attempt failed, but certain additional non-European polities were accepted as states during this era.[57] Further, statehood was not a pre-requisite for membership in the League of Nations. Collective entities similar to states, such as dominions and colonies, could join the League. That said, the fact that the League of Nations in the end remained true to the doctrine of recognition underlines that international law continuously embraced the distinction between civilized and uncivilized nations, where only the former could be a part of the international legal system.[58]

Section 2.3 articulates how classical international law was blind to collective entities other than states. Breaking with this tradition, in another attempt to reshape the international legal system, the League of Nations concerned itself with the situation of minorities and the principle of self-determination. Tensions between different ethnic and cultural groups that had become forced to share the same polity when the European states took form post-Westphalia was arguably the principal reason behind the outbreak of World War I. As a response, the League of Nations paid particular attention to ethnic groups that had been denied statehood when the European political map took shape. The League aimed to transform previously haphazard ideas on minority protection into a coherent normative system. A number of treaties were drafted that aspired to render it possible for ethnic minorities to preserve their cultural characteristics and traditions.[59] In the same vein, under the auspices of the League of Nations, the world community for the first time engaged in coherent discussions on the principle of self-determination. The President of the United States at the time, Woodrow Wilson, was the main promoter of this principle. He linked the principle of self-determination to rights of

[55] *Case of the S.S. 'Lotus'*, PJIC, Ser A, No 10, 1927 Sec III 4.

[56] Section 2.3 describes how under post-Westphalian international law, becoming a state was not a matter of fulfilling certain objective criteria, but rather of being accepted as a state by already existing as such.

[57] Anghie, *Imperialism* (n 5) 137–38.

[58] See Article 1(2) of the League of Nations Covenant; also Tarazona, 'The Civilized and the Uncivilized' (n 7) 3.

[59] James Crawford, 'The Right of Self-Determination in International Law: Its Development and Future', in Philip Alston (ed.), *Peoples' Rights* (Oxford University Press, 2005) 14–15; Hannum, *Autonomy, Sovereignty, and Self-Determination* (n 47) 52–54; Steven Wheatley, *Democracy, Minorities and International Law* (Cambridge Studies in International and Comparative Law, 2005) 8–10; Lerner, *Group Rights and Discrimination in International Law* (n 40) 10–13; Benedict Kingsbury, 'Reconciling Five Competing Conceptual Structures of Indigenous Peoples' Claims in International and Comparative Law', in Philip Alston (ed.), *Peoples' Rights* (Oxford University Press, 2005) 78; Raic, *Statehood and the Law of Self-Determination* (n 14) 191–92; Malcolm Shaw, 'Self-Determination and the Use of Force', in Ghanea and Xanthaki (eds.), *Minorities, Peoples and Self-Determination* (n 47) 37.

minorities. President Wilson went so far as to propose a League of Nations Covenant provision that proclaimed a fairly far-reaching right of racial groups to secession.[60] In the end, however, no right to secession was included in the League Covenant. Rather, the League of Nations Covenant introduced a Mandate System that remained true to classical liberalism's understanding of 'peoples'. The Mandate System pertained only to the aggregate populations of territories. It did not envision rights of culturally distinct groups within a territory.[61] In fact, the Mandate System sought to extinguish cultural practices viewed as backwards, such as those of 'native tribes'.[62] All in all, well into the 1900s, European lawyers and political thinkers understood international law as a normative system that was developed in Europe, and which provided the European states (and the United States) with rights over other, 'uncivilized', entities.[63]

Although the Mandate System and the League of Nations in general remained true to the conventional understanding of peoples and took an assimilatory approach towards indigenous peoples, international law of the era broke with the previous inhospitality towards minority rights and interests, as reflected in jurisprudence of the time. In its advisory opinion in the *Minority Schools in Albania Case* (1935), the PCIJ proclaimed that an ethnic minority in Albania had the right to preserve the traditions and national characteristics that distinguished the group from the majority population. The PCIJ held that equality in law precludes discrimination of any kind; whereas equality in fact may involve the necessity of different treatment in order to attain a result which establishes equilibrium between different situations. The Court further opined that '[t]he idea underlying the treaties for the protection of minorities is to secure for certain elements incorporated in a State, the population of which differs from them in race . . . the possibility of . . . preserving the characteristics which distinguish them from the majority, and satisfying the ensuing special needs.' The PCIJ elaborated that to achieve this end states should ensure that minority groups have 'suitable means for the preservation of their racial peculiarities, their traditions and their national characteristics.'[64] Notably, the Court did not merely underline that children belonging to minority groups have the same right to access education as children of the majority population, a position that in itself would only be firmly established in international law following the creation of the United Nations more than a decade later. Of even greater significance is the Court's distinction between 'equality in law' and 'equality in fact',

60 Hannum, *Autonomy, Sovereignty, and Self-Determination* (n 47) 27–32.

61 See the League of Nations Covenant, Article 22. For an extensive outline of the Leagues' Mandate System, see Anghie, *Imperialism* (n 5) 119–90.

62 See ibid., 168–69. See also Benedict Kingsbury, 'Legal Positivism as Normative Politics: International Society, Balance of Power; Lassa Oppenheim's Positive International Law' [2002] *European Journal of International Law* 13, reprinted in Evans and Capps (eds.), *International Law* (n 8) 412–13. Kingsbury discusses the writings of two legal scholars that exercised considerable influence on international law during the League of Nation epoch—Oppenheim and Westlake. They both asserted that native tribes were not legally capable of managing their own affairs. Therefore, it should be left to the conscience of the state to determine how to treat native tribes.

63 See, generally, Tarazona and also Koskenniemi, 'International Law in the World of Ideas' (n 17) 54.

64 *Minority Schools in Albania*, Advisory Opinion, PCIJ, Ser A/B, No 64, 1935.

as referred to above. This distinction led the PCIJ to conclude that minority childrens' different cultural background award them a right to be treated differently compared with the majority population, i.e. they are entitled to education accustomed to their distinct cultural and linguistic identity. The reader is wise to keep this aspect of the PCIJ's ruling in *Minority Schools in Albania* in mind when we return to the contemporary understanding of equality in Chapter 7.

As to the League of Nations epoch's view on the principle of self-determination, the findings of the Commission of Jurists in the *Åland Islands Case* (1920) are illustrative. The League appointed the Commission of Jurists to examine whether the population on the *Åland* Islands are entitled to a right to self-determination.[65] In deciding the case, the Commission of Jurists identified a relationship between the principle of self-determination and rights of ethnic and cultural minority groups. It noted that a common objective of self-determination and minority rights is to assure ethnic and cultural groups the possibility to maintain and develop their cultural and ethnic characteristics. According to the Commission, this end should whenever possible be achieved through secession. But when secession is for political reasons not possible, the ethnic group's right to preserve its cultural characteristics should be implemented through an extensive grant of liberty within the existing state. In the case at hand, the Commission of Jurists inferred that the *Ålanders* did not enjoy a unilateral right to secede from Finland. Therefore, the Commission concluded, the *Ålanders* were entitled to preserve their identity through a regime of autonomy. It underlined that the principle of self-determination must 'be brought into line with that of the protection of minorities'.[66]

As in *Minority Schools in Albania, Åland Islands* illustrates how minority groups enjoyed a relatively strong protection during the League of Nations era. *Åland Islands* further showcases the political force of the principle of self-determination in the inter-war period and highlights the interrelation between self-determination and protection of minority groups. True, the Commission of Jurists in the outset equated the principle to self-determination with a right to independence, and concluded that no such right exists under international law. But this did not leave the *Ålanders* without rights. On the contrary, the Commission still allowed itself to be guided by the spirit of self-determination. It inferred that international law awards

[65] The *Åland* Islands are a group of islands situated in the Baltic Sea between Finland and Sweden. The conflict concerned whether the *Åland* Islands where free to unilaterally secede from Finland to become a part of Sweden. Championing their claim, the *Ålanders* sought to invoke the principle of self-determination.

[66] See Report of the International Committee of Jurists Entrusted by the Council of the League of Nations with the Task of Giving an Advisory Opinion upon the Legal Aspects of the *Åland* Island Question, *Official Journal of the League of Nations*, Special Supplement No 3, October 1920. Regarding the Åland Island Case, see also Cassese, *Self-Determination of Peoples: A Legal Reappraisal* (Cambridge University Press, 1995) 27–31; Crawford, 'The Right to Self-Determination' (n 59) 13–14; Crawford, *The Creation of States* (n 6) 110–112; Christopher J Fromherz, '"Indigenous Peoples" Courts: Egalitarian Juridical Pluralism, Self-Determination, and the United Nations Declaration on the Rights of Indigenous Peoples' [2008] *University of Pennsylvania Law Review*, Vol 156 1355–56. For an extensive overview of the *Åland* Islands' autonomy arrangements, see Hannum, *Autonomy, Sovereignty, and Self-Determination* (n 47) 29–30, in particular 370–75.

minority groups a right to autonomy that allows them to preserve their cultural characteristics. In other words, the Commission of Jurists disentangled the principle of self-determination from secession. Having done so, it noted that the underlying rationale behind the principle of self-determination can also be met by a right to autonomy within existing state borders. The reader may bear in mind the Commission of Jurists' findings in *Åland Islands* when we return to the contemporary understanding of the right to self-determination in Chapter 6.

In sum, the League of Nations epoch partly broke with the clinical state-individual dichotomy professed by classical liberalism and post-Westphalian international law. The international legal order the League envisaged accepted rights of collectives other than states, including rights to be different and to autonomy. But the minority rights recognized by the League of Nations would not be long-lived. In the 1930s, the minority protection system started to implode, largely due to a combination of lack of oversight mechanisms and political unrest, including the rise of Nazism and Fascism.[67]

2.4.2 International law's position on indigenous land and natural resource rights during the League of Nations epoch

International law during the League of Nations' epoch upheld the *terra nullius* doctrine as a relevant international legal principle. The League's Covenant Article 23(a) included a 'Native inhabitants clause'. Pursuant to this provision, states undertook to 'secure the just treatment of the native inhabitants of territories under their control'. Clearly, the reference to 'under their control' affirmed the position that indigenous peoples lack capacity to legally occupy a territory, under the canon of the law of 'civilized' states.[68]

The League era's view on indigenous peoples' capacity, or rather lack thereof, to hold rights over land is further illustrated by the PCIJ ruling in the *Eastern Greenland Case*. Here, Denmark and Norway made competing claims of sovereignty over Eastern Greenland. In support of its position, Denmark sought to rely on affiliation with the indigenous Inuit population of the area. The argument did not convince the PCIJ. The Court held that the area in dispute had been *terra nullius* up and until the point when states claimed sovereignty over it. The PCIJ reached this conclusion although the area had indisputedly for a considerable time been inhabited by the Inuit.[69]

[67] Lerner (n 40) 1011, Hannum, *Autonomy, Sovereignty, and Self-Determination* (n 47) 53–55, and Makkonen, *Equal in Law, Unequal in Fact: Racial and Ethnic Discrimination and the Legal Response thereto in Europe* (Doctoral Dissertation presented at the Faculty of Law at the University of Helsinki) 5 March 2010 82.

[68] Gilbert, *Indigenous Peoples' Land Rights* (n 7) 34.

[69] See *Legal Status of Eastern Greenland (Den v Nor)*, 1933 PCIJ, Ser A/B, No 53) and compare the *Island of Palmas Case* which was decided by international arbitration a few years earlier. In *Island of Palmas*, the United States and the Netherlands held competing claims over the island. In his ruling, the arbitrator concluded that the Netherland's treaty with the indigenous inhabitants of the territory, as well as that population's actual occupation of it, were irrelevant for international legal purposes. What mattered under international law was states occupation of the island. See *Island of Palmas (US v Neth)*, 2 RIAA 831 (1928).

2.4.3 Generally on the *terra nullius* and various forms of discovery doctrines in the 19th and 20th centuries

Not all domestic jurisdictions of the era applied the *terra nullius* doctrine in its purest form. Already prior to the establishment of the League of Nations and continuously into the 1900s, some domestic courts developed more nuanced theories as to the legal effects of colonization of indigenous peoples' territories. Blake Watson divides the various approaches taken into four broad categories:

Approach 1: Indigenous peoples hold no rights over their territories whatsoever following colonization. All such rights vest with the colonizing entity.

Approach 2: Indigenous peoples continue to *possess* their territories, but following colonization no longer hold ownership or similar rights over these lands. Such territories are now owned by the colonizing entity. The colonizer is also entitled to transfer ownership of the land irrespective of indigenous peoples' possessions, and may further unilaterally extinguish all possessory rights of indigenous peoples.

Approach 3: Indigenous peoples continuously hold ownership or similar rights over their territories, but cannot transfer land without permission from the colonizing entity. In other words, the latter holds an exclusive right to acquire the territory from the indigenous people.

Approach 4: Indigenous peoples continuously hold ownership or similar rights over their territories, and are also free to transfer lands to whomsoever they see fit.[70]

As seen, the scale ranges from category 4, where indigenous peoples retain all proprietary rights over their traditional territories following colonization, to category 1, where no such rights remain. The latter category is hence the full *terra nullius* doctrine applied in practice. The two examples in between represent situations where indigenous peoples are deprived of most or some of their rights over land, but where they also retain certain rights to such.

2.4.4 Practical examples of applications of the *terra nullius* and discovery doctrines in the 19th and 20th centuries

Indigenous peoples retain no property rights whatsoever over their traditional territories following colonization (application of the genuine terra nullius *doctrine)*

In *Cooper v Stuart* (1889), the Judicial Committee of the Privy Council described the New South Wales region of Australia as 'practically unoccupied, without settled inhabitants or settled law',[71] despite the presence of the Aboriginal peoples there. According to the Council the British Crown not only asserted sovereignty over Australia, but claimed absolute ownership rights over lands, with no remaining rights

[70] Blake Watson, 'The Impact of the American Doctrine of Discovery on Native Land Rights in Australia, Canada, and New Zealand' [2011] 34 *Seattle U L Rev* 507 516–17.

[71] See *Cooper v Stuart* (1889) 14 App Cas 286 (PC) 291. In the same vein, see the Supreme Court of New South Wales' ruling in *Attorney General v Brown* (1847) 1 Legge 312.

of the Aboriginal peoples. The approach taken in Australia hence represents an application of a pure *terra nullius* doctrine.[72]

Indigenous peoples continue to possess its traditional land, but the land is declared owned by the colonizing entity which can also uninlaterally extinguish indigenous peoples' possessory rights

This position is normally referred to as one variation of the so-called doctrine of discovery. Former United States Chief Justice John Marshall formulated the best-known version of this doctrine in his rulings in the 'Marshall Trilogy'. In the first of the Trilogy cases, *Johnson v McIntosh*, Chief Justice Marshall did not take the most positive position towards Indian nations' rights over land (i.e. Category 4, above). But he did not align himself with the least favourable view either (i.e. Category 1, above). Rather, Chief Justice Marshall opted for an intermediate position. He ruled that following colonization the Indian nation maintained a right to possession over its territory. Still, the European 'discovery' gave the Federal state exclusive title over the land and the right to extinguish any rights of the Indian nation. In other words, Chief Justice Marshall applied the intermediate Category 2, above.[73]

To mention just one more application of 'Category 2', in 1847 the New Zealand Supreme Court essentially endorsed Chief Justice Marshall's ruling in *Johnson* in *The Queen v Symonds*. In *Symonds*, the Supreme Court held that the Crown's appropriation of New Zealand had not extinguished all Maori rights. Rather, the Court inferred, the Crown owns the land, but the Maori at the same time hold 'modified titles' to the land. The Maori retain customary rights to use and occupy their lands, but such titles are modified by Great Britain's sovereignty over New Zealand, the Court concluded.[74]

Indigenous people continue to own their traditional territories, but cannot transfer land without permission from the colonizing entity, which holds an exclusive right to acquire property from the indigenous people

The third of the Marshall Trilogy cases, *Worcester v Georgia*,[75] was decided eleven years after *Johnson*. Here, Chief Justice Marshall took a more positive view towards Indian nations' rights over land compared with the prior case. In *Worcester*, Marshall concluded that the Indian nation continued to own its traditional territory following colonization, but was not free to sell the land at will. Rather, due to its 'discovery', the Federal state held a pre-emptive right to acquire land from the Indians. In other words, different to *Johnson*, in *Worcester* Marshall employed the Category 3 approach towards the Indian nations' lands articulated above.[76]

72 Watson, 'The Impact of the American Doctrine of Discovery on Native Land Rights, (n 70) 512, 518.

73 See ibid., 507–11, and *Johnson v McIntosh*, 21 US 543 (1823).

74 See *The Queen v Symonds* (1847) NZPCC 387. See also Mark Hickford, 'Settling Some Very Important Principles of Colonial Law, Three "Forgotten" Cases of the 1840s' [2004] *Victoria University of Wellington Law Review* 35 1, Watson (n 70) 528–29; Gilbert, *Indigenous Peoples' Land Rights* (n 7) 59.

75 *Worcester v Georgia* (n 37).

76 See Anaya, *Indigenous Peoples in International Law* (n 1) 24–25; Blumm, 'Why Aboriginal Title is a Fee Simple Absolute' [2011] *Lewis & Clark Law School Legal Studies Research Paper* No 24; Watson, 'The Impact of the American Doctrine of Discovery on Native Land Rights (n 70) 507, 511–12. The

Indigenous peoples continue to own their traditional territories and are free to transfer land to whomsoever they see fit

The author has not come across any examples of this approach being taken towards colonized indigenous territories.

2.4.5 Final remarks

The intention with explaining how various jurisdictions nuanced the *terra nullius* doctrine is not to marginalize the impact this doctrine has had, and continues to have, on indigenous peoples. But at the same time, it is cardinal not to infer too quickly—as some tend to do—that applications of the *terra nullius* doctrine have necessarily resulted in complete extinguishment of indigenous peoples' proprietary rights over their traditional territories. It is one thing that philosophers, legal scholars, and the like develop *principles and theories* asserting that indigenous peoples' ways of life, including use of territories, can not result in rights over land. It is quite another that those authorized to create laws do so *with the effect* of excluding the possibility of indigenous peoples holding rights over their traditional territories. As Section 2.2 explains, and as the below returns to, that a state claims sovereignty over an indigenous people's traditional territory does not necessarily in itself result in extinguishment of the indigenous people's property rights over land. Rather, positive law to that effect is needed in order to transfer private rights from indigenous peoples to the state.

2.5 The Post-World War II Period—Return of Classical International Law's Position on Group Rights

2.5.1 Introduction

As mentioned, during the years that lead up to World War II, the League of Nations' minority protection system started to implode and eventually collapsed. In addition, the Nazi regime used alleged needs to protect German minority groups in neighbouring countries as justification for the aggressions that finally resulted in the outbreak of the war. To make matters worse, the general perception was that the German minorities had collaborated in these efforts. These factors together had

Marshall Trilogy has been subject to extensive study. A number of interpretations of Chief Justice Marshall's rulings have been presented. One reason behind the divergence of opinion as to what, more precisely, were Marshall's conclusions may be that the Marshall Trilogy includes numerous references to Indians as inferior people, or even as savages, with little progress in civilized occupations such as agriculture or manufacturing. See Williams, *Like a Loaded Weapon* (University of Minnesota Press, 2005) 51–70; Blumm, ibid.; Huff, 'Indigenous Land Rights and the New Self-Determination' (n 51) 299–300; Anaya, *Indigenous Peoples in International Law* (n 1) 23–26. All may hence not agree with the classification of *Johnson* and *Worcester* presented above. It does, however, seem to represent the dominant opinion. In any event, for the present purposes it is not necessary to provide an exact and complete analysis of the Marshall Trilogy or of other jurisprudence of the time. The point here is simply to show that colonization of indigenous peoples' territories needed not necessarily result in domestic legal orders that deprived indigenous peoples of all proprietary interests in land.

rendered the world community averse to minority rights when it embarked on crafting an improved world order in the wake of Word War II. Simultaneously, a belief emerged (probably partly spurred by the aversion to minority rights) that effective protection of individual civil and political rights does indirectly—yet adequately—protect the cultural characteristics of members of minority groups. Therefore, there should be no need for rights that explicitly target minority groups as such, it was argued.[77] Or perhaps one should rather say that such a belief re-emerged. Because the view that justice can be achieved through accurately formulating the state-individual relationship essentially implied a return to classical liberal values.

Another factor amplified the interest in individual human rights in the post World War II period. Many statesmen wished to weaken minority groups' potential to challenge state-power. The individual human rights approach fits this interest perfectly. It protects members of minorities as individuals, but not national groups' societal institutions through which collective (nationalistic) interests and aspirations could be chanelled. Thus disempowered, minorities were poorly equipped to resist deliberate nation-building processes of the state. As one observer put it: '[i]n a world where individuals were fully protected minority groups would disappear with time and the "nationality" problem would cease to pose any threat to world stability.'[78] Thus, when the foundation for a new world order was created in the wake of World War II, protection of minority rights that the League of Nations had promoted was substituted for a set of universal individual human rights. Joseph Kunz's observation illustrates the sentiment of the time well: '[a]t the end of the First World War international protection of minorities was the great fashion . . . [t]oday, the well dressed international lawyer wears "human rights"'.[79]

The notion that the principle of self-determination could be invoked to establish autonomy rights for groups within states suffered a fate similar to that of minority rights. True, in the post-World War II period, a few legal scholars suggested that peoples in the cultural/ethnic understanding of the term could also be beneficiaries of a right to self-determination. Still, faithful to classical liberalism, the overwhelming majority of international lawyers frowned at this idea. They submitted that understanding 'peoples' in such a manner constituted a contradiction in terms. Mainstream legal doctrine maintained that under international law, it is not possible to treat groups as political entities that are not already recognized as such. They asserted that by definition, polities that seek a right to self-determination can at

[77] Hannum, *Autonomy, Sovereignty, and Self-Determination* (n 47) 57; Will Kymlicka, *Multicultural Odysseys—Navigating the New International Politics of Diversity* (Oxford University Press, 2007) 29–30; Crawford, 'The Right to Self-Determination' (n 59) 14–15; Ana Filipa Vrdoljak, 'Self-Determination and Cultural Rights', in Francesco Francioni and Martin Scheinin (eds.), *Cultural Human Rights* (Martinus Nijhoff Publishers, 2008) 56; Kingsbury, 'Reconciling' (n 59) 78.

[78] See R E Hauser, as cited in Luis Rodríguez-Piñero, *Indigenous Peoples, Postcolonialism, and International Law* (Oxford University Press, 2005) 196; also Kymlicka, *Multicultural Odysseys* (n 77) 30–31, for a similar opinon.

[79] Josef Kunz, 'The Present Status of the International Law for the Protection of Minorities' [1954] *American Journal of International Law*, Vol 48 2 282.

present have no legal status and, as a consequence, enjoy no rights under international law.[80] In an oft used quote from 1956, Ivor Jennings is surely representative of the position of international lawyers of the era. He submitted that '[o]n the surface it seem[s] reasonable: let the people decide. [But] [i]t [is] in fact ridiculous because the people cannot decide until somebody decides who are the people.'[81] In a similar vein, the International Law Commission (ILC) opined that defining a 'state' or establishing what characteristics a community should possess to qualify as a state would serve no purpose.[82] Again, we see a return to classical international law. As Section 2.3 describes, classical international law held that the law should not, indeed cannot, concern itself with what polities make up a state, as the state pre-dates the law.

2.5.2 The United Nations Charter

Although, as mentioned, human rights ideas had surfaced centuries earlier, it was only in the post-World War II era that human rights formally became a concern of international law.[83] The United Nations (UN) Charter highlights the importance of respect for human rights, by declaring promotion of such rights as one of its objectives. Still, although the formal incorporation of human rights into the international legal system was significant, it did not reshape the basic structure of international law.

In conformity with the classical liberal legal tradition, post UN Charter law recognized only individuals as beneficiaries of human rights. The Charter further entrenches the centrality of the state in the international legal order. It underscores that international law rests heavily on the principle of state sovereignty. The UN Charter explicitly declares that human rights evolve only as a result of acceptance by states.[84] In addition, although the Charter was the first international legal instrument to refer to the principle of self-determination of peoples[85], it did not challenge the centrality of the state in the international legal order. Not all states favoured that the Charter refers to a principle of self-determination of peoples. They cautioned that such a reference might cause a threat to the state-centred world order and spur secession movements among national minorities. These concerns were allayed, however, by general statements that clarified that the reference to the principle of self-determination was not to be understood as conferring rights to minorities or other sub-segments of society. Comforted that the beneficiaries of the principle of self-determination were not peoples in any ethno-cultural meaning of the term—but rather states through their 'agent' peoples in the meaning the entire population of the state—all states agreed to the inclusion of references to the principle of self-determination in the Charter. Thus, although it is significant that the

[80] Crawford, *The Creation of States* (n 6) 124–25.
[81] Ivor Jennings, *The Approach to Self-Government* (Cambridge University Press, 1956) 56.
[82] ILC, Report 1949: A/925 9.
[83] Hannum, *Autonomy, Sovereignty, and Self-Determination* (n 47) 104.
[84] See Articles 2(4), 2(7), 13(1), 55(c). See also Cassese, *International Law* (n 13) 331–32, 336, 378.
[85] Articles 1(2), 55.

founding document of the UN refers to the principle of self-determination of peoples, the principle, as understood at the time, did not strengthen the situation of groups within the state, as it pertained only to state-to-state, and not group-to-state, relationships.[86] In sum, the references to the principle of self-determination of peoples in the UN Charter were not in any way intended to challenge the notion of the primacy of the state in international law. On the contrary, the Charter re-affirmed the state-individual dichotomy present in international law since the Peace of Westphalia, with the League of Nations epoch as the only small possible interruption.

2.5.3 The International Bill of Rights and other human rights instruments of the era

True to the objective set out in its Charter, following its establishment the UN embarked on crafting the first universally applicable human rights instrument. In 1948, the UN General Assembly (UNGA) adopted the Universal Declaration on Human Rights (UDHR).[87] The UDHR reflected the fashion of the time. It embraced only individual, and not group, rights.[88] Notwithstanding, the UDHR broke with the policies of racial supremacy that had underpinned colonization. With the adoption of the UDHR, the fundamental principle of human beings' equal value was codified into international law.[89] This development was of course significant in itself. But in addition, the adoption of the UDHR arguably spear-headed later developments in international law of greater relevance to the present purposes,[90] as the book shall return to below.

In 1948, the UNGA also adopted the Genocide Convention[91] as a response to the atrocities committed during World War II. A convention that outlaws genocide

[86] See UN GAOR, 6th session, Third Committee, 366th meeting 29 and 397th meeting 5–6, and UN Doc E/CN4/Sub2/L.625 77, 80. See also Philip Alston, 'Peoples' Rights: Their Rise and Fall', in Philip Alston (ed.), *Peoples' Rights* (Oxford University Press, 2005) 260–61; Cassese, *Self-Determination of Peoples* (n 66) 39–43; Crawford, *The Creation of States* (n 6) 112–14; Vrdoljak, 'Self-Determination and Cultural Rights', (n 77) 62.

[87] Adopted and proclaimed by UN General Assembly resolution 217 A (III) of 10 December 1948.

[88] See Kymlicka, *Multicultural Odysseys* (n 77) 30–31; and compare S James Anaya, 'The Capacity of International Law to Advance Ethnic or Nationality Rights Claims', in Kymlicka (ed.), *The Rights of Minority Cultures* (n 17) 326.

[89] As indicated, also prior to the adoption of the UDHR, liberal theories had for centuries celebrated equality of men in principle. But this equality had in practice been reserved for European men with means. See Sandra Fredman, 'Combating Racism with Human Rights: The Right to Equality', in Sandra Fredman (ed.), *Discrimination and Human Rights: The Case of Racism* (Oxford University Press, 2001) 14–15.

[90] See Kymlicka, *Multicultural Odysseys* (n 77) 89. Recognition of human rights in the aftermath of World War II did not only occur at a global level. At the same time as the UN engaged in drafting the UDHR, European and American states crafted regional human rights instruments. These instruments did not differ from their global counterparts in their principal approach towards human rights. In other words, the regional human rights instruments also proclaimed rights of individuals only. See the American Declaration of the Rights and Duties of Man, *OAS Res XXX*, the American Convention on Human Rights, *OAS Treaty Series No 36*, and the European Convention for the Protection of Human Rights and Fundamental Freedoms (Nov 4, 1950), ETS 5; 213 UNTS 221.

[91] Convention on the Prevention and Punishment of the Crime of Genocide, adopted by UNGA Resolution 260 (III) on 9 December 1948.

presented an apparent opportunity for the world community to break with the state individual dichotomy. Seemingly, the beneficiaries of a right not to be subject to genocide are peoples or other groups that share cultural and ethnic backgrounds, rather than individuals or aggregate populations of states with mixed ethnical origin. After all, by definition genocide is directed against a particular ethnicity or culture, rather than against individual members of that group or a population of a state. Notwithstanding, the language of the Genocide Convention does not speak in terms of rights of collectives. Rather, the Convention obliges states to punish persons guilty of acts defined as genocide. Consequently, if interpreting the Genocide Convention in the light of other human rights instruments adopted during the era, one can hardly refer to the Convention as evidence that international law at the time acknowledged human rights of peoples or other groups defined in terms of a common ethnicity and/or culture.[92]

Not long after the adoption of the UDHR, UN member states embarked on elaborating on and concretizing the rights enshrined in the Declaration in what was first supposed to be one, but which eventually ended up being two, legally binding human rights instruments. In 1966, the UNGA simultaneously adopted the International Covenant on Civil and Political Rights (CCPR) and the International Covenant on Economic, Social and Cultural Rights (CESCR).[93] As other international instruments of the era, the 1966 Covenants were true to the individual liberal tradition. The covenants underscore the centrality of the state in international law, and affirmed that human rights apply to individuals only.[94] CCPR Article 27, while frequently invoked in an indigenous rights context, illustrates well the individual nature of the rights enshrined in the CCPR, as these were understood at the time of the adoption of the instrument. Pursuant to this provision, individuals that belong to minority groups must not be denied the right to enjoy their own culture in community with other members of the group. The reference to individual members of the group, rather than to the group as such, highlights that the authors of the CCPR understood Article 27 to set forth a right to be enjoyed by individuals only. In addition, Article 27 is framed as a negative right. The state's duty, according to the wording of the provision, is to not interfere with, rather than to positively protect, cultural practices. That said, CCPR Article 27 does acknowledge that in certain circumstances, the right to culture can only be enjoyed in a meaningful manner in the context of other members of the group. Hence, Article 27 added an,

[92] See Alston, 'Peoples' Rights: Their Rise and Fall' (n 86) 261–62. See, however, also Rodolfo Stavenhagen, 'Cultural Rights: A Social Science Perspective', in Eide, Krause, and Rosas (eds.), *Economic, Social and Cultural Rights* (n. 38) 87, where he, referring to Buergenthal, asserts that the Genocide Convention recognizes the right of groups to exist.

[93] Both Covenants were adopted by UNGA through resolution 2200A (XXI) of 16 December 1966.

[94] That said, some argue that already at the time of the drafting of the CESCR, the crafters of the Covenant understood the economic, social, and culture rights the CESCR sets forth to be collective in nature. Mathew Craven submits that this is the reason why the CESCR was not equipped with the individual complaints mechanism that was incorporated into the CCPR. See Mathew Craven, 'The UN Committee on Economic, Social and Cultural Rights', in Eide, Krause, and Rosas (eds.), *Economic, Social and Cultural Rights* (n. 38) 458.

albeit limited, collective dimension to the individual right to culture, something that is absent in the UDHR.[95]

As mentioned, for most parts, the CCPR and CESCR build and elaborate on the UDHR. But in contrast to the UDHR, the 1966 Covenants also embrace the right to self-determination. The common Article 1.1 of CCPR and CESCR proclaims that 'all peoples have the right to self-determination . . . [b]y virtue of . . . which they freely determine their political status . . .'. The also common Article 1.2 then proceeds to lay out the so-called resource dimension of the right to self-determination. The provision stipulates that all peoples have the right to freely dispose of their natural resources and must not be deprived of their means of subsistence.[96] Through its inclusion in the 1966 Covenants, the principle of self-determination transcended from a principle into a legally binding right.[97]

The incorporation of the right to self-determination into the 1966 Covenants was preceded by a debate similar to the one that took place prior to the adoption of the self-determination provisions in the UN Charter. Again, some states were concerned that the Covenants proclaiming a right to self-determination of peoples could be interpreted as an endorsement of rights of ethnic and cultural groups. Such a recognition could, these states feared, potentially disrupt sovereign states. Notwithstanding, in the debate that ensued, the position that the 1966 Covenants should embrace a right to self-determination increasingly gained momentum. Eventually, concerned states agreed that it was sufficient to apply the same safety measures as when approving the UN Charter. Consequently, in connection with the adoption of the 1966 Covenants, a large number of states declared that the right to self-determination enshrined in common Article 1 cannot be interpreted as awarding rights to sub-segments of a state. Rather, the term 'peoples' should be understood as referring to the aggregate populations of states. Thus reassured, the UN member states proceeded to adopt the CCPR and the CESCR.[98] The continued understanding of peoples as aggregate populations of states implied that the common Article 1—at the time of its adoption—did not envisage recognition of human rights of groups in any meaningful understanding of the term. Again, when the beneficiary of the right is the entire population of a state, the right to self-determination becomes, if not formally, so at least for all practical purposes, essentially a right of the state vis-à-vis other states.

Even prior to the adoption of the 1966 Covenants, the UNGA had actually endorsed an instrument that elaborates on the right to self-determination's resource dimension. The Declaration on Permanent Sovereignty over Natural Resources[99]

95 Regarding the contemporary understanding of CCPR Article 27, see Section 5.5.

96 In the same vein, pursuant to the also identical CCPR Article 47 and CESCR Article 25, nothing in the Covenants shall be interpreted as impairing the right of all peoples to enjoy and utilize their natural resources.

97 That said, the UNGA had already referred to self-determination as a right in the 1960 UN Declaration on Granting Independence to Colonial Countries and Peoples (UN Resolution 1514 (XV), 14 December, 1960). See further Section 2.5.4.

98 Raic, *Statehood and the Law of Self-Determination* (n 14) 242–43; Cassese, *Self-Determination of Peoples* (n 66) 141–46.

99 GA Res 1803 (XVII), adopted on 14 December 1962.

(1962) proclaims a right of peoples over their natural resources. But the Declaration mixes references to a right of states to sovereignty over natural resources with such a right of peoples.[100] Consequently, for instance James Crawford doubts that the subjects of the rights enshrined in the Declaration are peoples in an ethnic/cultural meaning of the word. Rather, he submits, the more likely intended beneficiaries are entire populations of states.[101] Hence, it appears that the Declaration on Permanent Sovereignty over Natural Resources—at least at the time of its adoption—was understood to proclaim that natural resources of a state should benefit that state and not other states.[102] It did not, according to this interpretation, address who holds rights to natural resources within the state.

Thus, the incorporation of the right to self-determination in the 1966 Covenants did not intend to award political rights to peoples in the ethnic/cultural meaning of the term. That said, one should note that the drafters of common Article 1 consciously opted for rendering peoples, rather than states, the formal subjects of the right to self-determination. James Crawford points out that during the negotiations on the CCPR and the CESCR several proposals for a definition of the term 'peoples' were put forward. None of these were eventually included in the Covenants.[103] Still, the fact that a definition of peoples was considered underscores that the UN member states deliberately made peoples, and not states, subjects of the right to self-determination. The distinction is not without relevance. True, to formally view states and peoples as two distinct legal subjects might be of limited practical relevance when peoples are understood as the aggregate populations of states. As mentioned, under such circumstances, in all but formal terms, a state then exercises the right to self-determination through the 'agent' its people. But as the book shall return to in subsequent chapters, it has certainly been beneficial, perhaps even a pre-requisite, for subsequent developments within the self-determination discourse that at the time when the right was formulated, peoples, and not states, were viewed as the holders of the right. The inclusion of a right to self-determination of peoples in the 1966 Covenants would spur a debate on peoples' rights, including on who constitute peoples for international legal

[100] For instance, paras. 1 and 5 of the Declaration refer to peoples' rights and sovereignty over natural resources. At the same time, the *consideranda* to the Resolution refers to the inalienable rights of states to dispose of their wealth and resources. See also Ian Brownlie, *Principles of Public International Law* (6th edn., Oxford University Press, 2003) 515–16.

[101] See Crawford, 'The Right to Self-Determination' (n 59) 22. For a similar position, see also Cassese, *Self-Determination of Peoples* (n 66) 99–100.

[102] One can further note that in 1974, the UNGA adopted the Charter of Economic Rights and Duties of States (Res 3281 XXIX), a document which refers exclusively to states' (and not peoples') permanent sovereignty over natural resources.

[103] See Crawford, *The Creation of States* (n 6) 125–26. In the same vein, Antonio Cassese underlines that already at the time of the adoption of the 1966 Covenants, the right to self-determination was perceived to be geared towards peoples, and not states. See *Self-Determination of Peoples* (n 66) 143–44, 242, 285. See also Ian Brownlie, 'The Rights of Peoples in Modern International Law', in James Crawford (ed.), *The Rights of Peoples* (Clarendon Press, 1988) 3–5. Similarly, when crafting the African Charter on Human and Peoples' Rights, the 'Organization for African Unity' considered, but in the end deliberately omitted, a definition of 'peoples' in the African Charter. See Rapporteur's Report, OAU Doc CM/1149 (XXXVII), Ann 1, 4, para. 13 (1981).

purposes.[104] Perhaps, the rhetorical question posed by James Crawford sometime later would then be dignified with an answer; '[i]f the only rights of peoples are rights against other States, and if there is no change to the established position that the government of the State represents "the State" (i.e. the people of the State) for all international legal purposes irrespective of its representativeness, then what is the point of referring to the rights in question as rights of peoples?'[105]

Still, setting potential future developments aside, the international legal system the young UN set out to craft clearly broke with the League of Nations' interest in group rights inspired by the principle of self-determination. International law returned to classical liberal values. Three of liberal theory's most profound presumptions were incorporated into the contemporary international legal system that the UN and its member states set out to formulate in the wake of World War II. First, it was reiterated that it is self-evident that international legal standards emerge from the legal subjects themselves, in other words from states. State sovereignty was reaffirmed as the constitutional principle upon which the international legal system rests. It was again taken for granted that the creation of states pre-dates international law.[106] Second, UN member states accepted the notion that once created, the law binds states. A state cannot subsequently opt out of the law due to a change of mind. Finally, the UN Charter and the Bill of Rights implied a return to a firm application of the state-individual dichotomy. The group rights orientation of the League of Nations era was replaced with a complete belief in universal individual human rights. As Henry Reynolds puts it: '[w]hereas the League [of Nations] had thought a lot about minorities, the United Nations put the emphasis on the rights of individuals on one hand, and the rights of states on the other . . .'.[107]

2.5.4 The decolonization epoch

Following the transition from a principle into a right, the right to self-determination was instantly put into action. Colonies relied heavily on self-determination arguments when demanding independence from colonial

[104] For instance, Antonio Cassese observes that the acceptance of a right to self-determination of peoples in international law 'set in motion a restructuring and redefinition of the world community's basic "rules of the game"'; see Cassese, *Self-Determination of Peoples* (n 66) 1. Philip Alston also argues that despite its vagueness and ambiguity, the inclusion of the right to self-determination in the 1966 Covenants encouraged proponents of peoples' rights proper, and instigated an increased inclination to recognize the existence of such rights; see Philip Alston, *Peoples' Rights* (Oxford University Press, 2005) 1.

[105] James Crawford, 'The Rights of Peoples: "Peoples" or "Governments"?', in James Crawford (ed.), *The Rights of Peoples* (Clarendon Press, 1988).

[106] As Wolfgang Friedmann observes, the world during the Bill of Rights era was organized with states as the fundamental building blocks. Changes in international law could occur only due to state action and states were the repositories of legitimate authority over peoples and territories. See Wolfgang Friedmann, *The Changing Structure of International Law* (Columbia University Press, 1964) 213.

[107] See Henry Reynolds, 'Aborigines and the 1967 Referendum: Thirty Years On', in Department of the Senate Occasional Lecture Series, Parliament House, Australia (14 November 1997) 58. Similarly, Rupert Emerson notes that during the Wilsonian period, focus lay on rights of ethnic communities primarily defined by culture, whereas in the post-World War II era, ethnicity was essentially irrelevant. See Rupert Emerson, 'Self-Determination' [1971] *American Journal of International Law*, Vol 65 463.

states.[108] Section 2.5.3 touches upon how the decolonization process produced a number of legal sources that contributed to the transition of the principle of self-determination into a right, complementing the common Article 1 of the 1966 Covenants. As further touched upon, one of these instruments in fact pre-dated the adoption of the 1966 Covenants. Already in 1960, the UNGA Declaration on the Granting of Independence to Colonial Countries and Peoples proclaimed that peoples in colonized territories are entitled to the right of self-determination.[109]

The Declaration on the Granting of Independence to Colonial Countries and Peoples was immediately followed by UN Resolution 1541 (XV),[110] which extended the applicability of the right of self-determination to non-self-governing peoples. The International Court of Justice (ICJ) also contributed to the confirmation of self-determination as a right in a couple of cases decided around this time.[111] As revisited in subsequent chapters, it is worth noting that in doing so, the ICJ relied heavily on the formally non-binding Declaration against Colonization.[112] The mentioned resolutions thus collaborated to broaden the applicability of the right to self-determination. As a result of this process, at the end of the decolonization process, the right to self-determination not only addressed peoples in its meaning as aggregate populations of states. Now, international law understood the right to apply to in addition to populations of states, populations of territories that had not yet attained independence, as well as to populations of territories geographically separated from the state administering the territory and/or subject to foreign military occupation.[113]

The decolonization process resulted in international law no longer being essentially an internal Western affair. Sovereign states around the globe could now participate in the creation of international law. In that way, decolonization dramatically rewrote the political map of the world. Still, it did not challenge the centrality of the state in the international legal system. On the contrary, decolonization universalized the European state model as the supreme legal subject in the international community.[114] In addition, as Section 2.3.3 touches on, the new African and Asian states relied on the *uti possidetis* precedent set when Latin America

[108] Cassese, *Self-Determination of Peoples* (n 66) 71–74.

[109] See UNGA Resolution 1514 (XV); also Crawford, 'The Right to Self-Determination' (n 59) 17.

[110] Resolution 1541 (XV) on 'Principles Which Should Guide Members in Determining whether or not an Obligation Exists to Transmit the Information Called for under Article 73e of the Charter', 15 December 1960, UN GAOR, 15th Session, Supplement No 16 (A/4684).

[111] See e.g. the *Namibia Case*, Legal Consequences for States of the Continued Presence of South Africa in Namibia notwithstanding Security Resolution 276 (1970), ICJ Reports (1971) 31 and the *Western Sahara Case*, Advisory Opinion, ICJ Reports (1975) 12.

[112] Fromherz, '"Indigenous Peoples" Courts' (n 66) 1359.

[113] Crawford, 'The Right to Self-Determination' (n 59) 16–20; Cassese, *Self-Determination of Peoples*, (n 66) 59; Cassese, *International Law* (n 13) 61–62; Alexandra Xanthaki, 'The Right to Self-Determination: Meaning and Scope', in Ghanea and Xanthaki (eds.), *Minorities, Peoples and Self-Determination* (n 47) 16–17.

[114] See Koskenniemi, *The Gentle Civilizer of Nations* (n 15) 174–75; compare Barry Hindess, 'Sovereignty as Indirect Rule', in Trudy Jacobsen, Charles Sampford, and Ramesh Thakur (eds.), *Re-envisioning Sovereignty—The End of Westphalia?* (Ashgate Publishing, 2008) 307.

gained independence from Spain and Portugal to deny indigenous peoples both political and proprietary rights over lands and natural resources. As the Latin American states before them, African and Asian states continued to rely on the laws and policies towards indigenous peoples that the previous colonizers had established.[115] As Malcolm Shaw notes, the *ute possidetis* rule 'bestowed an aura of historical legality to the expropriation of the lands of indigenous peoples'.[116] The dominating view continued to be that the colonization of indigenous peoples' territories had been 'just'.[117] During the decolonization era, ideas that 'backward' indigenous societies should be integrated into the dominant political and social orders that engulf them were still common among states, including, or perhaps even particularly, among states that had just gained independence.[118] This position was backed by a sentiment that in any event, indigenous peoples were destined to slowly disappear and be integrated into the majority societies.[119] The integration prophecy served to legitimize the exclusion of indigenous peoples from the international regime of decolonization.[120]

Hence, the decolonization process had little or no impact on indigenous peoples' status in the international legal system, or rather on the lack thereof. The legal entities that were bestowed with the right to self-determination in the decolonization process were the entire populations of colonial territories, irrespective of pre-colonial ethnic and cultural patterns. Whether the colony hosted more than one culturally and ethnically distinct population lacked legal relevance, as did the fact that several of the colonies' borders had been haphazardly defined by the previous colonizers.[121] 'Territory, not "nationhood", was the determining factor' in the decolonization process.[122] In short, the decolonization regime by-passed indigenous peoples' societies. These simply became subjects of new forms of

[115] Ian Brownlie, *African Boundaries: A Legal and Diplomatic Encyclopedia* (Hurst & Co Publishers, 1979); Gilbert, *Indigenous Peoples' Land Rights* (n 7) 31, 36–37.

[116] Malcolm Shaw, 'The Heritage of States: The Principle of Uti Possedetis Juris Today' [1996] *British Yearbook of International Law* 97 67.

[117] Antonio Cassese observes that during the negotiations on the UNGA Resolutions that shaped the application of the right to self-determination to the former colonies, geopolitical considerations led developing countries, supported by socialist states and with no objections from Western states, to deny applicability of the right to self-determination to ethnic groups within colonial territories. Cassese labels the fact that the right to self-determination that emerged during the decolonization era was deemed inapplicable to ethnic groups a 'major flaw'. See Cassese, *Self-Determination of Peoples* (n 66) 72–74.

[118] James Tully, 'The Struggles of Indigenous Peoples for and of Freedom', in Duncan Ivison, Paul Patton, and Will Sanders (eds.), *Political Theory and the Rights of Indigenous Peoples* (Cambridge University Press, 2000) 40, 43–44.

[119] Hannum, *Autonomy, Sovereignty, and Self-Determination* (n 47) 81.

[120] Rodríguez-Piñero, *Indigenous Peoples, Postcolonialism, and International Law* (n 78) 143.

[121] Emerson, 'Self-Determination' (n 107) 463; Thomas M Franck, 'The Emerging Right to Democratic Governance' [1992] *American Journal of International Law* 86, reprinted in Evans and Capps (eds.), *International Law* (n 8) (Vol II) 5–55; Castellino, 'Territorial Integrity' (n 47) 511.

[122] Hannum, *Autonomy, Sovereignty, and Self-Determination* (n 47) 36 (with reference to Pomerance); Siegfried Wiessner, 'Indigenous Sovereignty: A Reassessment in Light of the UN Declaration on the Rights of Indigenous Peoples' [2008] *Vanderbilt Journal of Transnational Law* 41 1150; Raic, *Statehood and the Law of Self-Determination* (n 14) 209.

colonization.[123] An era that otherwise revolutionized the political map of the world left political thought, state policy, and international law on indigenous peoples and their rights largely the same.

The assimilatory approach taken towards indigenous peoples during the decolonization era is reflected in the first human rights instrument that specifically targets the situation of such peoples, which was adopted during this time. The International Labour Organization's (ILO) Convention (No 107) Concerning the Protection and Integration of Indigenous and Other Tribal and Semi-Tribal populations in Independent Countries (ILO 107)[124] (1957) was a child of its time. As the title suggests, ILO 107 focuses on rights of indigenous individuals.[125] What is more, the Convention aspired to integrate members of the 'less advanced' indigenous groups into the surrounding, developed, society, rather than to protect them as distinct ethnic and cultural entities.[126] Indeed, this position follows already from ILO 107's understanding of indigenous peoples. ILO 107 defines indigenous peoples as less-advanced groups *not yet integrated* into the society to which they 'belong'. In other words, the Convention rests on the assumption that indigenous peoples will eventually be integrated into the majority society, at which point ILO 107 ceases to apply to the group (rather naturally, as the indigenous population no longer exists according to the logic of the Convention).[127] Hence, international law's first attempt to define indigenous peoples aimed at seeing them disappear.[128] It was perceived that integration of the less advanced indigenous groups into the surrounding society was not only inevitable, but also in their best interest.[129]

Thus, at the time, the decolonization process did little to promote rights of indigenous peoples. That is not to say, however, that it was irrelevant to the indigenous rights discourse. Section 2.5.3 points to how the UDHR's confirmation of the equal value of all individuals, irrespective of the Declaration's focus on individual rights, probably paved the way for later progressive developments in

[123] Michael Reisman, 'Protecting Indigenous Rights in International Adjudication' [1995] *American Journal of International Law* 89 352–53; Kymlicka, *Multicultural Odysseys* (n 77) 269–70; Gilbert, *Indigenous Peoples' Land Rights* (n 7) 31.

[124] Adopted at 40th ILO Session on 26 June, 1957.

[125] See Alexandra Xanthaki, *Indigenous Rights and United Nations Standards—Self-Determination, Culture and Land* (Cambridge University Press, 2007) 73. True, ILO 107 does incorporate certain provisions that at first sight seems to address a collective aspect of indigenous rights, particularly within the sphere of lands and natural resources. But as Luis Rodríguez-Piñero observes, a closer examination of these provisions reveals that in fact, they aim to promote agrarian development, rather than respect for rights—see *Indigenous Peoples, Postcolonialism, and International Law* (n 78).

[126] Ibid., 174; see ILO 107 Article 1(a).

[127] Ibid., 164–65.

[128] Ibid., 172. For a detailed elaboration on why the ILO initially took such an integrationalist approach towards indigenous peoples, see ibid., 83–112, 181–99.

[129] See Athanasios Yupsanis, 'ILO Convention No. 169 Concerning Indigenous and Tribal Peoples in Independent Countries 1989–2009: An Overview' [2010] *Nordic Journal of International Law* 79 434–35; Lee Swepston, 'Indigenous Peoples in International Law and Organizations', in Joshua Castellino and Niamh Walsh (eds.), *International Law and Indigenous Peoples* (Martinus Nijhoff Publisher, 2005) 55. That said, Luis Rodrígues-Piñero notes that although ILO 107 takes an integrationist approach towards indigenous peoples, the Convention nonetheless made them *objects* of international law, something which would contribute to indigenous peoples becoming *subjects* of international law decades later (see ibid., 116, 139).

international law. The decolonization process was such a development.[130] In the same vein, the decolonization process, although itself blind to indigenous patterns of association, would decades later contribute to a belated decolonization process that would target indigenous peoples.[131]

In sum, by the end of the decolonization era, international law continuously understood 'peoples' as aggregate populations of states or territories. True, already then, a few scholars such as Richard Falk did argue that peoples in the ethnic/cultural understanding of the term are also bestowed with rights.[132] Still, this position enjoyed limited support among mainstream lawyers. Ian Brownlie's is surely a more representative view of the era. He labelled advocates of the existence of peoples' rights proper eccentric. Brownlie asserted that such rights would ignore the principle of non-intervention and diminish the right to self-determination. He held it self-evident that the 'peoples' that enjoy the right to self-determination are aggregate populations of states or territories.[133] Similarly, Hurst Hannum took for granted that there are no such things as collective human rights proper, wherefore the right to self-determination would have no relevance in the context of indigenous peoples.[134]

[130] Kymlicka, *Multicultural Odysseys* (n 77) 89.

[131] Ibid., and 269–70. Will Kymlicka submits that once the world community had accepted rights of former colonies, it was difficult to ignore indigenous peoples' claims that historic injustices directed at them should be addressed as well. For a similar opinion, see also Andrew Gray, 'The Indigenous Movement in Asia' in R H Barnes, Andrew Gray, and Benedict Kingsbury (eds.), *Indigenous Peoples of Asia* (Association for Asian Studies, 1995) 42–43; compare Mohsen al Attar, Nicole Aylwin, and Rosemary J Coombe, 'Indigenous Cultural Heritage Rights in International Human Rights Law', in Catherine Bell and Robert K Paterson (eds.), *Protection of First Nations Cultural Heritage, Laws, Policy, and Reform* (UBS Press, 2009) 315.

[132] Richard Falk, 'The Rights of Peoples (In Particular Indigenous Peoples)', in Jamess Crawford (ed.), *The Rights of Peoples* (Clarendon Press, 1988) 17–37, in particular 34, 35.

[133] Brownlie, 'The Rights of Peoples' (n 103) 4–16.

[134] Hannum, *Autonomy, Sovereignty, and Self-Determination* (n 47) 95–103.

3

Political Theory that Underpins the Law

3.1 Introduction

Chapter 2 outlines how liberalism emerged with the state, and presupposes it. The previous chapter articulates how liberal philosophy developed social contract theories to explain how groups of men came freely together to form states and agreed to be ruled by sovereigns. As further explained, these theories came to underpin the classical international legal system, and subsequently also the contemporary legal system the young United Nations (UN) embarked on shaping. As also seen, contemporary international law further endorsed the notion that peoples equal the aggregate populations of states (or territories). Moreover, it too rested on the assumption that states pre-date the law and are therefore free, in accordance with the principle of state sovereignty, to determine what international legal norms there are. Finally, the contemporary international legal system uncritically accepted the idea that human rights can apply to individuals only.

This chapter describes how more recent political theories have, however, seriously challenged the underlying fundaments of classical liberalism, and how this debate has resulted in the emergence of new schools of thought more hospitable towards the idea of group rights. Such an overview is relevant for the purposes of this book, since political theories exercise influence over international law. As Martti Koskenniemi notes, '[i]t is neither useful nor ultimately possible to work with international law in abstraction from descriptive theories about . . . normative views about the principles of justice which should govern international conduct.'[1] Or as the International Court of Justice (ICJ) has put it, '[l]aw exists . . . to serve a social need'.[2] A basic knowledge of trends within political philosophy therefore aids us in properly understanding international law. That said, this chapter does not purport to provide a comprehensive outline of relevant political philosophy theories. For the present purposes, a general overview of the core elements of these thoughts is sufficient.

[1] Martti Koskenniemi, *From Apology to Utopia—The Structure of International Legal Argument* (Cambridge University Press, 2005) 1.

[2] *South West Africa Case, South West Africa*, Second Phase Judgement, ICJ Reports 1966 6 34–35.

3.2 Further on Conventional Individual Liberalism

What has been articulated in Chapter 2 (and revisited above) may give the impression that classical liberalism is one single school of thought. To make such a claim would, however, be an oversimplification. Rather, there are various branches of liberal theory.[3] After centuries of fruitless attempts to formulate one coherent liberal theory of justice around which all liberals could unite, a work was published in 1971 that constitutes an elaborate attempt to present such a theory. *A Theory of Justice* by John Rawls revitalized the liberal school. It served as inspiration for various other contemporary liberal theories, almost always presented as a response to Rawls' ideas. Rawls' major innovation was a formula for redistributive justice not previously present in liberalism. He introduced a 'veil of ignorance' which he maintained a population of some kind of a fictional pre-state society would opt for if allowed to choose the principles that should govern it. Rawls submitted that the usual account of the state of nature is unfair, since some persons have more bargaining power than others due to better natural talents, more initial resources, and superior strength. This is unjust, he opined, since natural advantages are a result of chance, and not deserved. Rawls sought to address this perceived flaw in classical liberal theories by hypothetically blindfolding people so that they are not aware of their own talents and resources when formulating their position on what constitutes a just society. According to him, the population of a society should have to agree on the rules that should govern the society behind a 'veil of ignorance'.[4]

Even if ground-breaking in certain aspects, at its core *A Theory of Justice* remains true to classical individual liberalism. Despite adding the 'veil of ignorance' element to previous liberal theories, Rawls walks in the footsteps of the classical liberal tradition when assuming a hypothetical social contract.[5] As liberal scholars before him, Rawls uncritically accepts the presumption that due to uncertainties and scarcities of social life, groups of individuals in the original position would agree to cede decision-making power to a sovereign. True, according to Rawls, the social contract

[3] Some of the best known branches are utilitarianism, liberal equity, and libertarianism. See Will Kymlicka, *Contemporary Political Philosophy: An Introduction* (Oxford University Press, 2002) x–xi and Chapters 2–4. One should in addition note that while liberal thinkers have sought to formulate various theories based on fundamental liberal values, other philosophers have rejected the underlying premises of liberalism in whole or in part. These philosophers have sought to offer alternative concepts and principles to those provided by liberalism. Some of these theories, such as Marxism, have at times enjoyed considerable support. Notwithstanding, these schools of thought have exercised limited impact on the international legal system. Hence, they are not dealt with further in the present context.

[4] See John Rawls, *A Theory of Justice* (Oxford University Press, 1971) 11–12, 18–21, 74–80, 136–42. Compare also Stephen May, Tariq Modood, and Judith Squires, 'Ethnicity, nationalism and minority rights: charting the disciplinary debates', in Stephen May, Tariq Modood, and Judith Squires (eds.), *Ethnicity, Nationalism and Minority Rights* (Cambridge University Press, 2004) 1; David Lea, *Property Rights, Indigenous People and the Developing World: Issues from Aboriginal Entitlement to Intellectual Ownership Rights* (Martinus Nijhoff Publishers, 2008) 32.

[5] In fact, *A Theory of Justice* generated a revival of social contract theories. See Bardo Fassbender, 'The United Nations Charter As Constitution of the International Community' [1998] *Columbia Journal of Transnational Law* 36, reprinted in Malcom Evans and Patrick Capps (eds.), *International Law* (Vol I) (Ashgate Publishing, 2009) 559.

is only valid as long as the sovereign uses its powers to guard the individual against such scarcities and uncertainties. If the sovereign abuses this trust, the individual is no longer under duty to honour the social contract, he argues.[6] But *A Theory of Justice* is a social contract theory nonetheless. It presupposes the existence of a state and is ignorant to the fact that there may exist ethnically and culturally distinct groups within the state who hold preferences that may not coincide with those of the majority population.

The individual, liberal theories that were formulated as a response to *A Theory of Justice* are no more hospitable to group rights. For instance, another prominent contemporary liberal scholar—Ronald Dworkin—adds to Rawls' 'veil of ignorance' theory by accommodating for individuals that are disabled or otherwise naturally disadvantaged. Dworkin imagines an auction where all members of society start with the same share of resources to bid, and are at the same time unaware of their natural talents and shortcomings. Each person is fictionally asked how much he or she would spend on insurance against disadvantages. According to Dworkin, the amount of resources a society should utilize to compensate for natural disadvantages should equal the total amount paid by individuals for such insurances in the fictitious auction.[7] That said, irrespective of the fact that Dworkin arguably fine-tunes Rawls' 'veil of ignorance' theory, Dworkin's theory too rests on the notion of a social contract, assumes the nation-state, and does not accept group rights.[8]

Hence, as their classical counterparts, the articulated contemporary individual liberal theories also rest on the assumption that justice must be achieved within a polity—the state—whose borders and membership has been determined prior to the formulation of any theory of justice.[9] These individual liberal theories remain indifferent to ethno-cultural compositions of states. They acknowledge rights of individuals only, with no room for group rights. These theories remain true to classical liberalism when maintaining that the state shall not support cultural groups' aspirations to maintain and develop their distinct cultures.[10] The state shall—and, importantly, individual liberalism professes, can—remain neutral between cultures within the state. In this sense, one can view individual liberalism as apolitical, or

[6] Rawls, *A Theory of Justice* (n 4) 11–12, 21–22, 75.

[7] See Ronald Dworkin, *A Matter of Principle* (Harvard University Press, 1985) 206–13; also Kymlicka, *Contemporary Political Philosophy* (n 3) 75–82; Michael Hartney, 'Some Confusion Concerning Collective Rights', in Will Kymlicka (ed.), *The Rights of Minority Cultures* (Oxford University Press, 1995) 212.

[8] In passing, it is worth mentioning a contemporary liberal school that does not accept the assertion that redistribution among individuals is just. Libertarians criticize Rawls and Dworkin for rendering certain individuals mere resources for the good life of others. They submit that the state has no right to encroach upon the individual's right to freely dispose of her or his goods, even for the purpose of increasing equality. Libertarians assert that a just distribution of resources is simply a distribution that follows from people's free choices. See Robert Nozick, *Anarchy, State and Utopia* (Basic Books, 1974) 169–72; compare Kymlicka, *Contemporary Political Philosophy* (n 3) 103–09. Libertarianism does, however, share Rawls' and Dworkin's disinterest in group rights.

[9] Kymlicka, *Contemporary Political Philosophy* (n 3) 254–56.

[10] See, generally, Iris M Young, 'Structural Injustices and Politics of Difference', in T Christiano and J Christman (eds.), *Contemporary Debates in Political Philosophy* (Wiley-Blackwell, 2007); Kymlicka, *Contemporary Political Philosophy* (n 3) 343–45.

even as hostile to politics. Liberals may argue that liberalism 'merely' provides a simple framework within which political choices can be made, rather than a grand political theory.[11]

Individual liberals are, generally speaking, not concerned with whether minority groups share their liberal beliefs. In fact, to many individual liberals local fallacy is a main justification for championing an all-embracing theory of justice. They regard rights of ethnic and/or cultural groups as, by definition, political, in contrast to liberalism which, as mentioned, can be defined as apolitical.[12] Individual liberalism submits that the aim of political philosophy is precisely to provide a theory of justice universal to all societies which can assist in identifying practices that may be rooted in various groups' cultures but that are nonetheless unjust, restrict individual freedom, and should as a consequence be abolished.[13] To the individual liberal, the gradual disappearance of collective cultural identities is not a problem in itself. On the contrary, various forms of individual liberal theories share the assumption that the individual's interests are best promoted by allowing her or him to decide what life to pursue without cultural identity being imposed on the individual. According to individual liberalism, membership in any particular community does not define the individual. Rather, individuals can opt out of their cultural background. Consequently, community matters only to the extent it contributes to the well-being of the individual member. It has no value in its own right, and need therefore not exist in perpetuity, individual liberalism concludes.[14]

3.3 Criticism of Conventional Individual Liberalism

3.3.1 Generally

For centuries, the fact that conventional individual liberalism presupposes a state that pre-dates liberal theories was largely ignored. More recently, however, what impact this assumption may have on the relevance of liberal theory has been increasingly problematized.[15] More and more voices began to argue that conventional liberalism seems to support an abstract world that ignores the realities of current societies.[16] After all, in the real world, more than one ethnic and/or cultural group coinhabit almost all states. This raises the question; if a state is not ethnically

[11] Koskenniemi, *From Apology to Utopia* (n 1) 5–6.

[12] McDonald, 'Should Communities Have Rights? Reflections on Individual Liberalism' [1991] *Canadian Journal of Law and Jurisprudence*, Vol IV, No 2 228; Koskenniemi, *From Apology to Utopia* (n 1) 5–6.

[13] Kymlicka, *Contemporary Political Philosophy* (n 3) 211.

[14] Allan Buchanan, 'The Morality of Secession', in Kymlicka (ed.), *The Rights of Minority Cultures* (n 7) 358.

[15] Duncan Ivison, Paul Patton, and Will Sanders, *Political Theory and the Rights of Indigenous Peoples* (Cambridge University Press, 2000) 5–8; Ayelet Shachar, *Multicultural Jurisdictions—Cultural Differences and Women's Rights* (Cambridge University Press, 2001) 9; Kymlicka, *Contemporary Political Philosophy* (n 3) 61; Vernon Van Dyke, 'The Individual, the State, and Ethnic Communities in Political Theory', in Kymlicka (ed.), *The Rights of Minority Cultures* (n 7) 31.

[16] Michael Keating, 'So Many Nations, So Few States: Territory and Nationalism in the Global Era', in Alain G Gagnon and James Tully (eds.), *Multinational Democracies* (Cambridge University Press,

homogenous, how plausible is the notion that all its citizens have, at one point in time, come together to form the state through a social contract? Is it not more likely that all citizens of a state do not feel equal affinity to all other citizens or solidarity vis-à-vis other groups?[17] Indeed, might not a marginalized group even be adverse towards the majority culture? And if conventional liberalism presupposes a fictitious homogenous state that does not exist in reality, is it at all possible to formulate a coherent, all embracing, theory of justice?

Conventional individual liberals continue to answer the latter question in the affirmative. They retort that liberalism does not stand or fall with the existence of ethnically and culturally homogenous states.[18] Rather, conventional liberals submit, the two essential assertions of liberalism are (i) that a state shall and can be culturally neutral, i.e. has the capacity not to promote one culture over another, and (ii) that membership of a particular cultural background or community does not define individuals. Individuals are—conventional individual liberals continue to assert—free to question all their relationships, including cultural. The state can, conventional individual liberalism further posits, cater for an environment where all individuals, regardless of their cultural background, have equal opportunities to lead the life they wish, in accordance with the cultural parameters they opt for, if any. Seemingly, if these assertions can be substantiated, the claim that the ethnically and culturally homogenous state is a fiction would be less of a problem for individual liberalism. Under such circumstances, individuals are still free to lead the life they wish. However, more recent political philosophy theories have challenged these two conventional individual liberalism's assumptions as well.

If starting with the second assumption, political philosophers have increasingly come to hold that individuals are not the atomized generic objects that individual liberalism presumes. Rather, it is asserted, many individuals are rooted in, and their identity to a large degree defined by, their cultural background. All individuals are not free—as conventional liberalism argues—to question all their relationships, and in particular not their cultural affinity. Therefore, many philosophical scholars agree, it is not possible to formulate any relevant theory of justice without taking cultural identity into account.[19]

As to the first assumption, political theorists have increasingly come to argue that even if *formally* neutral, in the sense that it refrains from actively promoting the majority culture, the state is nonetheless incapable of being neutral *in practice*.[20] That is so, it is asserted, because the liberal understanding of being neutral is being

2001) 39–41; Carol C Gould, 'Diversity and Democracy', in Seyla Benhabib (ed.), *Democracy and Difference: Contesting the Boundaries of the Political* (Princeton University Press, 1996) 171.

[17] See, generally, Jeremy Waldron, 'Minority Cultures and the Cosmopolitan Alternative', in Kymlicka (ed.), *The Rights of Minority Cultures* (n 7) 95–96.

[18] Michael Walzer, *Spheres of Justice. A Defence of Pluralism and Equality* (Blackwell, 1983) 140.

[19] Kymlicka, *Contemporary Political Philosophy* (n 3) 221–22, 336–47.

[20] Dominique Arel, 'Political Stability in Multinational Democracies: Comparing Language Dynamics in Brussels, Montreal, and Barcelona', in Gagnon and Tully (eds.), *Multinational Democracies* (n 16) 72–73; Jeff Spinner-Halev, 'Multiculturalism and its Critics', in John S Dryzek, Bonnie Honig, and Anne Phillips (eds.), *The Oxford Handbook of Political Theory* (Oxford University Press, 2006); Koskenniemi, *From Apology to Utopia* (n 1) 5–6.

passive. But passive is, this line of thought argues, not necessarily the same thing as neutral. Rather, a passive state tends to cater for members of the dominant culture to use their institutional advantage over members of minority groups.[21] The state is almost inevitably, if not actively so at least implicitly, biased towards the needs and interests of the majority group, it is increasingly held. As Ayelet Shachar puts it, referring to Spinner, '. . . minority cultures often "come to the game after it has already begun", and do not define the governing standards of a society's institutions'.[22] Members of the majority people generally obtain disproportionate representation in cultural elites. State legislation, norms, and policies are in most instances based on the preferences, values, and interests of the majority culture.[23] As David Miller observes, 'majority voting as a way of implementing democratic principles applies only once the boundaries of the relevant constituency have been determined. A majority vote cannot be used to fix these boundaries, since the outcome of such a vote will itself depend on who is included in . . . the electorate . . .'.[24] In the same vein, Adene Addis notes that populations like the Aboriginal people of Australia can never achieve equal status in a marketplace of cultural values or through elections. She emphasizes that '[w]hat a seemingly neutral state purports not to affirm, is affirmed for it by a market that acts as its surrogate. In the matters of group affiliation, state neutrality, in the face of unequal circumstances between minorities and majorities, is nothing less than an affirmation of one particular way of life . . .'.[25] For instance, biased decision-making structures tend to result in decisions on what languages can be officially used that favour the language of the majority. Similarly, the educational system regularly promotes the majority culture. The dominating population's views and cultural assumptions are likely to become the norm in a state.[26] In sum, political philosophers have increasingly concluded that conventional individual liberalism fails to address entrenched inequalities in society. In the individual liberal state, all cultures do not enjoy the same chance to prosper, or even to survive. A passive state is necessarily not the same thing as a neutral state.

[21] Brian Walker, 'Plural Cultures, Contested Territories: A Critique of Kymlicka' [1997] *Canadian Journal of Political Science*, Vol 30, No 2 215–16; Ferran Requejo, 'Political Liberalism in Multinational States: The Legitimacy of Plural and Asymmetrical Federalism', in Gagnon and Tully (eds.), *Multinational Democracies* (n 16) 110–15.

[22] Shachar, *Multicultural Jurisdictions* (n 15) 73.

[23] Van Dyke, 'The Individual, the State, and Ethnic Communities in Political Theory' (n 15) 49–50; Shachar, *Multicultural Jurisdictions* (n 15) 23.

[24] David Miller, 'Nationality in Divided Societies', in Gagnon and Tully (eds.), *Multinational Democracies* (n 16) 316.

[25] Adeno Addis, 'Individualism, Communitarianism, and the Rights of Ethnic Minorities' [1992] *Notre Dame Law Review*, Vol 67, Issue 3 644–45.

[26] Susanna Mancini and Bruno De Witte, 'Language Rights and Cultural Rights; A European Perspective', in Francesco Francioni and Martin Scheinin (eds.), *Cultural Human Rights* (Martinus Nijhoff Publishers, 2008) 523; Arel, 'Political Stability in Multinational Democracies' (n 20) 78; Steven Wheatley, *Democracy, Minorities and International Law* (Cambridge Studies in International and Comparative Law, 2005) 4; Iris M Young, 'Together in Difference: Transforming the Logic of Group Political Conflict', in Kymlicka (ed.), *The Rights of Minority Cultures* (n 7) 163.

3.3.2 Nationalism

Indeed, criticism of the purportedly neutral liberal state has gone beyond submitting that the state passively favours the majority culture. It has been argued that state elites are in fact aware that the state is not ethnically and culturally homogenous. They know that not all segments of society feel the same solidarity vis-à-vis other segments. For effective rule and political stability, political leaders tend to correct this 'flaw'. Individual liberalism becomes a self-fulfilling prophecy. It is prone to nationalism; a calculated way for states to deal with shortcomings inherent in classical liberalism.[27] Liberal states—although purportedly neutral between cultures—tend to consciously nurture a national identity defined by the culture of the dominant population. The elite seek to convince the citizens of the state that they do in fact belong to one, homogenous, nation; thus the notion of the 'nation-state'. Nationalism seeks to erase cultural differences between various segments of the population of the state. It aims at eliminating any sense among minority groups of togetherness and otherness.[28] If successful, nationalism results in assimilation.

Several scholars maintain that nationalism is a fact, not a theory. For instance, Ernest Gellner notes that '[n]ations as a natural, God-given way of classifying men . . . are a myth; nationalism, which sometimes takes pre-existing cultures and turns them into nations, sometimes invents them, and often obliterates pre-existing cultures: that is a reality . . .'.[29] Will Kymlicka elaborates in depth on the interdependence between conventional liberalism, the notion of the nation-state, and nationalist policies. He concludes that virtually all Western democracies, former communist states, and former colonies have at one point or another pursued nationalization strategies.[30] In the same vein, Martti Koskenniem demonstrates

[27] Kymlicka, *Contemporary Political Philosophy* (n 3) 261–64.

[28] Wheatley, *Democracy, Minorities and International Law* (n 26) 2–3; Timo Makkonen, 'Minorities' Rights to Maintain and Develop Their Cultures: Legal Implications of Social Science Research', in Francesco Francioni and Martin Scheinin (eds.), *Cultural Human Rights* (Martinus Nijhoff Publishers, 2008) 193; and Makkonen, *Equal in Law, Unequal in Fact: Racial and Ethnic Discrimination and the Legal Response Thereto in Europe* (Doctoral Dissertation presented at the Faculty of Law at the University of Helsinki) 5 March 2010 34–35; Audra Simpson, 'Paths Toward a Mohawk Nation: Narratives of Citizenship and Nationhood in Kahnawake', in Ivison, Patton, and Sanders (eds.), *Political Theory and the Rights of Indigenous Peoples* (n 15) 122; S James Anaya, 'On Justifying Special Ethnic Group Rights', in Ian Shapiro and Will Kymlicka (eds.), *Ethnicity and Group Rights* (New York University Press, 1997); Kymlicka, *Contemporary Political Philosophy* (n 3) 311–12, 346, 348; Antony Anghie, *Imperialism, Sovereignty and the Making of International Law* (Cambridge University Press, 2004) 206.

[29] See Ernest Gellner, *Nations and Nationalism* (Oxford, Blackwell, 1983) 48–49. In a similar vein, David Raic argues that nationalism consciously fosters the illusion that states are ethnically and culturally homogenous. See David Raic, *Statehood and the Law of Self-Determination* (Kluwer Law International, 2002) 176. See also T K Oommen, 'New nationalisms and collective rights: the case of South Asia', in May, Modood, and Squires (eds.), *Ethnicity, Nationalism and Minority Rights* (n 4) 135, where he observes that nationalism tends to 'transform a state-nation into a nation-state'.

[30] See Will Kymlicka, *Multicultural Odysseys—Navigating the New International Politics of Diversity* (Oxford University Press, 2007) 5, 61–66. Alan Patten too points out that some liberals do admit that a certain amount of nationalism might be necessary to realize the liberal ideals. See Allan Patten, 'Liberal Citizenship in Multinational Societies', in Gagnon and Tully (eds.), *Multinational Democracies* (n 16) 281–82.

how already the liberal legal scholars that transformed the study of law into a 'science' in the 1800s identified nationalism as an integral part of their project.[31]

Recall how Section 2.5 explains how many post-World War II statesmen deliberately opted for an individual human rights approach rather than group rights orientation precisely because individual rights creates an environment prone to nationalism. It was convenient for nationalization theories to define peoples as the aggregate populations of states, regardless of its cultural and ethnic composition. International law followed suit. This is a concrete example of how political philosophy impacts on international law, and that also raises the question: has political philosophy subsequently become more hospitable towards group rights, and, if so, what relevance has this development had on the law?

3.4 Communitarianism

As indicated, the challenge of the basic premises of individual liberalism—i.e. (i) that states can remain culturally neutral, and (ii) that the individual is not defined by membership of a particular community—led a growing number of political philosophers to infer that it is incorrect to separate individuals' identities from their cultural background. A new school within political theory, communitarianism, emerged[32] as a response to individual liberalism. The label 'communitarianism', and its criticism of liberalism, invites one to revisit the cry of the French Revolution: 'liberté, egalité, *and* fraternité'. Early liberals celebrated freedom and equality—but also community. However, with time, ideas on community gradually disappeared from liberal thought.[33]

Communitarianism not only calls for community to recover its place alongside liberty and equality in theories of justice. It argues that community is in fact the most central of the three values the French Revolution celebrated. Communitarians disagree with the basic premises that underpin the various liberal theories of justice. In fact, they do not even share liberalism's main aspiration, i.e. to formulate one coherent theory of justice applicable to all societies. Communitarians submit that the search for a universal theory of justice is misguided. They posit that liberals misconstrue the individual's capacity to decide what ideals are best to pursue. Communitarianism holds that liberalism underestimates the importance of the individual's cultural background to her and his capacity to make meaningful choices as

[31] Martti Koskenniemi, *The Gentle Civilizer of Nations—The Rise and Fall of International Law 1870-1960* (Cambridge University Press, 2002) 63–64.

[32] Will Kymlicka has in one of his later works referred to 'communitarianism' as the 'traditional conception of multiculturalism', when underlining that multiculturalism, as he understands it, is rooted not in cultural conservatism, but in liberalism. See *Multicultural Odysseys* (n 30) 99–108. This book uses the term 'communitarianism' to clearly denote that communitarianism, unlike multiculturalism (which Section 3.6 addresses), is not a liberal theory. At the same time, communitarianism should not be confused with Marxism. The latter views community as something to be achieved through revolution. Communitarians, by contrast, believe that the communitarian society need not be created, only recognized and respected. See Kymlicka, *Contemporary Political Philosophy* (n 3) 208–09.

[33] Ibid., 208.

to how to lead a good life.[34] They assert that the self is embedded in established social practices particular to the community, which one cannot necessarily opt out of. Hence, the individual's attachment to her or his distinct culture greatly contributes to what sort of person he or she is, and to her or his own understanding of that person.[35] Consequently, it is not possible to develop one single relevant theory of justice applicable to all societies and cultures, communitarians conclude. They maintain that individual liberalism neglects that respect for the individual's rights, freedoms, and well-being are only possible within the context of a particular community.[36] Communitarianism argues that if one wishes to identify what justice is, one must first survey how a particular culture values social goods. What is just cannot be measured against one single theory of justice. Rather, a society acts just if it behaves in accordance with the shared values of its particular culture. All cultures should therefore be allowed to be self-governing polities, communitarianism concludes.[37] In its purest form, communitarianism submits that all cultures and societies should be left to their own devices.[38]

3.5 Criticism of Communitarianism

Liberals have largely been unconvinced by the communitarian argument. They disagree with the suggestion that an individual is irrevocably defined by her or his cultural background. Instead, liberals tend to assert that if cultural communities have successfully remained homogenous, this is normally not because individual members of the group have voluntarily opted to stay in the community and to protect the culture. More often, liberals argue, the group has maintained its distinctiveness because decision-making power within the group is restricted to men with means. Liberals claim that communities would not retain such like-mindedness if they were to fully include other segments of their societies, such as women, in decision-making processes. Liberals thus submit that communitarianism tends to entrench

[34] Spinner-Halev, 'Multiculturalism and its Critics' (n 20) 546–47; Jeffrey Weeks, 'The Value of Difference', in Jonathan Rutherford (ed.), *Identity—Community, Culture, Difference* (Lawrence and Wishart, 1990) 88; Margaret Moore, 'Liberalism, Communitarianism, and the Politics of Identity', in Thomas Christiano and John Christman (eds.), *Contemporary Debates in Political Philosophy* (Blackwell Publishing, 2009) 323–24; Kymlicka, *Contemporary Political Philosophy* (n 3) 212, 246–47.

[35] Jürgen Habermas, 'Three Normative Models of Democracy', in Seyla Benhabib (ed.), *Democracy and Difference: Contesting the Boundaries of the Political* (Princeton University Press, 1996) 23–30, Michael Sandel, 'The Procedural Republic and the Unencumbered Self', in Shlomo Avineri and Avner de-Shalit (eds.), *Communitarianism and Individualism* (Oxford University Press, 1992) 23.

[36] Darlene M Johnston, 'Native Rights as Collective Rights: A Question of Group Self-Preservation', in Kymlicka (ed.), *The Rights of Minority Cultures* (n 7) 180–81; Kymlicka, *Contemporary Political Philosophy* (n 3) 209–12.

[37] Walzer, *Spheres of Justice* (n 18); Avishai Margalit and Joseph Raz, 'National Self-Determination', in Kymlicka (ed.), *The Rights of Minority Cultures* (n 7) 88; Kymlicka, *Contemporary Political Philosophy* (n 3) 211, 221–24.

[38] That said, not all communitarians go as far as suggesting that cultures should be completely free from outside scrutiny. Some communitarians agree with liberals that the individual's personality is not completely determined by her cultural context. Still, this branch of communitarianism also maintains that choices of what constitutes a good life can only be meaningfully executed within the community's particular way of life. See Kymlicka, *Contemporary Political Philosophy* (n 3) 244–45.

social practices that marginalize certain groups within the community. They further assert that these practices have been designed for the precise purpose of keeping a small segment of society in power.[39]

The 'cosmopolitan'[40] liberal school completely reject communitarianism's assertion that an individual's cultural background is of importance to her or him. Cosmopolitans posit that one cannot simply claim that individuals are necessarily in need of their cultural roots. They argue that a person is capable of thinking of her or himself as not defined by her or his cultural background. Cosmopolitans admit that certain individuals may live a life heavily influenced by their cultural background. But the person nonetheless does not need this background, they assert. Indeed, some cosmopolitans submit that there is something artificial about seeking to preserve minority cultures. For instance, Jeremy Waldron suggests that in a world formed by technology, trade, mass immigration, and the dispersion of cultural influences, to engage in traditional practices of indigenous cultures might be a fascinating anthropological experiment, but nonetheless entails an artificial dislocation from what is going on in the world. Waldron submits that living in accordance with the tradition of an indigenous community in the modern world is like living in Disneyland believing that one's surrounding epitomizes what it is for a culture to really exist, at the same time as one demands funding to live in Disneyland and the protection from modern society for the boundaries of Disneyland.[41]

Not all cosmopolitans argue as pointedly as Waldron. But they largely agree that from the arguments outlined above, it naturally follows that there is no need to support or even protect minority cultures. Cosmopolitans suggest that cultures live and adapt to changes in their geographical and political surroundings. Sometimes a culture withers away. In other instances, the culture adapts and continues to thrive, or successfully blends with another culture. These are natural processes that the state shall not interfere with. In fact, cosmopolitans maintain, if one protects cultures, there is a risk that one artificially entrenches non-desired cultural practices, resulting in loss of individual freedom.[42]

Still, most liberals have not responded to communitarianism with cosmopolitanism. Even if unconvinced by the communitarian argument that the individual is necessarily defined by her cultural background, most liberals admit that communitarianism puts the finger on a paradox embedded in liberalism. How should a theory that celebrates individual freedom address individuals that genuinely—informed and freely—do view themselves as defined by their cultural background? As Joseph Carens notes, the individualistic assumption of conventional liberalism

[39] Kymlicka, *Contemporary Political Philosophy* (n 3) 258–61.

[40] As with communitarianism, 'cosmopolitanism' is not a term of art. Kwame Appiah, for instance, appears to refer to the school this book labels cosmopolitanism as 'universalism'. Appiah instead describes cosmopolitanism as 'universality plus difference'. See Kwame A Appiah, *Cosmopolitanism: Ethics in a World of Strangers*, (Penguin Books, 2007) 57, 151.

[41] Waldron, 'Minority Cultures' (n 17) 100–01, 109–10.

[42] Jan Pieterse, 'Ethnicities and multiculturalism: politics of boundaries', in May, Modood, and Squires (eds.), *Ethnicity, Nationalism and Minority Rights* (n 4) 43; Kymlicka, *Contemporary Political Philosophy* (n 3) 221–28; Thomas Hylland Eriksen, 'Ethnicity, class, and the 1999 Mauritian riots', in May, Modood, and Squires. (eds.), *Ethnicity, Nationalism and Minority Rights* (n 4) 78.

makes sense to persons from the West precisely because of their traditions.[43] In other words, how should liberalism address cultures where individuals do not value individual autonomy in the same way Western liberal thought does? By posing this question, communitarianism, although never a dominant school in itself, nonetheless impacted on political philosophy. Communitarianism sparked liberal thinkers to consider whether a relevant theory of justice should accommodate for the interests of groups that genuinely wish to remain distinct. In other words, communitarians inspired liberals to develop a theory with a space for ethnic and racial groups, in between those of states and individuals.[44]

3.6 Multiculturalism

3.6.1 Generally on multiculturalism

Rather than rejecting outright communitarianism's assertion that the individual's cultural background is important to her or his well-being, an increasingly larger group of liberal scholars have sought to reconcile the tension between individual liberalism and communitarianism. Multiculturalism rests on liberal values yet at the same time seeks to accommodate cultural diversity. In other words, it aims to combine respect for freedom of the individual with communities' interest in autonomy.[45] Multiculturalism asserts that liberalism can embrace community interests without compromising liberalism's basic individualistic premises.[46] At the same time, however, multiculturalism rejects the communitarian argument that her or his cultural background irrevocably defines an individual, wherefore communities should be free to manage their own affairs and to establish their own understanding of justice.[47] In short, multiculturalism seeks to accommodate for group rights without sacrificing the freedom of the individual. It does so through addressing the aforementioned two lines of criticism directed towards individual liberalism: (i) that this school of thought is ignorant of the fact that the identity of the individual is significantly tied to her cultural background; and (ii) that it takes for granted that the state can, and does, remain neutral between cultures.

[43] Joseph Carens, 'Aliens and Citizens: The Case for Open Borders', in Kymlicka (ed.), *The Rights of Minority Cultures* (n 7) 345.

[44] Moore, 'Liberalism, Communitarianism, and the Politics of Identity' (n 34) 325–32; compare Shachar, *Multicultural Jurisdictions* (n 15) 1–2, 22.

[45] Kymlicka, *Contemporary Political Philosophy* (n 3) 244, 284–87; May, Modood, and Squires (eds.), *Ethnicity, Nationalism and Minority Rights* (n 4) 4.

[46] Wayne Norman, 'Justice and stability in multinational societies', in Gagnon and Tully (eds.), *Multinational Democracies* (n 16) 95; James Tully, 'Identity Politics', in Terence Ball and Richard Bellamy (eds.), *The Cambridge History of Twentieth-Century Political Thought* (Cambridge University Press, 2003) 523; Ivison, Patton, and Sanders (eds.), *Political Theory and the Rights of Indigenous Peoples* (n 15) 5–6. In that sense, one can say that multiculturalism does take liberalism back to its origin, celebrating not only liberté and egalité, but also fraternité.

[47] Shane O'Neil, 'Mutual Recognition and the Accommodation of National Diversity: Constitutional Justice in Northern Ireland', in Gagnon and Tully (eds.), *Multinational Democracies* (n 16) 224–27.

Contrary to conventional liberals and cosmopolitans, multiculturalists agree that an individual's cultural background is important to her and him in a manner that any adequate theory of justice must consider. Humans have, they agree, a basic yearning to belong. Harkening back to the French Revolution cry, individuals want freedom and equality, but also community.[48] If the group as such is not well respected, the dignity and self-respect of its members is also at risk, multiculturalism asserts.[49] If the culture of the community is in decay, and/or if it is persecuted or discriminated against, the options and opportunities open to its members will shrink, and their pursuit of goals and happiness will be less successful. Thus, the individual's range of options for leading a good life is to some extent determined by her cultural heritage. This, multiculturalists argue, threatens the most basic premises of liberalism. It is cultural structures, multiculturalism submits, that provide us with 'a context of choice' when making informed decisions as to how to better our lives. Individual well-being depends on successful pursuit of goals and relationships that are culturally influenced. Membership in a cultural collective may therefore be a relevant criterion for justly distributing benefits and burdens within a society—the main purpose of all liberal theories of justice,[50] multiculturalists conclude.

With regard to the second line of criticism, multiculturalists concur that the state may be capable of remaining *formally* neutral between cultures, but maintain that in an individual liberal state cultural minorities nonetheless *in practice* face inequalities that are not a result of their own choices, but of decisions by others. Multiculturalists accept that behind the veil of formal objectivity, the state is rarely, if ever, neutral in reality. Rather, the state tends to—if not necessarily consciously then at least unconsciously—allow the values and practices of the majority culture to dominate in legislation, policies, and practices. The fact that the individual liberal state is not, and cannot be, neutral between cultures is another compelling reason to accept group rights, multiculturalists argue. A legitimate theory of justice cannot base its principles on the assumption that pre-existing societal structures provide for equal justice for all. Breaking with conventional individual liberalism, multiculturalists conclude that states should accept rights not only of individuals, but also of groups.[51]

[48] Young, 'Together in Difference' (n 26) 155–75; Van Dyke, 'The Individual, the State and Ethnic Communities in Political Theory' (n 15) 49; Spinner-Halev, 'Multiculturalism and its Critics' (n 20) 550.

[49] Ibid., 547; Kymlicka (ed.), *The Rights of Minority Cultures* (n 7) 7; O'Neil (n 47) 226.

[50] David Owen and James Tully, 'Redistribution and Recognition: Two Approaches', in Anthony Simon Laden and David Owen (eds.), *Multiculturalism and Political Theory* (Cambridge University Press, 2007) 270–71; Young, 'Structural Injustices' (n 10); Spinner-Halev, 'Multiculturalism and its Critics' (n 20) 547.

[51] Yvonne Donders, *Towards a Right to Cultural Identity?* (Intersentia, 2002) 41; Kymlicka, *Contemporary Political Philosophy* (n 3) 343–47; Will Kymlicka, *Multicultural Citizenship* (Oxford University Press, 1995) 108–15, 126–30, Dimitrios Karmis and Alain G Gagnon, 'Federalism, federation and collective identities in Canada and Belgium: different routes, similar fragmentation', in Gagnon and Tully (eds.), *Multinational Democracies* (n 16) 174–75.

3.6.2 Particularly on multiculturalism and indigenous peoples

In articulating his understanding of what is embedded in multiculturalism, Will Kymlicka distinguishes between 'national minorities' and 'ethnic groups'. In the former category, he places groups that are territorially concentrated to a particular land area, at one point were self-governing, and who wish to remain distinct cultural and self-governing entities. Ethnic groups, on the other hand are, according to Kymlicka, looser forms of association. Members of ethnic groups share certain cultural communalities, but the group as such cannot reasonably be said to constitute a political entity. If employing Kymlicka's classification, indigenous peoples constitute typical examples of national minorities, whereas for instance immigrant groups fall under the heading ethnic groups.

According to Will Kymlicka, only national minorities enjoy the full set of group rights, including rights to self-government.[52] Specifically on indigenous peoples, he submits that it might be necessary to award such peoples a right to self-determination to be exercised within existing state borders, should they enjoy the same freedom as others, given their distinct institutional, cultural, and spiritual history. Kymlicka argues that it is erroneous of liberals to simply assume that to subject indigenous governments to state jurisdiction is just.[53] Irism Young too asserts that legitimate interests of indigenous peoples cannot be accommodated within the conventional state-individual dichotomy that individual liberalism professes.[54] In the same vein, Allan Buchanan points out that a greater degree of self-governance is often the only practical way to avoid destruction of indigenous peoples' societies and cultures.[55] Similarly, James Tully agrees that a state can in fact consist of more than one people bestowed with self-determining rights. Consequently, he argues for recognition of an internal right to self-determination of indigenous peoples. Similar to Kymlicka, Tully views such a right as a pre-requisite, should indigenous peoples be genuinely free.[56]

In sum, multiculturalism asserts that liberal theories of justice can be combined with collective human rights of, among other national minorities, indigenous peoples. Multiculturalists further maintain that one such collective right to which indigenous peoples are entitled is a right to self-determination to be exercised within existing state borders.

3.6.3 Limitations of multiculturalism

As seen, multiculturalism breaks with conventional individual liberalism in that it accepts collective rights of ethnic and/or cultural groups. That said, multiculturalism's

[52] Kymlicka, *Multicultural Citizenship* (n 51) 10–14, 63, 95–97, 166; Kymlicka, 'American Multiculturalism and the "Nations Within"', in Ivison, Patton, and Sanders (eds.), *Political Theory and the Rights of Indigenous Peoples* (n 15) 221–22.

[53] Kymlicka, *Multicultural Citizenship* (n 51) 166–67.

[54] Iris M Young, 'Hybrid Democracy: Iroquois Federalism and the Postcolonial Project', in Ivison, Patton, and Sanders (eds.), *Political Theory and the Rights of Indigenous Peoples* (n 15) 247.

[55] Buchanan, 'The Morality of Secession' (n 14) 351–53.

[56] Gagnon and Tully (eds.), *Multinational Democracies* (n 16) 7–13, 30–33.

advocacy for group rights is far from unlimited. Rather, multiculturalists presuppose that in return for being bestowed with certain rights as groups, national minorities at the same time accept basic liberal values.[57]

As the liberal theory it is, multiculturalism emphasizes autonomy of the individual in a manner that limits the scope of protection it wishes to extend to groups. For instance, Will Kymlicka divides group rights into: (i) rights of the community vis-à-vis individual members of the group, and (ii) rights that aim to protect the group in its relationship with the larger society. He argues that groups are only entitled to the latter category of rights. The state, Kymlicka submits, should prevent among others indigenous peoples from using self-governing rights to limit the freedom of individual members of the group. According to him, rights of indigenous peoples are compatible with liberalism only insofar as such rights are exercised in ways that do not infringe on the freedom of individual members of the group. Indigenous peoples are entitled to pursue nation-building only to the extent such endeavours do not encroach upon the rights and liberties of individual members of the group. In sum, Kymlicka concludes, individual human rights always take precedent over collective such rights.[58]

Kymlicka's view is probably relatively representative of multiculturalists in general, albeit alternative proposals for how to solve potential conflicts between individual and collective rights have been put forward. For instance, Chandran Kukathas also stresses the fundamental importance of individual rights. He submits, however, that what is important is that the individual member has the right to exit the group. Provided that a right to exit exists, liberalism should likewise accept illiberal practices of a group, he posits.[59] Section 5.1.3 returns to the issue of potential conflicts between group and individual rights.

3.7 Criticism of Multiculturalism

Not everyone has accepted the multiculturalist argument.

Cosmopolitans maintain that the state can remain neutral between cultures and that to award specific rights to individuals based on membership in a particular group—or to the group as such—is by definition discriminatory.[60] This group of scholars further insist that a person's identity is not necessarily tied to her cultural background to the degree multiculturalists suggest.[61] Cosmopolitans also submit that extending protection to minority cultures is arbitrary, due to difficulties associated with (i) defining what groups deserve protection, (ii) determining who are the members of such groups, and (iii) deciding who identifies what cultural

[57] Kymlicka, *Contemporary Political Philosophy* (n 3) 256, 338–39.

[58] Ibid. (n 3) 340–43, 352; Kymlicka, *Multicultural Citizenship* (n 51) Ch 3.

[59] Chandran Kukathas, 'Are There Any Cultural Rights?', in Kymlicka (ed.), *The Rights of Minority Cultures* (n 7), in particular 238–39.

[60] See Thomas Pogge, 'Group Rights and Ethnicity', in Shapiro and Kymlicka (eds.), *Ethnicity and Group Rights* (n 28) 187–93, 196–215; Spinner-Halev, 'Multiculturalism and its Critics' (n 20) 548; compare Kymlicka, *Contemporary Political Philosophy* (n 3) 365–66.

[61] Spinner-Halev, 'Multiculturalism and its Critics' (n 20) 548.

practices are worthy of protection. In a similar vein, some cosmopolitans also reject multiculturalism due to a concern that recognition of collective rights might result in the collective violating the rights of individual members of the group, irrespective of the safeguards against such abuses that Will Kymlicka and other multiculturalists have proposed. Cosmopolitans argue that many indigenous cultures do not appreciate individuals' freedom of choice. Therefore, if freedom is what we value, cultural interference, not cultural protection, should be our choice, they submit.[62] Section 5.11 returns to these issues, and address the cosmopolitan concerns expressed here.

Communitarians, on their part, maintain that multiculturalism, as a liberal theory rooted in the notion of the nation-state, is—irrespective of its attempts to accommodate for certain interests of groups—still not sufficiently sensitive to cultural diversity.[63] For instance, Will Kymlicka has been accused of uncritically accepting the concept of the very same state he sets out to challenge.[64] This line of criticism has perhaps been particularly vocal in the context of indigenous peoples. Some have maintained that multiculturalism could and should be more observant to differences between indigenous peoples on one hand, and ethnic and cultural minorities on the other. For instance, Scott Idleman underlines that multiculturalism might work for minorities seeking respect for their cultural distinctiveness as part of the majority society. He asserts, however, that the limited group rights multiculturalism advocates do not match particularly well with indigenous peoples' aspirations, i.e. to remain as distinct societies.[65]

3.8 The Success of Multiculturalism and its Legal Relevance

Despite the articulated criticism, multiculturalism has established itself as the dominant school within contemporary political philosophy. In fact, it has been suggested that multiculturalism has evolved as almost a consensus position among liberals interested in cultural and community rights.[66] Thus, Bhikhu Parekh posits

[62] Ivison, Patton, and Sanders (eds.), *Political Theory and the Rights of Indigenous Peoples* (n 15) 8; Bhikhu Parekh, 'Redistribution or recognition? A misguided debate', in May, Modood, and Squires (eds.), *Ethnicity, Nationalism and Minority Rights* (n 4) 201–02; Kukathas, 'Are There Any Cultural Rights?' (n 59) 241–42.

[63] Dominic McGoldrick, 'Multiculturalism and its Discontents', in Nazila Ghanea and Alexandra Xanthaki (eds.), *Minorities, Peoples and Self-Determination—Essays in Honour of Patrick Thornberry* (Martinus Nijhoff Publishers, 2005) 219.

[64] Young, 'Structural Injustices' (n 10) 78.

[65] See Scott Idleman, 'Multiculturalism and the Future of Tribal Sovereignty' [2004] *Columbia Human Rights Law Review*, Vol 35 589–660, in particular 590–92. For a similar argument, see also Spinner-Halev, 'Multiculturalism and its Critics' (n 20) 548–49.

[66] See Kymlicka, *Contemporary Political Philosophy* (n 3) 340, 365–66. Other scholars that have noted the success of multiculturalism include McGoldrick, 'Multiculturalism and its Discontents' (n 63) 219; Daniel M Weinstock, 'Liberalism, Multiculturalism, and the Problem of Internal Minorities', in Laden and Owen (eds.), *Multiculturalism and Political Theory* (n 50) 245; Alain G Gagnon, 'The Moral Foundations of Asymmetrical Federalism: A Normative Exploration of the Case of Quebec and Canada', in Gagnon and Tully (eds.), *Multinational Democracies* (n 16) 320.

that today, a theory of justice that fails to recognize that people value and gain security from their cultural identity has a slim chance of finding support.[67]

The success of multiculturalism might be of significant relevance to this work. Following three centuries where conventional individual liberalism exercised virtually unchallenged influence over international law, a new political school of thought has become dominant. In contrast to conventional liberalism, this theory asserts that it is incorrect to take the state for granted as the only self-governing polity, and that group rights of indigenous peoples and other national minorities should be recognized. If this school of thought would come to exercise influence over international law in the manner that conventional individual liberalism has done until date, this could prove to be of cardinal importance to the indigenous rights discourse. As articulated above, multiculturalism identifies indigenous peoples as particularly strong candidates for self-governing rights. The subsequent chapters survey to what extent the new political philosophical ideas have indeed been matched by corresponding developments within international law.

[67] Parekh, 'Redistribution or recognition?' (n 62) 207.

4

International Law on International Legal Sources

4.1 Introduction

For two interrelated reasons, it may be pertinent for a book on indigenous peoples' rights under international law to devote more attention to international law on international legal sources than some may deem necessary at first glance.

First, Chapter 2 describes how classical international law, as well as many of the most central international legal sources that the young United Nations (UN) adopted in the wake of World War II, as understood at the time of their adoption, was not hospitable towards rights of indigenous peoples. International norms on international legal sources govern in what way and to what extent such sources have the capacity to evolve and take on new and/or expanded understandings. Norms on international law-making further regulate to what extent instruments and other documents that are formally speaking non-legally binding nonetheless can have normative effect and impact on our understanding of both international law and international law making. As indicated, that international legal sources, assisted by formally non-binding sources, can evolve to take on new understandings might be a prerequisite for the emergence of an international normative system of real relevance to indigenous peoples.

Second, the classical international law era clearly demonstrates how an international legal system that strictly upholds the principle of state sovereignty is not prone to develop norms favourable to indigenous peoples. Indeed, Chapter 2 explains how the classical international legal system was largely created precisely to substantiate the claim that European colonizers were legally entitled to place indigenous peoples' territories and natural resources under their hegemony and control. Consequently, for rights to evolve that recognize indigenous peoples as legal and political entities, and that protect their territories and cultures, it might be necessary that the contemporary international legal system does not uphold a strict adherence to the primacy of the principle of state sovereignty.

With these two articulated reasons in mind, this chapter analyzes international law on international legal sources.

4.2 What Are Relevant Legal Sources in the International Legal System?

4.2.1 Introduction

Chapter 2 describes how from the outset, the international legal system came to rest on the assumption that states pre-date the law, wherefore, as a consequence, no law can exist above states. With this understanding states are—by definition—the ultimate creators of international law. We further saw how this position became entrenched during the League of Nations epoch. Lassa Oppenheim, one of the most prominent legal scholars of the era, describes the sentiment of the time well: '[I]nternational law is a law not above but between states . . . there is no central authority above the sovereign states which could compel them to comply with the rules of international law . . . existing recognized rules of international law . . . are . . . found in customary practice of states or in law-making conventions.' Oppenheim further foresaw that this basic premise of the international legal system would last in perpetuity.[1] That said, also in the post-World War I period, some legal scholars argued against a strict application of legal positivism. For instance, Hersch Lauterpacht defended the continued role of natural law ideals in the international legal system.[2] This book will not probe deeper into the positivism–natural law debate of the early 1900s. It is sufficient to note that legal practice and mainstream doctrine clearly favoured positivism, even if many positivists nourished a belief that positive law also derives from international morality.[3] In any event, the reader is well advised to bear in mind Lauterpacht's argument that natural law theories should continuously be allowed to play a certain role in contemporary international law-making when going through this chapter.

Section 2.5 describes how Oppenheim's prediction at least proved correct when the UN was formed and the UN Charter adopted. As seen, the UN Charter largely codified the basic premises of the classical international legal system, including through reaffirming state sovereignty as the constitutional principle of international law. The UN Charter further established the International Court of Justice (ICJ). The ICJ Statute Article 38 provides what are relevant sources of international law for the purposes of the Court. Pursuant to Article 38.1, the ICJ shall, in its rulings, primarily apply (i) international conventions that establish rules expressly recognized by contracting states, (ii) international customary law, and (iii)

[1] See Lassa Oppenheim, 'The Science of International Law: Its Task and Method' [1908] *American Journal of International Law* 2, reprinted in Malcolm Evans and Patrick Capps (eds.), *International Law* (Vol I) (Ashgate Publishing, 2009) 321–22, 329–33. Parts of Oppenheim's article are actually written as a response to suggestions that natural law theories were still relevant to international law-making in the first half of the 1900s. Oppenheim submits that natural law theories have served the law in the past, but are now passé. He hence argues that to be useful, the international legal scholar should focus on analyzing and presenting positive law.

[2] Lauterpacht, 'The Grotian Tradition in International Law' [1946] *British Year Book of International Law* 23, reprinted in Evans and Capps (eds.), *International Law* (n 1).

[3] Dinah Shelton, 'Normative Hierarchy in International Law' [2006] *American Journal of International Law* 100, reprinted in Evans and Capps (eds.), *International Law* (n 1) 295, 302.

general principles of law recognized by civilized nations. Pursuant to Article 38.1 (d), the ICJ can apply judicial decisions and the teachings of the most highly qualified international legal scholars as secondary sources when primary sources offer insufficient guidance. The ICJ Statute Article 59 clarifies that judicial decisions, including by the Court itself, formally do not constitute primary sources, as they are binding only upon the parties to the dispute. In other words, the ICJ Statute essentially confirms Oppenheim's prediction that international law making will always be an affair of states. The ICJ Statute Article 38.1 does not rank the primary sources of international law. In practice, however, as Oppenheim further identifies, treaties and customary law are the central sources. ICJ Statue Article 38.1 is generally held to reflect customary international law on international legal sources.[4]

At first glance, the ICJ Statue would appear to offer a concrete and simple definition of what are relevant international legal sources. Still, the ICJ Statute Article 38.1 has been criticized both for formally listing at all what constitutes relevant sources of international law, and for failing to list enough sources.

Addressing the first criticism, some argue that the very idea of a closed list over what are relevant international legal sources contradicts the constitutional principle of international law-making, i.e. that only states can create law.[5] Martti Koskenniemi seemingly asserts that one could argue that a doctrine on international legal sources can at best *attempt* to describe what those sources are.[6] Scholars such as Alf Ross take this line of argument one step further. He posits that '[t]he basis of the doctrine of legal sources is in all cases actual [state] acceptance and that alone'.[7] If taking this position, there can be no meaningful doctrine on international legal sources. As the ultimate creators of international law, states can decide what constitute relevant sources of international law at any given time, irrespective of any 'pre-existing' normative system. With this understanding of international law-making, states are not bound to accept any definition of what constitutes relevant legal sources. In other words, the principle of state sovereignty provides not only that states are free to determine what the law is, but also what sources manifest the law at any particular point in time. This articulated line of criticism of the ICJ Statute Article 38.1 can be said to come from a position of pure legal positivism.

Addressing the second criticism, that of failing to list enough sources, others have, on the other hand, maintained that the ICJ Statute Article 38.1 takes a too positivistic and unrealistic approach towards what constitutes relevant international legal sources. This group of scholars criticizes ICJ Statute Article 38.1 for not accepting as indicative of international norms certain instruments, decisions, etc., that they argue are relevant to international law making irrespective of the view that

4 Brownlie, *Principles of Public International Law* (6th edn., Oxford University Press, 2003) 5.

5 Alexander Orakhelashvili, *The Interpretation of Acts and Rules in Public International Law* (Oxford University Press, 2008) 51–60.

6 Martti Koskenniemi, *From Apology to Utopia—The Structure of International Legal Argument* (Cambridge University Press, 2005) 165–67.

7 See Alf Ross, *A Textbook of International Law* (London, 1947) 195. For a similar argument, see also Prosper Weil, 'Towards Relative Normativity in International Law?' [1983] *American Journal of International Law* 77, reprinted in Evans and Capps (eds.), *International Law* (n 1).

these 'sources' are not necessarily, strictly speaking, immediately deducible from state consensus. Examples of sources that are often mentioned in this context are decisions by international organizations intended to be binding and UN declarations and other resolutions adopted by the UN General Assembly (UNGA).[8] Further, although the ICJ Statute Article 59 proclaims that rulings by the ICJ and other authoritative international tribunals formally only bind the involved parties, many maintain that such rulings are also relevant to the identification of international norms.[9]

Section 4.3 returns to the criticism directed against attempts to present international law as a formalized system that firmly defines what sources are reflective of international norms and those that are not. But before embarking on this analysis, the following sections briefly introduce the sources most commonly referred to as relevant sources of international law. Naturally, the sections take ICJ Statute Article 38.1 as the point of departure. They also address, however, certain instruments etc. not listed in the ICJ Statute, but which are nonetheless commonly discussed in the context of international law-making, as reflected in the articulated criticism directed against understanding the list of international legal sources the ICJ Statute Article 38.1 contains as exhaustive.

4.2.2 Peremptory norms

The ICJ Statute Article 38.1 makes no reference to peremptory norms, or *jus cogens*. This category of norms was formally introduced into the international legal system through the adoption (1969) and subsequent entering into force (1980) of the Vienna Convention on the Law of Treaties (VCLT). Pursuant to VCLT Article 53, a treaty provision is void if it conflicts with a peremptory norm. Although VCLT Article 53 only refers to treaties, it is widely accepted that international customary norms and unilateral state practice must also conform with peremptory norms.[10] The notion of *jus cogens* thus introduces a hierarchy among international legal sources and to which legal sources of this status rank first among, and take precedent over, them.[11] A peremptory norm can only be modified by a subsequent international norm of the same legal status.

As to their making, peremptory norms can be described as a particular form of international customary law.[12] Consequently, as Section 4.2.4 elaborates, a peremptory norm emerges through coherent state practice coupled with *opinio juris*, i.e. that states do not only act in a coherent manner but do so precisely because

[8] Antonio Cassese, *International Law* (2nd edn., Oxford University Press, 2005) 183.

[9] James Crawford, 'The Right of Self-Determination in International Law: Its Development and Future', in Philip Alston (ed.), *Peoples' Rights* (Oxford University Press, 2005) 32; Brownlie, *Principles of Public International Law*, (n 4) 19–21; Alan Boyle and Christine Chinkin, *The Making of International Law* (Oxford University Press, 2007) 268; Cassese, *International Law* (n 8) 194–95.

[10] James Crawford, *The Creation of States in International Law* (2nd edn., Clarendon Press, 2006) 107; Cassese, *International Law* (n 8) 199; David Raic, *Statehood and the Law of Self-Determination* (Kluwer Law International, 2002) 143.

[11] James Crawford and Martti Koskenniemi, *International Law* (Cambridge University Press, 2012) 11; Cassese, *International Law* (n 8) 199.

[12] Cassese, *International Law* (n 8) 199–202.

they subjectively perceive that their actions constitute a reflection of law. In addition, however, for a norm to acquire the status of *jus cogens*, there must also be *opinio juris* about the norm having such legal status.[13] As with customary international norms in general, it is sufficient that a significant majority of, but not necessarily all, states hold the opinion that a norm constitutes *jus cogens* for the norm to acquire such status.[14]

Viewed in light of the basic structure of the international legal system outlined above, it should come as no surprise that the notion of peremptory norms is not uncontroversial. Clearly, the idea that there are international norms that can be described to be of an absolute nature squares badly with the principle of state sovereignty. Because in an international legal system deeply rooted in the principle of state sovereignty, how may it be suggested that norms exist above those accepted by the ultimate creators of the law?[15] Rather unsurprisingly therefore, some positivist legal scholars have heavily criticized the entire idea of peremptory norms.[16]

Proponents of natural law theories, on their part, may argue that *jus cogens* is in fact a reflection of a continued relevance of natural law ideals to the contemporary international legal system.[17] Indeed, at the time of the adoption of VCLT Article 53, some states opined that the provision reflects a continued relevance of natural law.[18] Others, wishing to defend the peremptory norm foundation while still not giving in to natural law ideas, point out that VCLT Article 53 proclaims that for a norm to acquire the status of *jus cogens*, it must be accepted as such by the international community of states as a whole.[19] They argue that if only sovereign states can declare an international norm *jus cogens*, the notion of peremptory norms need not be viewed as conflicting with the principle of state sovereignty. To that, yet others retort however that one can seriously question the practical relevance of this caveat: Because must it not be a fiction that all states have at one particular point in time come together to give their consent to a norm acquiring the status of *jus cogens*? Instead, the argument goes, equity and reason, rather than explicit state consensus, are presumably in reality more plausible factors behind claims that an international customary norm has the status of *jus cogens*.[20]

Given the potential problems associated with reconciling the existence of peremptory norms with the principle of state sovereignty, it is perhaps not too surprising that there has been little agreement on what international norms amount to *jus cogens*, beyond obvious examples such as the prohibition of slavery and genocide. Peremptory norms have rarely been relied on in practice, including by the

[13] Paul Reuter, *Introduction to the Law of Treaties* (Kegan Paul International, 1995) 142–46.

[14] Stefan Talmon, 'The Constitutive Versus the Declaratory Theory or Recognition: *Tertium Non Datur?*' [2004] *British Yearbook of International Law* 75, reprinted in Evans and Capps (eds.), *International Law* (Vol II) (n 1) 131; Cassese, *International Law* (n 8) 201–02.

[15] Compare Koskenniemi, *From Apology to Utopia* (n 6) 322–25.

[16] For a particularly colourful example, see Prosper Weil, 'Towards Relative Normativity in International Law?' [1983] *American Journal of International Law* 77, reprinted in Evans and Capps (eds.), *International Law* (n 1) 423–30.

[17] Compare Evans and Capps (eds.), *International Law* (n 1) xiv.

[18] Boyle and Chinkin, *The Making of International Law* (n 9) 11.

[19] Shelton, 'Normative Hierarchy in International Law' (n 3) 301.

[20] Koskenniemi, *From Apology to Utopia* (n 6) 322–25, 391–93.

ICJ.[21] Yet two rights at the heart of this book are generally held to constitute peremptory norms: the rights to self-determination[22] and equality.[23] That said, one should recall that both these rights, at their core, reflect fundamental values, *and*, as conventionally understood, *only* these values. When the right to self-determination emerged in international law, it was essentially as a right of peoples to be free from foreign domination. And the traditional understanding of the right to equality was a right of individuals to be treated as equals. Most certainly, it is these core concepts of the rights to self-determination and equality, respectively, that have been considered *jus cogens*. As this book examines in depth in the following chapters, the rights to self-determination and equality have more recently evolved to take on broader understandings. It is far from certain, however, if these evolved understandings hold the status of *jus cogens* as well.[24]

4.2.3 International treaties

A treaty has been defined as 'any international agreement in written form . . . whatever its particular designation . . . concluded between two or more States or other subjects of international law and governed by international law'.[25] The term 'other subjects' refers to subjects of international law beyond states.[26] In this particular context we are, however, only concerned with treaties entered into by states. That said, as this book shall return to below, for the present purposes it is not irrelevant that international law on treaty making—and international law in general—envisage a role for international legal subjects other than states.

In one sense treaties are the most uncomplicated of the international legal sources. Treaty provisions are normally relatively straightforward in both content and reach. Further, treaties are binding only on the parties to the treaty, offering legal certainty. But this feature of treaties is at the same time their greatest disadvantage. It deprives them of the universal applicability denoting e.g. customary law. The result of different mixes of states being parties to various treaties is a fragmented legal structure, which ultimately breaks down to a network of binary state

[21] See International Law Association Final Report on the Impact of International Human Rights Law on General International Law (2008), Section 1.2. Dinah Shelton notes that while the concept of *jus cogens* might be much discussed in the legal doctrine, there is less reflection of such norms in state practice or judicial opinions—see 'Normative Hierarchy in International Law' (n 3) 292, 297.

[22] Antonio Cassese, *Self-Determination of Peoples: A Legal Reappraisal* (Cambridge University Press, 1995) 169–70; Cassese, *International Law* (n 8) 65–66; Brownlie, *Principles of Public International Law* (n 4) 489; Crawford, *The Creation of States* (n 10) 101.

[23] ILC, UN Doc A/56/10 284; Cassese, *International Law* (n 8) 65; Brownlie, *Principles of Public International Law* (n 4) 489.

[24] Raic, *Statehood and the Law of Self-Determination* (n 10) 146–47, 219; Marc Weller, 'Towards a General Comment on Self-Determination and Autonomy': *Working Paper submitted to the Sub-Commission on the Protection and Promotion of Human Rights, Working Group on Minorities*, UN Doc E/CN.4/Sub2/AC.5/2005/WP5 8; Timo Makkonen, *Equal in Law, Unequal in Fact: Racial and Ethnic Discrimination and the Legal Response thereto in Europe* (Doctoral Dissertation presented at the Faculty of Law at the University of Helsinki), 5 March 2010 83.

[25] See ILC Yrbk ILC (1962), ii 161; also Brownlie, *Principles of Public International Law* (n 4) 580. For an extensive discussion of all criteria present in the definition of treaties, see Anthony Aust, *Modern Treaty Law and Practice* (Cambridge University Press, 2007) 16–23.

[26] Brownlie, *Principles of Public International Law* (n 4) 580.

relationships. True, treaties tend to influence state practice in general, beyond those states that are formal parties to a treaty. To the extent such practice is matched by *opinio juris*, treaty provisions become reflective of customary international law. At this point, the rights enshrined in the treaty also become binding upon non-parties, thus providing them with a truly international character.[27] But when this is not the case, treaties result in complicated patchworks of rights and duties that bind different states to varying degrees.

4.2.4 Customary international law

As described above, international customary law emerges through discernible coherent state practice coupled with *opinio juris*, i.e. that states act coherently precisely because they perceive that they are legally obliged to do so and not simply because it is their will.[28] As further mentioned, complete uniformity in state practice is not required for an international customary norm to crystalize. It is sufficient that a substantial majority of states act in a coherent manner. Evidence of non-compliance, or even explicit rejection of the norm by a few states, does not necessarily preclude the emergence of a customary norm.[29] Moreover, consent to the norm can be tacit and/or implied, it need not be explicit.[30]

The existence of a customary norm can be deduced from essentially all acts and documents that evidence state practice and intent.[31] Customary international law can also often be identified through rulings by international tribunals. Rulings by the ICJ are naturally of particular relevance, but customary international law can also be reflected in findings by regional courts and other institutions, including by human rights courts and commissions.[32]

Obviously, treaty making constitutes a particularly relevant form of state practice. Indeed, under certain circumstances, the adoption of a treaty by a sufficient number of representative states can instantly create a customary norm.[33] More often, however, treaties are a source of evidence of the existence of customary international law.[34] If the same or similar treaty provision occurs in a number of treaties, this strongly indicates that the provision reflects a customary norm. That is particularly so if states that are not parties to the treaty still act in conformity with it, or at

[27] Ibid., 13.

[28] See the ICJ's ruling in the *North Sea Continental Shelf Case*, Judgement, *ICJ Reports*, 1969 3 73–74; also Cassese, *International Law* (n 8) 156; Brownlie, *Principles of Public International Law* (n 4) 6–9; Koskenniemi, *From Apology to Utopia* (n 6) 394–95.

[29] See the ICJ's ruling in Military and Paramilitary Activities in and against Nicaragua (*Nicaragua v United States of America)*, Merits, Judgement, *ICJ Reports* 1986 14; also Brownlie, *Principles of Public International Law* (n 4) 7; Cassese, *International Law* (n 8) 157.

[30] Jonathan Charney, 'Universal International Law' [1993] *American Journal of International Law* 87, reprinted in Evans and Capps (eds.), *International Law* (n 1) 536–37, and Orakhelashvili, *The Interpretation of Acts and Rules in Public International Law* (n 5) 71–75.

[31] Brownlie, *Principles of Public International Law* (n 4) 6.

[32] Boyle and Chinkin, *The Making of International Law* (n 9) 299–300.

[33] *North Sea Continental Shelf Case* (n 28) 73–74; and the *Barcelona Traction Case*, Barcelona Traction, Light and Power Company, Limited, Judgement, ICJ Report 1970 3 32.

[34] Brownlie, *Principles of Public International Law* (n 4) 13.

least do not object to the norm.[35] Even a treaty that has not yet entered into force can be indicative of a customary norm.[36] Similarly, treaties with only a limited number of ratifying states can nonetheless contribute to international customary law-making.[37]

But international customary norms are not only deducable from legally binding instruments. Additionally, formally non-binding instruments, such as UNGA declarations, can often be evidence of both state practice and *opinio juris*.[38] The fact that an instrument is formally non-legally binding need not mean that it lacks the capacity to reflect customary law. Treaties enshrine *opinio juris* not necessarily because of their legally binding nature. States' opinions can be equally evidenced by the position they take towards a non-binding instrument.[39]

In fact, as with treaties, formally non-binding UNGA resolutions can under certain circumstances instantly create customary international law, even if the examples are probably few. Still, in *Nicaragua*, the ICJ deduced the existence of *opinio juris* primarily from a non-binding UNGA resolution,[40] although some additional sources contributed to the Court's conclusions. Moreover, in reaching its conclusion, the ICJ first evaluated whether it could establish the existence of *opinio juris*. Only subsequently did the Court proceed to survey whether there was state practice that matched the subjective opinion of states.[41] The ICJ further declared that it 'does not consider that, for a rule to be established as customary, the corresponding practice must be in absolutely rigorous conformity with the rule . . . [T]he Court deems it sufficient that the conduct of states should, in general, be consistent with such rules, and that instances of state conduct inconsistent with a given rule should generally have been treated as breaches of that rule'.[42] The ICJ's ruling in *Nicaragua* thus gives significant weight to *opinio juris*, at the expense of state-practice. Prior to *Nicaragua*, it was generally thought that if one of the elements is more important than the other, it is state practice.[43] Instead, however, having established the existence of *opinio juris*, the ICJ subsequently presumed the existence of a customary norm, a presumption that then needed to be rebutted by contradicting state practice. Moreover, as to the quantity of state practice, the Court inferred that

[35] Reuter, *Introduction to the Law of Treaties* (n 13) 108–09, 139.

[36] See *Namibia Case*. Legal Consequences for States of the Continued Presence of South Africa in Namibia notwithstanding Security Resolution 276 (1970), Advisory Opinion, ICJ Reports 1971 47; also Brownlie, *Principles of Public International Law* (n 4) 14.

[37] Boyle and Chinkin, *The Making of International Law* (n 18) 234.

[38] See the ICJ's ruling in the *Nuclear Test Case*. Legality of the Threat or Use of Nuclear Weapons, Advisory Opinion, ICJ Reports 1996 226; also *Brownlie, Principles of Public International Law* (n 4) 14–15; Dinah Shelton, 'Law, Non-Law and the Problem of "Soft Law"', in Dinah Shelton (ed.), *Commitment and Compliance: The Role of Non-Binding Norms in The International Legal System* (Oxford University Press, 2007) 1; Boyle and Chinkin, *The Making of International Law* (n 9) 77, 212.

[39] Shelton, 'Normative Hierarchy in International Law' (n 3) 292–93, 320–21; Boyle and Chinkin, *The Making of International Law* (n 9) 215.

[40] UNGA Resolution 2625 (XXV) (The Friendly Relations Resolution).

[41] See *Nicaragua Case*, (n 29) 184–206; also Orakhelashvili, *The Interpretation of Acts and Rules in Public International Law* (n 5) 75–76.

[42] *Nicaragua Case* (n 29) 186.

[43] Bruno Simma and Philip Alston, 'The Sources of Human Rights Law' [1992] *Australian Year Book of International Law* 12 88.

a customary norm had materialized despite limited evidence of supporting such practice, and despite the fact that there were notable, if not numerous, examples of state-practice that contradicted the existence of a norm, something the ICJ also explicitly acknowledged.[44]

The ICJ's ruling in *Nicaragua* potentially significantly impacts on the understanding of how international law is created, for two interrelated reasons. First, the case submits that the UNGA has transcended its traditional recommendary role and can in fact instantly create international law.[45] As Fred Morrison notes, *Nicaragua* appears to change UNGA resolutions from 'soft law principles' to 'hard law prescriptions'.[46] Second, the UNGA's power is further enhanced by the ICJ's finding that if *opinio juris* can be demonstrated, the existence of a customary norm may be presumed. This implies that when there is *opinio juris*, there must be evidence of sufficient coherent *contradicting* state practice to deprive a declaration of its legal implications.[47]

As seen, the constitutive elements of customary law are relatively straightforward in principle. Still, to ascertain what constitutes concerted state practice, and in particular the collective subjective opinion of states, is often associated with practical difficulties. Evidence of state practice and *opinio juris* might be disperse, and difficult to assess and evaluate. As a consequence, one must often resort to secondary sources to identify a customary norm.[48] Martti Koskenniemi even suggests that to identify customary law is often not at all a process of deducing pre-existing rules. Rather, due to the difficulties associated with establishing state practice and *opinio juris* in an objective manner, international tribunals, including the ICJ, tend to resort to equity arguments when 'identifying' a customary international norm, he posits.[49] *In principle*, the *opinio juris* criterion implies that customary law creation,

[44] See *Nicaragua Case* (n 29) 186; also Hillary Charlesworth, 'Law-Making and Sources', in James Crawford and Martti Koskenniemi (eds.), *International Law* (Cambridge University Press, 2012) 193–94; Boyle and Chinkin, *The Making of International Law* (n 9) 235; compare Charney, 'Universal International Law' (n 30) 537–38.

[45] See John Tasioulas, 'In Defence of Relative Normativity: Communitarian Values and the Nicaragua Case' [1996] *Oxford Journal of Legal Studies* 16, reprinted in Evans and Capps (eds.), *International Law* (n 1) 96–100, 114; Charney, 'Universal International Law' (n 30) 546–47; Simma and Alston, 'The Sources of Human Rights Law' (n 43) 96–97. See also James Crawford, 'The Criteria for Statehood in International Law' [1976] *British Yearbook of International Law* 48 (1), reprinted in Evans and Capps (eds.), *International Law* (Vol II) (n 1) 152, where he notes that UNGA resolutions adopted by a large majority of states can have 'quasi-legislative effect'. Charney underlines, however, in the work referred to above, that formally speaking, the UNGA lacks independent legislative authority. Simma and Alston, also in their work referred to above (n 43), are critical of the ICJ's ruling in *Nicaragua*.

[46] See Fred L Morrison, 'Legal Issues in the Nicaragua Opinion' [1987] *American Journal of International Law* 81 161–62. He adds, however, that '[w]hether states are willing to accept this expanded view of the binding effect of resolutions remains to be seen'.

[47] *International Law Association's Final Report on the Impact of International Human Rights Law on General International Law* (2008), 73rd Conference of the ILA, Rio de Janeiro, Brazil, 17–21 August 2008 Section 2.

[48] Boyle and Chinkin, *The Making of International Law* (n 9) 163, 190.

[49] See Koskenniemi, *From Apology to Utopia* (n 6) 396–97, 409–11, 467–71. Boyle and Chinkin agree that to establish what constitutes customary international law is not an entirely scientific process. Rather, it involves political choices. See Boyle and Chinkin, *The Making of International Law* (n 9) 278–79.

as the making of treaties, respects the state sovereignty principle. But *in practice*, one can, noting Koskenniemi's observation, question how well customary law making complies with the notion that international norms emerge only as a result of state consent. As seen, *opinio juris*, and hence the presumption of a customary norm, can be deduced from non-legally binding instruments, despite the objection from and/or contradicting practice of a few states. A customary norm can hence emerge despite lack of consent, and then binds also objecting states.[50] In sum, the way in which customary law is made seems somewhat to contradict the position that international law rigidly upholds the principle of state sovereignty. Section 4.3 returns to this issue.

4.2.5 General principles of law recognized by civilized nations

As described above, the ICJ Statute Article 38.1 ranks 'general principles of law recognized by civilized nations' as primary international legal sources on a par with treaties and customary law. The idea behind general principles of law recognized by civilized nations as a legal source is that one can deduce such general principles through identifying common patterns in national laws.[51] The imprecise definition of what such principles are has led to some scholars questioning what practical role, if any, general principles of law recognized by civilized nations serve in the international legal system.[52] Against this backdrop, it appears safe to conclude that although formally recognized as primary international legal sources, in practice, such principles play a limited role in international law making. In addition, if evidence of general principles of law recognized by civilized nations is state practice (through domestic law making), one can question in what way such principles are possible to distinguish from customary international law.[53]

On a principal level, it is worth adding that seemingly, general principles of law recognized by civilized nations contradict the principle of state sovereignty to an even larger degree than customary international law. It would appear difficult to discern a general principle of law that supports one state's position over another. If international tribunals and the like were to apply general principles of law recognized by civilized nations, they would in practice have to resort to reason or equity to settle the dispute. Again, this would seem to imply that invoking general

[50] See the ICJ's rulings in the *Asylum Case*: Columbian-Peruvian asylum case, ICJ Reports 1950 276, 277; *Nicaragua Case* (n 29) 186; *North Sea Continental Shelf Case* (n 28) 74; also Koskenniemi, *From Apology to Utopia* (n 6) 395; Cassese, *International Law* (n 8) 157 and 162–63; Brownlie, *Principles of Public International Law* (n 4) 7.

[51] See Brownlie, *Principles of Public International Law* (n 4) 16. Principles of law recognized by civilized nations should not be confused with general principles of international law. While the former are identifiable through common patterns in *domestic legal systems*, the latter are general principles deduceable from *international legal sources*. General principles of international law are thus not legal sources per se, but assist us in understanding the international legal system. Examples of such principles are state sovereignty and respect for human rights. See Cassese, *International Law* (n 8) 188.

[52] For instance, Martti Koskenniemi points to that the ICJ has never explicitly applied general principles of law recognized by civilized nations in its rulings. See *From Apology to Utopia* (n 6) 402. In a similar vein, see also Brownlie, *Principles of Public International Law* (n 4) 16–17.

[53] Reuter, *Introduction to the Law of Treaties* (n 13) 141–42, 145.

principles of law recognized by civilized nations as legal sources in practice risks holding some states bound by norms to which they have not consented.[54]

4.2.6 'Soft law'

The term 'soft law' distinguishes a certain category of 'legal' sources from 'hard law'. If employing this distinction, the latter category refers to international legal sources that are formally legally binding, i.e. sources listed as primary sources in the ICJ Statute Article 38.1 and peremptory norms. Soft law, on the other hand, is a variety of sources that some may consider are relevant to international law making, although formally not legally binding.[55]

That said, as Section 4.2.1 indicates, to label certain sources 'soft law' has been criticized from two quite opposite angles. Some assert that it is wrong to refer to these sources as law at all. A source either enshrines law or not, it has been maintained. The constitutional principle of state sovereignty provides—at least in principle—that there can be nothing in between.[56] As to the opposite line of criticism, yet others might agree that formally speaking, the distinction between hard and soft law is valid. But they nonetheless question whether such a formalistic approach can be substantiated in practice. These scholars take a more 'sliding-scale approach'. They argue that there are shades of grey and that international legal sources carry relative weight. If taking this position, one might challenge the division of legal sources into hard and soft law as well, arguing that there is no clear distinction between the two. With these observations in mind, this book will continuously employ the vocabulary of 'hard' and 'soft' law, but will shortly return to the question as to whether it is appropriate to so strictly distinguish between two categories of international legal sources.[57]

Sources commonly referred to as soft law are e.g. declarations and other resolutions adopted by the UNGA or other bodies of international cooperation. Other examples include standards, principles, joint statements, etc., adopted by intergovernmental meetings or organizations.[58] Notably, soft law sources thus largely coincide with the sources from which customary international norms are deduced, as discussed above.

As further described, formally speaking the ICJ lacks power to formulate generally applicable international norms, as do UN treaty bodies through their individual complaint jurisprudence. Therefore, treaty body jurisprudence is sometimes also referred to as soft law.[59] Still, it is probably incorrect to use the label 'soft law', even in the most relaxed understanding of the term, to describe such case law. More

[54] Koskenniemi, *From Apology to Utopia* (n 6) 258–70, in particular, 402–05; Boyle and Chinkin, *The Making of International Law* (n 9) 286.

[55] Shelton, 'Normative Hierarchy in International Law' (n 3) 319–20; Boyle and Chinkin, *The Making of International Law* (n 18) 212–14.

[56] Jonathan Charney, 'Compliance With International Soft Law', in Shelton (ed.), *Commitment and Compliance* (n 38) 115.

[57] See Section 4.3, immediately below.

[58] Boyle and Chinkin, *The Making of International Law* (n 9) 212–13.

[59] Ibid., 156, 213.

correctly, jurisprudence from international tribunals and treaty bodies are sources that interpret hard law sources, thus informing us of their content.[60] As seen, rulings of the ICJ and other authoritative international tribunals are generally held to be of great importance to the identification of international customary norms. Indeed, it is often precisely through an ICJ ruling that we 'become aware' of the existence of an international norm. And, as subsequent chapters illustrate, treaty body jurisprudence in a similar fashion carries the capacity to inform us of the content of international law.[61] In a comparable vein, pursuant to ICJ Statute Article 38.1(d) the international legal doctrine constitutes only a secondary legal source. Still, the writings of leading legal scholars fulfil many of the same purposes as jurisprudence, and thus often inform us what constitutes relevant international law,[62] as do the findings of the International Law Commission (ILC).

In summary, formally speaking (i) 'soft law' sources proper, such as UN declarations, (ii) international legal sources interpreting hard law sources, such as rulings by international tribunals and treaty body jurisprudence, and (iii) secondary sources such as the legal doctrine, do not constitute 'hard law' sources. In fact, some posit that these 'sources' do not enshrine law at all. Still, such 'sources' seem to play a role in international law making. And to the extent they do, is it correct to claim that soft law sources lack legal relevance? It is emphasized that the answer to this question might be of particular relevance to the indigenous rights discourse, and is therefore addressed in depth in the following section.

4.3 Further on the Relative Status of Various International Legal Sources

4.3.1 The inherent juxtaposition of the liberal international legal system

The above explains how the international legal system rests on the premise that states are the ultimate creators of international law. No law can exist above them. As further seen, the international legal system is also based on a second precept, intrinsically connected to the first. Once the sovereign states have created a norm, the norm must be obeyed, including by states themselves. A state may not subsequently opt out of the norm due to a change in will. It is a keystone in the international legal system that once established, international law is objective and external to state behaviour, will, or interest. At first glance, this second premise seems straightforward. It appears to provide the foundation for a coherent theory of law. But if one examines the second premise more closely, does it not, to be

[60] Ibid., 156–57; but compare Dinah Shelton, 'Commentary and Conclusions', in Shelton (ed.), *Commitment and Compliance* (n 38) 451–52. Still, at the same time as Shelton takes a somewhat cautious position towards the status of treaty body jurisprudence as international legal sources, she argues that such jurisprudence can be more important for the formulation of international law than what she labels 'primary soft law sources' (p 461).

[61] Compare Boyle and Chinkin, *The Making of International Law* (n 9) 156–57.

[62] Talmon (n 14) 165.

operational in practice, rely on the first? It seems an illusion to talk about objective and external law *at the time when the law is applied*, if one cannot objectively determine how the norm became law *at the time of inception*. And at that point the law consists, it appears, only of that which those it is supposed to govern say. In this manner, it is more difficult to talk about the liberal international legal system as a coherent 'theory of law'.

In further examining this observation, this book relies heavily on Martti Koskenniemi's analyses in *From Apology to Utopia*. In this groundbreaking work, Koskenniemi observes that liberalism's first precept—the notion that international law is to be deduced from the actions and intent of the same polities the law is supposed to govern—embeds a juxtaposition that international lawyers have wrestled with since the advent of international law. Koskenniemi points out that a legal theory that assumes that the law can—and should—be deduced from state behaviour and intent is problematic since it presumes that state behaviour is correct. A legal theory which holds that state behaviour equates to the law—i.e. that state action/intent and the law, by definition, coincide—is easily accused of being in want of meaning. Can a legal theory that submits that the behaviour of those the law is supposed to govern, *is* the law, be called a legal theory at all? Moreover, is an exercise that aims to identify the law from state behaviour/intent not redundant under such circumstances? For all practical purposes, it would appear that it is the conduct/intent of states, rather than what can potentially be deduced therefrom, that is the 'law'. And if all this is true, is it correct and meaningful to even refer to international law as a legal system?

Koskenniemi notes that liberal lawyers have always been mindful that a rigid application of the principle of state sovereignty renders the international legal system vulnerable to questioning whether it is a legal system at all. Liberals accept that in order to constitute a legal system proper, international law should reasonably be binding upon states, something it is not—by definition—if state action/intent is the law. Should international law be 'law' in any meaningful understanding of the term, state action/intent must not define the law. But the alternative is also troublesome to liberals. If international law is not derived from state action/intent, i.e. from state consent, the implication is that the law has at some point acquired an autonomous status and has become disconnected from the sovereign. This, in turn, inevitably brings back the idea of some form of natural justice, a notion inherently contradictory to a positivist international legal system. Therein lies, Koskenniemi observes, the juxtaposition and the dilemma of a liberal international legal order firmly rooted in the principle of state sovereignty. Such a legal system cannot abandon the notion that law emerges only as a result of the exercise of state sovereignty. At the same time, one cannot ignore that a legal system where the norms are deduced from the action and intent of those the law is supposed to govern may come across as no legal system at all.

Attempting to defend the international normative order as a 'legal system', liberals have pointed to both the most concrete form of international law-making, i.e. treaties, and the most sweeping, i.e. general principles of law.

It has been argued that treaties create law in the way liberals imagine. One can objectively determine when and how treaties come into being, and once in force, a state that has accepted to be bound by a treaty cannot opt out of it. Koskenniemi accepts this observation, but points out that treaties emerge slowly, if at all, particularly in areas where they are most needed. Moreover, treaties only bind states that have explicitly agreed to be bound. In other words, as Section 4.2.3 explains, an international legal system that relies heavily on treaties is inevitably a fragmented one. It ultimately boils down to a patchwork of binary state relations that fails to bind many states to even the most needed and basic norms. Moreover, states whose behaviour the international community is presumably most keen to influence are often those least likely to sign on to treaties. To the extent one can label such an order a legal system, it is seemingly not an effective one.

Others have also sought to address the identified potential flaw in the international legal system by referring to general and fundamental principles that go beyond state practice and will, such as the principle of respect for humanity. The existence of such a principle evidences that the international normative order is indeed a legal system, one may argue, since this norm can be identified without resorting to state practice and intent. Koskenniemi accepts that principles such as the one of respect for humanity have been accepted as international law, but argues that why states do not differ in opinion on them is because of their general, obvious, and self-evident character. He argues that while these principles' general and self-evident nature protects them from state objection, it also deprives them of any practical applicability. Respect for humanity is simultaneously impossible to object to—and useless as a legal norm. The price paid for self-evidentness is incapability to regulate state behaviour in any meaningful manner. Ideals such as respect for humanity may be important as principles, but are equally unhelpful as law.

Koskenniemi rounds up his argument by concluding that to strictly uphold the principle of state sovereignty inevitably results in a risk that the international legal order is accused of being no legal system at all. According to him, the cure for this juxtaposition is pragmatism. Koskenniemi advises against both resorting to extreme formalism and treating international law as politics—or natural law. One should respect that the law is to be found in recognized legal sources, evaluated through methods lawyers have been trained to practice. But one should not, Koskenniemi posits, expect such processes to come up with clear-cut solutions to each and every dispute. Often, the international lawyer will, to some extent, have to rely on reason and equity. The international legal system is a legal system, albeit not a perfect one, he infers.[63]

[63] See Koskenniemi, *From Apology to Utopia* (n 6) 63, 85, 142, 158–67, 396–411, 467–71, 513–61, 568–69, 573–75, 583–84, 589, 616. He compares knowledge of international law with knowledge of a language. It is a set of rules that place constraints on the user, but nonetheless offers more than one correct option to her. See also Koskenniemi, *The Gentle Civilizer of Nations—The Rise and Fall of International Law 1870-1960* (Cambridge University Press, 2002) 502–17. Somewhat more recently, he has made the same point by asserting that 'although all the official justifications of decision-making are such that they may support contrary positions or outcomes, in practice nothing is ever that random'. See Martti Koskenniemi, 'The Politics of International Law' [2009] *The European Journal of International Law*, Vol 20, No 1 9.

For the present purposes, it is not necessary to critically analyze Koskenniemi's arguments in detail. It is sufficient to note that he seems to portray a reality, albeit somewhat pointedly. Section 4.2.2 describes how Koskenniemi is not alone in observing the apparent contradiction between a concept such as peremptory norms and the principle of state sovereignty. And as Section 4.2.4 articulates, others have pointed out that the idea that a customary norm can be identified through evidence of state practice and *opinio juris* alone is often a fiction. The description above of the nature of the international legal sources system supports Koskenniemi's assertion that in practice, the principle of state sovereignty has not been—and more importantly cannot be—strictly upheld. As Alan Boyle and Christine Chinkin observe, no international legal theory offers a complete scientific answer to international law-making.[64] In a similar vein, Malcolm Evans and Patrick Capps note that today, most international lawyers agree that there has been a substantial shift from strict positivism towards an international legal system 'which has a greater claim to be called a genuine system of "public" international law'.[65]

The question is then, if the principle of state sovereignty cannot be strictly upheld in reality, what are the implications for a stern distinction between 'hard' and 'soft' law sources? As noted above, this distinction (or, some would argue, the distinction between law and non-law) is a direct consequence of rigid reliance on the principle of state sovereignty.

4.3.2 Eggs d'droit—the soft and hard variety

The legal doctrine largely agrees that it is not possible to maintain a clear distinction between 'hard' and 'soft' law sources. Christine Chinkin notes that many legal scholars accept that if international law does not, and cannot, strictly uphold the principle of state consent in international law-making, it makes little sense to firmly categorize international legal sources into 'soft' and 'hard' or binding and non-binding.[66] Hillary Charlesworth largely concurs.[67] But equally important, it has been suggested, is that one does not resort to politics. Chinkin, together with Alan Boyle, submit that an 'enlightened positivist' should be mindful of the centrality of formal sources, at the same time as he or she recognizes wider methods for identifying what constitutes law. In an enlightened positivist's legal system, it is a 'fallacy' to dismiss soft law as non-law, they infer.[68] In a similar vein, Peter Haas notes that hard and soft law share the same objective, namely a need for states to signal

[64] Boyle and Chinkin, *The Making of International Law* (n 9) 19.

[65] Evans and Capps (eds.), *International Law* (n 1) xiii.

[66] Christine Chinkin, 'Normative Development in the International Legal System', in Shelton (ed.), *Commitment and Compliance* (n 38) 23.

[67] Charlesworth, 'Law-Making and Sources', in Crawford and Koskenniemi (eds.), *International Law* (n 44) 200.

[68] See Boyle and Chinkin, *The Making of International Law* (n 9) 12, 212. See also Mauro Barelli, 'The Role of Soft Law in the International Legal System: The Case of the United Nations Declaration on the Rights of Indigenous Peoples' [2009] *International and Comparative Law Quarterly*, Vol 58, where he makes similar observations.

their commitment to create a world order to other states.[69] Ian Brownlie too notes that the normative impact of an international instrument need not always depend solely on its formal legal status.[70] On that topic, Pieter van Dijk observes that '[t]he conclusion that the [Helsinki] Final Act is not a legally binding agreement does not mean that the matters agreed upon between the participating states . . . should not be binding'.[71] Finally, James Crawford and Martti Koskenniemi conclude that in settling international legal conflicts, the strict distinction between 'formal' and 'informal' legal sources as envisaged in ICJ Statute Article 38 is rarely employed. Rather, the international lawyer often has to resort to 'perceived equity' when settling such conflicts.[72]

Not only principal, but also practical, rationales render a rigid distinction between hard and soft law difficult. The above comments highlight that the formally recognized primary sources of international law—treaties, customary law, and general principles of law recognized by civilized nations—all have their deficiencies. Treaty law has the advantage of clarity, but suffers from gaps and fragmentation. Customary international law, on the other hand, benefits from universality, but is at the same time not easily identified. The latter is even more true with regard to general principles of law recognized by civilized nations, to an extent that it is unclear whether such norms are ever applied. Consequently, if one relies solely on formal hard law sources, one often receives limited guidance as to the content of the law.

With regard to (i) soft law sources, (ii) international legal sources interpreting hard law sources, and (iii) the international legal doctrine, the situation is often the opposite, compared with the formal hard law sources. The former groups of sources are formally not legally binding, but at the same time carry the advantages of being universal, concrete, and with the capacity to form a coherent pattern of law. For instance, as Chapters 5 and 8 return to, the UN Declaration on the Rights of Indigenous Peoples (UNDRIP) enshrines comparatively precisely-formulated, universally-applicable rights of indigenous peoples. Rulings by the ICJ and UN treaty body jurisprudence are also often clear, precise in their content, and reflective of globally applicable norms although formally binding only upon the parties to the conflict. And the very purpose of most writings by internationally recognized legal scholars is an attempt to both systemize international law and explain its details. In that sense, these sources can often be more informative as to the content of the law compared with the sometimes relatively obscure or fragmented hard law sources. Indeed, Sections 4.2.4 and 4.2.6 explain how state practice and *opinio juris* can at

[69] See Peter Haas, 'Choosing to Comply: Theorizing from International Relations and Comparative Politics', in Shelton (ed.), *Commitment and Compliance* (n 38) 43. For similar observations, see also Edith Brown Weiss, 'Understanding Compliance with Soft Law', also in Shelton (n 38) 535; Charney, 'Compliance with International Soft Law' (n 56) 116.

[70] *Brownlie, Principles of Public International Law* (n 4) 3–4, 534.

[71] Pieter van Dijk, 'The Implementation of the Final Act of Helsinki: The Creation of New Structures or the Involvement of Existing Ones?' [1989] *Michigan Journal of International Law*, Vol 10 110, 114.

[72] Crawford and Koskenniemi, *International Law* (n 11) 11.

times only be deduced from soft law sources, rulings by the ICJ, and the legal doctrine. In addition, it is often through treaty body jurisprudence one is informed about evolved understandings of treaty provisions that have crystalized into customary norms. Against this background, it appears to square badly with reality to label these sources 'soft law' or even non-law. If one can only identify the law through soft law sources, do not these sources, at least for all practical purposes, constitute legal sources?

As Section 4.2.4 discusses, this conclusion finds support in the ICJ's ruling in *Nicaragua*, which demonstrates that under certain circumstances, non-binding UN resolutions are not only indicative of, but indeed capable of instantly creating, customary international law. Frederic Kirgis submits that this power of the UNGA might be particularly present within the field of human rights. He adds that the more pressing the human rights issue, the less state practice should be needed to substantiate *opinio juris*.[73] Alan Boyle and Christin Chinkin agree that less evidence of state practice seems to be needed to establish customary law within the area of human rights.[74]

In sum, it would appear inappropriate to label certain international legal sources 'soft law'. Evidence shows that it is impossible—both in principle and in practice—to draw such a distinction between hard and soft law. As seen, sources often referred to as soft law create law through interplay with 'hard law' sources, and can even on rare occasions create law instantly by themselves.[75] For instance, provisions in UN declarations can reflect, indeed sometimes essentially clone, formally legally binding treaty provisions. UN declarations interacting with treaties in this manner indicate that the declaration provision reflects legally binding law, or at least that the right reflected in the provision is emerging into law.[76] In a similar fashion, soft law sources are often an important device for attributing meaning to international norms as well as for identifying changes in international law.[77]

Although enjoying broad support, the position that international law has strayed away from strict formal positivism is, however, not without criticism. In a famous article, Prosper Weil vehemently criticizes the notion that the principle of state sovereignty and formal positivism can be compromised, even in the slightest way. He maintains that a 'source' is either reflective of law or not, and that there is

[73] Fredric L Kirgis, 'Custom on a Sliding Scale' [1987] *American Journal of International Law*, 81 147–49.

[74] See Boyle and Chinkin, *The Making of International Law* (n 9) 285. To this assertion Bruno Simma and Philip Alston retort, though, that such reasoning 'seems to be a case of arriving at the wrong conclusion for the right reason'. See Simma and Alston, 'The Sources of Human Rights Law' (n 43) 96.

[75] Barelli, 'The Role of Soft Law in the International Legal System' (n 68) 959–60; Boyle and Chinkin, *The Making of International Law* (n 9) 220; Richard Bilder, 'Beyond Compliance: Helping Nations Cooperate', in Shelton (ed.), *Commitment and Compliance* (n 38) 70–72; Chinkin, 'Normative Development in the International Legal System' (n 66) 36–37.

[76] Boyle and Chinkin, *The Making of International Law* (n 9) 213.

[77] Ibid., 12.

nothing in between. Weil harshly criticizes the ICJ for accepting the existence of a customary norm despite insufficient evidence of state practice and *opinio juris*, and in spite of objections to the norm by some states.[78] A number of other legal scholars share this position.[79] Notwithstanding, the above appears to demonstrate that it is neither principally correct, nor practically feasible, to maintain a strict line between hard and soft law. Seemingly, international law has opted for a different path. As Hillary Charlesworth notes, 'Prosper Weil's [original] *cri de coeur* in the face of what he termed 'relative normativity' of international law . . . has now become a whisper.'[80]

The conclusion here is not that of Hersch Lauterpacht, that natural law theories still necessarily influence international law.[81] The point is rather that factual evidence suggests that Lassa Oppenheim's prediction that the principle of formal positivism would never be challenged, has been proven wrong. International law has moved beyond a strict reliance on those sources listed in ICJ Statue Article 38.1 as sole legal sources. It has strayed away from a formal division of law into hard and soft law. Consequently, the subsequent chapters will not employ this categorization. In line with the conclusions above, this work accepts that what some refer to as 'soft law' carries normative value. At the same time, it is mindful that not all international legal sources carry the same normative value. This work respects that in other than rare instances, in order for a formally non-binding source to reflect law, it needs to be backed up by treaties and/or customary law. International law is not politics.

The approach this work takes towards international law-making might be illustrated by a comparison between hard and soft law, on the one hand, and hard and soft boiled eggs, on the other. One can certainly identify some boiled eggs as being harder than others. But it is not possible to objectively classify eggs as hard or soft boiled. Furthermore, a soft-boiled egg can become hard-boiled. Soft law likewise has the capacity to develop into hard law, or wishes.

78 Weil, 'Towards Relative Normativity in International Law?' (n 16) 417–18, 423–42.

79 For some references, see Chinkin, 'Normative Development in the International Legal System' (n 66). In a similar vein, Richard Bilder, having noted that international normative arrangements often blend hard and soft law elements, points out that states may still find it useful to draw a relatively strict line between binding and non-binding norms. See Richard Bilder, 'Beyond Compliance: Helping Nations Cooperate', in Shelton (ed.), *Commitment and Compliance* (n 38) 71.

80 Charlesworth, 'Law-Making and Sources' (n 67) 200.

81 Some argue that natural law plays a role in international law-making today. See e.g. Orakhelashvili, *The Interpretation of Acts and Rules in Public International Law* (n 5) 60–66. He suggests that international law has a dualistic composition where positive law and natural law co-exist. Orakhelashvili submits that international law is primarily positive law, but that it is sometimes necessary to complement positive law with arguments going beyond state consent. He asserts that reason and perceptions of justice have a place in international law creation. Irrespective of whether one opts to label this aspect of the international legal system natural law, Orakhelashvili's seems to largely share Koskenniemi's position on international law-making.

4.4 Norms for Interpreting Treaties and Other International Legal Instruments

4.4.1 Treaties

VCLT[82] Article 31.1 proclaims that when interpreting a treaty, primacy should be given to the text of the instrument. A treaty provision shall as a general rule be given the content and scope that follows from an ordinary understanding of its wording, taking into account the context, object, and purpose of the treaty as a whole.[83] If the ordinary meaning of a treaty-provision is unclear, one may resort to preparatory works and other documentation that demonstrate the intent of the parties at the time of adoption of the instrument.[84] Importantly for the present purposes, the understanding of a treaty provision need not be static or bound to the parties' intentions at the time of the adoption of the treaty. Pursuant to VCLT Article 31.3(b), when interpreting a treaty, one shall take into account subsequent practice in the application of the treaty that demonstrates an evolved understanding of a provision.[85] It follows from VCLT Articles 31 and 32, when read together, that for treaty interpretation, preparatory works to the treaty and other documents that manifest the intention of the parties at the time of adoption of the treaty are sources secondary to subsequent practice.[86] The important role given to subsequent practice reflects that international law is a growing and an evolving body of law. The ICJ has confirmed that VCLT Articles 31 and 32 reflect customary international law.[87]

The evolving nature of treaties is particularly important in the context of human rights instruments. These are expected to be especially responsive to changed social conditions and evolved perceptions of justice.[88] In fact, human rights treaties should arguably respond to subsequent practice beyond what follows from VCLT Articles 31 and 32.

VCLT was crafted mainly with bilateral state treaties in mind. There is, however, a significant difference between such treaties and human rights instruments. The former can be compared with a contract between two parties, essentially serving the interest of those parties only.[89] Human rights treaties, on the other hand, are not primarily drafted with the intention to serve the parties. Indeed, human rights treaties are probably often viewed as a burden to the parties as such treaties limit state

[82] Two other Vienna conventions address treaty making between states and international organizations and treaties in the context of state succession, respectively. These instruments are, however, irrelevant for the present purposes.

[83] See also Reuter, *Introduction to the Law of Treaties* (n 13) 95–97; *Brownlie, Principles of Public International Law* (n 4) 602.

[84] VCLT Article 32; also *Brownlie, Principles of Public International Law* (n 4) 605–06.

[85] See also Reuter, *Introduction to the Law of Treaties* (n 13) 96–97.

[86] Compare also Cassese, *International Law* (n 8) 179; Boyle and Chinkin, *The Making of International Law* (n 9) 151 244–47; Reuter, *Introduction to the Law of Treaties* (n 13) 97–98.

[87] E.g. *Kasikili/Sedudu Island (Botswana/Namibia)*, Judgement, ICJ Reports 1999 1045; also Cassese, *International Law* (n 8) 187; Boyle and Chinkin, *The Making of International Law* (n 9) 191.

[88] Boyle and Chinkin, *The Making of International Law* (n 9) 151, 244–47.

[89] Frédéric Mégret 'International Law as Law', in Crawford and Koskenniemi (eds.) *International Law* (n 44) 69.

sovereignty.[90] Human rights treaties enshrine universal norms intended to benefit subjects other than the parties to the instrument. In that sense, human rights instruments are of a truly normative character, whereas treaties within other spheres of international law can, to varying degrees, be characterized as contracts.[91] When interpreting human rights treaties, the difference between the role and character of such treaties, on one hand, and of other treaties, on the other, justifies that one places greater emphasis on subsequent practice than the wording of VCLT Article 31.3(b) suggests.[92] In sum, human rights treaties have a greater capacity than other treaties to evolve and take on new and additional meanings.

The importance of subsequent practice to treaty interpretation is of particular relevance for the legal status of treaty body jurisprudence, which constitutes a form of subsequent practice pursuant to VCLT Article 31.3(b). This provision does not refer exclusively to *state* practice. Rather, it generically covers any subsequent practice in the application of a treaty provision. Treaty bodies are set up by the treaty they are supposed to monitor for the precise purpose of authoritatively contributing to subsequent practice that leads to evolved understandings of the treaty. By having consented to adhere to the findings of treaty bodies, state parties have recognized these bodies' role in making human rights treaties living instruments. Hence, treaty body jurisprudence constitutes important subsequent practice 'a lawyer would be foolish to ignore'.[93] Treaty body jurisprudence reflects the relevant understanding of a treaty provision, unless concerted state objection to the jurisprudence speaks in favour of another understanding. In other words, tacit state-approval qualifies treaty body jurisprudence as subsequent practice relevant to the interpretation of a treaty provision.[94]

Treaty bodies are not the only human rights institutions with the capacity to contribute to evolved understandings of treaties. James Anaya points to how the

[90] Cassese, *International Law* (n 8) 375–76.

[91] See Manfred Nowak, *Introduction to the International Human Rights Regime* (Brill, 2003) 33; Martin Scheinin, 'Characteristics of Human Rights Norms', in Catarina Krause and Martin Scheinin (eds.), *International Protection of Human Rights: A Textbook* (Institute for Human Rights, Åbo Academi University, 2009) 19; Olivier De Schutter, *International Human Rights Law* (Cambridge University Press, 2010) 48, 60, 89. The particular nature of human rights treaties is further illustrated by the fact that the most central human rights are considered to be *erga omnes*. *Erga omnes* norms constitute an exception to the general rule that only a directly aggrieved party may take action to rectify a violation of a treaty. Opposite to the general rule, every state is entitled, indeed obligated, to contribute to respect for and compliance with *erga omnes* rights, even when a violation does not directly impact on the state or its citizens. See ibid., 89–94; HRC General Comment No 31 [80], UN Doc CCPR/C/21/rev1/Add 13 2.

[92] See e.g. the European Court of Human Rights' rulings in *Soering v United Kingdom* (1989) 11 EHRR 439 87; *Ireland v UK* (1978) 2 EHRR 25 239. See also Makkonen, *Equal in Law, Unequal in Fact* (n 24) 76–77; Martin Scheinin, 'Impact on the Law of Treaties', in Menno T Kamminga and Martin Scheinin (eds.), *The Impact of Human Rights Law on General International Law* (Oxford University Press, 2009); *International Law Association's Final Report on the Impact of International Human Rights Law on General International Law*, 73rd Conference of the ILA, Rio de Janeiro, Brazil, 7; ILA Resolution No 4/2008, adopted at the same conference.

[93] Boyle and Chinkin, *The Making of International Law* (n 9) 156.

[94] Scheinin, 'Impact on the Law of Treaties' (n 92) 33; Makkonen, *Equal in Law, Unequal in Fact* (n 24) 78; Anthony Aust, *Modern Treaty Law and Practice* (Cambridge University Press, 2007) 241; ILA, Final Report (n 92) 8.

Inter-American Court on Human Rights (IACHR), when ruling in the *Awas Tingni Case*, 'was not deterred by the absence of any specific reference in the American Convention on Human Rights to indigenous peoples or collective rights [or] by the individualistic terms in which the right to property is expressed in the American Convention . . . '. He notes that the Court did not find itself bound by the mere wording of the property rights provision in the Convention. Rather, the IACHR looked at the core values of the right and matched these values with trends in the indigenous rights discourse. Anaya further observes that the IACHR took the same approach in the subsequent *Belize Case* and expanded on its ruling in *Awas Tingni*, as did the Inter-American Commission on Human Rights (IACommHR) in the *Dann Sisters Case*. Here the Commission relied on trends and developments in the international indigenous rights regime when interpreting the right to property in an indigenous context.[95] The position taken by the human rights institutions is only natural. The above demonstrates that formal positivism is not so rigidly upheld as to preclude adaptive understandings of international law, and in particular international human rights law. Hence, it is not only acceptable, but indeed expected, that international human rights courts and other institutions interpret human treaties in manners that correspond to developments within international law and evolved understandings of justice in general.

In summary, treaty body jurisprudence constitutes subsequent practice relevant to correct understandings of human rights treaty provisions. Absent coherent state objection, one can presume that such jurisprudence reflects international law. The same is largely true with regard to rulings by international human rights courts and institutions. Finally, Sections 4.2.4 and 4.3 describe how non-binding instruments such as UN declarations interplay with treaties to create international law. If a provision in a UN declaration addresses the same issue as an earlier treaty provision, the subsequent declaration provision can be indicative of an evolved understanding of the former. Naturally, an UNGA vote on a declaration constitutes subsequent practice relevant to the interpretation of a treaty, insofar as the parties to the treaty also participated in the vote on the declaration.[96]

4.4.2 Other international instruments

The VCLT directly applies only to treaties. It does not formally apply to UN declarations and other non-binding instruments. Still, as mentioned, VCLT Articles 31 and 32 reflect customary international law. Therefore, the universally accepted principles these provisions enshrine should reasonably be allowed to guide our understandings also of other instruments, similar in style with treaties and that

[95] See S James Anaya, 'Divergent Discourses About International Law, Indigenous Peoples, and Rights Over Lands and Natural Resources: Toward a Realist Trend' [2005] *Colorado Journal on International and Environmental Law and Policy*, Vol 16.2 253, 255. Regarding the mentioned cases, see further Section 8.6.4.

[96] Boyle and Chinkin, *The Making of International Law* (n 9) 212; Shelton, 'Law, Non-Law, and the Problem of "Soft Law"' (n 38) 1.

also carry the capacity to contribute to international law-making. That is particularly so against the backdrop of the conclusion above that there is no relevant reason to draw a strict line between formally binding and non-binding legal instruments. Presumably, therefore, the norms enshrined in VCLT Articles 31 and 32 are also relevant for the interpretation of formally non-binding international instruments, at least when such instruments are formulated in concrete and legalistic language, and hence do not deviate much from treaties in style.

4.5 Conclusions

Formally, treaties, customary law (including *jus cogens*), and general principles of law recognized by civilized nations constitute the primary sources of international law, or, if one prefers, hard law sources. But in practice, the doctrine on international legal sources has not upheld a clear distinction between hard and soft law. The reasons are both principal and practical. First, the international legal system has not strictly upheld the principles of formal positivism and state sovereignty in international law making. As a consequence, there is no principal reason to maintain a clear distinction between hard and soft law either. Second, formally primary sources of international law often offer insufficient guidance as to what is in fact the content of the law. Often, the practicing lawyer simply has no choice but to resort to secondary 'soft law' sources. The alternative would be to rely on subjective values. That said, one must still recognize that different legal sources carry different legal status in the international legal system. One cannot simply treat formally non-legally binding sources as binding. But to the extent the content of a formally non-binding source finds support in other sources, it is relevant when determining what constitutes law.

Subsequent practice is a relevant source when interpreting treaty provisions. That is particularly so with regard to human rights treaties, which are especially responsive to developments in society and evolved understandings of justice. Treaty body jurisprudence is a specific form of subsequent practice. States have agreed to respect the conclusions of treaty bodies when establishing it through the instrument the body is set up to monitor. In the absence of concerted state objections to a treaty body's interpretation of a treaty provision, one can presume that the findings of the body adequately reflect law. In a similar fashion, international tribunals contribute to evolved understandings of treaty provisions, not least within the field of human rights. Further, states voting on human rights instruments in the UNGA is also a state practice of relevance when one seeks to identify possible evolved understandings of a treaty provision.

In line with the above, the following chapters place considerable weight on treaty body jurisprudence, provided that there is no concerted state objection thereto. This book also considers the UNDRIP to be an important international legal source on indigenous peoples' rights, although the Declaration is, formally speaking, not legally binding. The work is, however, at the same time mindful that different international legal sources carry different normative authority. For instance, for an UNDRIP provision to be considered to be reflective of international law proper, it must normally find support in other sources of law, such as treaty provisions. Similarities between UNDRIP provisions and treaty provisions indicate that the former enshrines customary international law. Conversely, the UNDRIP can—as a UN declaration adopted with overwhelming support—also constitute such subsequent practice that informs us about evolved understandings of a treaty provision.[97]

[97] See Barelli, 'The Role of Soft Law in the International Legal System' (n 68) 966; Christopher J Fromherz, 'Indigenous Peoples Courts: Egalitarian Juridical Pluralism, Self-Determination, and the United Nations Declaration on the Rights of Indigenous Peoples' [2008] *University of Pennsylvania Law Review*, Vol 156 1342–43. Fromherz notes that if a UNDRIP provision matches UN treaty body jurisprudence, this indicates that the norm enshrined is legally binding.

PART II

INDIGENOUS PEOPLES' LEGAL STATUS AND THE RIGHT TO SELF-DETERMINATION

5

Indigenous Peoples' Legal Status under Contemporary International Law

5.1 Introduction

Chapters 2 and 3 describe how conventional individual liberalism came to underpin the classical international legal system from its advent in the wake of the Peace of Westphalia in 1648, and continued to do so up until the establishment of the United Nations (UN) and beyond. Those chapters explain how this legal system rests heavily on the constitutional principle of state sovereignty which professes that no law can pre-date or exist above the state. As sovereigns, states are the ultimate creators of international law.

We further saw how with time, the international normative order that got entrenched over the centuries embraced first human rights ideals and later human rights proper of the individual vis-à-vis the state, but throughout remained inhospitable towards the notion that indigenous peoples (and other groups) could be bestowed with rights. As a consequence, indigenous peoples did not enjoy political (or sovereign) rights as collectives, as the state remained the only collective legal subject (or polity) recognized by international law. Neither did indigenous peoples enjoy civil or other human rights as collectives, as these were reserved for individuals. In sum, in the state-individual dichotomy the classical international legal system advocated, there was no room for indigenous peoples.

At the same time, Chapter 3 describes how a school within contemporary political philosophy more hospitable towards rights of indigenous peoples (and other groups) has recently successfully challenged conventional individual liberalism, which has had to yield its previously dominating position within political thought. Moreover, Chapter 4 demonstrates how contemporary international law on international legal sources has not rigidly upheld the principle of state sovereignty, and, as a consequence, has not maintained a clinical distinction between hard and soft law sources either. This chapter surveys what impacts these more recent developments have had on the legal status of indigenous peoples. As mentioned, law does not exist in a vacuum. It should reasonably respond to new lines of thought and evolved understandings of justice in society at large.

5.2 Generally on Peoples' Rights during the 1970s and 1980s

Section 2.5 describes how although the contemporary international legal system initially did not embrace peoples' rights in any meaningful understanding of the term, the principal peoples' right, that of self-determination, was from the outset nonetheless deliberately geared towards peoples, and not towards states. It further indicates how this position may have planted a seed that would spur later debates on peoples' rights proper. The 1970s and 1980s witnessed the first, few, non-conclusive, but nonetheless discernible signs of acceptance of peoples' rights.

In 1970, the UN General Assembly (UNGA) adopted the Declaration on Friendly Relations among States.[1] The Friendly Relations Declaration essentially confirms the understanding of the right to self-determination established during the decolonization process. Notwithstanding, it has been suggested that it added an element to the scope of the right to self-determination, in that it requires the central government of the state to also represent the interests of minority populations within the state.[2] That is not to say that the Friendly Relations Declaration in any way suggested a right to self-determination in the meaning of self-governing rights of distinct segments of the population of a state. The Declaration still reflects a right where decision-making power vests solely with the state's political institutions, including with the new states that were formed following decolonization.[3] That said, a right to self-determination that encompasses a duty on states to take into account the specific interests of minority segments of society would appear to be a right that is not only formally but also in practice geared towards peoples, and not states, although the practical implications of this distinction are still admittedly limited.

In the 1980s, the International Court of Justice (ICJ) also had the opportunity to contemplate the scope and applicability of the right to self-determination. The *Frontier Dispute* did not involve a self-determination situation proper. Yet, in its ruling the ICJ opined that it is difficult to see how the principle of territorial integrity can be reconciled with that of self-determination.[4] The position taken by the ICJ seems to indicate that the Court thought of the right to self-determination in the context of peoples in the meaning sub-segments of the population of a territory. Because how can a right to self-determination that applies to the entire population of a territory be difficult to reconcile with the principle of territorial integrity of states? Seemingly, the right to self-determination can come into conflict with the principle of territorial integrity only if the right is deemed applicable to a particular

[1] GA Res 2526, UN GAOR, 25th Session, Supp 28 (1971), 9 ILM 1292.

[2] Antonio Cassese, *Self-Determination of Peoples: A Legal Reappraisal* (Cambridge University Press, 1995) 113–14.

[3] James Crawford, 'The Right of Self-Determination in International Law: Its Development and Future', in Philip Alston (ed.), *Peoples' Rights* (Oxford University Press, 2005) 16–17; Joshua Castellino, 'Conceptual Difficulties and the Right to Indigenous Self-Determination', in Nazila Ghanea and Alexandra Xanthaki (eds.), *Minorities, Peoples and Self-Determination—Essays in Honour of Patrick Thornberry* (Martinus Nijhsoff Publishers, 2005) 69.

[4] *Frontier Dispute (Burkina Faso v Mali)*, Judgement, ICJ Reports 1986 554 25.

group residing within a particular territory of the state which seeks to secede from the same.[5]

Further, in 1984, the UN Human Rights Committee (HRC) connected the right to self-determination to economic development. It confirmed that the right to self-determination applies beyond colonial situations. At the same time, the HRC did not go so far as to suggest that the right embraces self-governing rights of sub-segments of states.[6] In the same context, adopted two years later, the UNGA Declaration on the Right to Development proclaims a right of peoples—and not states—to economic, social, cultural, and political development.[7] Some proponents of peoples' rights argue that this Declaration evidences the existence of such rights. But similarly to other instruments of the era, it would appear that the term 'peoples' in the Declaration on the Right to Development does not refer to peoples in any ethnic/cultural meaning of the term. Rather, peoples were again understood as the aggregate populations (and thus agents) of states.

On a regional level, in 1975 the Conference on Security and Cooperation in Europe (CSCE) adopted the Helsinki Final Act, where participating states committed to respect the equal right of peoples to self-determination.[8] The Helsinki Final Act reaffirms that the right to self-determination stretches beyond a colonial context, and applies also to peoples in independent countries.[9] The Act further suggested a development within the field of minority rights. The Helsinki Final Act proclaims that states shall respect and protect rights of persons belonging to minorities. The reference to 'protect' seemingly points to a deviation away from the position that states should remain passive and neutral between cultures.

In summary, by the end of the 1980s international law still understood peoples in terms of aggregate populations of states. Notwithstanding, there were some indications, however still admittedly limited, that the world community was starting to entertain the notion of a right to self-determination that has relevance also to peoples in the meaning sub-segments of the populations of states.

5.3 The Seed to an Indigenous Rights Discourse

In the 1970s and 80s, the UN and its member states also took trembling steps towards addressing indigenous rights in earnest. Doing so, states soon came to acknowledge that the situation of indigenous peoples differs from that of ethnic and

[5] Compare Crawford, 'The Right to Self-Determination' (n 3) 36. In a similar vein, in *De Gasperi-Gruber* dispute concerning the Tyrol/Alto Adige province in Italy, the UNGA opined that ethnic groups can be beneficiaries of an internal aspect of self-determination that does not include a right to unilateral secession, but to autonomy within existing state borders. See Cassese, *Self-Determination of Peoples* (n 2) 104–07.

[6] General Comment No 12: The Right to Self-Determination of Peoples (Art 1): 13.03.1984.

[7] Declaration on the Right to Development, GA Res 41/128, 4 December 1986.

[8] See 14 ILM (1975) 1292. The CSCE is now called Organization for Security and Cooperation in Europe (OSCE).

[9] Crawford, 'The Right to Self-Determination' (n 3) 31; Alexandra Xanthaki, *Indigenous Rights and United Nations Standards—Self-Determination, Culture and Land* (Cambridge University Press, 2007) 139.

cultural minorities. It was recognized that despite colonization, assimilation, and similar policies, indigenous peoples had largely managed to preserve their distinct societies, cultures, and ways of life, which are deeply rooted in their ancestral lands. This characteristic, it was held, warranted the formulation of an indigenous rights discourse that specifically targets indigenous peoples, and not minorities. In other words, essentially from the very outset, the world community decided that international law should distinguish between indigenous peoples, on one hand, and minority groups, on the other.[10]

As indicated, states in particular recognized the clear connection between loss of lands and marginalization of indigenous peoples. Dispossessed of their lands, indigenous peoples are particularly vulnerable to pressure from the majority society. Continued access to their traditional territories is therefore paramount not only to indigenous peoples' cultural, but also to their physical, survival, the UN and its member states concluded.[11] For these reasons, from the very outset the indigenous rights discourse focused on allowing indigenous peoples to continue to exist as distinct polities, with particular attention being directed at their land and natural resource rights.[12] This principal position distinguishes indigenous peoples' rights from those of minority groups in a fundamental way. Indigenous rights are primarily directed at indigenous peoples as collectives, although indigenous individuals are of course also beneficiaries of human rights. Minority rights, on the other hand, are only rights of individual members of minority groups, never of the group as such.[13] In other words, whereas minority rights are always individual in nature, indigenous peoples' right have a collective dimension. The almost immediate decision to distinguish indigenous peoples from minority groups for international legal purposes would come to have a profound impact on how the indigenous rights discourse unfolded in subsequent decades, as the below elaborates.

The UN's work directed at indigenous peoples can be said to commence in earnest in 1971 when the UN Economic and Social Council (ECOSOC) authored the UN Sub-Commission on Prevention of Discrimination and Protection of Minorities (the Sub-Commission) to prepare a study on the 'Problem of Discrimination

[10] See Will Kymlicka, *Multicultural Odysseys—Navigating the New International Politics of Diversity* (Oxford University Press, 2007) 31, 272–93; compare Patrick Thornberry, 'The Convention on the Elimination of Racial Discrimination, Indigenous Peoples and Caste/Decent-based Discrimination', in Joshua Castellino and Niamh Walsh (eds.), *International Law and Indigenous Peoples* (Martinus Nijhoff Publisher, 2005) 17.

[11] Darlene M Johnston, 'Native Rights as Collective Rights: A Question of Group Self-Preservation', in Kymlicka (ed.), *The Rights of Minority Cultures* (Oxford University Press, 1995) 194; also the Inter-American Commission on Human Rights' (IACommHR) decision in the *Miskito Case*, Inter-American Commission on Human Rights, Report on the Situation of Human Rights of a Segment of the Nicaraguan Population of Miskito Origin, OEA/SerL/V/II.62, doc 10 and rev 3 (1983) and OEA/SerL/V/II62, doc 26 (1984).

[12] Paul Keal, 'Indigenous Sovereignty', in Trude Jacobsen, Charles Sampford, and Ramesh Thakur (eds.), *Re-envisioning Sovereignty—The End of Westphalia?* (Ashgate Publishing, 2008) 317–30; Patrick Macklem, 'Indigenous Recognition in International Law: Theoretical Observations' [2008] *Michigan Journal of International Law*, Vol 30 (1) 208.

[13] Regarding the nature of minority rights, see further Sections 5.4, and to a lesser degree, Section 5.5, immediately below.

against Indigenous Populations'.[14] The study, commonly referred to as the 'Cobo Report' after its formal author José Martinez Cobo, compiled a large amount of data on the situation of indigenous peoples around the globe. It consists of a series of partial reports, submitted between 1981 and 1983. The entire report was completed in 1986.[15] In his report, Special Rapporteur Cobo rejected the assimilation approach employed by, e.g. the International Labour Organization's (ILO) Convention (No 107) Concerning the Protection and Integration of Indigenous and Other Tribal and Semi-Tribal Populations in Independent Countries (ILO 107). He underscored that the UN's work directed at indigenous peoples should rather place emphasis on their ethno-development and self-determination, and not on integration.[16] The Cobo Report submits that self-governance is an inherent part of indigenous peoples' cultural and legal heritage, which contributes to the maintenance of their social and cultural traditions. The Report concludes that self-governance is a pre-condition should indigenous peoples be able to preserve, develop, and pass on to future generations their distinct cultural and ethnic identity. In addition to these principal recognitions, in his report Special Rapporteur Cobo presented a series of recommendations on how the UN could start to rectify past wrongs directed at indigenous peoples and to seriously address the situation of such populations.[17]

The Cobo Report profoundly impacted on the UN's attitude towards, and activities directed at, indigenous peoples.[18] Following the release of the Cobo Report, the UN intensified its information gathering on indigenous issues, arranged expert seminars, and engaged in other activities addressing the situation of indigenous peoples.[19] Even prior to the completion of the Cobo Report, the UN acted on some of the recommendations contained therein. In terms of institution-building, the most important outcome of the Cobo Report was the establishment in 1982 of the UN Working Group on Indigenous Populations (WGIP) as a

[14] See ESC Res 1589(L), May 21, 1971, UN ESCOR, 50th Session, Supp No 1, at 16, UN Doc E/5044 (1971). The Sub-Commission was later renamed the Sub-Commission on the Promotion and Protection of Human Rights, and subsequently abolished following the establishment of the UN Human Rights Council in 2006.

[15] The UN Sub-Commission on Prevention of Discrimination and Protection of Minorities, *Study of the Problem of Discrimination against Indigenous Populations*, UN Doc E/CN.4/Sub.2/1986/7 & Adds. 1–4 (1986). The original documents making up the study are UN Docs E/CN.4/Sub.2/476/Adds. 1–6 (1981), E/CN.4/Sub.2/1982/2/Adds. 1-7 (1982), and E/CN.4/Sub.2/1983/21/Adds. 1–7 (1983).

[16] E.g. the Cobo Report, E/CN.4/Sub.2/1983/21 10–44.

[17] The Cobo Report Add 4 UN Sales No E.86.XIV.3 (Vol 5, 'Conclusions and Recommendations'); and also S James Anaya, *Indigenous Peoples in International Law* (2nd edn., Oxford University Press, 2004) 62–63.

[18] In addition, the Cobo Report influenced activities outside the UN-system. It directed international legal experts' attention to the situation of indigenous peoples. The report further spurred indigenous peoples' representatives to engage at the international level in a larger, more organized and strategic manner than had previously been the case. See Henry Minde, 'The Destination and the Journey – Indigenous Peoples and the United Nations from the 1960s through 1985' [2007] Gáldu Čála, *Journal of Indigenous Peoples Rights*, No 4 12–35; compare Steve Kinnane, 'Indigenous Sustainability: Rights, Obligations, and a Collective Commitment to Country', in Castellino and Walsh (eds.), *International Law and Indigenous Peoples* (n 10) 182–83.

[19] Anaya, *Indigenous Peoples in International Law* (n 17) 62–63.

subsidiary body to the Sub-Commission.[20] The WGIP's mandate was to review developments pertaining to the situation of indigenous peoples and to develop international standards outlining the rights of such groups. The WGIP built on the Cobo Report and increased the awareness of, and focus on, indigenous issues in the UN system and beyond. Of even greater importance was the WGIP's work within standard-setting, in particular the initiative to develop a draft UN Declaration on the Rights of Indigenous Peoples (UNDRIP).

In 1985, the Sub-Commission approved the WGIP's decision to embark on crafting a draft UNDRIP for eventual adoption by the UNGA.[21] In 1993, the WGIP submitted a consensus draft UNDRIP to the Sub-Commission. The Sub-Commission adopted the draft and passed it on to its parent body the UN Commission on Human Rights (Commission HR). It is worth underlining that the very first draft UNDRIP included an Article 3 that proclaims that indigenous peoples have the right to self-determination. The fact that the Sub-Commission, which consisted of reknowned human rights experts, adopted a declaration that contained such a provision shows that already in the early 1990s, international legal experts had at least commenced contemplating a right to self-determination that applies not only to peoples in the meaning aggregate populations of states, but also to peoples in a cultural/ethnic meaning of the term, at least in the context of indigenous peoples. In 1995, the Commission HR established an ad-hoc working group, the Working Group on the Draft Declaration on the Rights of Indigenous Peoples (WGDD), tasked with reaching a political agreement on the UNDRIP.[22]

While the negotiations on the UNDRIP were on-going, international law relevant to indigenous peoples evolved based on the fundamental premise articulated above. In other words, the indigenous rights regime continued to rest heavily on the notion that indigenous rights shall first and foremost aim at allowing indigenous peoples to preserve and develop their distinct collective cultures and societies side by side with the majority society, where continued access to territories and natural resources traditionally used are of critical importance. Or to put it somewhat differently, from the outset the indigenous rights discourse came to build on two general premises: (i) that indigenous peoples have the right to make decisions regarding and maintaining their own societies (i.e. the right to self-determination); and (ii) that past and ongoing injustices caused by colonization of indigenous peoples' territories shall be rectified (i.e. land and resource rights, viewed through the prism of the right to equality).[23]

[20] See Commission on Human Rights Res 1982/19 (Mar 10, 1982); ESC Res 1982/34, May 7, 1982, Supp No 1 26, UN Doc E/1982/82 (1982). The WGIP met annually from its inception until it was abolished following the establishment of the UN Human Rights Council in 2006.

[21] Commission on Human Rights Res 1985/22.

[22] Commission on Human Rights Res 1995/32.

[23] For a similar observation, see Julian Burger, 'The UN Declaration on the Rights of Indigenous Peoples: From Advocacy to Implementation', in Stephen Allen and Alexandra Xanthaki (eds.), *Reflections on the UN Declaration on the Rights of Indigenous Peoples* (Hart Publishing, 2011) 43.

5.4 Minority Rights—'Collectivization' of Individual Rights

Chapter 3 outlines how by the early 1990s multiculturalism had successfully challenged some of the basic building blocks of conventional individual liberalism. By this time, political philosophers had increasingly come to question whether states can in fact remain neutral between cultures, or whether they are rather prone to indirectly favouring the majority culture, or even to outright nationalism. Mirroring this development, in the 1990s international law-makers came to increasingly doubt whether a human rights system that relies only on individual human rights that apply equally to all individuals regardless of their respective cultural backgrounds is apt to adequately address the interest and needs of those that do not belong to the majority culture. The world community started to consider whether instead particular legal measures might sometimes be necessary to satisfactorily target the situation of minority groups and their members.[24] In addition, political turmoil, such as the Balkan crisis, led many to argue that recognition, rather than denial, of minority rights promotes peace and order.[25] This new sentiment is well reflected in an observation made by the African Working Group of Experts on Indigenous Populations/Communities in 2005: 'What . . . creates conflict is that certain dominant groups force through a sort of "unity" that only reflects the perspectives and interests of certain powerful groups within a given state, and which seeks to prevent weaker marginalized groups from voicing their particular concerns and perspectives. Or, put another way: conflicts do not arise because people demand their rights but because their rights are violated.'[26]

As a result, the early 1990s saw the adoption of a number of international legal instruments that pertain to minorities, most notably the UN Declaration on the Rights of Persons Belonging to National or Ethnic, Religious and Linguistic Minorities (the Minority Declaration). The Minority Declaration proclaims that persons belonging to minority groups have the right to enjoy their own cultures freely, without discrimination, individually as well as in community with other members of the group.[27]

On a regional level, the Council of Europe considered but eventually refrained from adopting an additional protocol to the European Convention for the Protection of Human Rights and Fundamental Freedoms (ECHR) which, if adopted,

24 Crawford, 'The Right to Self-Determination' (n 3) 23–24, 65; Yvonne Donders, *Towards a Right to Cultural Identity?* (Intersentia, 2002) 4; Nathan Lerner, *Group Rights and Discrimination in International Law* (2nd edn., Martinus Nijhoff Publishers, 2003) 19–20; Kymlicka (ed.), *The Rights of Minority Cultures* (n 11) 18.

25 Ana Filipa Vrdoljak, 'Self-Determination and Cultural Rights', in Francesco Francioni and Martin Scheinin (eds.), *Cultural Human Rights* (Martinus Nijhoff Publishers, 2008) 64, 68–69; Lerner, *Group Rights and Discrimination in International Law* (n 24) 29; Crawford, 'The Right to Self-Determination' (n 3) 24–25; William Kurt Barth, 'Cultural Rights: A Necessary Corrective to the Nation State', in Francesco Francioni and Martin Scheinin (eds.), *Cultural Human Rights* (Martinus Nijhoff Publishers, 2008) 89–90.

26 UN Doc E/CN4/Sub2/AC5/2005/WP3 57.

27 UNGA Res 47/135, of 18 Dec 1992, Articles 1.2, 2.1, and 3.1.

would have addressed the situation of national minorities in Europe.[28] The Council did, however, adopt other instruments that aim to protect linguistic and other cultural rights of members of national and ethnic minorities, most notably the European Framework Convention for the Protection of National Minorities (EFCPNM).[29] Further, the CSCE declared that members of national minorities have the right to maintain and develop their culture, should be free from any attempt of assimilation, and allowed to participate in affairs that relate to the protection and promotion of their distinct identities.[30]

In line with what the above touches upon when distinguishing the indigenous rights discourse from that of minorities, none of the mentioned instruments confer rights to minority groups as such. For instance, recall the full title of the Minority Declaration—'Declaration on the Rights of Persons Belonging to National or Ethnic, Religious and Linguistic Minorities'. As the title reveals, the legal subjects of the Declaration are individual members of a minority group, rather than the group as such. All rights set forth in the Minority Declaration are individual in nature, as are the rights enshrined in the mentioned European instruments. None of these instruments contains any rights that pertain to the group as such. Indeed, the EFCPNM explicitly rejects the notion of collective rights.[31]

Irrespective of that the minority rights instruments proclaims individual and not collective rights, it has been suggested that these instruments can only be adequately implemented if coupled with some kind of separate authority of the minority group.[32] The potential value of autonomous administrations for national minorities has thus been acknowledged.[33] In the same vein, both the Council of Europe's Parliamentary Assembly and the UN Working Group on Minorities (UNWGM), in the latter's comment to the Minority Declaration, have submitted that minority rights might sometimes be most effectively implemented through the establishment of autonomous functions of the group.[34] Both institutions have, however, in line with international law's general understanding of the nature of minority rights, stopped short of suggesting that minority groups have a *right* to autonomy even when such arrangements might be useful. In fact, as noted, the EFCPNM explicitly rejects any such suggestion.

Having acknowledged the clearly individual nature of minority rights, including that they do not embrace a right to autonomy, it should be underlined that this

[28] Recommendation 1201 on an additional protocol on the rights of national minorities to the European Convention on Human Rights, Council of Europe Parliamentary Assembly Text.

[29] Council of Europe, H (94) 10 (1994).

[30] Concluding Documents of the Vienna Meeting (1989) 59; Document of the Copenhagen Meeting of the Conference on the Human Dimension of the CSCE (1990), Arts 32 and 35; Geneva CSCE Meeting of Experts on National Minorities (1991), Section 4; and Charter of Paris for a New Europe, CSCE, 30 ILM 193 (1991). Also John Packer, 'The OSCE High Commissioner on National Minorities: Pyrometer, Prophylactic Pyrosvestis', in Ghanea and Xanthaki (eds.), *Minorities, Peoples and Self-Determination* (n 3) 253.

[31] Article 3(2) and Explanatory Report annexed to the Framework Convention, 13, 31, 37.

[32] Packer, 'The OSCE High Commissioner on National Minorities' (n 30) 265.

[33] OSCE Charter for European Security, Istanbul, November 1999, 39 ILM 255 (2000) 19.

[34] Recommendation 1201 of the Council of Europe's Parliamentary Assembly (1993), Article 11 and UN Doc E/CN4/Sub2/AC5/2005/2 14, 20.

character of such rights need not deprive them of the capacity to indirectly extend certain protection also to the cultural identity of minority groups as such. Minority rights do incorporate, albeit implicitly, a recognition that protection of the individual member requires an amount of respect for the group per se. For instance, while the Minority Declaration only awards *rights* to individuals, Articles 1 and 2.1 positively oblige states to *respect* not only individual members of minority groups, but also the groups as such.[35] The UNWGM has underlined that states can only fully implement the rights the Minority Declaration enshrines if they ensure adequate conditions for the existence and identity of such groups to which minority individuals belong.[36] Similarly, the preamble to the EFCPNM proclaims that the Convention should not only ensure rights of persons belonging to minorities, but also protect minority groups as such. The Advisory Committee established to promote the implementation of the EFCPNM has called on states to take positive measures to dismantle structural injustices.[37]

The articulated view that in order to promote the rights of members belonging to minority groups, one need also respect the group as such, has also infiltrated European Union (EU) law. In 2000, the European Council (EC) adopted directive 2000/43. This directive confirmed that EU law *allows* member states to adopt measures that advance the situation of individuals belonging to disadvantaged ethnic and cultural groups.[38] Although directive 2000/43 is somewhat conservatively formulated, already at the time Christopher McCrudden submitted that EU law was about to embrace an *obligation* of member states to positively promote equality.[39] Subsequently, the European Court of Human Rights (ECtHR) has proven him right. The Court has on numerous occasions held that European states are positively obliged to take measures to prevent discrimination.[40] What is more, this is not only an obligation to bring disadvantaged members of a minority group up to the same level as members of the majority population. It is an obligation to promote their right to maintain their cultural and ethnic distinctiveness. As Chapter 7 elaborates, the distinction is cardinal.

In summary, one could say that the introduction of minority rights into the human rights system resulted in acceptance of a certain amount of 'collectivization' of formally speaking individual rights. The minority rights instruments of the 1990s broke with the classical liberal tradition in that they rejected the notion that states could and should remain neutral between cultures. Instead, international law came to hold that states are positively obliged to protect and promote the cultural

35 Ibid.; also Lerner, *Group Rights and Discrimination in International Law* (n 24) 23–24.

36 UN Doc E/CN4/Sub2/AC5/2005/2 14, 20.

37 ACFC Document ACFC/31 DOC (2008) 001.

38 OJ L 180 22; also Erika Szyszczak, 'Protecting Social Rights in the European Union', in Asbjørn Eide, Catarina Krause, and Allan Rosas (eds.), *Economic, Social and Cultural Rights – A Textbook* (2nd edn., Martinus Nijhoff Publishers, 2001) 501–02.

39 Christopher McCrudden, 'The New Concept of Equality' [2003] *ERA Forum*, Vol 4, No 3 21–24.

40 See *Andrejeva v Latvia* (2010) [GC] 51 EHRR 28 82. Similar conclusions follow also from *Thlimmenos v Greece* (2001) 31 EHRR 411; *Nachova and others v Bulgaria* [GC] (2005) 42 EHRR 933; to a lesser degree *Stoica v Romania* (Appl No 42722702). As the rulings by the ECtHR are binding on EU members, this position now constitutes EU law.

distinctiveness of members of minority groups. This, in turn, also extends an *indirect protection* to the group as such. Still, the minority rights system stopped short of establishing group *rights*. This is true also today and, as touched upon above and as elaborated below, distinguishes minority rights from those of indigenous peoples.[41]

5.5 The United Nations (UN) Covenant on Civil and Political Rights (CCPR) Article 27

5.5.1 Further on 'collectivization' of individual rights

'Collectivization' of human rights that are formally individual in nature has not been confined to international legal instruments that specifically target members of minority groups. Provisions in general human rights treaties that proclaim individual rights of such persons have more recently also been understood to have a collective dimension. Recall how CCPR Article 27 provides that persons belonging to minorities shall not be denied the right, in community with other members of the group, to enjoy their own culture. Section 2.5.3 outlines how, at the time of its adoption, CCPR Article 27, in accordance with its wording, envisaged only individuals as bearers of the right to culture. Moreover, at the time, the provision placed no positive obligation on states to promote or even protect minority cultures. On the contrary, the phrase 'shall not be denied the right' indicates that states were

[41] International law's firm distinction between minority groups and indigenous peoples—and between minority rights and indigenous rights—has only become entrenched during the last two decades. The development has not, however, occurred without criticism. For instance, Will Kymlicka admits that the distinction is appropriate if comparing indigenous peoples with new minorities such as immigrant groups. But he maintains that it makes less sense to legally separate what he labels old national minorities—ethnic groups that have lived in a state at least as long as the majority population, are large in number, culturally distinct, and have clear political organizations—from indigenous peoples. (The Basques and the Kurds are probably good examples of such groups Kymlicka refers to.) Kymlicka argues that political, and not principal, rationale, explains this distinction. Unlike indigenous peoples, 'old national minorities' are often perceived as threats to national security, he posits. For this reason, states have been reluctant to recognize collective rights of such groups. See Kymlicka, *Multicultural Odysseys* (n 10) 272–93. Kymlicka maintains that states have allowed indigenous peoples' rights to evolve far beyond those of minority groups based on the precise premise that collective rights of indigenous peoples can and should not spread to minorities. He asserts that states have created a 'firewall' between indigenous and minority rights. See Will Kymlicka, 'Beyond the Indigenous/Minority Dichotomy?', in Allen and Xanthaki (eds.), *Reflections on the UN Declaration on the Rights of Indigenous Peoples* (n 23) 187. Helen Quane seems to concur. She posits that states have accepted self-governance rights of indigenous peoples based on the understanding that such rights do not extend to other groups, although she admits that alternative interpretations are also plausible. See Helen Quane, 'The UN Declaration on the Rights of Indigenous Peoples: New Directions for Self-Determination and Participatory Rights?', in Allen and Xanthaki (eds.), *Reflections on the UN Declaration on the Rights of Indigenous Peoples* (n 23) 267–69. Kymlicka is critical of the 'firewall' between indigenous and minority rights, which he finds both morally unjustifiable and untenable in practice—see Kymlicka, 'Beyond the Indigenous/Minority Dichotomy?' (cited above) 183–208. Kymlicka's observations may not be without merit. Irrespective of the quality of Kymlicka's arguments, however, it is beyond the scope of this book to survey whether the rights analyzed here should reasonably also apply to groups other than indigenous peoples.

supposed to remain neutral and not actively protect any particular culture within the state.[42]

Although the wording of CCPR Article 27 suggests that the provision has limited applicability when it comes to protecting minority groups as such, the UN Human Rights Committee (HRC) has in a series of observations gradually 'collectivized' the individual right the provision sets forth in the context of indigenous peoples. True, the Committee has respected that the right to culture CCPR Article 27 enshrines is formally individual. Still, the HRC has interpreted the provision as also extending an, albeit indirect, protection to the cultural integrity of indigenous peoples as such, with a particular focus on traditional livelihoods and other culturally based land uses. The HRC has further repeatedly underlined that states have a positive obligation to promote the right reflected in CCPR Article 27, irrespective of the fact that the provision's wording suggests only a negative duty.

The articulated development started with the *Kitok Case* (1988). Here, the HRC confirmed that although CCPR Article 27 does not explicitly refer to indigenous peoples, the provision nonetheless applies to member of such groups, and then is of particular relevance in the context of their traditional livelihoods.[43] In *Ominayak v Canada* (1990), the Committee confirmed its finding in *Kitok* and held that the exploitation of timber, gas, and oil in the aboriginal Lubicon Lake Band's traditional territory amounted to a violation of CCPR Article 27 as such industrial activities prevented the exercise of the Band's traditional land uses such as hunting and fishing.[44] In 1994, the HRC reaffirmed that culture manifests itself in many forms, for instance in the particular way of life of indigenous peoples. Doing so, the Committee underlined that certain cultural rights, even though formally applying to individuals only, lose all relevance if disconnected from the community as such.[45] The HRC has subsequently on a number of occasions repeated that CCPR Article 27 encompasses a dimension that extends indirect protection to indigenous peoples' collective cultures, e.g. in the two *Länsman Cases*[46] and in *Apirana Mahuika* et al *v New Zealand*.[47] The Committee has further on several occasions

[42] Article 30 of the Convention on the Rights of the Child (CRC) (General Assembly Resolution 44/25 of 20 November 1989) is essentially a clone of CCPR Article 27. The provision hence proclaims that children of ethnic minority origin shall not be denied the right to, in community with other members of the group, enjoy their own culture. Different when compared with CCPR Article 27, CRC Article 30 explicitly affirms that the right applies to indigenous children. But as with CCPR Article 27, CRC Article 30 embraces only individual rights.

[43] *Ivan Kitok v Sweden*, Comm No 197/1985, views adopted 27 July 1988.

[44] *Bernard Ominayak, Chief of the Lubicon Lake Band v Canada*, Comm No 167/1984, views adopted 26 March 1990; also Benedict Kingsbury, 'Reconciling Five Competing Conceptual Structures of Indigenous Peoples' Claims in International and Comparative Law', in Alston (ed.), *Peoples' Rights* (n 3) 80.

[45] HRC General Comment No 23: The Rights of Minorities (Art 27) 08.04.1994. CCPR/C/21/Rev1/Add5; compare Fredricio Lenzerini, 'Indigenous Peoples' Cultural Rights and the Controversy over Commercial Use of Their Traditional Knowledge', in Francioni and Scheinin (eds.), *Cultural Human Rights* (n 25) 124–25.

[46] *Ilmari Länsman* et al *v Finland*, Comm No 511/1992, views adopted 26 October 1994; *Jouni E Länsman* et al *v Finland*, Comm No 671/1995, views adopted 30 October 1996.

[47] *Apirana Mahuika* et al *v New Zealand*, Comm No 547/1993, views adopted 27 October 2000.

confirmed that states are positively obliged to respect and implement the collectivized rights of indigenous peoples enshrined in CCPR Article 27, irrespective that the wording of CCPR Article 27 suggests differently.[48]

The HRC has probably gone as far in 'collectivizing' the right to culture enshrined in CCPR Article 27 as is possible without formally declaring that the right applies also to collectives. For instance, in *Ominayak* the formal applicant was an individual. Still, the findings of the Committee were clearly, in everything but formal terms, directed towards the indigenous community as such. The community had formulated its claim as a violation of the collective right to self-determination pursuant to CCPR Article 1. The HRC translated the claim into an assertion of a violation of the (formally) individual right to culture pursuant to CCPR Article 27. Doing so, the Committee indirectly confirmed the interdependence of the two rights, at least when applied in an indigenous context. In *Apirana Mahuika* the HRC took one step further. Having reaffirmed that the right to culture CCPR Article 27 enshrines is formally individual in nature, the HRC explicitly underlined the interdependence between CCPR Article 27 and Article 1. The Committee submitted that the right to culture enjoyed by indigenous individuals must be understood in light of the collective right to self-determination. This conclusion by the HRC must reasonably be understood as an acknowledgement of that, albeit not formally, so at least in practice, Article 27 in addition to protecting the indigenous individual's right to culture, extends informal protection to the cultural identity of indigenous groups as such.[49] In summary, the 'collectivized' version of the individual right to culture that CCPR Article 27 enshrines does not formally amount to a collective human right. Notwithstanding, for all practical purposes it extends a protection, albeit an indirect one, also to indigenous communities and peoples as such. Through reading a collective element into CCPR Article 27, the HRC took the development towards recognition of indigenous peoples' rights proper one step further.

States appear largely to have accepted the HRC's understanding of CCPR Article 27. In recent instances when indigenous individuals (almost always indirectly representing groups) have brought states before the Committee claiming a breach of CCPR Article 27, states have argued that the competing activity does not seriously harm the indigenous people's culture. But they have rarely denied that the right enshrined in Article 27 has a collective dimension. Hence, states have indirectly accepted the HRC's interpretation of the provision, wherefore it constitutes such subsequent practice pursuant to the Vienna Convention on the Law of Treaties (VCLT) Article 31.3(b) that implies that the provision has evolved to take on

[48] See e.g. HRC General Comment No 23: The Rights of Minorities (Art 27) 08.04.1994. CCPR/C/21/Rev1/Add5 6.1; also Concluding Observations on Finland, UN Doc CCPR/C/79/Add91 10; on New Zealand, UN Doc CCPR/C/75/NZL 4; on Guatemala, UN Doc CCPR/CO/72/GTM; on the Philippines, UN Doc CCPR/CO/79/PHIL. See also Martin Scheinin, 'Indigenous Peoples' Rights under the International Covenant on Civil and Political Rights', in Castellino and Walsh (eds.), *International Law and Indigenous Peoples* (n 10) 4.

[49] See *Apirana Mahuika v New Zealand* (n 47) 9.2; also Scheinin, 'Indigenous Peoples' Rights' (n 48) 9. (Martin Scheinin is a former member of the HRC.) This book will return to the applicability of the right to self-determination to indigenous peoples in Sections 5.7–5.12 and Chapter 6.

a new meaning. The basic features of CCPR Article 27, as interpreted by the HRC, have also been confirmed in other international legal sources.[50] Consequently, it has been suggested that the articulated evolved understanding of CCPR Article 27 forms part of customary international law.[51]

5.5.2 The material content of CCPR Article 27—indigenous land and resource rights as cultural rights

In addition to the explained principal importance of HRC's collectivization of the right to culture, through the Committee's progressive interpretation of CCPR Article 27 there has emerged a concrete material right to culture that protects indigenous peoples' and communities' traditional livelihoods and other culturally based land uses. This book focuses on indigenous peoples' rights over land as property rights. Still, it is pertinent to briefly outline the content and scope of indigenous peoples' rights over lands and natural resources under the right to culture.

As touched upon, in *Kitok* the HRC held that in the context of indigenous peoples, the right to culture CCPR Article 27 enshrines embraces traditional livelihoods, irrespective of the fact that the wording of the provision may be understood to suggest that the original intention was rather to target language and similar rights. In *Ominayak*, the HRC reaffirmed its principal conclusion in *Kitok*, and also found a violation of this aspect of the right to culture. As mentioned, the Committee inferred that the exploitation of timber, gas, and oil in the aboriginal Lubicon Lake Band's traditional territory amounted to a violation of CCPR Article 27, as these activities caused the destruction of the community's traditional hunting and fishing grounds. In other words, the HRC established that competing activities that prevent indigenous communities from pursuing culturally based livelihoods are forbidden. In addition, in *Ominayak* the Committee further confirmed that although CCPR Article 27 is negatively formulated, states are positively obliged to intervene and prevent private enterprises from engaging in resource extraction that violates the right to culture. In General Comment No 23, the HRC reaffirmed that the right to culture, when applied in an indigenous context, must be understood against the backdrop that indigenous cultures manifest themselves in many forms, and are inevitably intrinsically connected to indigenous peoples' traditional lands and natural resources. The Committee further confirmed that states are positively obliged to intervene and prevent violations of this aspect of the right to culture.

In *Länsman x 2*, the HRC nuanced the picture as to what extent CCPR Article 27 outlaws natural resource extraction and other activities that compete

[50] See e.g. the UN Committee on the Elimination of Racial Discrimination General Recommendation No 23: Indigenous Peoples: 18/08/97; the UN Committee on Economic, Social and Cultural Rights General Comments No 17, Article 15.1(c), and No 21, Article 15.1(a); International Labour Organization's Convention No 169 on Indigenous and Tribal Peoples in Independent Countries Articles 2.2(b) and 5(a); the African Commission on Human and People's Rights' decision in *Endorois People v Kenya Centre for Minority Rights Development (Kenya) and Minority Rights Group International on behalf of Endorois Welfare Council v Kenya*, Comm 276/2003.

[51] Steven Wheatley, *Democracy, Minorities and International Law* (Cambridge Studies in International and Comparative Law, (2005) 15.

with indigenous peoples' traditional livelihoods and other culturally based land uses. The Committee held that restricted activities are not limited to those that completely prevent the indigenous people or community from continuously exercising its traditional land uses. Rather, in the view of the HRC, CCPR Article 27 also prohibits competing activities that effectively destroy the possibility to engage in traditional livelihoods or other culturally based land uses. The Committee underlined that states enjoy essentially no margin of appreciation with regard to competing activities with negative impacts of such scale. In *Länsman No 1*, the HRC declared that 'the scope of [a state's] freedom to [allow economic activities by enterprises] is not assessed by reference to a margin of appreciation, but by reference to the obligations it has undertaken in article 27. Article 27 requires that a member of a minority shall not be denied his right to enjoy his own culture. Thus, measures whose impact amounts to a denial of the right will not be compatible with the obligations under article 27. However, measures that have a certain limited impact on the way of life of persons belonging to a minority will not necessarily amount to a denial of the right under article 27.'[52] In other words, no proportionality test is allowed. If a competing activity effectively prevents an indigenous people or community from the pursuit of traditional land uses, it is forbidden even if it would generate huge incomes or for other reasons would be of substantial value to society as a whole.[53]

A final step in evolving the understanding of CCPR Article 27 came with *Poma Poma v Peru*. In *Poma Poma*, the HRC built on previous cases, in particularly *Länsman x 2*, as well as on earlier observations such as 'when planning actions that affect members of indigenous communities, the State party must pay primary attention to the sustainability of the indigenous culture and way of life . . . '.[54] Doing so, it reaffirmed that no proportionality test is allowed. The Committee underscored that 'economic development may not undermine the rights protected by article 27'. Most importantly, however, the HRC elaborated on to what extent activities that compete with indigenous peoples' and communities' culturally based land uses are forbidden. In this context, the Committee held that an activity with 'substantive negative impact' on the right to culture must be discontinued unless the community has consented to the activity.[55] In other words, the HRC lowered the previously employed 'effectively destroy' threshold somewhat further. Now, already a resource extraction or other competing activity that substantially negatively impacts on a culturally based land use is forbidden.

[52] *Ilmari Länsman* (n 46) and *Jouni E Länsman* (n 46) 9.4.

[53] For an in-depth outline of how the HRC has contributed to an evolved understanding of CCPR Article 27 up to and including the Committee's decisions in *Apirana Mahuika*, see former HRC member Martin Scheinin, 'The Right to Self-Determination under the Covenant on Civil and Political Rights', in Pekka Aikio and Martin Scheinin (eds.), *Operationalizing the Right of Indigenous Peoples to Self-Determination* (Åbo Akademi University, 2000) 193–207; also Jérémie Gilbert, *Indigenous Peoples' Land Rights Under International Law: From Victims to Actors* (Transnational Publishers, 2006) 131–32.

[54] Concluding Observations with regard to Chile, UN Doc CCPR/C/79/Add104 22.

[55] *Ángela Poma Poma v Peru*, Comm No 1457/2006, views adopted on 27 March 2009 7.4–7.6.

5.6 International Labour Organization's (ILO) Convention No 169 on Indigenous and Tribal Peoples in Independent Countries (ILO 169)—Recognition of Collective Rights Proper of Indigenous Groups

Sections 5.4 and 5.5 describe how the adoption of minority rights instruments and the evolved understanding of CCPR Article 27 through the HRC's active interpretation of the provision resulted in acceptance of rights that indirectly protect the cultural identity of groups. Still, as further seen, minority rights formally remain rights of individuals only. At the same time, Section 5.3 explains how when the UN started to address the situation of indigenous peoples in earnest, it immediately acknowledged that the particular characteristics of indigenous peoples warrant that international law distinguishes between rights of such peoples, on one hand, and of minority groups, on the other. This principal divide between minority and indigenous rights became visible when ILO decided to re-examine ILO 107 in the 1980s, which resulted in the adoption of ILO 169 in 1989.

ILO 169 breaks sharply with the integrationist approach employed by its predecessor. In contrast to integration, ILO 169 focuses on promoting respect for indigenous groups' distinct societies, cultures, and ways of life, with the aim that these groups should have the opportunity to continuously exist side by side with the majority society.[56] ILO 169's approach towards indigenous rights has been labelled 'ethno political self-government',[57] as the Convention foresees self-governing rights of indigenous peoples[58] and calls for respect of their collective traditions and customary laws.

ILO 169's focus on collective rather than individual rights is arguably underscored by the Convention, unlike its predecessor ILO 107, employing the term 'indigenous peoples' throughout. The ILO's own guide to ILO 169 affirms that the term 'peoples' is used precisely to denote that indigenous peoples constitute organized societies with an identity of their own, rather than mere groupings with some shared ethnic or cultural characteristics.[59] Be that as it may despite the conscious use of the term peoples, it follows explicitly from ILO 169 that at the time of the

[56] Manuela Tomei and Lee Swepston, *Indigenous and Tribal Peoples: A Guide to ILO 169* (ILO, 1996); Lee Swepston, 'Indigenous Peoples in International Law and Organizations', in Castellino and Walsh (eds.), *International Law and Indigenous Peoples* (n 10) 53, 57; Athanasios Yupsanis, 'ILO Convention No. 169 Concerning Indigenous and Tribal Peoples in Independent Countries 1989-2009: An Overview' [2010] *Nordic Journal of International Law* 79 436; Federico Lenzerini, 'Sovereignty Revisited: International Law and Parallel Sovereignty of Indigenous Peoples' [2006] *Texas International Law Journal*, Vol 42 178; Kymlicka, *Multicultural Odysseys* (n 10) 32.

[57] Kristian Myntti, 'National Minorities, Indigenous Peoples and Various Models of Political Participation', in Frank Horn (ed.), *Minorities and the Right to Political Participation* (Northern Institute for Environmental and Environment Law, 1996) 24.

[58] See Christopher J Fromherz 'Indigenous Peoples Courts: Egalitarian Juridical Pluralism, Self-Determination, and the United Nations Declaration on the Rights of Indigenous Peoples' [2008] University of Pennsylvania Law Review, Vol 156 1367; for a similar position, see Lenzerini, 'Sovereignty Revisited' (n 56) 178.

[59] Tomei and Swepston, *Indigenous and Tribal Peoples* (n 56) 7.

adoption of the Convention, states were not ready to acknowledge indigenous groups as peoples proper, with rights as such. For this reason, the drafters of the Convention consciously excluded the right to self-determination from ILO 169.[60] Moreover, to avoid any uncertainty, ILO 169 Article 1(3) underlines that '[t]he use of the term 'peoples' in this Convention shall not be construed as having any implications as regards the rights which may attach to the term under international law.' Having reassured themselves that indigenous peoples could not invoke ILO 169 to claim the right to self-determination or other peoples' rights, states apparently felt confident to accept collective rights limited in their applicability to indigenous populations.

Although ILO 169 fell short of recognizing peoples' rights, the fact that states acknowledged that indigenous peoples hold collective rights *sui generis* to them is still significant. For the first time, an international legal human rights instrument recognized that collectives others than aggregate populations of states (or territories) can be beneficiaries of rights proper. In that sense, ILO 169 confirmed the particular status of indigenous peoples in international law.[61]

Of the material rights contained in ILO 169, Articles 13–15 on rights over lands and natural resources are of the greatest interest. Chapter 8 examines these provisions.

5.7 Contemporary International Law on Indigenous Peoples' Rights

5.7.1 Introduction

As described above, by the mid-1990s two developments had challenged the state-individual dichotomy integral to the post-Westphalian international legal order that was readily adopted by the contemporary international legal system following the establishment of the UN. Minority rights had been 'collectivized' to also protect, albeit indirectly, minority groups as such. In addition, international law had come to recognize that indigenous peoples and communities hold collective rights

[60] Swepston, 'Indigenous Peoples in International Law' (n 56) 57.

[61] As follows already from its title, ILO 169 defines its beneficiaries not as 'indigenous' but as 'indigenous and tribal' peoples. As Section 6.4 elaborates, albeit no official definition exists, 'indigenous peoples' is almost a term of art. By contrast, it is uncertain what are 'tribal peoples'. In any event, for the present purposes it is not necessary to examine the distinction between indigenous peoples and tribal peoples, whoever the latter are in an international legal context, as this book only examines rights of the former category of peoples. Still, one may note in passing that the developments in international law this book analyzes will assumingly require a clearer distinction between indigenous 'peoples' and other indigenous and/or tribal groups. When international law acknowledges rights of indigenous peoples, including the right to self-determination, one must reasonably be able to identify what groups qualify as such peoples. For a similar line of thought, see Benedict Kingsbury, 'Indigenous Peoples as an International Legal Concept', in R H Barnes, Andrew Gray, and Benedict Kingsbury (eds.), *Indigenous Peoples of Asia* (Association for Asian Studies, 1995) 30–31; and Martin Scheinin, 'The Right of a People to Enjoy its Culture: Towards a Nordic Saami Rights Convention', in Francioni and Scheinin (eds.), *Cultural Human Rights* (n 25) 154–58.

sui generis to them, as reflected in ILO 169. Still, international law was yet to recognize indigenous peoples as peoples proper, with rights as such. This section surveys the development in international law beyond mere recognition of collectivized individual rights and *sui generis* indigenous group rights.

5.7.2 Universally applicable international legal sources: generally

The Political Declaration adopted by the UN World Conference on Human Rights[62] (1993) essentially affirmed the conventional understanding of peoples in international law, as did General Recommendation No 21 on self-determination[63] (1996) of the UN treaty body established to oversee the implementation of the Convention on the Elimination of Racial Discrimination (CERD Convention), the Committee on the Elimination of Racial Discrimination (CERD Committee). These documents borrow language from the Friendly Relations Declaration, and declare that the right to self-determination should not be construed as authorizing any action that impairs the territorial integrity of states possessed with a government that represents the whole people belonging to the territory. The reference to 'the whole people' in singularity shows that the drafters of the instruments understood 'peoples' as aggregate populations of states only,[64] in line with the conventional understanding of that term in international law. That said, the reference to governments representing the whole populations of states in addition seemingly affirms the Friendly Relations Declaration's position that the right to self-determination does apply to peoples, and not states. Moreover, having underscored that international law does not recognize a general right for people to secede, the CERD Committee in its recommendation on the right to self-determination stated that this does not preclude political arrangements for groups within the state. Hence, the Committee foresaw that the implementation of the right to self-determination could include autonomy and similar arrangements for segments of the entire population of a state.

Section 5.4 describes how, when 'collectivizing' the right to culture, the HRC stopped short of formally proclaiming that indigenous peoples are beneficiaries of the right to self-determination and other peoples' rights. At the same time, as further seen, the Committee also flirted with the idea of recognizing indigenous peoples as 'peoples'. It did so when positing that there is an intrinsic connection between the right to culture as enshrined in CCPR Article 27 and the right to self-determination as reflected in Article 1, when these provisions are applied in an indigenous context. Pursuing this line of thought, in the late 1990s the HRC was ready to take one step further. Since then, the Committee has on numerous occasions employed language that demonstrates that it is its view that the right to self-determination CCPR Article 1 proclaims applies to indigenous peoples. The

62 Vienna Declaration and Programme of Action, 25 June 1993, 32 ILM.

63 General Recommendation No 21 Right to Self-Determination: 23/08/96.

64 Crawford, 'The Right to Self-Determination' (n 3) 30–31; Anne-Christine Bloch, 'Minorities and Indigenous Peoples', in Asbjørn Eide, Catarina Krause, and Allan Rosas (eds.), *Economic, Social and Cultural Rights – A Textbook* (2nd edn., Martinus Nijhoff Publishers, 2001) 374–75.

HRC has systematically applied the right of self-determination to indigenous peoples in reports on states that recognize the existence of such peoples within their borders. This has resulted in a rather coherent jurisprudence on the relevance of the right, as reflected in the CCPR, to indigenous peoples.

In some instances, the HRC has simply referred to indigenous groups in the context of CCPR Article 1, often coupled with a request that the state party report on what measures it has taken to implement the right to self-determination of the indigenous people in forthcoming reports to the Committee.[65] Even though such statements by the HRC have limited material content, the fact that the Committee considers indigenous peoples in the context of CCPR Article 1 evidences that it holds the position that the right to self-determination applies to indigenous groups that qualify as peoples for international legal purposes. Martin Scheinin, former member of the HRC, affirms that the Committee has taken the position that certain indigenous groups do constitute peoples for the purposes of the common Article 1 of the 1966 Covenants.[66] In other instances, the HRC has gone one step beyond and explicitly applied the right to self-determination to indigenous peoples, often with emphasis on the resource dimension of the right. For instance, the HRC has, with explicit reference to the aboriginal peoples in Canada, emphasized that 'the right to self-determination requires, *inter alia*, that all peoples must be able to freely dispose of their natural wealth and resources and that they may not be deprived of their own means of subsistence.'[67] In the same vein, the HRC has, with explicit reference to CCPR Article 1(2), called on Australia to allow indigenous peoples a stronger role in decision-making over their traditional lands and natural resources.[68] It has been further concerned that Sweden does not allow the Sami people a significant role in decision-making processes that affect their traditional lands and economic activities.[69]

[65] See e.g. CCPR/C/79/Add112 (Norway); CCPR/CO/82/FIN (Finland); CCPR/CO/75/NZL (New Zealand).

[66] Scheinin, 'Indigenous Peoples' Rights' (n 48) 3, 10–11; Scheinin, 'What Are Indigenous Peoples?', in Ghanea and Xanthaki (eds.), *Minorities, Peoples and Self-Determination* (n 3) 6.

[67] CCPR/C/79/Add105 8. [68] A/55/40 498-528.

[69] See CCPR/CO/74/SWE 15. Additionally, the HRC has called on Mexico to respect indigenous peoples' collective right over their traditional patterns of living and to settle the question of self-determination of indigenous groups (CCPR/C/79/Add109 19), has concluded that extinguishment of aboriginal rights in Canada may amount to a violation of CCPR Article 1 (CCPR/C/CAN/CO/5 8), and has commended Norway for enacting legislation that furthers the Sami people's right to self-determination pursuant to CCPR Article 1 (CCPR/C/NOR/CO/5 5). It is also worth noting the HRC's conclusions in *Marie-Hélèn Gillot* et al *v France* (Comm No 932/2000). The CCPR provision invoked in *Gillot* was not Article 1, but Article 1(2) on the right to participate in general elections. The case is nonetheless relevant to the question of what groups constitute peoples for international legal purposes. The Caledonians had decided that a referendum on independence from France should be open only to persons with sufficient ties to the territory. Gillot, an ethnic Frenchwoman, submitted that this violated her right to participate in political processes pursuant to CCPR Article 25(b). The HRC disagreed. It interpreted the provision in light of CCPR Article 1 and concluded that since the referendum was arranged in a process of decolonization and self-determination, it was legitimate to restrict participation in the referendum to persons with sufficient ties to New Caledonia. The decision reflects the Committee's view that a 'people' need not be understood as the entire population of a territory, as the HRC defined the ethnic Caledonians as a people. Regarding *Gillot*, see also Scheinin, 'Indigenous Peoples' Rights' (n 48) 14–15.

The HRC's sister body, the UN Committee on Economic, Social and Cultural Rights (CESC), that has been established to authoritatively interpret the Convention on Economic, Social and Cultural Rights (CESCR), including its Article 1 on the right to self-determination, has been more careful in applying this right to indigenous peoples. Still, it has done so on a few occasions, thus concurring with the HRC's position that the right to self-determination does apply to indigenous groups that constitute peoples for international legal purposes.[70]

In sum, the two UN expert bodies that are mandated to oversee compliance with the most central self-determination provision in international law both concur that the right applies to indigenous peoples.

Recognition of indigenous peoples' rights proper has not been confined to the right to self-determination. A few years after its General Recommendation on self-determination, the CERD Committee issued a General Recommendation on the rights of indigenous peoples. The CERD Convention, as human rights conventions in general, does not contain any provisions that specifically target indigenous peoples. Moreover, the rights the Convention enshrines are all formulated as rights of individual only. Notwithstanding, in General Recommendation No 23, the CERD Committee holds that the CERD Convention is relevant to indigenous peoples, and further that the rights enshrined in the Convention have a collective dimension when applied to them. The Committee encourages states to recognize and respect indigenous peoples' distinct cultures, ways of life, and cultural identities. It calls on states to ensure that indigenous peoples can exercise their right to practice and revitalize their cultural traditions and customs. Of particular interest for the present purposes, the CERD Committee calls on states to recognize and protect indigenous peoples' right to own, develop, control, and use their communal lands, territories, and resources. Finally, the CERD Committee declares that no decisions that directly relate to indigenous peoples' rights and interests may be taken without their consent.

The right to benefit from the moral and material interests resulting from one's scientific and artistic production enshrined in CESCR Article 15.1(c) is, as other human rights provisions of the time, formulated as an individual right. Still, the CESC has concluded that CESCR Article 15.1(c) has evolved to take on a new understanding pursuant to which the provision awards rights to indigenous peoples as such. The Committee holds that in addition to protecting the creativity of individuals, CESCR Article 15.1(c) safeguards indigenous peoples' collective cultural heritage. The CESC further proclaims that states shall respect indigenous peoples' right to consent before non-members access elements of their cultural heritage. The CESC reaches these conclusions irrespective of it explicitly recognizing that the drafters of CESCR Article 15.1(c) had not foreseen that the provision could apply to collectives. The Committee infers that a progressive interpretation of the provision is necessary in light of recent developments in international law.[71]

[70] See e.g. UN Doc E/C12/1/Add94 11 and 39.
[71] General Comment No 17 2, 7, 10, 12, 32.

The CESC has subsequently reiterated that indigenous peoples are entitled to control their respective cultures. In doing so, the Committee reaffirms that although at the time of its adoption, CESCR Article 15 was held to apply to individuals only, against the backdrop of recent developments in international law, the provision must today be understood to embrace rights of groups as such as well. The CESC calls on states to protect and respect the cultural identity of indigenous peoples, and reiterates that states are obligated to obtain indigenous peoples' consent before taking measures when the preservation of their cultural resources is at risk.[72]

The UN system is not alone in having acknowledged the existence of collective rights of indigenous peoples. In its Operative Policy on indigenous peoples, OP 4.10, the World Bank infers that international law imbues indigenous peoples with peoples' rights.[73] Pursuant to paras. 10 and 11 of OP 4.10, the World Bank should only provide funding for industrial projects in indigenous peoples' territories when there is broad community support. A footnote clarifies that individual members of the community do not have a right to veto the project, only the community as such.

To conclude, the three core human rights treaties the UN has adopted have all been interpreted, by bodies authoritatively entrusted to do so, as embracing rights of indigenous peoples as such. As mentioned, of particular relevance is that the two treaty bodies that oversee the implementation of the most important of peoples' right, the right to self-determination, have both concluded that this right applies to indigenous peoples. The articulated development has occurred irrespective that at the time of their adoption, none of the surveyed human rights instruments were understood to envelope rights of indigenous peoples as such. As Chapter 4 demonstrates, the fact that human rights instruments evolve and take on new understandings does not, however, contradict international law on international legal sources. Treaty body jurisprudence constitutes such subsequent practice that contributes to evolved understandings of treaty provisions. This progressive development has also been confirmed by sources beyond treaty bodies. The sources surveyed are coherent. They assert in chorus that indigenous peoples constitute 'peoples' for international legal purposes, enjoying the right to self-determination and other peoples' rights.

But even if the treaty body jurisprudence outlined above seems to have received at least tacit support from states, it is legal sources that emanate from expert bodies, and not from states—the ultimate creators of international law as Chapters 2 and 4 discusses in depth. However, in 2007 states were provided with the opportunity to take an explicit position on indigenous peoples' status in the contemporary international legal system.

[72] General Comment No 21 7, 9, 36, 55 (e).

[73] The World Bank Operational Manual, Bank Procedures OP 4.10 (January 2005).

5.7.3 Universally applicable legal sources—particularly on the United Nations Declaration on the Rights of Indigenous Peoples (UNDRIP)

After almost a quarter of a century of negotiations, the UNGA adopted the UNDRIP (the United Nations Declaration on the Rights of Indigenous Peoples) in 2007. In addition to land and natural resources rights, the most controversial issue in the UNDRIP deliberations was what position the Declaration should take on indigenous peoples' rights in general, and on the right to self-determination in particular. When the UNDRIP finally was adopted, it reaffirmed the developments in international law outlined above.

UNDRIP Article 3 proclaims that '[i]ndigenous peoples have the right to self-determination. By virtue of that right they freely determine their political status and freely pursue their economic, social and cultural development.' It is worth noting that UNDRIP Article 3 is largely a clone of the common CCPR/CESCR Article 1.1. The only difference is that where the latter provision refers to 'all peoples', UNDRIP Article 3, naturally, specifically targets indigenous peoples. The fact that UNDRIP borrows language from Article 1.1 of the 1966 Covenants suggests that the right the Declaration enshrines is the general right to self-determination already recognized in international law and not a right *sui generis* to indigenous peoples.

The right to self-determination is not the only collective right reflected in the UNDRIP. The Declaration proclaims a vast array of material rights of indigenous peoples and communities as such. In addition, Articles 1 and 2 as well as preambular paragraph (pp) 22 spell out the Declaration's principal position on peoples' rights, as they pertain to indigenous peoples. Pursuant to UNDRIP Article 1, '[i]ndigenous peoples have the right to the full enjoyment, as a collective or as individuals, of all human rights and fundamental freedoms as recognized in the Charter of the United Nations, the Universal Declaration of Human Rights and international human rights law.' Article 2, in pertinent parts, proceeds to proclaim that '[i]ndigenous peoples and individuals are free and equal to all other peoples and individuals . . . '. Finally, pursuant to relevant parts of pp 22, ' . . . indigenous individuals are entitled without discrimination to all human rights recognized in international law, and . . . indigenous peoples possess collective rights . . . '. Clearly, the outlined provisions could have been drafted in a more elegant and straightforward manner. Notwithstanding, if one studies the provisions carefully, in light of one another and and against the backdrop of the Declaration as a whole, their content and meaning appears clear.

As already seen, having initially proclaimed that 'indigenous peoples have the right to full enjoyment . . . of all human rights', Article 1 then goes on to add, somewhat confusingly, that indigenous peoples enjoy this right 'as a collective or as individuals'. In doing so, the provision seemingly ignores that it would appear difficult for a 'people' to enjoy rights 'as individuals'. The question then becomes, can this ambiguity result in a conclusion that Article 1 does not after all affirm that indigenous peoples are the beneficiaries of peoples' rights? International law on international legal sources seems to answer the posed question in the negative. Despite its odd reference to individuals, the main thrust of Article 1 does proclaim that indigenous peoples, as collectives, are indeed bearers of human rights. As Section 4.4 explains, an UNDRIP provision shall, in case of doubt, be interpreted in a manner that gives the provision a reasonable understanding, in light of the context of the instrument as a whole. Therefore, as the language that suggests that peoples enjoy rights as individuals is incoherent and illogical, a reasonable understanding appears to be that the part of UNDRIP Article 1 that speaks about indigenous peoples enjoying rights as individuals does not nullify the unambiguous language in the central message of the provision that provides that indigenous peoples enjoy peoples' human rights.

As further seen, in a similar manner as UNDRIP Article 1, pp 22 first unambiguously declares that 'indigenous peoples possess collective rights'. The provision then proceeds, however, to explicitly refer to individual rights as human rights, something it notably does not do with regard to peoples' rights. One could therefore argue *e contrario* that pp 22 intends to suggest that indigenous peoples' collective rights do not constitute human rights. Still, pp 22 does proclaim that indigenous peoples are bearers of rights. The fact that these rights are found in a human rights instrument certainly suggests that most, if not all, of these rights are in fact also human rights. Hence, similar to the ambiguity built into UNDRIP Article 1, it is somewhat confusing that pp 22 explicitly confirms that individual rights are human rights, at the same time as the provision omits to do so with regard to collective rights. Still, nothing in the wording of pp 22 can be said to preclude an understanding of the provision pursuant to which indigenous peoples' rights contained in the UNDRIP are human rights. And given that the alternative interpretation results in the implausible conclusion that the majority of the rights enshrined in a human rights instrument are in fact not human rights, the reasonable understanding of pp 22 appears to be that the provision at least does not exclude the conclusion that indigenous peoples' collective rights can also be human rights.

As indicated, the UNDRIP encompasses a number of material provisions that proclaim collective rights of indigenous peoples (or, alternatively, of indigenous communities, see further Chapter 8). In fact, the vast majority of the Declaration's articles envelope rights where the beneficiaries of the right are indigenous peoples as such, rather than individual members of the group. In summary, although certain ambiguities are built into UNDRIP Article 1 and pp 22, these provisions can hardly be understood to rebut what follows from UNDRP's material provisions, i.e. that indigenous peoples hold collective human rights.[74]

[74] For similar conclusions, see S James Anaya, 'The Right of Indigenous Peoples to Self-Determination in the Post-Declaration Era', in Claire Charters and Rodolfo Stavenhagen (eds.), *Making the Declaration Work: The United Nations Declaration on the Rights of Indigenous Peoples* (IWGIA, 2009) 186–87; compare Mauro Barelli, 'The Role of Soft Law in the International Legal System: The Case of the United Nations Declaration on the Rights of Indigenous Peoples' [2009] *International and Comparative Law Quarterly*, Vol 58 961.

This conclusion gains further support from UNDRIP Articles 2 and 3, read in conjunction. Article 2 provides that 'indigenous peoples are equal to all other peoples.' True, the provision does not explicitly stipulate that indigenous peoples have equal *rights* with other peoples. Still, a people can hardly be said to be equal to other peoples if enjoying less rights than them. Further, as seen, UNDRIP Article 3 proclaims that indigenous peoples have the right to self-determination. The right to self-determination is undoubtedly a human right enjoyed by peoples.

To conclude, read in light of one another and against the backdrop of the rest of the UNDRIP provisions, UNDRIP Articles 1–3 and pp 22 must be understood as confirming that indigenous peoples do enjoy peoples' human rights. This conclusion finds further support if one reads the Declaration in the context of the international legal sources the sections above survey. UNDRIP affirms the position taken by UN treaty bodies and other institutions, namely that indigenous peoples have emerged as 'peoples' for international legal purposes, with rights as such.

5.7.4 Further on the legal status of the UNDRIP

In order to properly evaluate the legal status of the UNDRIP, it is pertinent to recall the conclusions drawn in Chapter 4 on international law on international legal sources. The UNDRIP *as such* is, as other UNGA resolutions, formally not a legally binding instrument. But Chapter 4 explains how this fact alone need not result in the conclusion that individual UNDRIP *provisions* cannot be reflective or at least indicative of binding international norms. As Chapter 4 discusses, if an UNDRIP provision sufficiently mirrors other legal sources, that suggests that the provision reflects an international legal norm. As seen, UNDRIP provisions that relate to collective rights, in particular Article 3 on the right to self-determination, do interplay with formally legally binding international legal sources. As Mauro Barelli observes, 'the strong relationship between the content of the Declaration and existing law should be recognized.' He infers that this characteristic of the Declaration underscores the UNDRIP's legal relevance and significance.[75] In the same vein, Javaid Rehman notes that many UNDRIP provisions, including those on self-determination, self-government, and autonomy, represent customary international law.[76]

The fact that in UN practice, the format of Declarations is restricted to 'formal and solemn' instruments on 'rare occasions when principles of great and lasting importance are being enunciated' further supports the conclusion that one may assume that many UNDRIP provisions are reflective or at least indicative of international law. When the Declaration format is opted for, there is 'a strong expectation that members of the international community will abide by it'.[77] In this context, it is worth noting that pursuant to UNDRIP Article 38, '[s]tates shall

[75] Barelli, 'The Role of Soft Law in the International Legal System, (n 74) 966.

[76] Javaid Rehman, 'Between the Devil and the Deep Blue Sea: Indigenous Peoples as the Pawns in the US "War on Terror" and the Jihad of Osama Bin Laden', in Allen and Xanthaki (eds.), *Reflections on the UN Declaration on the Rights of Indigenous Peoples* (n 23) 561.

[77] See UN Doc E/CN.4/832/Rev1 105; also Willem van Genugten, 'The African Move towards the Adoption of the 2007 Declaration on the Rights of Indigenous Peoples: The Substantive Arguments behind the Procedures', <http://ssrn.com/abstract=1103862> accessed on 30 July 2012 9.

... take the appropriate measures, including legislative measures, to achieve the end of [the] Declaration.' The use of the mandatory term 'shall' suggests that states, when adopting the Declaration, have undertaken to abide by the UNDRIP.[78] Christopher Fromherz asserts, with reference to the UN Secretary-General, that the fact that the Declaration was adopted with such overwhelming support gives it particular authority.[79] Clive Baldwin and Cynthia Morel concur.[80] As seen, UNGA Declarations adopted with overwhelming support are often indicative of international customary law. Subsequent to Fromherz's, Baldwin's, and Morel's observations, the four states that voted against the adoption of the UNDRIP have all reversed their position and now endorse the Declaration.[81] This of course gives further strength to these authors' arguments.

As indicated, the process that led up to the adoption of the UNDRIP was an extraordinary complex, and time-consuming standard-setting exercise. It proceeded during largely the same time-period when UN treaty bodies and other institutions increasingly came to take the position that indigenous peoples are 'peoples' for international legal purposes, with rights as such. States were of course well aware of this development, and of its relevance to the UNDRIP process. While the Declaration was under negotiation, states generally refrained from taking a position on indigenous peoples' legal status in other international forums and processes. Rather, they declared that the matter would be resolved by the WGDD and the UNDRIP. The question of whether indigenous peoples enjoy peoples' rights in general, as reflected e.g. in UNDRIP Article 1, and in particular the right to self-determination, as mirrored in Article 3, were among the most contentious in the UNDRIP negotiations. This demonstrates an awareness among states that their final position on Articles 1, 3, and other related UNDRIP provisions would be significant for how we understand indigenous peoples' rights in general and their right to self-determination in particular. As mentioned, the voting on the UNDRIP in the UNGA offered states the opportunity to provide their previously lacking *explicit* response to the question of the legal status of indigenous peoples in the international legal system.[82] Thus informed, states advanced to adopt a Declaration

[78] Ibid., 9–10.

[79] See Fromherz, Indigenous Peoples Courts (n 58) 1344. The Declaration was adopted with 143 votes in favour, 4 against, 11 abstentions, and 34 UN member states being absent. See UNGA Resolution 61/295.

[80] Clive Baldwin and Cynthia Morel, 'Using the United Nations Declaration on the Rights of Indigenous Peoples in Litigation', in Allen and Xanthaki (eds.), *Reflections on the UN Declaration on the Rights of Indigenous Peoples* (n 23) 123–24.

[81] These states are Australia, Canada, New Zealand, and the United States. They have all made public official statements in which they formally endorse the Declaration.

[82] See Barelli, 'The Role of Soft Law in the International Legal System (n 74) 969. Similarly, Emmanuel Voyakis asserts that the complexity of the UNDRIP negotiations, which, as mentioned, took more than 20 years to complete, suggests that the negotiating states were aware that once adopted, the UNDRIP would be considered to be reflective of customary international law. He argues that it was precisely this perception among states that delayed the adoption of the Declaration. See Emmanuel Voyakis, 'Voting in the General Assembly as Evidence of Customary International Law?', in Allen and Xanthaki (eds.), *Reflections on the UN Declaration on the Rights of Indigenous Peoples* (n 23) 222–23. For a dissenting view, however, see Stephen Allen, 'The UN Declaration on the Rights of Indigenous Peoples and the Limits of the International Legal Project', in Allen and Xanthaki (eds.), *Reflections on the UN Declaration on the Rights of Indigenous Peoples* (n 23) 229, 254.

that affirms indigenous peoples as international legal subjects that are beneficiaries of the right to self-determination and other peoples' rights.[83] In summary, when adopting the UNDRIP, states gave their political consent to UN expert bodies' and other international institutions' recognition of indigenous peoples as subjects of international law, with rights as such. As Alexandra Xanthaki notes, in that sense the UNDRIP can be said to constitute an agreed interpretation of various relevant pre-existing international legal sources.[84]

5.7.5 Endorsement of the UNDRIP by the UN system and beyond

Since its adoption, several UN and other institutions have endorsed the UNDRIP, indicating its conformity with international law. CESC has underlined that several of the rights the UNDRIP enshrines are reflected in CESCR Article 15, understood in light of recent developments in international law.[85] The CERD Committee has allowed itself to be guided by the UNDRIP when examining state compliance with the CERD Convention in country-specific reports,[86] as has the Committee on the Rights of the Child (CRC).[87]

In compliance with the treaty bodies, then UN Special Rapporteur on the rights of indigenous peoples, James Anaya, shortly following the adoption of the Declaration, observed that '[UNDRIP] represents an authoritative common

[83] However, a few interpretative statements delivered in connection with the UNGA's adoption of the UNDRIP did reject the notion that indigenous peoples are peoples for international legal purposes. Australia expressed dissatisfaction with the Declaration's reference to self-determination, claiming that this right applies only in decolonization and secession contexts. India opined that the right to self-determination applies only in a colonial context and not to segments of sovereign independent states, emphasizing the principle of territorial integrity of states. Iran made a similar comment. Nigeria registered a general dissatisfaction with the UNDRIP's self-determination provisions. The United States opined that the Declaration does not recognize collective human rights, a position shared by the United Kingdom. The latter delegation added that beyond the right to self-determination, the United Kingdom does not accept the existence of collective human rights. Sweden declared that it recognizes collective rights only to the extent such rights are not human rights. Comments from a relative low number of states cannot, however, reasonably be considered to impact on the conclusions above, i.e. that the UNDRIP affirms that indigenous peoples constitute subjects of international law, with rights as such. For a similar opinion, see Siegfried Wiessner, 'Indigenous Sovereignty: A Reassessment in Light of the UN Declaration on the Rights of Indigenous Peoples' [2008] *Vanderbilt Journal of Transnational Law* 41 1162. In addition to the statements referred to above, a number of states commented on the relationship between the right to self-determination and the principle of territorial integrity of states. This issue is, however, of limited relevance to the rights addressed in this book as it is not suggested here that indigenous peoples' right to self-determination awards them with a right to unilaterally secede from the states in which they find themselves residing today. See further Section 6.1. With this understanding of the right to self-determination as it applies to indigenous peoples, the right cannot conflict with the principle of territorial integrity of states.

[84] See Alexandra Xanthaki, 'Indigenous Rights in International Law over the Last 10 Years and Future Developments' [2009] *Melbourne Journal of International Law* 10 (1). For an extensive analysis of what resulted in the adoption of the UNDRIP, see Mattias Åhrén, 'The UN Declaration on the Rights of Indigenous Peoples – How Was It Adopted and Why Is It Significant?' [2007] *Gáldu Čála, Journal of Indigenous Peoples Rights*, No 4.

[85] Concluding Observations, UN Doc E/C12/NIC/CO/4 35.

[86] See e.g. CERD/C/USA/CO/6 29 (United States); CERD/C/FJI/CO/17 13 (Fiji); CERD/C/CAN/CO/18 27 (Canada).

[87] See e.g. General Comment No 11, CRC/C/GC/11 82; CRC/C/BOL/CO/4 3 (c) (Bolivia).

understanding, at the global level, of the minimum content of the rights of indigenous peoples, upon a foundation of various sources of international human rights law.'[88] Comforted by this observation, Anaya further declared that from then and onwards, he would measure state conduct vis-à-vis indigenous peoples by the yardstick of the UNDRIP. In a similar vein, the Office of the High Commissioner on Human Rights has underlined that it shall assist states and indigenous peoples in implementing the UNDRIP.[89] The UN Development Group, which includes all UN system organizations and programs that work with development, has also acknowledged that the UNDRIP provides the relevant legal framework for these organizations' and programs' work directed at indigenous peoples.[90] For its part, in its Policy on Indigenous and Tribal Peoples, the UN Food and Agriculture Organization (FAO) has recognized its 'responsibility to observe and implement UNDRIP' in all its activities vis-à-vis indigenous peoples.[91] Also, the UN Global Compact has produced a business reference guide to the UNDRIP, thus underscoring the relevance of the rights contained therein to business and beyond.[92]

Regional organizations of states have also embraced the UNDRIP. The Organization of American States (OAS) uses the Declaration as 'the baseline for negotiations and . . . a minimum standard' for the deliberations on an OAS American Declaration on the Rights of Indigenous Peoples.[93] Section 5.7.6 further discusses this process. In an American context, it is also worth noting that the IACHR relied in part on UNDRIP in its ruling in *Saramaka*,[94] as did the African Commission on Human and Peoples' Rights (AfCommHPR) in its decision in *Endorois*.[95]

In summary, a vast number of UN system organizations have officially and explicitly endorsed the UNDRIP. Others have demonstrated that they accept the Declaration as at least indicative of binding international law through applying

[88] UN Doc A/HRC/9/9 85.

[89] Expert Mechanism on the Rights of Indigenous Peoples, 'Statement by Ms Kyung-wha Kang, Deputy High Commissioner for Human Rights', 1st session, Geneva (1 October 2008).

[90] See UN Development Group, Guidelines on Indigenous Peoples' Issues (1 February 2008). In the same vein, the 31 UN specialized agencies that make up the Inter-Agency Support Group to the UN Permanent Forum on Indigenous Issues have pledged to advance the spirit and letter of the UNDRIP. See Statement on the UN Declaration on the Rights of Indigenous Peoples, adopted at the Annual Meeting of the Inter-Agency Support Group in September 2007.

[91] See FAO Policy on Indigenous and Tribal Peoples (2010) 2 and Chapter IV, 'Objectives for Engagement with Indigenous Peoples'. FAO particularly emphasizes the need to respect indigenous peoples' right to self-determination (4–5), the principle of free, prior, and informed consent (5), and other collective rights, including such that pertain to lands and natural resources (6).

[92] UN Global Compact, 'UN Declaration on the Rights of Indigenous Peoples; A Business Reference Guide', December 2013.

[93] OEA/SerK/XVI, GT/DADIN/doc321/08 (14 January 2008) 3.

[94] *Saramaka People v Suriname*, Judgement of November 28, 2007, Inter-Am Ct HR (Ser C) No 172 (2007); Judgement of November 28, 2008, Inter-Am Ct HR (Ser C) No 172 (2008), in particular 131.

[95] See *Endorois* (n 50) 232. The African Commission on Human and Peoples' Rights has also officially welcomed the adoption of the UNDRIP, noting that the Declaration is in line with the position and work of the Commission. See Communiqué on the UN Declaration on the Rights of Indigenous Peoples, Doc No ACHPR/Res 121 (XXXXII, of 28 November 2007). The Commission has further made specific references to the UNDRIP when discussing indigenous peoples' rights to lands and natural resources. See 'Draft Principles and Guidelines on Economic, Social and Cultural Rights in the African Charter on Human and Peoples' Rights'.

rights enshrined in the UNDRIP in country-specific situations, as have regional human rights institutions. This jurisprudence and documentation indicate that parts of the UNDRIP have become accepted as reflective of customary international law.[96]

5.7.6 Regional legal sources

Regional human rights institutions have not only accepted indigenous peoples as international legal subjects by endorsing the UNDRIP. Already prior to the adoption of the Declaration, the developments on the international level that Section 5.7.2 articulates had been matched in regional processes.

As the title suggests, the African Charter on Human and Peoples' Rights (AfCHPR) contains a range of provisions proclaiming peoples' rights. Similar to the global level, questions have been raised as to what is understood with the reference to 'peoples' in the title of this instrument.[97] Again, it appears that at the time of its adoption, the term 'peoples' in the AfCHPR referred to the aggregate populations of states.[98] But again matching developments at the global level, the understanding of the AfCHPR has also progressed. The African Commission on Human and Peoples' Rights (AfCommHPR) has subsequently interpreted the term 'peoples' in the Charter as not necessarily referring to the aggregate population of states. The term can also, the Commission submits, refer to ethnic/cultural subgroups of a state. For instance, in *Katangese*, the AfCommHPR initially reiterated that all peoples have the right to self-determination. Having subsequently noted that 'there may . . . be controversy as to the definition of peoples', the Commission went on to declare that '[t]he issue in the case is not self-determination for all Zairians as a people but specifically for the Katangese.' The AfCommHPR thus clearly took the position that the right to self-determination can attach to a people understood as a segment of the population of the state. In addition, it clarified that the Katangese should exercise its right to self-determination through self-government within the state of Zaire.[99] In a similar vein, it follows from the AfCommHPR's decision in *Ogoni* that the Commission held that the Ogoni in Nigeria constitute a

[96] For similar conclusions, see Timo Koivurova, 'Jurisprudence of the European Court of Human Rights Regarding Indigenous Peoples: Retrospects and Prospects' [2011] *International Journal on Minority and Group Rights* 18 32; and Baldwin and Morel, 'Using the United Nations Declaration on the Rights of Indigenous Peoples in Litigation' (n 80) 123–24; and compare van Genugten, 'The African Move towards the Adoption of the 2007 Declaration on the Rights of Indigenous Peoples (n 77) 11.

[97] Richard N Kiwanuka, 'The Meaning of "People" in the African Charter on Human and Peoples' Rights' [1988] *American Journal of International Law*, Vol 82 80–101; Peter Nobel, 'The Concept of "Peoples" in the African Charter on Human and Peoples' Rights', in Peter Nobel (ed.), *Refugees and Development in Africa* (Scandinavian Institute on African Studies, 1987) 9–17.

[98] David Raic, *Statehood and the Law of Self-Determination* (Kluwer Law International, 2002) 232–33; Gilbert, *Indigenous Peoples' Land Rights* (n 53) 210; Hurst Hannum, *Autonomy, Sovereignty, and Self-Determination: The Accommodation of Conflicting Rights* (Revised edn., University of Pennsylvania Press, 1996) 46–47.

[99] See *Katangese Peoples' Congress v Zaire*, Comm No 75/92 (1995) 3, 6. See also John Dugard and David Raic, 'The Role of Recognition in the Law and Practice of Secession', in Marcelo G Cohen (ed.), *Secession: International Law Perspectives* (Cambridge University Press, 2006) 107–08.

people for international legal purposes. In doing so, the AfCommHPR refers to the *Ogoni* and *Ogoniland* throughout, referring to that people's right to control its own land and natural resources,[100] underlining its position that the Ogoni constitute a people for international legal purposes.

The AfCommHPR findings have not been confided to peoples' rights in general. In addition, the AfCommHPR has explicitly held that the right to self-determination applies to indigenous peoples. The Commission has elaborated that when applied to indigenous peoples, the right to self-determination encompasses a right to self-government, to pursue their traditional way of life, and to preserve and develop their respective distinct cultures.[101] AfCommHPR member Barney Pitnaya notes the resemblance between the AfCHPR Article 20 (on self-determination) and the corresponding provision in the then draft UNDRIP.[102] In a similar vein, the AfCommHPR's Working Group on Indigenous Peoples/Communities infers that indigenous peoples' rights are collective rights, crucial to their capacity to survive as distinct peoples.[103] In summary, the AfCommHPR has through subsequent practice contributed to an evolved understanding of the AfCHPR. According to the Commission, today this instrument must be understood as recognizing indigenous peoples as peoples, with rights as such.[104] The AfCommHPR has specifically confirmed that the AfCHPR awards indigenous peoples with a right to self-determination, to be exercised through autonomous arrangements within the state. As Section 4.4 explains, such an evolved understanding of the African Charter is in conformity with the law of treaties. The AfCommHPR fulfills a similar function with regard to the AfCHPR as treaty bodies do with regard to globally applicable human rights instruments.

On the American Continent, the Inter-American Commission on Human Rights (IACommHR) has explicitly recognized the collective aspect of indigenous peoples' rights. It has proclaimed that indigenous peoples' cultures shall in part be protected through peoples' rights,[105] adding that states must not engage in acts detrimental to indigenous peoples' ethnic identity.[106] The IACommHR, as well as the IACHR, have in particular emphasized states' obligations to protect indigenous peoples' cultures in a number of cases concerning indigenous peoples' land and resource rights. In doing so, the Court and the Commission have underscored that

[100] *Ogoni Case. Social and Economic Rights Action Center and the Center for Economic and Social Rights v Nigeria*, Comm No 155/96 (2001).

[101] Advisory Opinion on the United Nations Declaration on the Rights of Indigenous Peoples, Adopted at 41st Ordinary Session (May, 2007) 27.

[102] N Barney Pityana, 'The Challenge of Culture for Human Rights in Africa: The African Charter in a Comparative Context', in Malcolm Evans and Rachel Murray (eds.), *The African Charter on Human and Peoples' Rights: The System in Practice, 1986-2000* (Cambridge University Press, 2002) 232.

[103] Conceptual Framework Paper (2nd Draft) by the Working Group on the Rights of Indigenous Peoples/Communities in Africa of the African Commission on Human and Peoples' Rights, 20 December, 2002.

[104] For a concurring opinion, see Wheatley, *Democracy, Minorities and International Law* (n 51) 82–83.

[105] IACHR, The Human Rights Situation of Indigenous Peoples of the Americas, OEA/SerL/V/II/108, doc 62 (2000) 125.

[106] Third Report on the Situation of Human Rights in the Republic of Guatemala OEA/Ser1/V/II 67, doc 9 (1986) 114.

indigenous peoples hold collective rights that require respect for their cultural identity, culture, and way of life.[107] The Caribbean Community has also committed to protect the rights of indigenous peoples as well as to respect their cultures and way of life.[108]

In 1995 the IACommHR approved a draft declaration on the rights of the indigenous peoples of the Americas to serve as a basis for further negotiations. Since then, American states and indigenous peoples have been negotiating a declaration on the rights of the indigenous peoples of this continent, although activities have been limited during recent years. Notwithstanding, the most recent draft[109] contains a number of provisions that are interesting for the present purposes. For instance, Article 3 proclaims that '[w]ithin the States, the right to self-determination of the indigenous peoples is recognized . . .'. Article 20.1 elaborates that indigenous peoples have a right to autonomy and self-government, and pursuant to Article 10.1 such peoples are entitled to develop their cultural identity. Finally, with regard to the rights of greatest relevance for the present purposes, Article 24 provides that indigenous peoples have the right to recognition of property and ownership rights over lands traditionally occupied or used.

The 'Eleventh Meeting of Negotiations in the Quest for Points of Consensus', held by the Working Group to Prepare the OAS Declaration, identified parts of the Declaration on which there is consensus.[110] The status document shows that agreement has been reached on Article 10.1 (cultural identity) and Article 20 (autonomy /self-government, on the parts of the provision relevant to the present work). The status document further records that agreement is yet to be reached on Article 3 (self-determination) and Article 24 (property rights to land). A vast majority of the participants in the Working Group agree that where there is no agreement on a provision, the UNDRIP shall be used as the baseline for further negotiations.[111]

In an American context, it is further worth mentioning the Supreme Court of Canada's ruling in the *Quebec Secession Case*. It is uncommon, if not unique, that domestic courts get the opportunity to consider the applicability of the right to self-determination. In an exceptional case, the Supreme Court of Canada was requested to rule on whether the province of Quebec (or perhaps more correct the population thereof) is in possession of a right to self-determination that encompasses a right to unilaterally secede from Canada. Deciding under what circumstances, if any, Quebec has a right to secession, the Canadian Supreme Court *obiter dicta* touched upon whether this right, under such circumstances, could additionally apply to the indigenous peoples within the province. After a thorough analysis, the Supreme Court concluded that a people, for international legal purposes, may make up a portion of the total population of a state. The Supreme Court thus rejected the conventional understanding that peoples, for international legal purposes, necessarily

107 Regarding these cases, see further Section 8.6.4.

108 Article XI of the Caribbean Charter of Civil Society (1997).

109 'Record of the Current Status of the Draft American Declaration on the Rights of Indigenous Peoples', OEA/SerK/XVI, GT/DADIN/doc334/08 rev 3, 30 December 2008.

110 Ibid.

111 Report of the Chair, 14 January 2008, document OEA/SerK/XVI, GT/DADIN/doc321/08, Section II G.

equal aggregate populations of states. According to the Supreme Court, such a narrow definition of 'peoples' would render the right to self-determination largely duplicative (as such a definition of 'peoples' would result in the right to self-determination being, for all practical purposes, a right of states rather than of peoples). In the same vein, in conformity with its conclusion that a state can host more than one people, when borrowing language from the Friendly Relations Declaration's safeguard clause, the Supreme Court referred not to a government that represents 'the whole of *the people* of the state', but rather to a government that represents the whole of 'the people *or peoples*' [emphasis added] residing within its territory.

To conclude, the Supreme Court of Canada concurs that indigenous populations can be 'peoples' for international legal purposes, and as such be beneficiaries of the right to self-determination. The Court also agrees with the conclusion that indigenous peoples must exercise this right through autonomy arrangements within existing state borders.[112]

Compared with its Inter-American counterpart, the ECtHR has had few chances to consider what rights indigenous peoples possess under international law. As Europe hosts few indigenous populations, indigenous rights are not at the forefront of the European human rights debate in the same way as they are in the Americas. Yet, on the rare occasions when the ECtHR has been challenged with indigenous issues, it has taken a fairly conservative approach, in line with the cautious stand generally taken by the European human rights institutions towards minority rights.[113] Still, in *G and E v Norway*, the European Commission on Human Rights opined that ECHR Article 8 awards indigenous peoples a right to have their particular lifestyles respected,[114] thus at least indicating an openness towards rights of indigenous peoples. Moreover, in its Northern Dimension Action Plan, the EU accepts that indigenous peoples of the Arctic are beneficiaries of the 'inherent right to self-determination'.[115]

Given the small number of European states that host indigenous peoples, Europe has naturally not embarked on crafting a European indigenous rights instrument. Still, in the northern part of the continent, Finland, Norway, and Sweden are in the process of agreeing on a Nordic Sami Convention which aims to specify how the

[112] See [1998] 1 SCR 217. Regarding the *Quebec Secession Case*, see also Crawford, 'The Right to Self-Determination' (n 3) 47–50, 59–60; and Patrick Dumberry, 'Lessons Learned from the Quebec Secession Reference before the Supreme Court of Canada', in Marcelo G Kohen (ed.), *Secession: International Law Perspectives* (Cambridge University Press, 2006).

[113] María Amor Martín Estébanez, 'Council of Europe Policies Concerning the Protection of Linguistic Minorities and the Justiciability of Minority Rights', in Ghanea and Xanthaki (eds.), *Minorities, Peoples and Self-Determination* (n 3) 279; Alston (ed.), *Peoples' Rights* (n 3) 275–76.

[114] See *G and E v Norway*, Appl no 9278/81 and 9415/81 (Commission Decision, 3 October 1983). The ECourtHR seems to affirm this position in its ruling in *Handölsdalen Sami Village AO v Sweden*, App no 39013/04 (ECtHR, 30 March 2010).

[115] See Commission of the European Communities COM (2003) 343 final, adopted on 10 June 2003. Further, when Finland and Sweden joined the EU in 2004, the EU accepted an exception to the Union's general competition rules. According to this exception, Finland and Sweden are allowed to render reindeer herding as a sole right of the indigenous Sami people, due to reindeer herding's importance and intrinsic connection to the Sami culture. See Article 1 of Protocol 3 to Finland's and Sweden's acceding treaty to the EU.

human rights the indigenous Sami people possess under international law materialize themselves in the particular context of the Sami. A draft Convention, prepared by a group of experts appointed by the three governments and the three Sami Parliaments, was presented in 2005. The draft Convention contains a number of provisions that underline that the Sami people enjoy rights as a people, including the right to self-determination.[116] When presenting its proposal, the Expert Group underlined that it had drafted the Sami Convention in a manner so that the Convention, in the Expert Group's opinion, conforms with relevant international norms.[117] On a more practical level, the Nordic states have further affirmed that the Sami people are entitled to the right to self-determination through the establishment of the Sami Parliaments in their respective countries as tools for operationalizing this right, as it applies to the Sami people.[118] As to the other indigenous people of the European Arctic, the Inuit, Denmark has also affirmed that the Inuit constitute a people with rights as such, including the right to self-determination, most recently through the adoption of the Act on Greenland Self-Government.[119]

In Asia, regional processes that address indigenous peoples' rights are lacking.[120] The absence of such initiatives can probably largely be explained by the fact that historically, a relative low number of Asian states have recognized the existence of indigenous peoples within their borders. In addition, the Asian region has traditionally not engaged in standard-setting activities within the sphere of human rights.[121] There are signs, however, that Asian collective activities within the sphere of human rights are about to pick up. Asian states have relatively recently embarked on drafting a general Asian human rights declaration. Still, they are yet to engage in standard-setting activities that specifically target the human rights situation of the indigenous peoples of the continent, something that will most likely not occur within the foreseeable future. Against this background, lack of documented support for indigenous rights from within Asia need not be taken as evidence of the region necessarily being adverse towards such rights. Rather, disinterest may explain the inaction so far. What is more, Asian states are increasingly recognizing that they are host to indigenous peoples. This recognition may with time spur Asian standard -setting activities within the sphere of indigenous peoples' rights.

As with Asia, Oceania has not undertaken regional standard-setting activities that address the specific rights of indigenous peoples. Contrary to Asia, however, the inaction may not be explained by lack of recognition of the existence of indigenous peoples. Rather, the reason is presumably the limited number of Oceanian states. In any event, as in Europe, in Oceania domestic processes confirm that the

116 Article 3 of the Draft Nordic Sami Convention, with commentary.

117 For an in depth outline of the Draft Sami Convention, see Mattias Åhrén, Martin Scheinin, and John B Henriksen, 'The Nordic Sami Convention: International Human Rights, Self-Determination and other Central Provisions' [2007] *Gáldu Cála, Journal of Indigenous Peoples Rights*, No 3.

118 Finnish Constitution (731/1999), Article 17.3 and Act on the Sami Parliament (974/1995), Norwegian Sami Act (12 juni 1987 nr 56); Swedish Sami Parliament Act (1992:1433).

119 Act no 473 of 12 June 2009.

120 Some Asian states have, however, recognized indigenous peoples' rights in their national legislation. See e.g. the Philippine Indigenous Peoples Rights Act, Republic Act No 8371 (1997).

121 Li-ann Thio, 'International Law and Secession in the Asia and Pacific Regions', in Kohen (ed.), *Secession: International Law Perspectives* (n 114) 303, 345.

states of the region recognize indigenous peoples as legal subjects with rights as such.[122]

In summary, four continents have witnessed developments that closely mirror the outlined trend in globally applicable international legal sources. African and American human rights institutions have affirmed that indigenous peoples are beneficiaries of peoples' rights, including the principal peoples' right, that of self-determination. With regard to the latter right, these institutions have further affirmed that when applied in an indigenous peoples' context, the right to self-determination is to be exercised through autonomy and self-governance arrangements. The OAS Declaration process is yet to be completed. Still, the deliberations so far have resulted in agreements on, for instance, that indigenous peoples are entitled to collective rights, including autonomy and self-government within existing states. On a regional level, Europe has been less active within the sphere of indigenous rights. Yet the EU has confirmed that the indigenous peoples of the Arctic are entitled to the right to self-determination. Further, all countries in Europe that are host to indigenous peoples have taken practical steps towards the implementation of a right to self-determination to be exercised through autonomy and self-government. The situation in Oceania mirrors that of Europe, both when it comes to recognition and acceptance of rights. The only Continent that has largely omitted to address indigenous peoples' rights on a regional level is Asia. Natural reasons may, however, explain this inactivity. The lack of regional initiatives should therefore not necessarily be interpreted as an aversion against indigenous peoples' rights. Moreover, certain signs indicate that also the Asian region may in the future engage in standard-setting activities on indigenous peoples' rights. To infer then: regional legal processes, jurisprudence, and institutions support the conclusion that follows from globally applicable legal sources, i.e. that international law has evolved to recognize indigenous peoples as subject of international law, with rights as such, including the right to self-determination. This conclusion finds further support in UN institution building and proceses.

5.7.7 Recognition of indigenous peoples as international subjects in UN institutions and processes

The outlined recent development within the indigenous rights discourse has been mirrored in UN processes and institution building. The particular status of indigenous peoples within the international legal system was, for instance, reflected in the UNDRIP process. The UNDRIP is probably the only globally applicable international legal instrument that has been formulated through direct negotiations

[122] In New Zealand, this position was confirmed already by the Treaty of Waitangi of 1840. The status of the Treaty of Waitangi was shortly after affirmed in the Constitution Act of 1852 and then in the Maori Land Act of 1862. The Treaty of Waitangi continues to serve as the foundation for the relationship between British decendants of New Zealand and the Maori people. The Treaty's confirmation of the Maori as a people remains uncontested. With regard to Australia's recognition of the Aboriginal populations as peoples, see e.g. the Aboriginal Affairs Act of 1973 (No 115, 1973); the Aboriginal and Torres Strait Islanders Commission Act of 1989 (No 150, 1989); the Council for Aboriginal Reconciliation Act of 1991 (No 127, 1991).

between states and the beneficiaries of the document. Although under UN rules of procedures, states formally owned the process, in practice, indigenous peoples' representatives participated in the UNDRIP negotiations essentially on par with state negotiators. From the outset of the process, it was generally understood that the UNDRIP could only be adopted if enjoying broad support not only among states, but also among indigenous peoples' representatives. This feature of the UNDRIP process arguably reflects indigenous peoples' particular legal status in the international normative system.[123]

As to institution building, in 2000 the UN established the Permanent Forum on Indigenous Issues (the Permanent Forum), as a subsidiary body to the Economic and Social Council (ECOSOC).[124] Of the Permanent Forum's 16 members, eight are appointed by states and eight by indigenous peoples (although formally all members serve in their personal capacity). This feature of the Permanent Forum, i.e. that member states share decision-making power with representatives of non-state forming peoples,[125] is indicative of indigenous peoples enjoying status as international legal subjects.[126]

The way in which the UNDRIP was negotiated, and the structure of the Permanent Forum, may also contribute to the creation of material law. Alan Boyle and Christine Chinkin observe that the way in which indigenous peoples' participated in the UNDRIP process and their representation on the Permanent Forum on par with state representatives seem to establish a principle, backed by state practice. This practice underscores, they submit, that today, rights of indigenous peoples cannot be determined without their participation and consent,[127] a right that would seemingly attach to indigenous peoples only if they are indeed international legal subjects.

5.8 The Legal Doctrine

The legal doctrine largely concurs with the conclusion drawn above that indigenous peoples have been recognized as peoples for international legal purposes, with rights as such, including a right to self-determination to be exericised through autonomy and self-government arrangements. The first UN Special Rapporteur on the Rights of Indigenous Peoples, Rodolfo Stavenhagen, notes, in his capacity as an academic, that the UNDRIP awards indigenous peoples with collective human rights bestowed to them due to their specific identities. He adds that international law has found it more fruitful to move towards a redefinition of the concept 'nation'

123 See Barelli, 'The Role of Soft Law in the International Legal System, (n 74) 970, with references.

124 Res E/RES/2000/22.

125 Alan Boyle and Christine Chinkin, *The Making of International Law* (Oxford University Press, 2007) 50.

126 For concurring opinions, see Anaya, *Indigenous Peoples in International Law* (n 17) 154, 219–20; Lola Garcia Alix, *Handbook, The Permanent Forum on Indigenous Issues* (IWGIA, 2003).

127 Boyle and Chinkin, *The Making of International Law* (n 125) 50.

than to stick firmly to the classical state-individual dichotomy.[128] In a similar vein, Simon Wiessner observes that a survey of state practice and *opinio juris* reveals that international law recognizes a right to self-governance of indigenous peoples that bestow them with a right to manage their internal affairs.[129] Jérémie Gilbert too posits that recent developments within international law, in particular the UNDRIP and treaty body jurisprudence, confirm that indigenous peoples have the right to self-determination to be exercised through self-government. He further observes that this right is confirmed by a large number of autonomy arrangements at the national level.[130] Federico Lenzerini concurs that indigenous peoples have emerged as distinct subjects of international law,[131] as does Luis Rodrígues-Piñero.[132] Clive Baldwin and Cynthia Morel note that most states today accept that indigenous peoples are indeed 'peoples', for legal purposes, and thus beneficiaries of the right to self-determination and other peoples' rights.[133]

Already prior to the adoption of the UNDRIP, Marc Webber had concluded that indigenous peoples enjoy a right to self-determination to be exercised by autonomy and self-government arrangements. Following the adoption of the UNDRIP, he has affirmed this position.[134] Alexandra Xanthaki shares this view. She asserts that the UNDRIP affirms that indigenous peoples are entitled to the right to self-determination.[135] Helen Quane concurs. She adds that UNDRIP may represent one of the most significant evolvements in how we understand the right to self-determination since colonization.[136] Similarly to Weller, Will Kymlicka had

[128] Rodolfo Stavenhagen, 'Cultural Rights: A Social Science Perspective', in Asbjørn Eide, Catarina Krause, and Allan Rosas (eds.), *Economic, Social and Cultural Rights—A Textbook* (2nd edn., Martinus Nijhoff Publishers, 2001) 96, 108; Stavenhagen, 'Making the Declaration on the Rights of Indigenous Peoples Work: The Challenge Ahead', in Allen and Xanthaki (eds.), *Reflections on the UN Declaration on the Rights of Indigenous Peoples* (n 23) 150.

[129] Wiessner, 'Indigenous Sovereignty' (n 83) 1156–57.

[130] See Jérémie Gilbert, 'Indigenous Rights in the Making: The United Nations Declaration on the Rights of Indigenous Peoples' [2007] *International Journal on Minority and Group Rights* 14; Gilbert, *Indigenous Peoples' Land Rights* (n 53) 231–46. For a similar opinion, see also Anaya, *Indigenous Peoples in International Law* (n 17) 140–41.

[131] Lenzerini, 'Sovereignty Revisited' (n 56) 181.

[132] See Luis Rodríguez-Piñero, 'The Inter-American System and the UN Declaration on the Rights of Indigenous Peoples: Mutual Reinforcement', in Allen and Xanthaki (eds.), *Reflections on the UN Declaration on the Rights of Indigenous Peoples* (n 23) 6–7. Patrick Dumberry draws the same conclusion with regard to the indigenous peoples of North America. See Dumberry, Lessons Learned from the Quebec Secession Reference before the Supreme Court of Canada', in Kohen (ed.), *Secession: International Law Perspectives* (n 114) 431–35.

[133] Baldwin and Morel, 'Using the United Nations Declaration on the Rights of Indigenous Peoples in Litigation' (n 80) 129.

[134] Marc Weller, 'Settling Self-Determination Conflicts: Recent Developments' [2009] *European Journal of International Law*, Vol 20, No 1'; Marc Weller, 'Towards a General Comment on Self-Determination and Autonomy': Working Paper Submitted to the Sub-Commission on the Protection and Promotion of Human Rights', Working Group on Minorities, UN Document E/CN4/Sub2/AC5/2005/WP512 16.

[135] Xanthaki, 'Indigenous Rights in International Law' (n 84); and Xanthaki, 'The Right to Self-Determination: Meaning and Scope', in Ghanea and Xanthaki (eds.), *Minorities, Peoples and Self-Determination* (n 3) 22–23.

[136] Helen Quane, 'The UN Declaration on the Rights of Indigenous Peoples: New Directions for Self-Determination and Participatory Rights?', in Allen and Xanthaki (eds.), *Reflections on the UN Declaration on the Rights of Indigenous Peoples* (n 23) 259–60.

already prior to the adoption of the UNDRIP inferred that states have largely endorsed the notion that indigenous peoples are entitled to the internal aspect of self-determination. Following the adoption of the UNDRIP, he notes that the Declaration affirms that this right applies to indigenous peoples. In support of his conclusion, Kymlicka points to how essentially all Western countries with indigenous populations have accepted that these peoples enjoy rights to various forms of self-government. He adds that by now, most Latin America countries have introduced cultural autonomy arrangements for indigenous peoples today residing within the state and that the remaining countries of the continent are moving in the same direction.[137] Kymlicka further concludes that the UNDRIP confirms that international law recognizes collective group-differentiated rights.[138] Christian Tomuschat joins the choir. He too concludes that indigenous peoples constitute self -determining peoples.[139] James Anaya elaborates that the human rights character of the right to self-determination must no longer be obscured by a state-centred world. He underscores that self-governance is the key feature of indigenous peoples' right to self-determination. Anaya adds that this right should be exercised through indigenous peoples' own political institutions that allow them to develop their societies with respect for their distinct cultural characteristics.[140] Similarly, Joshua Castellino posits that international law has come to hold that the right to self-determination applies to peoples in the ethnic/cultural meaning of the word. He adds that such peoples shall exercise their right to self-determination right through constructive arrangements within the state.[141] Christopher Fromherz concurs that indigenous peoples are entitled to the internal aspect of the right to self -determination and that this right is to be exercised through self-governing and autonomy functions.[142] Timo Koivurova agrees that indigenous peoples are beneficiaries of a right to internal self-determination that embraces among other things a right to manage their natural wealth and resources.[143] Martti Koskenniemi adds, perhaps somewhat more cautiously, that the internal aspect of the right to

[137] Kymlicka, *Multicultural Odysseys* (n 10) 80–81, 103–104, 108, 249; Kymlicka, 'American Multiculturalism and the "Nations Within"', in Duncan Ivison, Paul Patton, and Will Sanders (eds.), *Political Theory and the Rights of Indigenous Peoples* (Cambridge University Press, 2000) 225–27; Kymlicka, 'Beyond the Indigenous/Minority Dichotomy?' (n 41) 186.

[138] Ibid., 186.

[139] Christian Tomuschat, 'Secession and Self-Determination', in Kohen (ed.), *Secession: International Law Perspectives* (n 114).

[140] Anaya, *Indigenous Peoples in International Law* (n 17) 150–53; Anaya, 'The Capacity of Inter- national Law to Advance Ethnic or Nationality Rights Claims', in Kymlicka (ed.), *The Rights of Minority Cultures* (n 11) 325–27.

[141] Castellino, 'Conceptual Difficulties' (n 3) 67–68.

[142] See Fromherz, Indigenous Peoples Courts (n 58) 1370–71. For similar positions, see Natalia Loukacheva, 'On Autonomy and Law', <https://www.claonet.org/wps/ighc/000/546/f_000/456_6419.pdf> accessed on 2 February 2010); Barelli, 'The Role of Soft Law in the International Legal System (n 74) 961; Stefania Errico, 'The UN Declaration on the Rights of Indigenous Peoples is Adopted: An Overview' [2007] *Human Rights Law Review* 7:4 757–58.

[143] Timo Koivurova, 'Jurisprudence of the European Court of Human Rights Regarding Indigenous Peoples: Retrospects and Prospects' [2011] *International Journal on Minority and Group Rights* 18 36.

self-determination requires that the majority society respects the distinct cultural identities of indigenous peoples.[144] On his part, former member of the CERD Committee Patrick Thornberry notes that the Committee has in light of recent developments in international law confirmed that the CERD Convention endorses that indigenous peoples are beneficiaries of collective human rights.[145]

Some legal scholars have been more hesitant to definitively conclude that indigenous peoples have emerged as international legal subjects, with rights as such. They note that international law is about to embrace rights of indigenous peoples as peoples, and are in many instances positive towards such an evolvement, but have nonetheless not yet been ready to infer that this development has reached its end. For instance, Benedict Kingsbury posits that in order to adequately address the needs and aspirations of groups, one should reinvent international law and add concepts that go beyond the state-individual dichotomy.[146] In a similar vein, James Crawford asserts that it is increasingly acknowledged that conventional individual human rights are inadequately defined to protect those that want to be different. He adds that a complete focus on individual human rights may promote assimilation. Crawford posits that to acknowledge that peoples are beneficiaries of the right to self-determination, only to in the same breath submit that the right applies solely to peoples understood as aggregate populations of states, reduces the right to a 'cruel deception'. He identifies a trend in international law towards recognizing a right to self-determination of peoples in the ethnic/cultural understanding of the term, in particular in the context of indigenous peoples.[147] Similarly, David Raic notes that the internal aspect of the right to self-determination has conventionally been understood to amount to a mere right of all citizens of the state to participate in the decision-making processes of the state on an equal basis. He envisages, however, other ways in which the internal aspect of the right to self-determination could be exercised, including through autonomy arrangements for ethnic and cultural groups within the state. In support of this argument, Raic asserts that applying the right to self-determination to groups within a state in the described manner would be in line with the rights' *raison d'être*.[148]

A third category of legal scholars all together rejects the notion that indigenous peoples constitute peoples for international legal purposes. (Again, this position might not in all instances necessarily be reflective of these scholars' personal opinion as to what the law *should* be, but rather of an evaluation of the law *de lege lata*.)

[144] Martti Koskenniemi, 'National Self-Determination Today: Problems of Legal Theory and Practice' [1994] *International & Comparative Law Quarterly*, Vol 43 267.

[145] Patrick Thornberry, 'Integrating the UN Declaration on the Rights of Indigenous Peoples into CERD Practice', in Allen and Xanthaki (eds.), *Reflection on the UN Declaration on the Rights of Indigenous Peoples* (n 23) 88.

[146] Benedict Kingsbury, 'Reconciling Five Competing Conceptual Structures of Indigenous Peoples' Claims in International and Comparative Law', in Alston (ed.), *Peoples' Rights* (n 3).

[147] Crawford, 'The Right to Self-Determination' (n 3) 24, 26, 39–40, 64; James Crawford, *The Creation of States in International Law* (2nd edn., Clarendon Press, 2006) 120–21.

[148] Raic, *Statehood and the Law of Self-Determination* (n 98) 146, 239, 248, 255–57, 283–85, 446.

Already mentioned have been the positions of Ian Brownlie[149] and Hurst Hannum. The latter author notes, however, that although most states automatically negatively react to the notion of a right to self-determination of indigenous peoples, there is some evidence that the issue could be considered with flexibility.[150] Marcelo Kohen too maintains that international law only acknowledges one category of peoples, i.e. peoples understood as aggregate populations of states (or territories).[151] Stephen Allen concurs. He infers that the orthodox position remains valid still today, i.e. that people-hood equates to the aggregate populations of states.[152] Similarly, as touched upon, Antonio Cassese submits that the right to self-determination does not yet apply to segments of the state such as ethnic and cultural groups. At the same time, however, he adds that international law does not specify in what ways members of such groups may exercise the internal aspect of the right to self-determination beyond taking part in national decision-making processes on par with other citizens of the state. The latter observation indicates that Cassese may envisage that one, and more meaningful, way of doing so could be through autonomy and self-governance.[153] Gudmundur Alfredsson is of a similar view. He equates the internal aspect of the right to self-determination with democratic governance. In other words, Alfredsson maintains that this right amounts to nothing more than an equal right of all citizens of the state to a government that represent the entire population of a territory, irrespective of whether the territory contains several ethnic and/or cultural groups.[154] In a neighbouring vein, Malcolm Shaw seemingly accepts that the right to self-determination formally can apply to segments of the state such as indigenous peoples, but in the same breath suggests that is not to say that the right necessarily envelopes a right to autonomy or self-government.[155]

In summary, a large majority of legal scholars infer that indigenous peoples constitute peoples for international legal purposes, with rights as such, including the right to self-determination. In addition, with few exceptions, scholars that have been hesitant to join this chorus have made their observations prior to the adoption of the UNDRIP. Perhaps this hesitance can therefore, in some instances at least, be

[149] Ian Brownlie, *Principles of Public International Law* (6th edn., Oxford University Press, 2003) 540–41, 553; Brownlie 'The Rights of Peoples in Modern International Law', in James Crawford (ed.), *The Rights of Peoples* (Clarendon Press, 1988) 4–16.

[150] Hannum, *Autonomy, Sovereignty, and Self-Determination* (n 98) 95–103.

[151] That said, Kohen may take this position because he equates the right to self-determination with a right to secession. See Marcelo G Kohen, *Secession: International Law Perspectives* (n 114) 9, 16. As mentioned, and as the below elaborates upon, when applied to indigenous peoples, the right to self-determination will be about self-government and autonomy within existing states, and not about secession.

[152] Stephen Allen, 'The UN Declaration on the Rights of Indigenous Peoples and the Limits of the International Legal Project', in Allen and Xanthaki (eds.), *Reflections on the UN Declaration on the Rights of Indigenous Peoples* (n 23) 242.

[153] Antonio Cassese, *International Law* (2nd edn., Oxford University Press, 2005) 63–64; Cassese, *Self-Determination of Peoples* (n 2) 53–54, 64–65, 101, 124, 131, 298.

[154] Gudmundur Alfredsson, 'The Right to Self-Determination and Indigenous Peoples', in Christian Tomuschat (ed.), *Modern Law of Self-Determination* (Nijhoff, 1993) 41–54.

[155] Malcolm Shaw, 'Self-Determination and the Use of Force', in Ghanea and Xanthaki (eds.), *Minorities, Peoples and Self-Determination* (n 3) 41–43.

explained by the fact that at the time legal sources that suggest that indigenous peoples have emerged as international legal subjects largely originated from expert bodies and international tribunals. As mentioned, many states had explicitly deferred their position on the legal status of indigenous peoples to the UNDRIP process. Consequently, following the adoption of the UNDRIP, one may perhaps expect the previously doubting legal scholars to again consider their position as to what extent the right to self-determination and other peoples' rights apply to indigenous peoples. That is particularly so since, as seen above, several of these scholars have already opined that international law *should* head in the direction the UNDRIP submits.[156]

To conclude, there seems to be broad support within the legal doctrine for the position that international law has come to recognize indigenous peoples as legal subjects, with rights as such, including the most prominent of peoples' rights, that of self-determination.

5.9 Conclusions

Based on what has been articulated above, it would appear reasonable to conclude that international law has come to affirm that indigenous peoples constitute international legal subjects. As such, they enjoy peoples' rights, including the foremost of these rights, i.e. the right to self-determination. The HRC and the CESC—the two UN expert bodies that have been entrusted to authoritatively oversee the implementation of the right to self-determination—have both concluded that this right does apply to indigenous peoples. Moreover, these and other UN treaty bodies have also applied other human rights to indigenous peoples as such, thereby taking the position that indigenous peoples are entitled to peoples' rights. There appears to be no concerted state objections to the conclusions the HRC, the CESC, and other treaty bodies have drawn in this regard. Rather, states largely seem to have accepted this subsequent practice, most notably through their adoption of the UNDRIP, including its Article 3 on the right to self-determination and Articles 1 and 2 on peoples' rights in general. In addition, states have affirmed that a right to self-determination—to be implemented through autonomy and self-governance arrangements within existing state borders—applies to indigenous peoples through domestic recognition and action. Moreover, legal sources emanating out of regional

[156] For instance, already in 1995 Antonio Cassese noted a tendency in international law to recognize that the internal aspect of the right to self-determination should apply to, at least in some respects, minority groups. He observed that several states had agreed to discuss how this right could be more effectively implemented in the particular context of populations within the state other than the majority people. With these observations as point of departure, Cassese recommended that the concept of self-determination be remodelled so as to better apply to ethnic and cultural groups. He asserted that when applied to peoples in this understanding of the term, the right should encompass a right to autonomy and a broad measure of self-government. See Cassese, *Self-Determination of Peoples* (n 2) 104, 107, 330, 339, 349–51, 354–55, 362. Similarly, Hurst Hannum has observed a trend in international law to accommodate for autonomy and self-determination of, among others, indigenous peoples. In doing so, he has added that often only group rights can adequately promote the interests of indigenous peoples. See Hannum, *Autonomy, Sovereignty, and Self-Determination* (n 98) 473–75.

human rights courts and other institutions support the conclusion that indigenous peoples have emerged as peoples for international legal purposes, with rights as such, as does, largely speaking, the legal doctrine.

The UNGA's adoption of the UNDRIP ended decades of debate and negotiations on the understanding of 'peoples' under international law, insofar as indigenous peoples are concerned. One must now reasonably conclude that the term 'peoples' can no longer be understood to exclusively refer to aggregate populations of states. Rather, also populations with certain distinct cultural and ethnic characteristics within a state can also be peoples for international legal purposes, at least in an indigenous peoples' context. In other words, in states with indigenous populations there can be more than one people in a state, and the territory of a people can also stretch across state borders.

The outlined development cannot be described as anything less than a paradigm shift in international law. In the international legal and political order that equated 'peoples' with aggregate populations of states, for all practical purposes, states were the only relevant international polities. With this understanding of peoples, there could be no peoples' rights in any meaningful understanding of the term, since a people in practice, if not formally, coincided with the state. The political map changes dramatically, however, when the conventional understanding of 'peoples' becomes complimented by peoples in the meaning cultural/ethnic segments of the state. The emergence of peoples' rights proper challenges the primacy of the state in unprecedented ways. Within the state, indigenous peoples on one hand, and state representative institutions on the other, then compete for jurisdiction. This development requires international law to define people-state relationship in previously unknown ways.[157] Chapter 6 elaborates on what this process may entail. Prior to that, it is, however, pertinent to address some principal concerns that have been raised in the debate as to what extent indigenous peoples possess peoples' rights, or collective rights in general.

5.10 The Compatibility between State Sovereignty and a Right to Self-Determination of Indigenous Peoples

5.10.1 Introduction

Having reached the conclusion that indigenous peoples have emerged as beneficiaries of the right to self-determination, it is relevant to add a few words on the compatibility between this right and the (i) external and (ii) internal aspects of state sovereignty, i.e. on the compatibility between a right to self-determination of indigenous peoples and (i) the principle of territorial integrity of states, and (ii) state

[157] Will Kymlicka concurs that recognition of a right to self-determination of indigenous peoples fundamentally reshapes the notions of state sovereignty and nationhood. He agrees that autonomy and self-governance arrangements of indigenous peoples include a genuine transfer of power, or of sovereignty if one wishes, from the state to the indigenous people. See Kymlicka, *Multicultural Odysseys* (n 10) 4–5, 33, 206–11; Kymlicka 'American Multiculturalism' (n 137) 225–27.

jurisdiction.[158] It is proper to do so, since it is sometimes argued that a right to self-determination of indigenous peoples would violate the fundamental principle of state sovereignty.

5.10.2 The external aspect—territorial integrity of states

Chapters 2 and 3 explain that 'state' is not a term of art. Humans must take a political decision as to what polities constitute states. Chapter 2 describes how traditionally, international law did not define states. A polity became a state if accepted as such by already existing sovereign states. Following the failed attempt by the League of Nations to objectively define states, lawyers debated whether recognition by other sovereign states should—as under the classical international legal system—be the determinative element of a state coming into existence, or whether rather what amounts to a state should be defined by law. With time, the latter argument prevailed. International law now objectively defines what polities qualify as states.[159] That said, it should be underlined that this does not change the fact that it is still a political decision what polities qualify as states. States can at any point amend the presently valid definition of states.

Irrespective of how defined, states are the only legal persons under international law and remain, at least formally,[160] the sole creators of such. Out of self-interest, but also motivated by a perception that the presence of states are the best guarantee for peace and order,[161] states are notoriously sceptical towards developments in international law that would challenge their position. Hence, the principle of territorial integrity of states continues to be a cornerstone in the international legal system. Interest in maintaining respect for this principle has also exercised a certain influence on the indigenous rights discourse.

The above outlines how historically, states have been hesitant to acknowledge a right to self-determination of indigenous peoples. As touched upon, a major reason for this scepticism has been a fear that such a development in international law would result in, or at least encourage, separatist movements and aspirations. States' inhospitality towards an expanded understanding of the right to self-determination has been motivated at least partly by an assumption that the right encompasses a right to statehood, or at least could be understood to do so by the new beneficiaries

[158] Sovereignty has been described as states' (i) jurisdiction over their territory and their permanent population, (ii) a duty on other states not to intervene in the state's area of exclusive jurisdictions, and (iii) the dependence of obligations arising from international law on the consent of the obligator. See Brownlie, *Principles of Public International Law* (n 149) 106–07, 119, 287; and Cassese, *International Law* (n 153) 49–51. In other words, sovereignty is essentially about independence (or territorial integrity) externally and of self-determination (or jurisdiction) internally. See Martti Koskenniemi, *From Apology to Utopia—The Structure of International Legal Argument* (Cambridge University Press, 2005) 240.

[159] See Arbitration Commission of the Hague Conference on Yugoslavia, Opinion No 1 [*Disintegration of the SFRY*] (1991) 92 ILR 162, 164–65; also Cassese, *International Law*, (n 153) 73–77; and Raic, *Statehood and the Law of Self-Determination* (n 98) 29–37.

[160] Compare the conclusions in Section 4.3.

[161] Cassese, *International Law* (n 153) 71–72; Boyle and Chinkin, *The Making of International Law* (n 125) 17, 41; Raic, *Statehood and the Law of Self-Determination* (n 98) 18, 26; Crawford, *The Creation of States* (n 147) 252.

of the right.[162] The concern is understandable, to some extent. Section 2.5.4 describes how the right to self-determination has most effectively, and visibly, been invoked in a decolonization context. As a consequence, it may be easy to get the impression that the right to self-determination equals a right to secession and independence. Against this backdrop, it is not entirely unsurprising that states initially feared that a right to self-determination of indigenous peoples would result in a second wave of decolonization, or secessionist, movements. True, most states are reasonably aware that secession is an unlikely and impractical option for most indigenous peoples. Nevertheless, states may have harboured a fear that if indigenous peoples gained recognition that they are entitled to the right to self-determination this might inspire other, more combative and separatist oriented, segments of states to move for independence.

Thus, from a political perspective, it is understandable that states were concerned that recognition of a right to self-determination of indigenous peoples might encourage secessionist aspirations, if not by the indigenous peoples themselves so at least among other groups. From a legal perspective, however, such fears are unfounded. Under international law, the right to self-determination does not encompass a right to secede, save in extreme circumstances. It is generally held that only if the state is guilty of gross human rights violations that render it impossible to exercise the right to self-determination in any meaningful manner within state borders is secession allowed as a last resort. Absent such abnormal circumstances, however, international law requires that indigenous peoples exercise their right to self-determination through autonomy arrangements within existing state borders. No peoples, including indigenous peoples, are legally entitled to a general right of unilateral secession.[163]

In sum, when applied to indigenous peoples, the right to self-determination is to be exercised within existing state borders. It therefore follows that recognition of such a right does not, by definition, conflict with the principle of territorial integrity of states.

5.10.3 The internal aspect—jurisdiction

As mentioned, states remain the only *legal persons* recognized by international law. That does not necessarily mean, however, that states are also the sole international

[162] Anaya, *Indigenous Peoples in International Law* (n 17) 7–8; Raic, *Statehood and the Law of Self-Determination* (n 98) 242–43, Hannum, *Autonomy, Sovereignty, and Self-Determination* (n 98) 96, 473.

[163] See Crawford, 'The Right to Self-Determination' (n 3) 49–60; Crawford, *The Creation of States* (n 147) 383–418; Cassese, *Self-Determination of Peoples* (n 2) 167, 283, 334, 349; Allan Buchanan, 'The Morality of Secession', in Kymlicka (ed.), *The Rights of Minority Cultures* (n 11) 352; Tomuschat (n 154) 35–36, 84–86; Dugard and Raic (n 99); 102–08; Antello Tancredi, 'A Normative "Due Process" in the Creation of States through Secession', in Kohen (ed.), *Secession: International Law Perspectives* (n 114) 175–84; Patrick Thornberry, 'Self-Determination and Indigenous Peoples: Objections and Responses', in Pekka Aikio and Martin Scheinin (eds.), *Operationalizing Self-Determination* (Institute for Human Rights, Åbo Akademi University, 2002) 53. That indigenous peoples' right to self-determination does not embrace a right to secession also follows explicitly from UNDRIP Article 46.

legal subjects. Already at the advent of the contemporary international legal system, Hersch Lauterpacht observed that '[t]here is no rule in international law which precludes . . . bodies other than states . . . [from] becoming subjects of [international law].'[164] Since then, international law has come to recognize a number of entities as international legal subjects, beyond states. In *Reparation for Injuries*, the ICJ proclaimed that the UN enjoys status as an international legal subject.[165] More recently, and more relevant for the present purposes, in *East Timor* the ICJ held that the population of East Timor, at a time when it formed part of Indonesia, constituted an international legal subject. In doing so, the Court underlined that although international law primarily regulates state behaviour, it also recognizes rights of other entities, such as peoples.[166]

The legal doctrine concurs that the fact that states remain the sole international legal persons does not preclude the possibility that other entities can acquire status as subjects of international law. Bin Cheng observes that it follows already from the principle of state sovereignty that states are free to endow other entities with such status.[167] In the same vein, Ian Brownlie notes that the world community should be, and historically has been, ready to demonstrate flexibility when it comes to awarding political entities other than states with status as subjects of international law. International law opens up for—indeed foresees— situations where legal entities beyond states perform tasks conventionally associated with the state, he asserts.[168] James Crawford too posits that the fact that the state remains the principal international legal subject does not preclude that other distinct territorial communities can be international legal subjects as well. Such entities can still hold rights to diverse arrangements of secession less sovereignty, he submits.[169]

In summary, international law has the capacity to accept polities other than states as international legal subjects. Consequently, no principal reason precludes the possibility of indigenous peoples emerging as international legal subjects,[170] as the presentation in Sections 5.7–5.9 indeed suggests that they have. The question that remains is then whether a right of indigenous peoples to self-determination and other peoples' rights is compatible with the internal aspect of state sovereignty, i.e. with states' rights to manage their own affairs, internally.

Chapter 2 describes how the principle of state sovereignty follows from the assumption that no law can pre-date the emergence of the state. Since no law can derive from an authority above states, law that binds states must emanate from states. As further explained, in that sense, the principle of state sovereignty represents the constitutional doctrine of international law.

164 Hersch Lauterpacht, *The Subjects of the Law of Nations* (LQR, 1947) 444.

165 *Reparation for Injuries Case. Repartition for Injuries Suffered in the Services of the United Nations*, Advisory Opinion: ICJ Reports 1949 174.

166 *East Timor (Portugal v Australia)*, Judgement, ICJ Reports 1995 90.

167 Bin Cheng, 'Introduction to Subjects of International Law', in Mohammed Bedjaoui (ed.), *International Law: Achievements and Prospects* (UNESCO, 1991) 24–25.

168 Brownlie, *Principles of Public International Law* (n 149) 59, 63, 77.

169 Crawford, *The Creation of States* (n 147) 197, 254; also, for a similar opinion, Ivison, Patton, and Sanders (eds.), *Political Theory and the Rights of Indigenous Peoples* (n 137) 14.

170 Macklem, 'Indigenous Recognition' (n 12) 178–79.

The principal understanding of sovereignty, including its internal aspect jurisdiction, is hence straightforward. The state is free to run its internal affairs without outside interference. The state itself determines its relationship with the international community by agreeing, or not, to the creation of international norms and, at least in the case of treaties, by determining to what extent it should accept to be bound by such norms. From this understanding of sovereignty it further follows that albeit *the concept* of sovereignty is clear, what *more precise powers* are included in a particular state's sovereignty vary. Sovereignty has the capacity to respond to needs and interests of the society, and to limit its own applicability. It is in the process of constant erosion, as international law places more and more obligations on states. Indeed, to limit what actions a state can undertake with reference to its sovereignty is the precise purpose of international law. That is particularly so in the sphere of human rights.[171] Sovereignty implies nothing more than that a state shall be free from outside interference in its internal affairs *as long as its international undertakings do not provide differently.*[172] By accepting international obligations a state voluntarily limits its own jurisdiction to the extent such undertakings require the state to act or not to act in certain manners in its internal affairs. Needless to say, states may be reluctant to cede jurisdiction in such a manner. But it happens nonetheless, as Chapter 6 and in particular Section 6.3, elaborates.

It follows from the above that indigenous peoples being beneficiaries of the right to self-determination (and other peoples' rights) fully conforms also to the internal aspect of state sovereignty, i.e. jurisdiction. Indigenous peoples having emerged as holders of the right to self-determination simply constitutes one example among others of state jurisdiction having been 'eroded' by the creation of an international norm. This particular erosion has resulted in the scope of indigenous peoples' right to self-determination—or *their* jurisdiction if one wants—having expanded to an extent that corresponds to decreased state jurisdiction. To infer, recognition of a right to self-determination of indigenous peoples is compatible with the internal aspect of state sovereignty.[173]

[171] Cassese, *International Law* (n 153) 98, 123; Brownlie, *Principles of Public International Law* (n 149) 291–93; Andrea Bianchi, 'Immunity versus Human Rights: The Pinochet Case' [1999] *European Journal of International Law* 10, reprinted in Malcolm Evans and Patrick Capps (eds.), *International Law* (Vol II) (Ashgate Publishing, 2009) 261, 265; Frédéric Mégret, 'International Law as Law', in Crawford and Koskenniemi (eds.), *International Law* (Cambridge University Press, 2012) 67, 83; Raic, *Statehood and the Law of Self-Determination* (n 98) 25–26; Bardo Fassbender, 'The United Nations Charter As Constitution of the International Community' [1998] *Columbia Journal of Transnational Law* 36, reprinted in Malcom Evans and Patrick Capps (eds.), *International Law* (Vol I) (Ashgate Publishing, 2009) 582; Wiessner, 'Indigenous Sovereignty' (n 83) 1146–49; Hersch Lauterpacht, 'The Problem of Jurisdictional Immunities of Foreign States' [1951] *British Yearbook of International Law*, 28, reprinted in Malcolm Evans and Patrick Capps (eds.), *International Law* (Vol II) (Ashgate Publishing, 2009) 394; Francis Hinsley, *Sovereignty* (Basic Books, 1966) 219; Joshua Castellino, 'The Protection of Minorities and Indigenous Peoples in International Law' [2010] *International Journal on Minority and Group Rights* 17 409; Anaya, 'The Capacity of International Law' (n 140) 326–27.

[172] Lenzerini, 'Sovereignty Revisited' (n 98) 158–60.

[173] Arguably, a right to self-determination of indigenous peoples also conforms to the liberal theories that underpin the international legal system. Chapter 2 articulates how liberal social contract theories profess that states are formed through agreements by groups of men. But Chapter 3 shows how it is highly unlikely that random groups of men, without ethnic or cultural kinship, come together and form states. Certainly, if one accepts the notion of a social contract it appears more realistic that groups

5.11 The Relationship between Indigenous Peoples' Rights and (i) Group Rights in General, and (ii) the Rights of Individual Members of the Group

5.11.1 Introduction

As mentioned, before turning attention to the content and scope of indigenous peoples' right to self-determination, this work shall briefly address two other lines of arguments that have been raised against the notion that indigenous peoples are bestowed with rights as collectives. Some are sceptical to the idea of group rights in general, asserting that it is impossible to draw a line between groups that are worthy of rights and those that are not. Others may have less principal problem with the notion that indigenous peoples can be beneficiaries group rights, but are concerned that the exercise of such right may be harmful to and result in violations of rights of individual members of the group.

5.11.2 The relationship between indigenous peoples' rights and group rights in general

Naturally, if one wishes to bestow groups with rights, it is necessary to identify what groups are worthy of such. Some reject the notion of group rights based, or at least partly based, on the argument that collectives are not fixed entities. Consequently, they posit, it is not possible to define what groups constitute such collectives that should be entitled to rights. For instance, Chandran Kukathas posits that ethnic identity has a contextual character. An ethnic group is defined based on its relationship with other groups. It can form and dissolve in response to changes in its surrounding environment. Kukathas argues that this instability renders it difficult to identify such groups that should be possessors of rights. He points to the fact that ethnic and cultural minorities are not the only groups facing inequalities. Kukathas criticizes Kymlicka for failing to explain how groups entitled to protection distinguish themselves from other collectives not worthy of rights. In a similar vein, Anne Phillips asserts that arguments in favour of recognizing rights of ethnic and cultural minority groups could readily also be made with regard to other collectives, such as religious, sexual, and class groups.[174]

of men ethnic and cultural ties would enter into such contracts. An ethnic/cultural group that is aware of its vulnerable position appears as an unlikely candidate to sign a social contract with the majority group. Compare Philip N Petit, 'Minority Claims under Two Conceptions of Democracy', in Ivison, Patton, and Sanders (eds.), *Political Theory and the Rights of Indigenous Peoples* (n 137) 205; Vernon Van Dyke, 'The Individual, the State, and Ethnic Communities in Political Theory', in Kymlicka (ed.), *The Rights of Minority Cultures* (n 11) 45; Bhiku Parekh, 'The Rushdie Affair: Research Agenda for Political Philosophy', in Kymlicka (ed.), *The Rights of Minority Cultures* (n 11); Packer, 'The OSCE High Commissioner on National Minorities' (n 30) 265.

[174] See Chandran Kukathas, 'Are There Any Cultural Rights?', in Kymlicka (ed.), *The Rights of Minority Cultures* (n 11) 232, 244–45; and Anne Phillips, 'Democracy and Difference: Some Problems

It may be correct that, generally speaking, to define what groups are entitled to and/or in need of rights can be associated with certain, or even substantial, difficulties. Perhaps it is true that sometimes it is not entirely easy to justify why certain groups should enjoy rights while others, seemingly equally disadvantaged, should not. For the present purposes, it is, however, not necessary to examine the validity of the articulated line of argument in any depth.

The developments within political philosophy that Chapter 3 outlines have surely exercised influence on the indigenous rights discourse. As seen, it appears that multiculturalism contributed to a development within international law that rendered it more hospitable towards group rights. Importantly, however, this chapter explains how international law has drawn a clearer line than political philosophy between indigenous peoples, on one hand, and minority groups, on the other. As the above outlines in depth, international law sharpbly distinguishes between indigenous peoples and other groups that are in a minority and/or vulnerable position vis-à-vis the majority population. Indigenous peoples' rights have largely evolved not because of a comparison with minorities and other groups, but because of a comparison with peoples' rights in general. Therefore, it would be conceptually incorrect to argue against the existence of indigenous peoples' rights by invoking difficulties associated with identifying minorities and other similar groups.[175] This problem simply does not present itself in the context of indigenous peoples, at least not from a legal perspective. The entire indigenous rights discourse rests on the position that indigenous peoples are clearly distinguishable compared with minority groups (although that might perhaps not always be the case in practice). Consequently, even if it should be correct that it is hard to determine what various kinds of minority groups should be entitled to rights, this argument has, from a legal perspective, no relevance in the context of indigenous peoples.

5.11.3 Potential Conflicts between Indigenous Peoples' Rights and those of Individual Members of the Group

Chapter 3 describes how some argue that collective rights can pose threats to the well-being of individual members of the group. Proponents of this line of thought fear that acceptance of group rights may lead to systematic discrimination and maltreatment of vulnerable sub-segments of the group, where women and the girl-child are often referred to as examples. To recognize collective rights, it is submitted, may often be equivalent to accepting that a majority or elite within the minority group has a right to dominate vulnerable elements of the group. A collective right to cultural privacy could potentially be used to shield the culture in question from much needed outside scrutiny, the argument goes. Some add that acceptance of

for Feminist Theory' [1992] *The Political Quarterly* (63) 1. For a similar line of thought, see also Vernon Van Dyke, 'Collective Entities and Moral Rights: Problems in Liberal-Democratic Thought' [1982] *The Journal of Politics*, Vol 44, Issue 01 32.

[175] Ivison, Patton, and Sanders make a similar argument, in *Political Theory and the Rights of Indigenous Peoples* (n 137) 20–21.

group rights tends to freeze cultures in a state where cultural practices that appear offensive to most outsiders are nonetheless accepted by the group. Group rights may deny the minority within the minority the possibility to reshape the rules and culture of the group, it is sometimes posited.[176]

As mentioned, the outlined concerns have led some liberal scholars to infer either that there can be no group rights at all, or, alternatively, that group rights must always yield to the human rights of the individual. For instance, recall how Section 3.6 describes how Will Kymlicka distinguishes between group rights that (i) are directed towards members of the group, and (ii) those that aim to protect the group from society at large, and further how he submits that only the latter set of rights shall be accepted. In case of conflict, Kymlicka posits, human rights of the individual always take precedent over collective human rights, including in the context of indigenous peoples and individuals. It is pertinent to consider, however, how well this line of argument conforms to the general logic of liberalism.

Chapters 2 and 3 outline how a collective—the state—is a keystone in liberal theory. Liberalism professes—indeed assumes—that the state can with authority impose decisions on its members, i.e. its citizens. Also within a state, actions undertaken by the majority (or other forms of authority) can cause harm to marginalized segments of the group, as indeed many, if not all, indigenous peoples can bear witness to. In other words, the same concern that some raise with regard to rights of groups—i.e. that the exercise of collective rights may result in a limitation of freedom of individual members of the group—could in fact be raised against the powers exercised by a state. Kymlicka and other liberals seemingly fail to explain why limitation of freedom as a result of state action is more morally acceptable than authority exercised within an indigenous group. Why should indigenous peoples, unlike state-forming peoples, not have the right to determine the course of their societies just because all members of the group might not look favourably upon a particular action?

Perhaps even more importantly, however, in addition to being morally questionable, to take the position that indigenous peoples' rights must always yield to those belonging to individual members of the group seems to contradict the underlying rationale of indigenous peoples' rights. As underscored throughout, at their core, indigenous peoples' rights aim to allow such peoples to form and control their own societies. Indigenous peoples can hardly effectively do so if the exersice of the right to self-determination is curtailed in the manner Kymlicka and others suggest. Until multiculturalism—and other liberal theories—has responded in a relevant manner

176 Daniel M Weinstock, 'Liberalism, Multiculturalism, and the Problem of Internal Minorities', in Simon Laden and David Owen (eds.), *Multiculturalism and Political Theory* (Cambridge University Press, 2007) 246–47; Ayelet Shachar, 'Feminism and Multiculturalism: Mapping the Terrain', in Laden and Owen, ibid., 115–47; and *Multicultural Jurisdictions* (n 149) 2–3, 19, 28–29; Jeff Spinner-Halev, 'Multiculturalism and its Critics', in John S Dryzek, Bonnie Honig, and Anne Phillips (eds.), *The Oxford Handbook of Political Theory* (Oxford University Press, 2006) 549; Kukathas, 'Are There Any Cultural Rights?' (n 174) 236; Susan M Okin, 'Is Multiculturalism Bad for Women?' [1997] *Boston Review* 22 26; Xanthaki, *Indigenous Rights and United Nations Standards* (n 9) 20–21.

to the articulated counter-arguments, their concern over vulnerable segments of indigenous societies is less convincing.[177]

Multiculturalists might retort that individual human rights have been elaborated exactly to place checks and balances on states. States are bound to respect all individual human rights. Is it then not reasonable to expect indigenous peoples to do the same? For instance, Ayelet Shachar at least indirectly acknowledges that multiculturalism is vulnerable to arguments that there is no major principal difference between a state, on one hand, and an indigenous authority, on the other, imposing its will on its subjects/members. Still, she prefers the state-individual dichotomy over group rights precisely because states are obliged to respect individual human rights.[178] This argument does not, however, address the fact that indigenous peoples' rights are partly a reaction to that the state–individual dichotomy does not adequately take into account the needs, aspirations, and concerns of indigenous peoples, and, that this failure indirectly harms also the individual members of the people. Arguably rights of indigenous peoples as such should be recognized precisely because individual rights cannot sufficiently protect either indigenous peoples or their members. That is why hitherto dominating political and legal structures are being reshaped in their foundations, as they apply to indigenous peoples. Under such circumstances, it makes little sense to impose an entire pre-existing set of rights that was developed during a time-period when international law was blind to indigenous societal structures, on indigenous peoples. Rather, a more flexible approach is called for.

The argument here is not that all sorts of cultural practices within indigenous societies shall be accepted. Certain individual human rights should never be encroached upon for the benefit of protecting group rights.[179] But setting such principal individual rights aside, what right prevails in instances of conflict between a collective and an individual right should reasonably be determined on a case-by-case basis. No fixed formula should provide that any individual right, however

[177] In this context, see Martin Scheinin, 'How to Resolve Conflicts Between Individual and Collective Rights?', in Martin Scheinin and Reeta Toivanen (eds.), *Rethinking Non-Discrimination and Minority Rights* (Institute for Human Rights, Åbo Academy University, 2004) 222, 238. Martin Scheinin points to how liberal political theory fails to convince when advocating constant precedent of individual rights over collective rights at the same time as multiculturalism takes for granted that the state has the power to impose burdens on its 'members'—in some countries to the extent that it can execute its own citizens. Scheinin asserts that one should logically uphold the same conditions for restrictions of individual rights, irrespective of which authority, i.e. a state or an indigenous people, seeks to impose limitations on such rights. In a similar vein, Iris M Young posits that the collective's and the individual's interests need to be balanced against one other—regardless of whether the collective is a state or an indigenous people. See Iris M Young, 'Two concepts of self-determination', in Stephen May, Tariq Modood, and Judith Squires (eds.), *Ethnicity, Nationalism and Minority Rights* (Cambridge University Press, 2004) 187–89, 192–93.

[178] Shachar, *Multicultural Jurisdictions* (n 176) 2–3, 19, 28–29.

[179] Martin Scheinin lists as examples of such rights the rights to life, to be free from torture and inhuman, degrading, or cruel treatment, to be free from slavery, to be free from arbitrary deprivation of liberty, and to be free from grave forms of discrimination. See Scheinin, 'How to Resolve Conflicts Between Individual and Collective Rights?' (n 177) 233–34.

insignificant, always take precedent over collective rights cardinal to the survival of indigenous peoples as collectives. This approach also has the added value that it allows indigenous peoples to take responsibility for their own cultures. Timo Makkonen notes that all cultures have at some point included elements of which they are less proud today. But peoples are not slaves to their cultures and histories. All peoples, including indigenous peoples, are likely to grind out dysfunctional cultural practices, if offered the opportunity.[180]

Consequently, international law has not accepted the argument that individual human rights always take precedent over collective human rights of indigenous peoples. Rather, under international law, the two sets of rights shall, as argued above, be balanced against one another. For instance, the HRC has held actions that otherwise could potentially amount to violations of individuals' rights pursuant to CCPR Article 27 to be permissible precisely because the actions served to protect the collective cultural identity of the group.[181] In other instances, the HRC has found that the interest of the group could not outweigh the interest of the individual.[182] In short, the Committee has sought to weigh rights of the indigenous people as such and those of the members of the group against one another. At the same time, the HRC has declared certain individual rights absolute, such as fundamental rights of women.[183] In the same vein, the CERD Committee has held that collective and individual rights must be balanced against one another, but that fundamental individual human rights must always be respected.[184] Similarly, ILO 169 Article 8.1 calls for respect for indigenous peoples' cultural practices, while Article 8.2 clarifies that respect for such practices should prevail only when compatible with *fundamental* individual human rights.[185] The UNDRIP takes the same approach to the potential conflict of rights.

180 See Timo Makkonen, 'Minorities' Rights to Maintain and Develop Their Cultures: Legal Implications of Social Science Research', in Francioni and Scheinin (eds.), *Cultural Human Rights* (n 25) 205. For a similar argument, see also Scheinin, 'How to Resolve Conflicts Between Individual and Collective Rights?, (n 177) 223–24. It should be added that at the same time as defending the primacy of individual human rights, Will Kymlicka concurs with this observation. He accepts, with reference to Speed and Collier, that it is hypocritical of a state to deny indigenous peoples self-governing rights that allow their cultural practices to evolve, at the same time as the state labels these practices barbaric. See Kymlicka, *Multicultural Odysseys* (n 10) 151–53.

181 *Kitok v Sweden* (n 43); *Apirana Mahuika v New Zealand* (n 47).

182 *Lovelace v Canada*, Comm No R.6/24, views adopted 30 July 1981.

183 See General Comment No 28: Equality of Rights between Men and Women (Article 3): 29.03.2000. CCPR/C/21/Rev1/Add10 5. See also Xanthaki, *Indigenous Rights and United Nations Standards* (n 9) 36; Alexis P Kontos, 'Aboriginal Self-Government in Canada: Reconciling Rights to Political Participation and Indigenous Cultural Integrity', in Castellino and Walsh (eds.), *International Law and Indigenous Peoples* (n 10) 211–15; S James Anaya, 'On Justifying Special Ethnic Group Rights: Comments on Pogge', in Ian Shapiro and Will Kymlicka (eds.), *Ethnicity and Group Rights* (New York University Press, 1997) 224–27; Scheinin, 'How to Resolve Conflicts Between Individual and Collective Rights?' (n 177) 232–33.

184 See CERD/C/62/CO/6; and also former CERD Committee member Patrick Thornberry, 'The Convention on the Elimination of Racial Discrimination' (n 10) 23–24.

185 Compare Michael Freeman, 'Are There Collective Human Rights?' [1995] *Political Studies*, XLIII.

In sum, international law does not support the argument that individual rights should always prevail in conflicts with the rights of indigenous peoples as such. It has taken a more flexible approach. Only fundamental individual rights automatically take precedent over collective rights.[186] In other instances, the collective and the individual right must be weighed against one another in instances of conflict.

[186] It might be worth adding that it is not new to the human rights system that rights must sometimes be balanced against one another. The human rights system does not form a perfect patch-work. Individual rights too sometimes contradict. When this occurs, individual human rights must be weighed against one another, on a case to case basis. There is nothing dramatic about undertaking the same exercise with regard to collective rights. For a concurring opinion, see Freeman, 'Are There Collective Human Rights?' (n 185) 29.

6
The Content and Scope of the Right to Self-Determination When Applied to Indigenous Peoples

6.1 The External Aspect of the Right to Self-Determination

As touched upon in the previous chapter, the right to self-determination has an internal and an external aspect. The latter aspect allows a people to freely determine its political status vis-à-vis other peoples. Sections 2.5.4 and 5.10.2 explain how the right to self-determination has hitherto most concretely, effectively, and visibly been applied in a decolonization context. With regard to territories geographically separated from the colonizing state, the external aspect of the right to self-determination has largely been applied in a manner that entails the aggregate population of a colony to determine whether it should secede and form a state, or, alternatively, seek other political arrangements with it. In the case of already existing states, the external aspect of the right to self-determination has conventionally been understood as a right of the entire population of the state to require that other states recognize its sovereignty, including its territorial integrity.

Clearly, the external aspect of the right to self-determination cannot manifest itself in the described manner when applied to indigenous peoples. Section 5.10.2 articulates how the principle of territorial integrity of states provides that the right to self-determination does not envelope a right of segments of a state to unilaterally secede from it, save in extreme circumstances. The fact that the right to self-determination now applies also to indigenous peoples does not impact on this fundamental principle in international law. Conequently, as a general rule, indigenous peoples must exercise their right to self-determination within existing state borders.

Secession is, however, not the only element embedded in the external aspect of the right to self-determination. A people's right to freely determine its political status vis-à-vis other peoples also entails a right of the people to represent itself in relation to other peoples. Hence, the external aspect of self-determination awards indigenous peoples a right to represent themselves on the international level, including at the United Nations (UN) and other international institutions. Section 5.7.7 gives a couple of examples as to how this right has been reflected in practice in UN standard setting processes and institutions.

6.2 Generally on the Internal Aspect of the Right to Self-Determination—A Mere Right of Indigenous Individuals to Participate in the Political Life of the State on Equal Footing with Other Citizens?

As seen, the internal aspect of the right to self-determination, as conventionally understood, entails a right of all citizens of the state—regardless of ethnic and cultural background—to participate in the political life of the state on an equal basis. Thus understood, the internal aspect, when applied to indigenous peoples, would imply a right of indigenous individuals to vote and run for election in state democratic processes, without discrimination. Recent developments within the indigenous rights regime, as outlined above, do, however, rule out such a narrow understanding of the internal aspect of the right to self-determination when applied to indigenous peoples.

Chapter 5 describes how, more or less since its inception, the indigenous rights discourse has focused on allowing indigenous peoples to preserve and develop their own distinct societies, to exist side-by-side with the majority society. Indigenous rights aim to advance autonomous functions of indigenous peoples' societies, rather than to integrate indigenous individuals into the majority society. Chapter 5 further elaborates how international legal sources on indigenous peoples' right to self-determination reflect this core feature of the indigenous rights regime. These sources envisage that indigenous peoples are to operationalize their right to self-determination through autonomous and self-governing arrangements within states.

For instance, when elaborating on the content and scope of the right to self-determination when applied to indigenous peoples, the UN Declaration on the Rights of Indigenous Peoples (UNDRIP) echoes international law's general approach towards indigenous peoples' rights. Following UNDRIP Article 3's general affirmation that indigenous peoples have the right to self-determination, Articles 4 and 5 proceed to articulate how the right should be implemented. Article 4 provides that '[i]ndigenous peoples, in exercising their right to self-determination, have the right to autonomy or self-government in matters relating to their internal and local affairs . . .'. Complementing Article 4, pursuant to Article 5, '[i]ndigenous peoples have the right to maintain and strengthen their distinct political, legal . . . and cultural institutions . . .'. The provision subsequently proceeds to clarify that indigenous peoples participate 'in the political . . . and cultural life of the state' only to the extent '. . . they so choose . . .'. Hence it follows explicitly from Articles 4 and 5 that the right to self-determination, when applied to indigenous peoples, is primarily exercised through their own decision-making institutions. Only as a secondary, optional, consideration, do indigenous peoples exercise their right to self-determination through their members' participation in the political life of the state. As mentioned, this understanding of indigenous peoples' right to self-determination is backed up by a multitude of other international legal sources.

In summary, indigenous peoples are beneficiaries of an internal aspect of the right to self-determination that goes beyond the conventional understanding of that aspect. Indigenous peoples are entitled to first and foremost exercise the right to self-determination through autonomy and self-government arrangements within the state. The following sections survey how far-reaching this right to autonomy and self-government might be.

6.3 Further on the Internal Aspect of Self-Determination

6.3.1 Introduction

This section aims to survey what is, more precisely, the content and scope of the autonomy and self-government arrangements that indigenous peoples are entitled to under international law, as examined above. This section first responds to claims that when applied to indigenous peoples, the internal aspect of the right to self-determination only embraces elements that are entirely internal to indigenous peoples. The section then proceeds to outline, as far as possible given the limited guidance offered by international legal sources at present, what is the content and scope of this right, when applied in an indigenous context.

6.3.2 Is the scope of the right to self-determination limited to affairs completely internal to an indigenous people?

To establish the more precise content and scope of the internal aspect of self-determination when applied to indigenous peoples is not an entirely easy task at this point. As indicated, international law-makers and legal scholars have, until relatively recently, focused on whether indigenous peoples qualify as legal subjects that are entitled to the right to self-determination. Understandably during the time-period when this issue was subject to debate, far less attention has been paid to the content and scope of the right when applied not to the aggregate population, but to a segment, of the state. Consequently, international legal sources offer limited guidance as to the content and scope of the internal aspect of the right to self-determination, when applied to indigenous peoples.[1] Nevertheless, certain conclusions may be drawn.

Although legal sources are scarce, following the adoption of the UNDRIP, there have been certain discussion as to what is the scope and content of the right to

[1] For a concurring opinion, see Helen Quane, 'The UN Declaration on the Rights of Indigenous Peoples: New Directions for Self-Determination and Participatory Rights?', in Stephen Allen and Alexandra Xanthaki (eds.), *Reflections on the UN Declaration on the Rights of Indigenous Peoples* (Hart Publishing, 2011) 260–61, 267, 275–77.

self-determination, when applied to indigenous peoples. In this discussion, some states have suggested that the right has a rather narrow scope. For instance, when the Special Rapporteur on the Rights of Indigenous Peoples gathered information for his report on the situation of the indigenous Sami people, the governments of Finland, Norway, and Sweden suggested that indigenous peoples enjoy a genuine right to self-determination only in affairs entirely internal to them. In other words, the assertion is that when applied to indigenous peoples, the internal aspect of the right to self-determination embraces only such affairs that are of no relevance whatsoever to the majority population or to the state as such. In all matters that are also relevant to society at large, irrespective of whether to a very insignificant degree, indigenous peoples lack genuine decision-making power, these states purported. In such affairs, the argument goes, indigenous peoples' right to self-determination is in fact a mere right to consultation. If consultation leads to no agreement, the position of the state always prevails. This position thus suggests that UNDRIP Article 4's reference to 'internal and local affairs' envelopes only a right to take part in decision-making processes. The assertion is that indigenous peoples never have a right to effectively impact on the material outcome of decision-making processes in instances when differences in opinion between the state and the indigenous people cannot be reconciled.

It might prove difficult, however, to substantiate the outlined position on the content and scope of the internal aspect of the right to self-determination, when applied to indigenous peoples. To suggest that the right applies only in cases of no conflict of interest would appears to constitute a contradiction in terms. And to posit that the right to self-determination only amounts to a right to consultation seems to confuse two different rights.

The suggestion that the right to self-determination, when applied to indigenous peoples, is only a genuine right to be self-determining in instances where there are no competing interests whatsoever reduces the applicability of the right to situations where the right lacks any effective meaning. If there is no conflict of interests, there is simply no situation to regulate. Under such circumstances, the indigenous people will simply organize matters its own way—irrespective of the right to self-determination or any other right. Therefore, it appears to be a contradiction in terms to claim that a genuine right to self-determination applies only in instances where there is no conflict of interest. A right can—by definition it would seem—exist only in a relationship between two or more legal subjects. Consequently, only in situations where there is divergence of opinion between the majority people and the indigenous people can the latter group's right to self-determination come into play. In such instances—and only in such instances—does the right to self-determination offer guidance as to how to settle the conflict. Consequently, to suggest that the right to self-determination applies only in situations where there is no conflict of interest appears to be akin to saying that the right does not exist at all. As Chapter 5 infers, such an understanding of the internal aspect of the right to self-determination must be ruled out.

The second line of the argument, i.e. that the internal aspect of the right to self-determination, when applied to indigenous peoples, is in fact a right to consultation, i.e. only a right to be involved in decision-making processes, but not to determine the outcome of such, can seemingly not be substantiated either. This position appears to contradict the law of treaties as well as reason.

Although there are certain overlaps in their respective contents, at their core the rights to self-determination and consultation differ fundamentally. That indigenous peoples have a right to be consulted in decision-making processes of relevance to them has been well established in international law for decades. The right to consultation is, for instance, a cornerstone of the International Labour Organization (ILO) Convention No 169 on Indigenous and Tribal Peoples in Independent Countries (ILO 169).[2] The right to consultation provides that indigenous peoples are allowed to *participate* in decision-making processes of relevance to them. The right does in no way ensure, however, that indigenous peoples can exercise genuine influence over the *material outcome* of the decision-making process. Indigenous peoples' right to consultation obliges states to seek, in good faith, indigenous peoples' consent before taking a decision that affects them. In other words, efforts must be made to reach consensus. But if no agreement is reached at the end of the day, the right to consultation is of no use to the indigenous people. The right to consultation always vests ultimate decision-making power with a party other than the indigenous people.

As indicated, the right to self-determination also includes participatory rights elements. As the right to consultation, it requires that indigenous peoples are allowed to be involved in decision-making processes of relevance to them. In that sense, the rights to self-determination and consultation overlap. Notwithstanding, the right to self-determination is, at its core, not a mere right to *participate* in decision-making processes. The central element of the right to self-determination is the right to *exercise genuine influence over the material outcome* of the decision-making process. In other words, while the right to consultation is a *right to a process* the right to self-determination is, although it also embeds process right elements, first and foremost a *material right*. In stark contrast to the right to consultation, which offers a process, but no consolation when the process fails, the right to self-determination can materially determine the outcome of a decision-making process in favour of indigenous peoples—also in absence of agreement.[3]

Section 5.10.2 explains how certain states feared that recognition of a right to self-determination of indigenous peoples could spur secession movements and aspirations. It further describes how this fear contributed to certain states being

[2] See in particular ILO 169 Article 6; S James Anaya, *Indigenous Peoples in International Law* (2nd edn., Oxford University Press, 2004) 153–54; Manuela Tomei and Lee Swepston, *Indigenous and Tribal Peoples: A Guide to ILO 169* 8. Also, as Chapter 5 explains, treaty bodies have repeatedly affirmed that indigenous peoples enjoy the right to consultation. Consequently, James Anaya, among others, infers that indigenous peoples' right to consultation forms part of international customary law. See Anaya, *Indigenous Peoples in International Law* (n 2) 155–56.

[3] For an elaboration of the differences between the rights to self-determination and consultation, see the UN Expert Mechanism on the Rights of Indigenous Peoples' (EMRIP) Expert Advice No 2 (2011): Indigenous Peoples and the Right to Participate in Decision-Making, paras. 2, 20, 21, 34.

hesitant to accept that indigenous peoples are indeed beneficiaries of that right. This in turn, was a main factor behind it taking almost a quarter of a century to complete the UNDRIP deliberations. That said, the articulated fundamental difference between the right to consultation, on one hand, and the right to self-determination, on the other, is probably the primary reason why states have only recently acknowledged that the latter right applies to indigenous peoples. This is a more understandable rationale from a legal perspective since, as Section 5.10.2 further explains, the fear of secession is from an international legal point of view unfounded, something that most states, although their rhetoric suggested otherwise, must surely have been aware of. More than with secession, states' hesitance with regard to UNDRIP Article 3 was presumably associated with having to share jurisdiction within the state with indigenous peoples.[4] As the above indicates and the below elaborates, concern over having to share jurisdiction with indigenous peoples makes much more sense from a legal perspective, since this aspect of the right to self-determination when applied to indigenous peoples does reshape the political map of states that host such peoples. This in itself argues against the notion that the right to self-determination enshrined in the UNDRIP amounts to nothing more than a right to consultation. It seems unlikely that states that participated in the UNDRIP negotiations would have found the right to self-determination contentious if it in fact means nothing more than a right that has been well-established in international law for twenty years, is well defined, uncontroversial, and ensures indigenous peoples no influence over the material outcome of decision-making processes. The reasonable conclusion, based on state behaviour, is rather that the content and scope of the right to self-determination enshrined in the UNDRIP goes beyond that of the right to consultation.[5]

That indigenous peoples' right to self-determination cannot be understood as a right to consultation also follows from the law of treaties. Section 4.4 outlines how the law of treaties provides that a provision in an international instrument shall, absent convincing evidence to the contrary, be given a meaning that follows from an ordinary understanding of its wording, in light of the instrument as a whole. As mentioned, pursuant to common Article 1 of the Covenants on Civil and Political Rights (CCPR) and Economic, Social and Cultural Rights (CESCR), respectively, and UNDRIP Article 3 '[[a]ll/[i]ndigenous] peoples have the right to self-determination'. A reasonable interpretation of this language can hardly result in a conclusion that the provisions set forth a right to consultation. The same is true for the wording '[i]ndigenous peoples, in exercising their right to self-determination, have the right to autonomy or self-government . . .' in UNDRIP Article 4. Had the intention been to reaffirm the already existing right to consultation, language to that effect would presumably have been opted for in UNDRIP Articles 3 and 4. The

[4] This conclusion finds further support in the fact that the inclusion of a reference to the principle of territorial integrity of states in UNDRIP Article 46.1 far from dispersed states' uneasiness with the UNDRIP Article 3 proclaiming right to self-determination of indigenous peoples.

[5] Although presenting a somewhat different line of argument, Helen Quane concurs that it is unlikely that indigenous peoples and states negotiated for more than two decades only to arrive at status quo. See Quane, 'The UN Declaration on the Rights of Indigenous Peoples' (n 1) 275–77.

ordinary understanding of UNDRIP Article 3, in particular if read in light of Articles 4 and 5, is clear. No evidence supports an interpretation other than that which follows from a normal understanding of the provisions' wording, understood in light of the Declaration as a whole; i.e. that indigenous peoples are entitled to a genuine right to self-determination, to be exercised through autonomy and self-government arrangements within existing state borders.[6]

As indicated, the conclusion that the internal aspect of the right to self-determination, when applied to indigenous peoples, is a right that should be exercised primarily through autonomy and self-government arrangements also finds support in other legal sources as well as in the legal doctrine. Recall how James Anaya underscores that self-governance is the key feature of indigenous peoples' right to self-determination, and that this right should be implemented through their own political institutions within existing states.[7] Recall further Will Kymlicka's submission that a right to self-determination of indigenous peoples fundamentally reshapes the understanding of state sovereignty, since autonomy and self-government arrangements of indigenous peoples do include genuine transfer of power, or jurisdiction if one wants, from state institutions to indigenous peoples' decision-making bodies.[8] As explained above, a 'right to self-determination' that is understood to amount to nothing more than a right to be consulted would not transfer any power.

In sum, the suggestion that the internal aspect of the right to self-determination, when applied to indigenous peoples, is only a genuine right to self-determination in affairs without any relevance to the majority people and/or the state, appears to be difficult to substantiate. Neither can one convincingly argue that the right

[6] This conclusion finds further support in the safeguard clause in UNDRIP Article 46.1. If UNDRIP Article 3 were to be understood to proclaim a right to consultation, there would have been no need to even discuss a provision that calls for respect for the principle of territorial integrity of states, since there is no link between this principle and the right to consultation.

[7] See Anaya, *Indigenous Peoples in International Law* (n 2) 150–53; Anaya, 'The Capacity of International Law to Advance Ethnic or Nationality Rights Claims', in Will Kymlicka (ed.), *The Rights of Minority Cultures* (Oxford University Press, 1995) 325–26. For similar opinions see also Martin Scheinin, 'Indigenous Peoples' Rights under the International Covenant on Civil and Political Rights', in Joshua Castellino and Niamh Walsh (eds.), *International Law and Indigenous Peoples* (Martinus Nijhoff Publisher, 2005) 9–15; Martin Scheinin, 'How to Resolve Conflicts Between Individual and Collective Rights?', in Martin Scheinin and Reeta Toivanen (eds.), *Rethinking Non-Discrimination and Minority Rights* (Institute for Human Rights, Åbo Academy University, 2004) 236–37; Alexandra Xanthaki, 'Indigenous Rights in International Law over the Last 10 Years and Future Developments' [2009] *Melbourne Journal of International Law* 10 (1); Marc Weller, 'Towards a General Comment on Self-Determination and Autonomy: Working Paper submitted to the Sub-Commission on the Protection and Promotion of Human Rights', Working Group on Minorities, UN Document E/CN4/Sub2/AC5/2005/WP5 12, 16; Marc Weller, 'Settling Self-Determination Conflicts: Recent Developments' [2009] *European Journal of International Law*, Vol 20, No 1; Siegfried Wiessner, 'Indigenous Sovereignty: A Reassessment in Light of the UN Declaration on the Rights of Indigenous Peoples' [2008] *Vanderbilt Journal of Transnational Law* 41 1156; Mauro Barelli, 'The Role of Soft Law in the International Legal System: The Case of the United Nations Declaration on the Rights of Indigenous Peoples' [2009] *International and Comparative Law Quarterly*, Vol 58 961. For a possible dissent, see, however, Quane, 'The UN Declaration on the Rights of Indigenous Peoples' (n 1) 271.

[8] Will Kymlicka, *Multicultural Odysseys—Navigating the New International Politics of Diversity* (Oxford University Press, 2007) 3–5; Will Kymlicka, 'American Multiculturalism and the "Nations Within"', in Duncan Ivison, Paul Patton, and Will Sanders (eds.), *Political Theory and the Rights of Indigenous Peoples* (Cambridge University Press, 2000) 225–27.

amounts to a mere right to consultation. Rather, also when applied to indigenous peoples, the right to self-determination must be understood as a genuine material right in instances where an indigenous people's interests conflict with those of society at large. It cannot be a mere right to a process. In other words, the core element of the internal aspect of the right to self-determination is not a right to participate in decision-making processes, but to effectively determine the material outcome of such. That said, the right is obviously not absolute either. When applied to indigenous peoples, the right to self-determination must be accustomed to the fact that it applies to segments, and not to entire populations, of states. Indigenous peoples' right to self-determination must be reconciled with the right to self-determination that applies to peoples in the meaning aggregate populations of states.

This seems to lead to the conclusion that in instances when good faith consultations between states and indigenous peoples fail to produce consensus, the right to self-determination provides that the position of the indigenous people prevails over that of the majority people/the state in certain, but far from all, instances. This conclusion also reflects the general understanding of autonomy in the legal doctrine. For instance, Hurst Hannum and Richard Lillich posit that autonomy amounts to 'independence of action on the internal or domestic level'. But autonomy need not mean unlimited jurisdiction. There is room for cooperative arrangements between the central government of the state and the autonomous people on issues of joint interest.[9] Still, it is inherent in the concept of autonomy that the autonomous people enjoy considerable decision-making powers, albeit within the framework of the state.[10] In affairs concerning both the indigenous people and the majority people, international law calls for shared jurisdiction between the two peoples.[11] What remains, then, to survey is what this general feature of the internal aspect of the right to self-determination implies for the more precise scope and content of the right, when applied to indigenous peoples.

6.3.3 A proposed principle for establishing the content and scope of the internal aspect of the right to self-determination when applied to indigenous peoples—the sliding scale

The above establishes that indigenous peoples shall first and foremost exercise the internal aspect of the right to self-determination through autonomy and self-government arrangements within existing state borders. In contrast to the right to consultation, which is a right to a process only, the right to self-determination is primarily a material right. It is a right that allows indigenous peoples to exercise

9 Hurst Hannum and Richard B Lillich, 'The Concept of Autonomy in International Law' [1980] *American Journal of International Law*, Vol 74, No 4 858–61 (quote from p 860).

10 Weller, 'Towards a General Comment on Self-Determination and Autonomy' (n 7) 5–6.

11 See James Tully, 'The Struggles of Indigenous Peoples for and of Freedom', in Duncan Ivison, Paul Patton, and Will Sanders (eds.), *Political Theory and the Rights of Indigenous Peoples* (Cambridge University Press, 2000) 53. For similar, although somewhat more cautious, conclusions, see the Special Rapporteur on the Rights of Indigenous Peoples Report on the situation of the Sami people in the Sápmi region of Norway, Sweden and Finland (A/HRC/18/35/Add.2), 76; and Quane, 'The UN Declaration on the Rights of Indigenous Peoples' (n 1) 275–77.

genuine influence over the material outcome of decision-making processes. This is far from saying, however, that in all instances where an indigenous people and a majority people disagree, the will of the indigenous people prevail. Rather, indigenous peoples must exercise the right to self-determination with respect for, and their will must therefore sometimes yield to, the right to self-determination enjoyed by peoples in the meaning aggregate populations of states.

This is essentially the guidance existing international legal sources provide us with as to the content and scope of the internal aspect of the right to self-determination, when applied to indigenous peoples. As mentioned, until relatively recently, the indigenous rights discourse focused on whether indigenous peoples are at all beneficiaries of the right to self-determination. Only now have discussions on what is implied in this right commenced in earnest. As a consequence, at present international legal sources that address the more precise scope and content of the internal aspect of the right to self-determination when applied to indigenous peoples are scarce, in fact almost non-existing. Notwithstanding, perhaps the formula suggested below can be argued for.

Arguably, it may make sense to think in terms of a 'sliding scale' when considering whose will should prevail in instances of insoluble differences in opinion between an indigenous people and the majority people/the state. As a strong candidate for a criterion to settle such conflicts one could put forward the relative importance of the issue to the respective people. It perhaps make sense to posit that the more important the issue to the indigenous people's culture, society, and way of life, the greater influence the people should be allowed to exercise over the decision-making process. Conversely, if the matter is of little significance to the indigenous people, but important to the welfare of society at large, indigenous peoples' right to self-determination may only award the indigenous people with limited influence over the decision-making process. Obviously, there are also matters in between.[12] The proposed formula can be illustrated with a few examples.

Decisions on school curricula for their children are normally of significant importance to indigenous peoples. In order for indigenous societies to survive and develop, it is crucial that the children are educated in an environment accustomed to their particular culture. Indigenous peoples themselves are in the best position to take informed decisions as to how school curricula should be designed to suit the cultural background of their children. Conversely, the majority population and the state should have a limited interest in overruling indigenous peoples' aspirations in this regard (lest the state is engaged in nationalist practices). True, states will normally want to ensure that indigenous children acquire a basic knowledge in fundamental subjects such as math, the majority language, and natural and social sciences. But beyond that, states should reasonably have no legitimate issue with indigenous childrens' school curricula being accustomed to their cultural background. Consequently, perhaps one can make a strong argument for—in cases of conflict between the will of an indigenous people and the state on school curricula

[12] In its Expert Advice No 2 (2011), The Expert Mechanism on the Rights of Indigenous Peoples (EMRIP) envisions a similar model for determining the scope and content of indigenous peoples' right to self-determination. See in particular para. 22.

for children that belong to the indigenous group—that the will of the indigenous people should be allowed to prevail.

At the opposite end of the sliding scale, one may find decisions on issues with little or even marginal impact on indigenous peoples' traditional societies, even if also such matters might be of relevance to certain indigenous individuals. It is difficult to argue that indigenous peoples' right to self-determination should award them a decisive say in such affairs. For instance, unemployment should normally have no greater impact on indigenous persons compared to persons belonging to the majority population. Therefore, measures to combat unemployment are presumably best designed by decision-making bodies representing the entire population of the state.

In between the two polar examples, but probably closer to the employment policy example, one can probably place decisions pertaining to formulation of health care services. It makes sense that the state has the right to decide on the general design of such services. At the same time, it is important, both out of respect for the cultural identity of the individual, and for adequate health care being provided to her or him, that the cultural and genetic background of indigenous patients be taken into consideration. Against this background, one may argue that this motivates that indigenous peoples are provided with the opportunity to determine over measures to be taken that aim to ensure that culturally (and genetically) appropriate health care is provided to members of their respective groups.

Finally, it is pertinent to add a few words on how the envisioned sliding scale could possibly materialize itself in the context of the resource dimension, which is a core element of the right to self-determination, not least for indigenous peoples. Here, it makes sense to distinguish between lands and natural resources traditionally used by indigenous peoples, on the one hand, and natural resources situated on, or perhaps more often under, indigenous peoples' territories, but which the people in question have not used historically, on the other.

With regard to the former category of lands and resources, if accepting the sliding scale argument, indigenous peoples' decision-making power must reasonably be relatively extensive. As emphasized throughout this book, from the very outset the indigenous rights discourse has recognized that indigenous peoples' societies, cultures, and ways of life are intrinsically rooted in lands and natural resources traditionally used. Traditional livelihoods and other culturally-based land uses constitute the basis of indigenous societies and cultures, without which they cannot exist. The above infers that even when applied to indigenous peoples, the right to self-determination is a genuine material right. This leads to the conclusion that in some (but far from all) instances, an indigenous people's position must be allowed to prevail in case of an insoluble conflict of interest with the majority population/the state. The above further suggests that this right is presumably most far-reaching in affairs of fundamental importance to indigenous peoples. To the extent that these conclusions are correct, as a general rule, indigenous peoples should reasonably have far-reaching decision-making power in affairs that impact on their traditional lands, livelihoods and other forms of culturally-based land uses. This conclusion finds support in UNDRIP Article 32.2, which provides that '[s]tates shall . . . obtain [indigenous peoples'] free and informed consent prior to the approval of any project affecting their lands and territories and other resources, particularly in connection with the development, utilization or exploitation of mineral, water or other resources.'

The relevance of the argument above is not limited to decisions with a direct impact on indigenous peoples' territories and/or livelihoods. Again, if accepting the sliding scale argument, indigenous peoples must in addition reasonably be allowed to exercise considerable influence over decisions that are not explicitly directed at their lands, natural resources, or livelihoods, but that nonetheless have the capacity to result in negative impacts on such lands and livelihoods. One example of such decisions might be policies for resource extraction in indigenous territories that compete with, and often negatively impact on, indigenous peoples' traditional land uses.

As to natural resources situated on or under territories traditionally used by indigenous peoples, but which have not been used by them historically, indigenous peoples reasonably possess less decision-making power. As these resources do not form part of, and hence are assumingly not of vital importance to, indigenous peoples' societies and cultures, it is difficult to argue that indigenous peoples should have a decisive say over such resources. It makes more sense that such natural resources are, at least as a starting point, managed by institutions that represent the entire population of the state. That is particularly so in instances when the natural resource is of great interest to the welfare of society at large, which is often the case with regard to resources such as oil, gas, and minerals. That said, these resources have not conventionally formed part of the majority population's society either. And they are situated on or under the indigenous, and not the majority, people's traditional territory. The argument can therefore be made that indigenous peoples should be entitled to some form of co-management role with regard to non-traditional natural resources, as well as to a share in the proceeds the extraction of such resources generates. Moreover, to the extent such resource extraction negatively impacts on indigenous peoples' traditional livelihoods, and other culturally-based land uses, their right to influence the decision-making process should increase substantially in line with what the above outlines.

Having thus articulated the 'sliding scale argument', it bears repeating that this is only a proposal by the author. As mentioned, at present few international legal sources exist that offer support for any conclusions as to the more precise scope and content of the right to self-determination when applied to indigenous peoples. At this point, the only conclusion one can draw for sure is that this is a right to be exercised though autonomy and self-government arrangements within existing states that goes beyond a mere right to be consulted. The internal aspect of indigenous peoples' right to self-determination awards them with a right to exercise genuine influence over the material outcome of decision-making processes of relevance to them, sometimes at the expense of the will of the majority people and the state.[13]

[13] Some might argue that UNDRIP Articles 46.2 and 46.3 suggest a more restrictive understanding of the scope and content of indigenous peoples' right to self-determination than the one that has been presented here. Pursuant to UNDRIP Article 46.2, in implementing the Declaration, 'human

6.3.4 Territorial *and* cultural autonomy

Chapter 5 describes how an intrinsic link to a fairly identifiable traditional territory is the characteristic that most clearly distinguishes indigenous peoples from minority groups. The more precise design of the various indigenous peoples' autonomy and self-government arrangements will necessarily differ somewhat, depending on regional and national, cultural, geographical, and legal contexts. Still, given that all indigenous peoples—by definition—maintain an intrinsic connection to their traditional territories, their autonomy arrangements will always have a territorial base.

At the same time, relevant international legal sources suggest that indigenous peoples' autonomy and self-government arrangements need not be purely territorial. Rather, indigenous peoples' right to self-determination must presumably also often embrace an element of cultural (non-territorial) autonomy, i.e. an autonomy that applies to all members of the people, irrespective of their physical residence. This element of indigenous peoples' autonomy and self-government arrangements thus applies beyond the borders of their traditional territory.[14] A right of an indigenous people to decide over or at least influence the school curricula also with regard to children that belong to the people, but that reside outside the peoples' traditional territory, can be mentioned as one example of the exercise of cultural autonomy.

rights of . . . all should be respected' and the rights the UNDRIP sets forth may be subject to limitations that are 'non-discriminatory and strictly necessary . . . for the purpose of securing due . . . respect for the rights . . . of others . . . and for meeting the just and most compelling requirements of a democratic society'. UNDRIP Article 46.3, on its part, proclaims that UNDRIP shall be 'interpreted in accordance with the principles of justice, democracy, respect for human rights, equality, non-discrimination, good governance and good faith'. Hence, pursuant to UNDRIP Article 46.2, the right to self-determination must only be limited for the purposes of (i) securing rights of others, and (ii) meeting compelling needs for society at large. As to the first qualifier, recognition of a right to self-determination of indigenous peoples does not per se infringe on rights of others. True, the exercise of this right may to some extent limit human rights of individuals, including of individual members of the indigenous people, as Section 5.11 explains. However, as Section 5.11 further infers, international law has accepted that individual and collective rights must sometimes be weighed against one another. Thus, the outlined understanding of the right to self-determination does not violate rights of individuals. Neither does it fail to respect compelling needs of society as a whole. As seen, indigenous peoples' right to self-determination must be balanced against the right to self-determination of peoples in the meaning aggregate populations of states. As to UNDRIP Article 46.3, the described content and scope of the right to self-determination meet all the criteria listed in this provision. True, one can discuss how a right to self-determination of indigenous peoples conforms to the criteria 'democracy', 'equality', and 'non-discrimination', *as these concepts were understood under the Westphalian international legal system.* But when international law has evolved to recognize that there can exist more than one polity within a state, the right to self-determination actually advances, rather than threatens, democratic governance. Similarly, in an international legal system that does not equate equality with conformity, a right to self-determination of indigenous peoples promotes equality as well. Regarding the evolved understanding of equality, see Chapter 7.

[14] See Marc Weller, 'Towards a General Comment on Self-Determination and Autonomy: Working Paper Submitted to the Sub-Commission on the Protection and Promotion of Human Rights', Working Group on Minorities, UN Document E/CN4/Sub2/AC5/2005/WP5 5–7. Weller distinguishes between cultural (non-territorial) and territorial autonomy, where cultural autonomy awards the autonomous people the right to foster the preservation and further development of its cultural identity. Territorial autonomy, on the other hand, as the title suggests, refers to autonomy within a distinct territorial area within the state.

6.3.5 The closing of a circle

As a final note, it is interesting to compare the contemporary understanding of the content and scope of the right to self-determination, when applied to indigenous peoples, with the Commission of Jurists' conclusions in *Åland Islands*.[15] Recall how the Commission emphasized the relationship between the principle of self-determination and rights of ethnic groups. It noted that when secession is not an option, ethnic groups' right to preserve their cultural characteristics should be implemented through extensive amounts of autonomy within states. The Commission of Jurists' position in *Åland Islands* differs from the conclusions in this chapter and Chapter 5 in that the Commission did not award the *Ålanders* a right to self-determination (as this right did not form part of international law at the time). But irrespective of the formal labelling of the rights, the content and scope of the *Ålanders* right to autonomy as identified by the Commission is strikingly similar to the content and scope of indigenous peoples' right to self-determination under contemporary international law, as presented above. Thus, almost a century after *Åland Islands* was decided, international law has closed the circle. It again acknowledges autonomy and self-government rights of ethnic and cultural groups, at least in the context of indigenous peoples.

6.4 On the Definition of 'Indigenous Peoples'

International law does not formally define 'indigenous peoples'. In one sense, this is only natural, since indigenous peoples have only recently emerged as international legal subjects. When indigenous peoples could not hold rights under international law there was, from a legal perspective, less of a need to define what groups qualify as such peoples (although already at that time indigenous individuals of course derived their individual rights from membership of the group). The situation changes when international law embraces indigenous peoples as legal subjects. Then it is necessary to define what groups can claim rights as indigenous peoples. One can therefore perhaps expect a formal legal definition of indigenous peoples to emerge relatively soon, despite the practical difficulties associated with such an endavour. If states are to recognize, concretize, and realize indigenous peoples' rights, including the right to self-determination, reasonably they need a clear understanding of what groups are beneficiaries of such rights.

When articulating a formal definition of 'indigenous peoples', one need not look far for guidance. As indicated, although no formal definition exists, there is a general understanding of what groups constitute indigenous peoples for international legal purposes. In line with this general understanding, various working-definitions collaborate to paint a relatively clear picture of what groups qualify as indigenous peoples. The working definitions differ in their details, but are coherent in their core elements. The surely most relied upon working-definition is also the original

[15] See Section 2.4.1.

one—the so called Cobo-definition, introduced by then UN Special Rapporteur Martinez Cobo in the report that lay the foundation for the contemporary indigenous rights regime.[16] Special Rapporteur Cobo's definition of indigenous peoples reads as follows:

Indigenous communities, peoples and nations are those which, having a historical continuity with pre-invasion and pre-colonial societies that developed on their territories, consider themselves distinct from other sectors of the societies now prevailing in those territories, or parts of them. They form at present non-dominant sectors of society and are determined to preserve, develop and transmit to future generations existence as peoples, in accordance with their own cultural patterns, social institutions and legal systems.

The historical continuity may consist of the continuation, for an extended period reaching into the present, of one or more of the following factors:

(a) Occupation of ancestral lands, or at least of part of them;
(b) Common ancestry with the original occupants of these lands;
(c) Culture in general, or in specific manifestations (such as religion, living under a tribal system, membership of an indigenous community, dress, means of livelihood, life-style, etc);
(d) Language (whether used as the only language, as mother-tongue, as the habitual means of communication at home or in the family, or as the main, preferred, habitual, general or normal language);
(e) Residence in certain parts of the country, or in certain regions of the world;

Other relevant factors. [17]

If one summarizes, according to the Cobo-definition an 'indigenous people' is a population (i) that had established itself in a fairly definable territory prior to invasion and/or colonization, (ii) that continues to have a firm attachment to that territory, (iii) that self-identifies as a people and consider its own society distinct from that of the majority society, and (iv) have distinct common cultural characteristics such as common language, traditional livelihoods, and belief system. Other working definitions of indigenous peoples include those adopted by Food and Agriculture Organization (FAO)[18] and the World Bank.[19] In addition, it can be mentioned that on a regional level, the African Commission on Human and Peoples' Rights (AfCommHPR) has sought to outline the key characteristics which identifies the indigenous peoples of Africa.[20] ILO 169, Article 1.1–1.3 also defines what groups qualify as indigenous and tribal peoples for the purposes of that particular convention. The issue of a definition of indigenous peoples was contentious in the deliberations on the UNDRIP, which in the end came to include no such definition. Instead, as a compromise solution, the Declaration's preambular paragraph 23 merely states that the situation of indigenous peoples vary from region to region and from country to country.

As indicated, the definitions referred to above largely repeat the core elements of the Cobo-definition. In summary, international law thus has a clear understanding

[16] See Section 5.3.
[17] UN Doc E/CN4/Sub2/1986/7 and Add 1–4 379–82.
[18] FAO Policy on Indigenous and Tribal Peoples (2010) 4.
[19] The World Bank Operational Manual, Operational Policy (OP) 4.10, Indigenous Peoples.
[20] *Indigenous Peoples in Africa: The Forgotten Peoples?—The African Commissions Work on Indigenous Peoples in Africa* (2006) 9–10, 13.

of what populations qualify as indigenous peoples. As touched upon, of the elements that define indigenous peoples, the presence of a distinct society that exists parallel to the majority society and an intrinsic connection to a fairly definable territory are clearly at the core. As Sections 5.3 and 5.4 points to, these are also the elements that distinguish indigenous peoples from minority groups.[21]

A final observation in context of the definition of indigenous peoples may be pertinent. Irrespective of that, as the above has addressed thoroughly, with the exception of indigenous peoples, international law at present only recognizes peoples in the meaning aggregate populations of states (or territories), some attempts have been made to define non-state forming 'peoples' more generally. Rather naturally, these working definitions do not deviate significantly from those of indigenous peoples. Of the working definitions of 'peoples' understood in terms of common ethnicity/culture, the 'Kirby-definition' is probably the best known.[22] The Kirby-definition is strikingly similar to the working-definitions of indigenous peoples. It too focuses on common cultural characteristics and adds a connection to an identifiable territory.[23] The similarity between the working definitions of 'peoples' and 'indigenous peoples' underlines both indigenous peoples' legal status under international law and their distinction from minorities.

[21] International law does not define minorities either. The UN Sub-Commission on Prevention of Discrimination and Protection of Minorities suggested that minorities should be defined as '[a] group of citizens of a State, constituting a numerical minority and in non-dominant position in that State, endowed with ethnic, religious or linguistic characteristics which differ from those of the majority of the population, having a sense of solidarity with one another . . .'. See UN Doc E/CN4/Sub2/1985/31 & Corr 1 (1985). The definition was never adopted, but nonetheless underscores the difference between minority groups and indigenous peoples.

[22] For instance, the United Nations Economic, Social and Cultural Organization (UNESCO) endorses the Kirby-definition. See UNESCO International Meeting of Experts on Further Study of the Concept of the Rights of Peoples, UNESCO HQ, Paris, November 27–30, 1989.

[23] Other working definitions of peoples include the same basic elements as the Kirby-definition. See e.g. a more recent UN study, UN ESCOR, 137 UN doc E/CN4/Sub2/404 (vol 1).

PART III

THE RIGHT TO EQUALITY AND RIGHTS OVER LANDS AND NATURAL RESOURCES TRADITIONALLY USED

7
The Right to Equality

7.1 Introduction

The previous part demonstrates how indigenous peoples having been recognized as peoples for international legal purposes can be described as nothing less than a paradigm shift in international law. Having examined the international legal status of indigenous peoples and the principal peoples' right, that of self-determination, this book now turns its attention to a second paradigm shift within the indigenous rights discourse. This chapter surveys how the right to equality has evolved to take on a second facet. This development is of critical importance for the present purposes for three reasons. First, it confirms the development in international law towards recognition of group rights, as presented in Chapter 5. Second, it forms the basis for essentially all human rights that indigenous individuals possess. Third, and arguably most significantly, the expanded understanding of equality underpins recent developments towards recognition of indigenous communities' property right over lands and natural resources traditionally used (set out further in Chapters 8 and 9).

7.2 The Right to Equality in International Legal Instruments

The right to equality is one of the most central rights in the contemporary human rights system. It was 'incorporated' into contemporary international law already through its inclusion in the Universal Declaration on Human Rights (UDHR). UDHR Article 2 proclaims that '[e]veryone is entitled to all the rights and freedoms set forth in this Declaration, without distinction of any kind, such as race...'. Further, pursuant to Article 7, '[a]ll are equal before the law and are entitled without any discrimination to equal protection of the law.' A number of subsequently adopted human rights treaties also incorporate the right to equality, including the International Covenant on Civil and Political Rights (CCPR) (Articles 2.2 and 26) and the International Covenant on Economic, Social and Cultural Rights (CESCR) (Article 2.2).

In addition, an entire human rights treaty—the Convention on the Elimination of Racial Discrimination (CERD Convention)—is devoted to the right to equality, thereby underscoring the centrality of the right. Pursuant to CERD Article 1.1 '... the term "racial discrimination" shall mean any distinction, exclusion, restriction or preference based on race . . . or ethnic origin which has the purpose or effect of nullifying or impairing the recognition, enjoyment or exercise, on an equal footing, of human rights and fundamental freedoms . . .'. Article 5 elaborates on this general definition of discrimination by explicitly listing a number of rights which all are entitled to, without distinction as to e.g. race and ethnic origin. Articles 1.4, 2, 4, 6, and 7 outline measures that states are expected to take to combat discrimination. Of these, Articles 1.4 and 2 are of particular relevance for the present purposes, as these provisions instruct states how to address minority groups in the context of discrimination.

7.3 The Conventional Understanding of the Right to Non-Discrimination—The Requirement that Equal Cases Be Treated Equally

In line with the individual liberal tradition, as conventionally understood, the right to equality was geared towards individuals only. At the time when the right was incorporated into the human rights system, 'special' rights for particular segments of society were perceived as inherently discriminatory. International law of the era obligated states to disregard the fact that its population was not culturally and/or ethnically homogenous when designing their laws and policies. It was sufficient, indeed expected, that the state provided one educational system, one set of health care service etc. The only requirement placed on states by the right to equality, as understood at the time, was that all citizens, irrespective of ethnic and cultural background, had equal access to such services. In short, the right to non-discrimination required, and only required, that equal cases be treated equally. This understanding of equality can be illustrated with the following example. It is equality if all children in a country—regardless of their cultural and/or ethnic background—have the same right to access an educational system that provides education in and on the majority language and that is also otherwise accustomed to the majority culture.

True, the CERD Convention incorporates a couple of provisions that may be understood to suggest that already the drafters of the Convention envisaged special measures aiming at protecting and promoting minority cultures. Pursuant to Article 2.1 (a), states must not engage in actions that discriminate racial groups. Further, Article 2.2 proclaims that states shall, when circumstances so warrant, take special measures to ensure the protection not only of individuals belonging to a minority group, but also of the racial group as such. At first glance, these provisions may give the impression that the CERD Convention prohibits discrimination not only of individuals, but also of groups. However, Article 2.2 proceeds to underline that special measures must not result in maintenance of separate rights of the group. In the same vein, pursuant to Article 1.4, special measures taken must not result in lasting group rights. Thus, at the time of its adoption, the CERD Convention did not extend any protection to minority cultures.[1] Indeed, the Convention explicitly prohibited the use of special measures to protect and promote the cultural distinctiveness of members of minority groups.[2] At the time, the CERD Convention only allowed special measures that aimed at bringing members of minority cultures up to the same level as the majority population. In other words, the special measures that the drafters of the CERD Convention foresaw should have the purpose of integrating members of minority groups into the majority society. Measures that aspired to preserve such individuals' cultural distinctiveness were not allowed and neither were, obviously, measures aiming at protecting the group as such. As former member of the UN Committee on the Elimination of Racial Discrimination (CERD Committee) Patrick Thornberry observes, at the time of its adoption, the CERD Convention was 'dedicated to eliminating discrimination [as conventionally understood] rather than positively recognizing diversity'.[3] Similarly, Timo Makkonen notes that the CERD Convention was a child of its time. For instance, it does not envelope any explicit references to cultural rights, and did not foresee any such rights with a collective or even collectivized nature.[4] This fact is underscored by the wording of CERD Convention, Article 2. The provision only speaks of state's obligations vis-à-vis groups, thereby deliberately avoiding any reference to rights of the latter. Moreover, the core material provision of the CERD Convention, Article 5, only speaks of 'everyone's' right to non-discrimination, indicating its intended applicability to individuals only.

The outlined conventional understanding of the right to equality corresponds well to the traditional interpretation of the right to culture as enshrined in CCPR Article 27. At the time of the adoption of the CERD Convention and the International Convention on Civil and Political Rights (CCPR), both rights were perceived to benefit individuals only, and further expected states to remain neutral between cultures and abstain from positively promoting cultural diversity. As seen, the wording of CCPR Article 27 suggest that the provision only sets forth a negative right, calling on states not to interfere with individuals' cultural practices. Similarly, under the CERD Convention, only such special measures were accepted that aimed to bring members of minority groups up to the same level of development as the majority population, thereby integrating the minority culture into the majority culture. No measures aspiring to support minority cultures' efforts to continuously

[1] See Sandra Fredman, 'Combating Racism with Human Rights: The Right to Equality', in Sandra Fredman (ed.), *Discrimination and Human Rights: The Case of Racism* (Oxford University Press, 2001) 23; Patrick Thornberry, 'The Convention on the Elimination of Racial Discrimination, Indigenous Peoples and Caste/Decent-based Discrimination', in Joshua Castellino and Niamh Walsh (eds.), *International Law and Indigenous Peoples* (Martinus Nijhoff Publisher, 2005) 18; Nathan Lerner, *Group Rights and Discrimination in International Law* (2nd edn., Martinus Nijhoff Publishers, 2003) 57; compare Antonio Cassese, *Self-Determination of Peoples: A Legal Reappraisal* (Cambridge University Press, 1995) 329.

[2] Patrick Thornberry, '*International Law and the Rights of Minorities* (Oxford University Press, 1993) 266–68; Timo Makkonen, *Equal in Law, Unequal in Fact: Racial and Ethnic Discrimination and the Legal Response thereto in Europe* (Doctoral Dissertation Presented at the Faculty of Law at the University of Helsinki) 5 March 2010 95.

[3] Thornberry, 'The Convention on the Elimination of Racial Discrimination' (n 1) 18.

[4] Makkonen, *Equal in Law, Unequal in Fact* (n 2) 92.

thrive and develop were envisaged.[5] Indeed, at the time, such measures were deemed inherently discriminatory.

7.4 The Contemporary Understanding of the Right to Equality—Different Cases Be Treated Differently

As understood at the time of their adoption, the right to equality enshrined in the CERD Convention, CCPR, and CESCR was clearly of limited relevance to indigenous peoples. But as Section 4.4 explains, understandings of treaties need not be static. In particular human rights treaties have a capacity to evolve to take on new understandings. Indeed, such treaties are expected to respond to new conceptions of justice. Further, Chapter 5 outlines how, subsequent to the adoption of the CERD Convention, international law came to embrace a minority rights system that calls on states to actively promote and protect the cultural identity of members of minority groups. In addition, we saw how this protection of the cultural identity of individuals also extended an, albeit indirect, protection to the cultural identity of the group as such. This development occured particularly through the UN Human Rights Committee's (HRC) application of CCPR Article 27 to indigenous peoples. During roughly the same time-period, the understanding of the right to equality came to evolve in a corresponding manner.

In tandem with its progressive interpretation of the right to culture as enshrined in CCPR Article 27, the HRC contributed to an evolved understanding of the equality provisions in the Convention as well. In 2004, the Committee opined that CCPR Article 26 embraces a positive duty on states to prevent discrimination.[6] The HRC has subsequently applied and elaborated on this understanding of equality, thereby confirming that CCPR Article 26 encourages states to take relatively far-reaching positive measures to prevent discrimination.[7] The HRC has since repeatedly held that the right to equality need not mean identical treatment of persons with different cultural backgrounds in every instance. The Committee has stressed that differential treatment does not amount to discrimination as long as the criteria for differentiation are reasonable and objective.[8] In other words, the HRC has not gone as far as to call for differential treatment. It has, however, legitimized such action. In a similar vein, the UN Committee on Economic, Social and Cultural Rights (CESC) has inferred that combating discrimination requires paying sufficient attention to systemic discrimination of groups of individuals which suffer

[5] Will Kymlicka concurs that the right enshrined in CCPR 27, as understood at the time of its adoption, essentially equalled the conventional understanding of the right to equality. See Kymlicka, *Multicultural Odysseys—Navigating the New International Politics of Diversity* (Oxford University Press, 2007) 34–35.

[6] General Comment No 31: Nature of the General Legal Obligation Imposed on States Parties to the Covenant: 26.05.2004 CCPR/C/21/Rev1/Add13 8.

[7] *Jacobs v Belgium*, Comm No 943/2000, views adopted on 7 July 2004.

[8] General Comment No 18: Non-Discrimination, UN Doc HRI/GEN1/Rev 1 9–13; *Süsser v Czech Republic*, Comm No 1488/2006, views adopted 25 March 2008; *X v Colombia*, Comm No 1361/2005, views adopted on 30 March 2007.

from historic and persistent discrimination. Further, according to CESC, pursuant to CESCR Article 2.2, states are obligated to take special measures to halt such forms of discrimination when warranted.[9]

In a manner corresponding to the practices of its sister treaty bodies, the CERD Committee has progressively interpreted the right to equality set forth in the CERD Convention. The Committee has underlined that the Convention is a living instrument that must be interpreted in light of evolved understandings of justice.[10] The way in which the CERD Committee has gradually developed its understanding of equality, as articulated below, should be understood against the backdrop of this general principle.

As an initial step, the CERD Committee—as HRC and CESC—observed that differential treatment need not amount to discrimination provided that the criteria for differentiation are legitimate.[11] The Committee then inferred that the CERD Convention Article 2.2 embraces an obligation on states to take affirmative action to prevent discrimination of members of vulnerable groups when the circumstances so warrant.[12] In General Recommendation No 20, the CERD Committee then proceeded by clarifying that states are positively obliged to intervene and prevent discrimination caused by private entities.[13] Finally, in 2009 the CERD Committee summarized its previous findings, and reaffirmed that the CERD Convention includes a positive obligation on states to take special measures to ensure equality not only in law, but also in practice.

More importantly for the present purposes, however, in General Recommendation No 32, the CERD Committee firmly and repeatedly underscores that it is of critical importance to draw a clear distinction between temporary special measures targeting vulnerable groups that do not result in permanent rights, on the one hand, and permanent rights of among others indigenous peoples and individuals to maintain and develop their distinct cultural identities, on the other. The CERD Committee further reiterates that '[t]o treat in an equal manner persons or groups whose situation are objectively different will constitute discrimination in effect' and further that '[t]he Committee has also observed that the application of the principle of non-discrimination requires that the characteristics of groups be taken into consideration.'[14] In other words, the CERD Committee takes the position that rights of groups such as indigenous peoples and their members are embedded in the CERD Convention, and further that under the Convention, states have a positive duty to promote among others indigenous peoples and their members in their

[9] See General Comment No 20, Non-Discrimination in Economic, Social and Cultural Rights (Article 2, para. 2), E/C12/GC/20, 10 June 2009 8–9, 12, 36, 39. See also Makkonen, *Equal in Law, Unequal in Fact* (n 2) 120.

[10] Communication (*Hagan v Australia*), Comm 26/2002, UN Doc A/58/18, Annex III, Sec A, 7.2.

[11] General Recommendation No 14: Definition of Discrimination (Art. 1, par. 1): 22/03/1993 2.

[12] See e.g. Concluding Observations on Uruguay, CERD/C/304/Add 78 13; on Fiji, CERD/C/62/CO/3 15.

[13] General Recommendation No 20: Non-Discriminatory Implementation of Rights and Freedoms (Art. 5) 15.03.96.

[14] General Recommendation No 32: The Meaning and Scope of Special Measures in the International Convention on the Elimination of All Forms of Racial Discrimination, CERD/C/GC/32 8 (quote from this paragraph) 15, 26.

efforts to maintain their cultural distinctiveness. Clearly, such a positive duty on states to respect and promote the cultural identity not only of indigenous individuals but also of indigenous peoples is a quite different duty, compared with the special measures envisioned at the time of the adoption of the Convention. As articulated above, the latter measures had the opposite intention. They aimed at integrating indigenous individuals into the majority society, thus also resulting in the destruction of the group as such. In stark contrast to this position, the Committee now seemingly hold the position that the right to equality calls on states to take positive measures that actually protect and promote indigenous individuals'—as well as indigenous peoples'—permanent right to preserve their cultural identities.

On a regional level, the European Court of Human Rights (ECtHR) first noted an emerging international consensus that states are positively obligated to protect the lifestyles and cultural identities of minorities,[15] although on the merits, the Court did not find the norm to be sufficiently clear to find a violation of the right in the particular instance. In the same vein, the European Court of Justice (ECJ) acknowledged that treating instances differently that are significantly different need not amount to discrimination.[16]

The ECtHR has subsequently taken one step further. It has not stopped at the conclusion that treating different cases differently *need* not amount to discrimination. Rather, in *Thlimmenos*, the ECtHR held that the right to non-discrimination does not only entail that equal cases must be treated equally. Rather, according to the Court, in addition different cases *shall be* treated differently. Having initially noted that '[t]he Court has so far considered the right [to non-discrimination] ... violated when States treat differently persons in analogous situations without providing an objective and reasonable justification' (i.e. the conventional understanding of equality), the ECourtHR proceeded and declared that it '... now considers that this is not the only facet of the [right to non-discrimination]. The right not to be discriminated against ... is also violated when States without an objective and reasonable justification fail to treat differently persons whose situations are significantly different.'[17] Recent interpretations of the European Social Charter confirm that European law embraces a second facet of the right to equality according to which different situations call for differential treatment.[18]

[15] *Chapman v The United Kingdom* [GC] (1999) 27 EHRR 667 55–59, 90.

[16] See e.g. Case 210/03, *Swedish Match* [2004] ECR 11893 70; compare also Christopher McCrudden, 'The New Concept of Equality' [2003] *ERA Forum*, Vol 4, No 3 20.

[17] See *Thlimmenos v Greece* (2001) 31 EHRR 411 44. The ECtHR has reaffirmed this position in subsequent case-law, although it has been careful to apply this facet of the right to equality. See e.g. *Nachova and others* v *Bulgaria* [GC] (2005) 42 EHRR 933, and, to a lesser degree, *Stoica v Romania* (Appl No 42722702); also Makkonen, *Equal in Law, Unequal in Fact* (n 2) 127–28; Oddny Arnardóttir, *Equality and Non-Discrimination under the European Convention on Human Rights* (Kluwer Law International, 2003) 10–13. Arnardóttir seemingly argues that *Thlimmenos* shall be interpreted as implying that while relevant equalities demand equal treatment, only highly relevant inequalities require unequal treatment.

[18] The European Committee on Social Rights, tasked with interpreting and implementing the Social Charter, has noted that discrimination occurs also when states, without objective and reasonable justification, fail to treat differently persons whose situation is different. See *ERRC v Italy*, decision of 7 December 2005 36, and *Autisme-Europe v France*, decision of 4 November 2003, 52.

In summary, the ECtHR and other European institutions have proclaimed that the right to non-discrimination no longer merely entails that equal cases be treated equally. European law has come to acknowledge that the right to equality in addition embraces a right of individuals that are significantly different compared with the majority population to be treated differently. This position corresponds to recent developments in the findings of the UN treaty bodies that have been established to authoritatively interpret the right of equality. The HRC and the CESC have not explicitly required that states treat differently those that are culturally different. But these UN expert bodies have affirmed that differential treatment of such individuals whose cultural background is different compared with the majority population is a legitimate aspect of the right to equality, and have encouraged such state action. Moreover, CESC has opined that states must take measures to eliminate systemic discrimination of groups in a manner that recognizes their cultural differences, a position that resembles a call for a positive duty to treat different those that are culturally different. The CERD Committee, the principal UN expert body on the right to equality, has taken a step further. First, it has concurred with the ECtHR when proclaiming that a correct understanding of the right to equality requires states to respect cultural differences, and to treat those differently that have a different cultural background compared with the majority population. Second, the CERD Committee has taken the position that the right to equality the CERD Convention enshrines has a collective dimension, when proclaiming that the right requires that states take the characteristics of groups into account when operationalizing the right.

To infer, international legal sources sing the same hymn when positing that the right to non-discrimination no longer merely entails that equal cases be treated equally, but rather in addition calls for differential treatment of those that are culturally different. This position is in line with the recently emerged new understanding of justice within political theory.[19] More importantly, there is little evidence that it does not have the acceptance of states. In conclusion, one must reasonably infer that the second facet of the right to equality that entails that different cases be treated differently has crystalized into a customary international norm.[20] As Hurst Hannum notes, '[a] fundamental state obligation under international human rights norm is to eliminate discrimination, not to destroy all differences.'[21]

As touched upon, this conclusion finds further support in what has been inferred in Sections 5.4 and 5.5 on the contemporary understanding of the right to culture. Recall how these sections conclude that international customary law now provides that the right to culture requires a state to positively support members of minority cultures' endeavours to maintain and develop their distinct cultural identities and further that the right to culture also extends an, albeit indirect, protection to the

[19] Sections 3.6–3.8.

[20] In this context, recall how Chapter 4 explains that treaty body jurisprudence constitutes such subsequent practice that the Vienna Convention on the Law of Treaties prescribes can result in evolved understandings of treaty provisions and that regional human rights courts, such as the ECtHR, can also contribute to such developments.

[21] Hurst Hannum, *Autonomy, Sovereignty, and Self-Determination: The Accommodation of Conflicting Rights* (Revised edn., University of Pennsylvania Press, 1996) 476.

cultural identity of the group to which the individual belong. In other words, the scope and content of the right to equality as articulated above appears to—for all practical purposes—essentially match a contemporary understanding of the 'collectivized' right to culture. These common features of the rights to culture and equality, respectively, entail that the conclusions drawn in Sections 5.4 and 5.5 find support in the above and vice versa.

The second facet of the right to equality is, as touched upon in the introductory Section 7.1, highly relevant to the indigenous (and minority) rights discourse. If returning to the language example above, on the individual level the second facet of the right to non-discrimination implies that it is no longer equality if all children in a country—regardless of cultural and/or ethnic background—have the same right to education in and on the majority language. Today, it is equality if children belonging to minority cultures have the same opportunity to access education in and on their own mother tongue, as children belonging to the majority population do. The right to equality further requires that education is also otherwise accustomed to the cultural background of children belonging to indigenous (and minority) cultures.

7.5 A Formal Collective Right of Indigenous Peoples to Equality?

The section above explains how the CERD Committee in General Recommendation No 32 'observe[s] that the application of the principle of non-discrimination requires that the characteristics of groups be taken into consideration'. Some might want to interpret this statement as the CERD Committee acknowledging a right to equality that not only indirectly, but formally, extends protection to minority groups as such. This is, however, probably to stretch the position the CERD Committee has taken on the applicability of the right to equality too far.

First, the CERD Committee does not talk about a right of minority groups to equality. It 'merely' underlines that states shall take the characteristics of such groups into account in an equality context. In addition, the Committee does so through referring to the 'principle', and not the 'right', to non-discrimination. Presumably, this is a conscious choice of wording. In summary, there seems to be insufficient evidence to support a conclusion that the CERD Committee has gone as far as suggesting that the CERD Convention enshrines a formal collective right to equality. This conclusion also finds firm support in the general features of the indigenous and minority rights discourses, respectively. As Sections 5.3–5.5 elaborate, international law has drawn a clear distinction between minority and indigenous rights, where only the latter embrace collective rights. To interpret General Recommendation No 32 as acknowledging a collective right to equality of minority groups would thus violate a fundamental international norm. That the CERD Committee should reach such a conclusion therefore appears far-fetched. With regard to indigenous peoples, on the other hand, no formal objections preclude *the possibility* that such peoples *could* be beneficiaries of the right to equality.

In General Recommendation No 23 that specifically targets indigenous peoples, the CERD Committee interprets the right to equality the CERD Convention enshrines as applying not only indirectly, but also formally, to indigenous peoples as such. The opening paragraph of General Recommendation No 23 proclaims that 'discrimination against indigenous *peoples* falls under the scope of the [CERD] Convention . . .'. (emphasis added) Thus understood the right to equality is not only a right of indigenous individuals to have all human rights applied to them on an equal basis with other individuals; it is also a right of indigenous peoples to enjoy peoples' rights on an equal basis with other peoples.[22] As seen, a similar conclusion follows from UNDRIP Article 2.[23]

As touched upon, however, parts of the subsequent General Recommendation No 32 also explicitly address the situation of indigenous peoples. Still, as further discussed above, General Recommendation No 32 notably refrains from echoing General Recommendation No 23's proclamation that the right to equality applies not only indirectly, but also formally, to indigenous peoples.[24] Rather, as seen, the CERD Committee explicitly distinguishes between collective human rights and the right to equality. Albeit affirming that the latter right can only be effectively implemented in an indigenous (and minority) context if the characteristics of the group are being considered, the Committee stops short of repeating the suggestion that indigenous peoples have a formal right to equality.

Neither are there other international legal sources that suggest that the right to equality formally applies to indigenous peoples, with the possible exception of the mentioned UNDRIP Article 2. As seen, UNDRIP Article 2 proclaims that indigenous peoples are equal to other peoples. Certainly, one might interpret UNDRIP Article 2 as a reflection of the right to equality as enshrined e.g. in the CERD Convention. But other interpretations are also plausible. As Section 5.7.3 leans towards, UNDRIP Article 2 can, and probably should, be understood more as a general and principal affirmation of indigenous peoples status as 'peoples' for international legal purposes than as an explicit reference to the right to equality as presently understood in international law. True, having emerged as 'peoples' for international legal purposes, it is only natural that indigenous peoples are treated equally with other peoples, as Section 5.7.3 concludes. But that is not the same thing as to say that the right to equality as articulated in the CERD Convention applies to indigenous peoples. As follows, from the above, the right is not understood to attach to peoples in the meaning aggregate populations of states either, although also such peoples have legitimate expectations to be treated on par with one another. In other words, a right to equal treatment of collectives does not necessarily correspond to the right to equality formally applying to them. In any event, without more support in other international legal sources, one can hardly draw the conclusion simply from

22 Compare Katarina Tomasevski, 'Indicators', in Asbjørn Eide, Catarina Krause, and Allan Rosas (eds.), *Economic, Social and Cultural Rights—A Textbook* (2nd edn., Martinus Nijhoff Publishers, 2001) 533, and Asbjørn Eide, 'The Use of Indicators in the Practice of the Committee on Economic, Social and Cultural Rights', in ibid., *Economic, Social and Cultural Rights—A Textbook* (2nd edn., Martinus Nijhoff Publishers, 2001) 549.

23 Section 5.7.3.

24 Compare Makkonen, *Equal in Law, Unequal in Fact* (n 2) 95.

UNDRIP Article 2 that a formal right to equality of indigenous peoples has crystalized into a customary international norm. The legal doctrine seems largely to concur with this assessment.[25] To conclude, it appears doubtful that the right to equality has evolved to such an extent as to apply also *formally* to indigenous peoples. As a final observation in this context, one can note that this conclusion further highlights the corresponding nature between the rights to equality and culture. As seen, the latter right has not been understood to formally apply to indigenous peoples either, but nonetheless protects them.

The comparison with the right to culture also reminds us that one should probably be careful not to overestimate the practical implications of the conclusion that the right to equality does not formally apply to indigenous peoples. Whether such is the case might be a largely academic question. As seen, the second facet of the right to non-discrimination implies that those individuals that are culturally different are entitled to differential treatment. As touched upon, this entails, for all practical purposes, that the right also protects groups as such. On the collective level, the formal right to differential treatment on the individual level corresponds to an informal right of the group to receive protection for its cultural characteristics. If all members of an indigenous people receive education, health care, social services etc. that are respectful of and promote their cultural identities then this will further the cultural identity also of the group. Thus understood, the right to equality protects the cultural identity of indigenous peoples as such, and it becomes a less relevant question whether the right applies formally to such peoples.

The articulated conclusion finds broad support in the legal doctrine.[26] It is also in line with Dimitrina Petrova's and Bhiku Parekh's observations that racial discrimination—by definition—presupposes the existence of ethnic and/or racial groups in society. Even if an individual might be the victim of racial discrimination,

[25] For instance, Timo Makkonen, in his doctoral dissertation on the right to non-discrimination, concludes that the right to equality, irrespective of recent developments, formally remains individual in nature. See *Equal in Law, Unequal in Fact* (n 2) 178–79.

[26] See e.g. the 2008 'Declaration of Principles of Equality' at <www.equalrightstrust.org> accessed on 25 April, 2010, signed by 128 human rights experts, in particular principles 5 and 9; and also McCrudden, 'The New Concept of Equality' (n 16) 22–23. Former CERD Committee member Patrick Thornberry concurs that a collective right to culture is indeed very similar to an individual right to be treated differently—see Thornberry, 'The Convention on the Elimination of Racial Discrimination' (n 1) 23; Thornberry 'Integrating the UN Declaration on the Rights of Indigenous Peoples into CERD Practice', in Stephen Allen and Alexandra Xanthaki (eds.), *Reflection on the UN Declaration on the Rights of Indigenous Peoples* (Hart Publishing, 2011) 64. For similar comments, see Steven Wheatley, *Democracy, Minorities and International Law* (Cambridge Studies in International and Comparative Law, 2005) 22; David Lea, *Property Rights, Indigenous People and the Developing World: Issues from Aboriginal Entitlement to Intellectual Ownership Rights* (Martinus Nijhoff Publishers, 2008) 20; Joshua Castellino, 'Conceptual Difficulties and the Right to Indigenous Self-Determination', in Nazila Ghanea and Alexandra Xanthaki (eds.), *Minorities, Peoples and Self-Determination—Essays in Honour of Patrick Thornberry* (Martinus Nijhoff Publishers, 2005) 61; Michael Hartney, 'Some Confusion Concerning Collective Rights', in Will Kymlicka (ed.), *The Rights of Minority Cultures* (Oxford University Press, 1995); 220; Rodolfo Stavenhagen, 'Cultural Rights: A Social Science Perspective', in Asbjørn Eide, Catarina Krause, and Allan Rosas (eds.), *Economic, Social and Cultural Rights—A Textbook* (2nd edn., Martinus Nijhoff Publishers, 2001) 98; S James Anaya, *Indigenous Peoples in International Law* (2nd edn., Oxford University Press, 2004) 139; Makkonen, *Equal in Law, Unequal in Fact* (n 2) 180–81.

she or he is not so because of her or his own characteristics but because of association with a particular group. Consequently, racial discrimination cannot be disassociated from the group as such. It can simply not be discussed in individual terms.[27]

In summary, contemporary international law provides that the right to equality requires that state law and policy positively distinguish between indigenous individuals and members of the majority population. Such laws and policies must provide for differential treatment to the former based on their cultural distinctiveness. Moreover, the differential treatment of the individual level must be applied in a manner that provides protection of the cultural characteristics also of the indigenous people as such.

Against the outlined background, it is ironic that governments not uncommonly use the equality argument to *reject* indigenous peoples' calls for protection of their distinct cultures. Governments often respond to such cries by arguing that it cannot offer special treatment to the indigenous people or its members, as this would amount to discrimination of the members of the majority population. As is clear from the above, this argument is blind to the paradigm shift that has occurred with regard to how the right to equality must be understood in a contemporary context. Governments are now not only allowed to treat indigenous individuals, and indirectly also indigenous peoples, differently. The right to equality requires them to do so.

7.6 Conclusions—The Relevance of the Evolved Understanding of the Right to Equality to the Indigenous Rights Discourse

As already described, the evolved understanding of the right to equality is of paramount importance to the indigenous rights discourse for three reasons, where the first two are clearly interrelated.

As to the first reason, the outlined evolved understanding of equality affirms the conclusions drawn in Chapter 5, i.e. that international law has come to recognize a collectivized right to culture that extends an, albeit indirect, protection also to indigenous peoples as such. This is of profound importance, as, particularly when understood in light of one another, the evolved understandings of the rights to culture and equality entail a break with the state-individual dichotomy present in the international legal system since its inception. The strict reliance on this dichotomy implied that until recently, the human rights system was of limited relevance to indigenous peoples. This has now changed, as the rights to

[27] See Dimitrina Petrova, 'Racial Discrimination and the Rights of Minority Cultures', in Sandra Fredman (ed.), *Discrimination and Human Rights: The Case of Racism* (Oxford University Press, 2001) 67; Bhikhu Parekh, 'Redistribution or recognition? A misguided debate', in Stephen May, Tariq Modood, and Judth Squires (eds.), *Ethnicity, Nationalism and Minority Rights* (Cambridge University Press, 2004) 210. In a similar vein, Sandra Fredman notes that in order to determine whether an individual has been discriminated against one must often first determine whether the group she belongs to has historically been disadvantaged. See Sandra Fredman, 'Providing Equality' [2005] *South African Journal on Human Rights* 21 177–79.

equality and culture extend protection also to the cultural identity of indigenous collectives as such.

As to the second reason, as the language-education example above illustrates, the evolved understanding of the right to equality underpins essentially all rights of relevance to indigenous individuals. As seen, the second facet of the right to equality can be invoked to require that essentially all forms of societal services be accustomed to the cultural background of indigenous individuals. As has already been demonstrated, the evolved understanding of non-discrimination demands that indigenous children receive education in and on their mother tongue. Health care services must also be accustomed to indigenous patients' cultural and ethnical background. In a similar vein, a contemporary understanding of the right to equality requires that services for indigenous elders are accustomed to their cultural background. There must be personnel that speak their language and at least attempts must be made to adapt food services etc. to their traditional nutrition. The examples go on and on and can be chosen from essentially all spheres of human activity.

Finally, Chapter 8 elaborates on how the evolved understanding of the right to equality has been of cardinal importance to international law's position on to what extent indigenous communities have established property rights over lands and natural resources through traditional use. That is so, since the right to property essentially is a particular aspect of the right to equality. As a consequence, as Chapter 8 explains, the fact that the right to equality now requires that domestic laws and policies take cultural differences into account within all aspects of society has profound effects within the sphere of property rights over territories. But before returning to this matter, a few additional final observations shall be offered with regard to the right to equality.

7.7 The Closing of a Circle

Having established what is the contemporary understanding of equality, it is interesting to briefly revisit the Permanent Court of International Justice's (PCIJ) interpretation of the right in *Minority Schools in Albania*. Recall how Section 2.4 explains how in this case, decided about a century ago, the PCIJ's opined that 'equality in fact may involve the necessity of different treatment in order to attain a result which establishes equilibrium between different situations' and further that '[t]he idea underlying the treaties for the protection of minorities is to secure for certain elements incorporated in a State, the population of which differs from them in race . . . the possibility of . . . preserving the characteristics which distinguish them from the majority, and satisfying the ensuing special needs.' The resemblance between these statements by the PCIJ and the position international law returned to more than three quarters of a century later is certainly striking. In a similar vein, recall further how the PCIJ in *Minority Schools in Albania* noted the similarities between the individual right to equality and the cultural rights of groups. As the above elaborates, this comparison could have been taken from a legal source of today. In short, after almost a century adrift, international law is back at the position taken by the PCIJ in *Minority Schools in Albania*.

7.8 Briefly on the Relationship between the Right to Equality and the Principle of Universality of Human Rights

Human rights are generally understood to be universal. The principle of universality of human rights provides that such rights apply equally to all individuals around the globe. It is hardly surprising therefore, that it has been argued that the recent recognition that indigenous peoples and communities are beneficiaries of rights particular to them, and that individuals belonging to ethnic and cultural groups that significantly differ from the majority are entitled to differential treatment, violate the principle of universality of human rights. Because if human rights are in fact universal, is it not a paradox to suggest that they apply differently depending on cultural context? As Dominic McGoldrick puts it, 'while international human rights is a universal doctrine, multiculturalism can appear to be a localising doctrine.'[28] Given the weight that has conventionally been given to the principle of universality of human rights, it may be pertinent to briefly respond to this assertion.

James Anaya responds to the articulated concerns by simply noting that if it is a paradox that universally applicable rights can extend particular protection to certain groups and individuals, as has been argued, then contemporary human rights law has embraced this paradox.[29] It is easy to accept this argument. As this book underlines throughout, international law, and in particular human rights law, is not caste in stone. Rather, it has the capacity to constantly evolve. Chapter 5 and this chapter survey such developments within the fields of peoples' rights and the right to equality, respectively. Provided that the conclusions in these chapters are correct, it is of little use to suggest that these developments contradict a human rights principle as it has been conventionally understood. As Anaya observes, if the notion of universality of human rights cannot be reconciled with indigenous peoples' rights and the right to differential treatment, then international law has simply opted for the latter. As the above has further addressed in depth, international law has done so exactly due to increased recognition that a human rights system that focuses solely on the universality of individual human rights is prone not to adequately protect the interest, concerns, and needs of ethnic and cultural groups—as well as of their members. Indeed, we have seen that an international legal system that relies solely on universal individual human rights runs the risk of erasing cultural diversity. As James Crawford seemingly notes, accepting the universality of human

[28] Dominic McGoldrick, 'Multiculturalism and its Discontents', in Nazila Ghanea and Alexandra Xanthaki (eds.), *Minorities, Peoples and Self-Determination—Essays in Honour of Patrick Thornberry* (Martinus Nijhoff Publishers, 2005) 233.

[29] Anaya, *Indigenous Peoples in International Law* (n 26) 133.

rights without accommodating for cultural differences can be viewed as akin to accepting that human rights do not protect against assimilation.[30] Taking this line of argument one step further, Sandra Fredman posits that the conventional understanding of the right to equality 'is based on an assumption of conformity to a given norm, and therefore of assimilation'. A human rights norm that provides that equal cases be treated equally, but nothing more, asserts, she points out, that she or he who seeks non-discrimination protection must agree to be considered to be 'like' the standard model, i.e. like members of the majority population.[31]

The notion that human rights apply to individuals only—and in the same manner to all individuals—may seem to be incompatible with the notion of peoples' rights and differential treatment. Notwithstanding, this and the previous chapters demonstrate how recently international law has simply evolved. It has come to embrace rights of indigenous peoples' as such and has come to hold that individuals belonging to ethnic and culturally distinct groups, such as indigenous peoples, are entitled to differential treatment.

As a final note in this context, it is underscored that acceptance of indigenous peoples' rights and of differential treatment need not necessarily be understood to contradict the principle of universal human rights—in the sense that human rights no longer apply equally to all.

The right to equality might very well still be understood to have universal applicability. The only thing that has changed is an acknowledgment that when the universally applicable right to equality is being *implemented*, this need not result in mainstreaming, i.e. only in *equality in law*. Rather, the right should be implemented in a manner that takes different cultural contexts into account in the form of differential treatment that caters for the preservation of distinct ethnic and/or cultural identities, i.e. *equality in fact*. In other words, the right to equality still *applies* universally. But that is no longer to say that the right must necessarily *materialize itself* in the same manner in every context. As Willem van Genugten observes, '[u]niversality of human rights standards is not necessarily uniformity as to the ways to realize them.'[32]

As far as indigenous rights as peoples' rights are concerned, one can simply note that peoples' rights have been well established in the international legal system for decades without any questions being raised as to their compatibility with the principle of universality of human rights. This can hardly change simply because indigenous peoples have now been recognized as 'peoples' as well.

30 James Crawford, 'The Right of Self-Determination in International Law: Its Development and Future', in Philip Alston (ed.), *Peoples' Rights* (Oxford University Press, 2005) 24.

31 See Sandra Fredman, 'Combating Racism with Human Rights: The Right to Equality', in Sandra Fredman (ed.), *Discrimination and Human Rights: The Case of Racism* (Oxford University Press, 2001) 16. In a similar vein, compare Dianne Otto, 'Rethinking the "Universality" of Human Rights Law' [1997] *Columbia Human Rights Law Review* 29 7–8.

32 Willem van Genugten, 'The African Move towards the Adoption of the 2007 Declaration on the Rights of Indigenous Peoples: The Substantive Arguments behind the Procedures', at <http://ssrn.com/abstract=1103862> accessed on 30 July 2012.

8

Indigenous Communities' Property Rights over Lands and Natural Resources Traditionally Used

8.1 Introduction

Albeit perhaps not in so many words, Section 5.5.2 explains how in its early years the indigenous rights discourse essentially couched indigenous peoples' rights over lands and natural resources in terms of cultural rights. Land and resource rights were essentially defined as rights that should allow indigenous communities (although formally speaking the beneficiaries of the right are indigenous individuals) to preserve and develop their distinct cultures, including culturally-based land and natural resource uses. But the above also indicates how more recently indigenous peoples' rights over territories traditionally used have increasingly come to be viewed through the prism of property rights. As further touched upon, and as elaborated below, the right to property is intrinsically connected to the right to equality.

Section 8.2 outlines some key features of property rights theory of particular relevance to the present purposes and also identifies what understanding of the right international law has accepted. Examining the nature of the right to property assists us in understanding precisely why the right is so heavily rooted in the right to equality. The subsequent sections then proceed to survey how the evolved understanding of the right to equality has impacted on to what extent indigenous communities have established rights over lands and natural resources traditionally used. This chapter's focus is mostly on territories traditionally and *continuously used*, but Section 8.8 on the right to restitution does address what property rights interests indigenous communities may still hold in territories traditionally used, *but subsequently taken without their consent*. Chapter 9 investigates the more precise content and scope of indigenous land and resource rights, when understood as property rights.

8.2 The Basic Nature of the Right to Property

8.2.1 Property rights theory

For the present purposes, it is not necessary to embark on a lengthy exposé over the rather extensive discussions within property rights theory. But it is pertinent to briefly touch upon the basic theories that underpin the right to property. As indicated, that is so, since property right theories contribute to a correct identification of what understanding of the right international law has embraced.

The basic premise that underpins the argument that there should be a right to property is that it would appear reasonable that human beings hold certain rights over lands and chattels that they, by some measure of legitimacy, have reduced to their own control.[1] If accepting this basic premise, property rights can be described as norms governing in what ways rights over property can be established, and to what extent the holder of a property right can exercise control over and use her or his property.[2] This understanding of the right to property further leads to the conclusion that the right should be viewed not as one, but rather as a catalogue, of rights.[3]

For the purposes of this book, Jeremy Waldron's dissection of the right to property into certain broad categories can serve as a useful illustration of the various potential elements philosophical theory ascribes to the right to property. Waldron divides the right to property into the categories 'Immunities against expropriation', 'Natural property rights', 'Eligibility to hold property', and 'The general right to have private property'.[4] The second category is of less relevance here. But a comparison of the other three—which are also the property rights elements that have attracted most property rights theory attention—reflects well the most important dividing line within such theory.

One liberal philosophical school argues that individuals should be bestowed with a positive right to be provided with a minimum amount of property. This position is based on a belief that being in possession of property has a moralizing effect on the holder. It is suggested that the individual needs a minimum amount of property in order to develop a complete identity and personality. Proponents of this understanding of the right to property place the right on an equal footing with other civil rights. They hold that having property is critical to the freedom of the individual.[5]

But far from all political thinkers have accepted the idea that the right to property should embrace a positive right to be provided with property. A competing property rights theory focuses on the first and third of Waldron's elements, i.e. on '[i]mmunities against expropriation' and '[e]ligibility to hold property'. These elements could be described as a more modest property right, compared with the category '[t]he general right to have private property'. Eligibility to hold property merely implies that all should have an equal right to acquire property. And once property has been thus acquired, 'immunities against expropriation' provides that one must not be arbitrarily deprived of that property. The fact that a formal equal opportunity to acquire property will in practice probably never result in even close

[1] S James Anaya, *Indigenous Peoples in International Law* (2nd edn., Oxford University Press, 2004) 141.

[2] Jermy Waldron, *The Right to Private Property* (Clarendon Paperbacks, 1998) 33–37.

[3] Stephen R Munzer, *A Theory of Property* (Cambridge University Press, 1990) 23.

[4] Waldron, *The Right to Private Property* (n 2) 16–24.

[5] Ibid., 15–56.

to an even distribution of property and that rather some individuals are likely to end up with little property is not a concern to the proponents of this line of argument. Philosophers such as John Locke and Robert Nozick are often associated with this school of thought. They maintain that property rights are rights that should occur, and occur only, as a result of special relationships based on contingent events such as original acquisition.[6] The question then becomes—which of these lines of thought find support in international law?

8.2.2 The general understanding of the right to property under international law

The right to property was incorporated into the contemporary human rights system at its inception. The Universal Declaration of Human Rights (UDHR) Article 17 proclaims that '[e]veryone has the right to own property' and further that '[n]o one shall be arbitrarily deprived of the same'. The right to property was also included in the regional human rights instruments that were adopted during this era. The American Convention on Human Rights (ACHR) Article 21.1 recognizes a right to property that can only be encroached upon subject to payment of just compensation. In the same vein, Article 1 of Protocol 1 to the European Convention on Human Rights (ECHR) proclaims that everybody has the right to peaceful enjoyment of her or his possessions. The European Court of Human Rights (ECtHR) has clarified that the phrase 'right to peaceful enjoyment of possessions' shall be understood as a right to property.[7] Notably, the right to property was subsequently included in the Convention on the Elimination of Racial Discrimination (CERD Convention) through its Article 5(d)(v). Having initially provided that states are obliged to prohibit and eliminate racial discrimination, the provision proceeds to specifically prescribe that one way in which states shall promote equality is through guaranteeing 'the right of everyone, without distinction as to race . . . or ethnic origin, to equally before the law [enjoy] . . . the right to . . . property'. CERD Convention Article 5(d)(v) thus explicitly underlines the link between the rights to equality and property. The right to property has subsequently been incorporated into other regional human rights instruments such as the African Charter on Human and Peoples' Rights (AfCHPR) and the Arab Charter on Human Rights.[8] In conclusion, one can safely conclude that the right to property forms part of customary international law.

The manner in which the drafters have formulated the right to property in the mentioned human rights instruments clearly answers which of the two understandings of the right in property right theory international law endorses. The right to

[6] David Lea, *Property Rights, Indigenous People and the Developing World: Issues from Aboriginal Entitlement to Intellectual Ownership Rights* (Martinus Nijhoff Publishers, 2008) 15; Waldron, *The Right to Private Property* (n 2) 131, 136–38.
[7] *Marckx v Belgium* (1979) 2 EHRR 330 50.
[8] *International Human Rights Reporter*, Vol 4, No 3 (1997) 850–57, Article 25.

property known to international law is undoubtedly a right to acquire property on equal basis with others, and, once property has been thus acquired, not to be arbitrarily deprived of the same. There is no right to be provided with property under international law. In other words, if returning to Jeremy Waldron's categorization, international law embraces the elements '[e]igibility to hold property' and '[i]mmunities against expropriation', but rejects the element a '[g]eneral right to have property'.[9]

As a consequence of this understanding of the right to property, international law essentially accepts any domestic position as to what extent property and chattel can be subject to private property rights—as long as it is non-discriminatory. Domestic legal systems stand free to recognize private property rights to various extents, as long as all have (i) the same opportunity to acquire property, and (ii) enjoy equal recognition and protection of their thus established property rights. As indicated, in other words, the right to property is at its core a particular aspect of the right to equality.

8.2.3 Generally on the relevance of international law's understanding of the right to property to indigenous property rights over territories

The fact that the right to property is 'nothing more' than a particular aspect of the right to equality suggests a profound relevance of the right to indigenous communities' rights over lands and natural resources traditionally used. That is so since the intrinsic connection between the rights to equality and property suggests that (i) the initial incorporation of the former right into the international legal system, and (ii) the subsequent evolved understandings of the right, should both directly impact on indigenous communities' property rights over territories traditionally used. The sections below survey to what extent this assumption is correct. In doing so, when analyzing to what extent international law acknowledges that indigenous communities hold property rights over land, it might be useful to look at what position three different time-periods took towards the right to equality.

Chapter 2 describes how the early international legal system that emerged in the centuries that followed the Peace of Westphalia held indigenous territories to be *terra nullius*. We saw that the *terra nullius* doctrine professes that although indigenous territories are literally speaking inhabited, they were from an international legal perspective empty. As a consequence, European colonizers were legally entitled to place such territories under their hegemony and control. Chapter 2 further explains how in more recent times, some countries continued to invoke the *terra nullius* doctrine in its purest form, while others formulated various

[9] Compare Richard Lillich, 'Global Protection of Human Rights', in Theodor Meron (ed.), *Human Rights in International Law: Legal and Policy Issues* (Clarendon Press, 1984 [reprint 1992]); Catarina Krause, *The Right to Property*, in Asbjørn Eide, Catarina Krause, and Allan Rosas (eds.), *Economic, Social and Cultural Rights—A Textbook* (2nd edn., Martinus Nijhoff Publishers, 2001) 191–92.

forms of 'discovery doctrines'. The latter theories, although somewhat more nuanced than the *terra nullius* doctrine, are still inhospitable towards the notion that indigenous peoples hold property rights over lands and natural resources. As that chapter also elaborates, states continued to rely on *terra nullius* and discovery doctrines well into the 1900s, doctrines that professed that indigenous peoples, by the very nature of their societies, could hold no, or only limited, rights to land. From an international legal perspective, it was unproblematic to do so during a time-period when the international legal system was yet to embrace a right to equality. With no right to equality to consider, states were free to determine that certain groups and individuals were entitled to property rights over land, while others were not.

The previous chapter also describes, however, how when the United Nations (UN) commenced to elaborate the contemporary human rights system, the right to equality immediately became an integral part, indeed a core right, of that system. The acceptance of the right to non-discrimination as a central human right was an immediate challenge to the *terra nullius* and discovery doctrines. When the right to equality is considered a core human right, it is clearly problematic to argue that indigenous communities' traditional land uses, by their very nature can—by definition—not result in establishment of property rights. Consequently, with the introduction of a right to equality in the international human rights system, a formal recognition that indigenous communities' traditional land uses can indeed result in property rights must reasonably and necessarily follow. Notwithstanding, when the right to non-discrimination is understood to merely provide that equal cases be treated equally, i.e.that states provide for formal equality only, it may still be difficult for indigenous communities to have property rights over lands and natural resources traditionally used acknowledged in practice, as Section 8.4 elaborates.

Of the three time-periods of international law's position towards indigenous property rights over territories traditionally used the above refers to, the era when the right to non-discrimination merely entailed that equal cases be treated equally can be described as the second time-period. Sections 8.3 and 8.4 outlines this period. The third time-period starts when the right to equality evolves and takes on a second facet that calls for differential treatment of those that are ethnically and/or culturally different compared with the majority population. Section 8.5 addresses the relevance of this development to indigenous communities' property rights over lands and natural resources traditionally used.

8.3 Rejection of the *Terra Nullius* Doctrine

8.3.1 Introduction

As mentioned, it is difficult to uphold *terra nullius* and similar doctrines against the backdrop of the right to equality. As a consequence, following the incorporation of the right into the contemporary international human rights system, when international and domestic courts were faced with matters relating to indigenous communities' rights over territories traditionally used, they found it increasingly hard to uphold the *terra nullius* and similar doctrines. A few examples below illustrate this development. The section first addresses the shifted view on the *terra nullius* doctrine in general. Subsequently, it directs its attention to how this doctrine has been viewed specifically in an indigenous rights context.

8.3.2 *Western Sahara*

In *Western Sahara* (1975), Morocco and Spain both claimed sovereignty over the Western Sahara territory in Northern Africa. The dispute provided the International Court of Justice (ICJ) with the opportunity to address the validity of the *terra nullius* doctrine under the contemporary international legal system.

Morocco based its claim on 'legal ties' with nomadic Saharan tribes in Western Sahara. In other words, Morocco argued, contrary to what the *terra nullius* doctrine professes, that it should be legally relevant that tribal peoples have historically inhabited Western Sahara, and that the country should have rights to the territory due to its connection with the tribes. The ICJ, accepted Morocco's argument, and thus parted with the *terra nullius* doctrine, in the sense that the Court underlined that a geographical area is not necessarily uninhabited for international legal purposes simply because its inhabitants are being perceived by some as primitive and in want of a governmental structure. Some form of social and political organization is sufficient, the ICJ concluded. Still, *Western Sahara* did not as such contribute to an evolved understanding of indigenous communities' rights to land. Having inferred that the land area in dispute was not *terra nullius*, the ICJ did nonetheless not find that the tribes that traditionally inhabited the land had established rights thereto. Rather, the Court found that the invoked link between the tribes and the Sherifian State, the predecessor to modern Morocco, allowed Morocco to rely on the tribes' land use to claim sovereign rights over Western Sahara.[10]

Western Sahara is important in the sense that it was the first time an international tribunal parted with the *terra nullius* doctrine and held that a doctrine that proclaims that a territory is uninhabited simply because its population does not pursue a European style agrarian life-style can not form part of contemporary international law. Still, the case did not support indigenous claims to rights over territories traditionally used. True, the ICJ held the Western Sahara tribes' occupation of land to be of legaly relevant. But the tribes were nonetheless not treated as holders of land in their own right, but rather as mere pawns in a game between Morocco and Spain.[11]

[10] *Western Sahara Case*. Advisory Opinion, ICJ Reports 1975 12.

[11] For similar opinions, see Joshua Castellino, 'Territorial Integrity and the "Right" to Self-Determination: An Examination of the Conceptual Tools' [2008] *Brooks Law Journal of International Law*, Vol 33:2 517, 535–36; Jérémie Gilbert, *Indigenous Peoples' Land Rights Under International Law: From Victims to Actors* (Transnational Publishers, 2006) 28–29.

8.3.3 Rejection of the *terra nullius* doctrine in the indigenous rights discourse

Perhaps as a response to a contemporary international legal system that outlawed discrimination, domestic courts in countries hosting indigenous peoples gradually commenced to reject the *terra nullius* doctrine. This trend accelerated following the ICJ's ruling in *Western Sahara*. For the present purposes, it is not necessary to provide an extensive outline of this case law. Rather, one example illustrates well the impact the inclusion of a right to equality in the international human rights system had on the validity of the *terra nullius* doctrine.

Probably the most referred to case as an example of the rejection of the *terra nullius* doctrine in an indigenous context is the High Court of Australia's ruling in *Mabo v Queensland* [No 2].[12] In *Mabo*, the High Court explicitly broke with the *terra nullius* doctrine, which Australia had relied on well into the 1990s.[13] The Court held that 'the fiction by which the rights and interests of indigenous inhabitants in land were treated as non-existent was justified by a policy which has no place in contemporary law . . . Whatever the justification advanced in earlier days for refusing to recognise the rights and interests in land of the indigenous inhabitants . . . an unjust and discriminatory doctrine of that kind can no longer be accepted.'[14] It is worth noting that, as indicated, the High Court of Australia explicitly allowed itself to be inspired by *Western Sahara* when ruling in *Mabo*.[15]

As is clear from the quote above, it was equality rationales that convinced the High Court of Australia to reject the *terra nullius* doctrine and conclude that the nature of indigenous communities' land uses does not disqualify them from being holders of property rights over lands and natural resources. Rather, the Court underscored that if the state recognizes in general that private entities can establish property rights over land, at the same time as it fails to accept that indigenous communities' traditional land uses can result in such rights, this is discriminatory. In other words, and rather natural given the general understanding of the right to property as articulated above, the right to land the High Court of Australia recognizes in *Mabo* is not an outcome of what Jeremy Waldron labels a '[g]eneral right to hold property'.[16] Rather, what we see is an application of the '[e]ligibility to hold property' element. The property right endorsed is one rooted in historical entitlement, only with a contemporary view on who are historically entitled.[17] The right

[12] *Mabo v Queensland* [No 2] (1992) 175 CLR 1.

[13] Compare Andrew Huff, 'Indigenous Land Rights and the New Self-Determination' [2005] 16 *Colo J Int'l Envtl L Pol'y* 295 299–300.

[14] See also Eric Dannenmaier, 'Beyond Indigenous Property Rights: Exploring the Emergence of a Distinctive Connection Doctrine' [2008] *Washington University Law Review*, Vol 86:53 68.

[15] Anaya, *Indigenous Peoples in International Law* (n 1) 198.

[16] See Section 8.2.1.

[17] See also S James Anaya, 'The Right of Indigenous Peoples to Self-Determination in the Post-Declaration Era', in Claire Charters and Rodolfo Stavenhagen (eds.), *Making the Declaration Work: The United Nations Declaration on the Rights of Indigenous Peoples* (IWGIA, 2009) 193. James Anaya observes that recent developments that acknowledge that indigenous communities' use of land results in property rights derive from the general right to property. One should note, however, that at the same

to equality does not allow states to continuously rely on doctrines that provide that indigenous land uses by definition do not result in property rights. The legal doctrine concurs that international law has firmly rejected the *terra nullius* doctrine.[18]

8.4 The Right to Property When Rooted in the Conventional Understanding of the Right to Equality

Perhaps contrary to what some had expected, the rejection of the *terra nullius* doctrine did not open up the floodgates to extensive domestic recognition of property rights of indigenous communities over territories traditionally used. *Formal* recognition is not necessarily the same thing as acknowledgment of rights *in practice*. Although the *terra nullius* doctrine had been formally rejected, most states with indigenous peoples continued to rely on the legacy of the doctrine. State laws and policies tended to continuously treat indigenous communities' traditional territories as the property of the state, often without offering any justification for this position. Rather, states tended to hide behind a 'veil of ignorance', simply ignoring the questionable legal basis for its claims to rights over indigenous territories.[19] In other words, although the *terra nullius* doctrine and other doctrines with similar effects had been rejected as inherently discriminatory, most states did little to address the remnants of such regimes.

For some time, the articulated position of states was not necessarily problematic under international law. When the right to property was viewed against the backdrop of the conventional understanding of the right to equality, it allowed states to rely on the legacy of *terra nullius* and other similar doctrines when formulating their

time as the High Court of Australia held that Aboriginal communities' traditional land uses can result in property rights, the Court further inferred that Australia's sovereign rights allows it to extinguish Aboriginal communities' property rights interests in land. Moreover, although the ruling in *Mabo* rejected the *terra nullius* doctrine, the land right the Hight Court of Australia awarded to the Aboriginal community is one hard to establish. In order to have property rights over land recognized under the norm established in *Mabo*, Aboriginal communities not only have to prove that at the time of colonization, their own customary laws conferred them with rights to land. In addition, the communities must demonstrate that observance of those customary laws are still intact today. See Kent McNeil, 'Judicial Treatment of Indigenous Land Rights in the Common Law World', in John V Cioffi and Peer Zumbansen (eds.), *Indigenous Peoples and the Law: Comparative and Critical Perspectives* (Hart Publishing, 2009) 36; Lindsay Robertson, *Conquest by Law: How the Discovery of America Dispossessed Indigenous Peoples of their Lands* (Oxford University Press, 2005) 144.

18 Siegfried Wiessner, 'Indigenous Sovereignty: A Reassessment in Light of the UN Declaration on the Rights of Indigenous Peoples' [2008] *Vanderbilt Journal of Transnational Law* 41 1154; Federico Lenzerini, 'Sovereignty Revisited: International Law and Parallel Sovereignty of Indigenous Peoples' [2006] *Texas International Law Journal*, Vol 42 167; Patrick Macklem, 'Indigenous Recognition in International Law: Theoretical Observations' [2008] *Michigan Journal of International Law*, Vol 30 (1) 185; James Tully, 'The Struggles of Indigenous Peoples for and of Freedom', in Duncan Ivison, Paul Patton, and Will Sanders (eds.), *Political Theory and the Rights of Indigenous Peoples* (Cambridge University Press, 2000) 54; Antony Anghie, *Imperialism, Sovereignty and the Making of International Law* (Cambridge University Press, 2004) 111–12; Joshua Castellino, 'The Right to Land, International Law & Indigenous Peoples', in Joshua Castellino and Niamh Walsh (eds.), *International Law and Indigenous Peoples* (Martinus Nijhoff Publisher, 2005) 92–101.

19 Duncan Ivison, Paul Patton, and Will Sanders, (eds.); *Political Theory and the Rights of Indigenous Peoples* (Cambridge University Press, 2000) 12.

law and policy on indigenous property rights over territories traditionally used or perhaps rather lack thereof. As seen, at the time the right to property was viewed through the prism of a right to non-discrimination that merely required states to treat equal cases equally. In such a legal environment, it proved extremely difficult *in practice* for indigenous communities to establish property rights over land in courts of law, irrespective of that domestic jurisdiction *formally* recognized that indigenous communities' traditional land uses could result in property rights. These difficulties followed from what sorts of land uses where deemed to result in property rights.

Clearly, not just any form of haphazard land use can reasonably result in the establishment of property rights. As seen, international law provides that a land area shall have been 'traditionally' used for a property right to crystalize. That a territory shall have been 'traditionally' used indicates that a certain amount of continuity and pattern in the utilization is required. How such criteria are formulated more precisely naturally vary from jurisdiction to jurisdiction, and this is something international law accepts, within certain boundaries of course. Generally speaking, domestic legal systems tend to require that three objective criteria be fulfilled in order to establish property rights over lands and natural resources through traditional use. To establish a property right in the form of usufruct right, it is normally expected that the use has been sufficiently (i) intense and (ii) continuous. For an ownership right to materialize, the use must in addition have been sufficiently (iii) dominating (or exclusive).[20]

When the right to property was understood against the backdrop of a right to non-discrimination that merely required that equal cases be treated equally, the way in which the intensity, continuity, and exclusivity criteria were applied rendered it difficult for indigenous communities to establish property rights over land in practice. Criteria such as 'intensity', 'continuity', and 'exclusivity' are not terms of art. They are not, and cannot be, objectively defined. What is considered intense, continuous, and exclusive use is determined by a cultural context. For instance, a nomadic Sami reindeer herder naturally has a very different conception of what amounts to intense, continuous, and exclusive use, compared with a Scandinavian farmer that keep cattle stationary within fences.

Chapter 7 explains how the conventional understanding of the right to equality does not require states to take cultural differences into account in their respective laws and policies. That chapter illustrates this understanding of the right with an example from the sphere of education. Recall how according to the conventional understanding of the right to equality, it is sufficient (indeed expected) that a state provides one educational system—based on the majority culture. The right to equality, as conventionally understood, only requires that all children, irrespective of cultural background, have the same right to access that one educational system. The above outlines how the right to property is essentially a particular aspect of the

[20] In addition to objective criteria, some jurisdictions demand that a subjective good faith criterion be fulfilled. The good faith criterion prescribes that a user must not only objectively have used a land area to a sufficient degree. The user must in addition have done so based on a subjective belief that it has a right to do so.

right to equality. Hopefully, the reader now starts to see how fundamentally relevant the link between the rights to property and equality is for indigenous communities' possibility to establish rights over lands and natural resources through traditional use.

As seen, the conventional understanding of the right to equality does not oblige states to culturally adjust education to the cultural background of children belonging to among others indigenous groups. Neither does, in a comparable manner, the conventional understanding of the right to equality require states to culturally adjust the criteria one needs to fulfil in order to establish property rights over territories through traditional use—i.e. the intensity, continuity, and exclusivity criteria—to indigenous cultures, even in disputes that concern their right to land. A 'translation' of the educational example above to the sphere of land rights could read as follows: It is equality [under the conventional understanding of the right to equality] if a Sami reindeer herder has the same opportunity as a Scandinavian farmer to establish property rights over land through purchasing a cow, building a fence around a plot of land, and placing the cow within the confines of the fence. In other words, a right to non-discrimination that merely requires states to treat equal cases equally accepts a domestic legal system that provides that only land uses with the same sort of continuity, intensity etc. as land uses common to the majority culture results in property rights. Thus, indigenous communities can establish property rights over land by adapting to the majority people's way of life (and if in doing so, the right to equality obliges the state to acknowledge the community's property right irrespective of its different cultural background), but the community cannot establish property right over land if continuously pursuing land uses that do not meet the majority culture's understanding of what amounts to intense, continuous etc. use. To conclude, the conventional understanding of the right to equality allows states to employ only one understanding of what constitutes intense, continued, and dominating use, an understanding derived from standards set by the majority culture, in the same manner as it allows the state to provide only one educational system rooted in the majority culture and language.

For the articulated reasons, irrespective of that in the second time-period, international law formally recognized that indigenous communities could establish property rights over land and natural resources through traditional use, such communities nonetheless faced great difficulties when seeking to have such rights recognized in practice. Indigenous communities were often unable to gain acknowledgement that their land use had been sufficiently intense etc. when measured against standards set by land utilizations common to the majority culture. The lingering problem can again be illustrated by building on the Sami example above. Under the conventional understanding of the right to equality, when examining whether Sami nomadic reindeer herding communities had established property rights over land through traditional use, Scandinavian courts applied standards as to what amounts to intense, continued, and dominating land uses derived from land utilizations common to Scandinavian style stationary agriculture. Naturally, under such circumstances Sami reindeer herding communities were rarely, if ever, successful when seeking to have rights to land recognized. The same were true for other indigenous cultures as well.

8.5 The Right to Property When Rooted in the Evolved Understanding of the Right to Equality

Chapter 7 explains how the right to non-discrimination has evolved to require not only that equal cases be treated equally, but also that different cases be treated differently. Formal equality is no longer sufficient. There must also be equality in practice. As further seen, although the right to equality does not formally apply to collectives, for all practical purposes, the evolved understanding of the right does indirectly extend a protection also to the cultural distinctiveness and identity of indigenous group as such.

In addition, Section 8.2.2 explains how the right to property, at its core, essentially is a particular aspect of the right to equality. Therefore, an evolved understanding of the latter right should reasonably directly impact on how we understand the content and scope of the former. Section 7.4 illustrates how the evolved understanding of the right to equality compares with the conventional one by using an example from the sphere of education. It explains that under the evolved understanding of equality, it is no longer non-discrimination if indigenous children have the right to equal access to education in and on the majority language. Rather, the right to equality now requires that states provide an educational system that offers indigenous children the same right to access education in and on their mother tongue compared with children belonging to the majority culture. As with regard to the conventional understanding of equality, the example derived from the sphere of education is translatable to the area of land and natural resource rights.

Viewed through the prism of the evolved understanding of the right to equality, it is no longer sufficient that domestic property law is formally neutral between cultures. It must also be non-discriminatory in practice. To the extent domestic law and policy generally provides that private entities can hold property rights over lands and natural resources, the fact that different spheres of society use lands in different manners must be taken into account. Purportedly neutral property right laws and policies are discriminatory if nonetheless indirectly favouring land uses typical to the majority culture.[21] In other words, a domestic property rights regime is discriminatory if it accepts that property rights over land arise as a result of land uses common to the majority culture at the same time as land uses customary to an indigenous culture are held to fail to meet the criteria necessary to fulfil in order to establish property rights over land.

To illustrate how the recent developments within the sphere of equality must impact on how we understand the right to property, it may be useful to return to the example of Sami reindeer herding as contrasted against Scandinavian style agriculture. The above shows how a right to non-discrimination that merely requires states to treat equal cases equally accepts a property right law that is designed so that

[21] As James Anaya notes, 'the fundamental norm of non-discrimination requires recognition of the forms of property that arise from the traditional or customary land tenure of indigenous peoples, in addition to the property regimes created by dominant society.' See *Indigenous Peoples in International Law* (n 1) 142.

property rights over lands can in practice only be established through agricultural practices common to the Scandinavian culture. According to the evolved understanding of the right to equality, on the other hand, it is equality if Sami reindeer herders have the same opportunity to establish property rights over land through land uses common to their culture, i.e. through herding reindeer over mountains and through forests, as Scandinavian farmers have through agriculture. To be more specific, the contemporary understanding of the right to equality requires domestic legal systems, and those that apply the law, to adjust the intensity, continuity, and exclusivity criteria to the culture of the people whose property rights over lands and natural resources are being examined. For instance, if a domestic court surveys whether an indigenous community has established property rights over land through traditional use, the evolved understanding of equality prescribes that the court should evaluate whether the use has been sufficiently intense, continued, and, if an ownership right is at stake, dominating, *based on what constitutes intense, continued (and dominating) use according to that indigenous culture*. Again turning to the Sami for illustration, if a Sami reindeer herding community seeks to have property rights over its traditional territory recognized, the domestic court must evaluate whether the reindeer herding pursued has been sufficiently intense, continued, (and dominating) based on what is common to the Sami nomadic reindeer herding culture. The right to equality provides that the court must not apply standards on what amounts to intense, continued, (and dominating) use set by Scandinavian style agriculture or other forms of stationary land uses.

In summary, at least in theory, recent developments as to how we understand the right to equality suggest that indigenous communities should be able to realize property rights over territories traditionally used also in practice. What remains to survey is to what extent this theoretical conclusion is reflected in legal sources.

8.6 International Legal Sources on Indigenous Land Rights

8.6.1 International Labour Organization's (ILO) Convention No 169 on Indigenous and Tribal Peoples in Independent Countries

The adoption of the International Labour Organization's (ILO) Convention No 169 on Indigenous and Tribal Peoples in Independent Countries (ILO 169) was indicative of a development towards recognition that indigenous communities hold property rights over territories traditionally used. Pursuant to ILO 169 Article 14.1, '[t]he right to ownership and possession of the peoples concerned over the lands which they traditionally occupy shall be recognized. In addition, measures shall be taken in appropriate cases to safeguard the right of the peoples concerned to use lands not exclusively occupied by them, but to which they have traditionally had access for their subsistence and traditional activities.'

The wording of the provision thus submits that indigenous peoples hold property rights in the form of ownership rights over lands they occupy by means of traditional use. (Again, in the term 'traditional' one must read in that the use has been sufficiently intense and continuous.) The first sentence of Article 14.1 does not explicitly require that the use has been dominant. But that follows from the second sentence, which speaks of territories indigenous peoples today share with the majority population. This makes it clear that the first sentence only addresses such territories where the indigenous land use has been, and continues to be, dominant, resulting in ownership rights. The second sentence of ILO 169 Article 14.1, on the other hand, is not explicit as to what kind of right it addresses. But as the first sentence clearly proclaims a property right, one can safely assume that the second sentence does so as well. To conclude, pursuant to ILO 169 Article 14.1, indigenous peoples hold property rights in the form of usufruct rights over territories traditionally used, but which they today share with the majority population. Insofar as the land area is not shared but rather the use still dominant, the right held is one of ownership.

Section 4.4 describes how pursuant to the Vienna Convention on the Law of Treaties (VCLT) Article 31.1, a treaty provision shall, in absence of overwhelming evidence to the contrary, be given a meaning that follows from an ordinary understanding of its wording. As seen, the wording of ILO 169 Article 14.1 is straightforward, including its proclamation that indigenous peoples hold ownership rights to land areas traditionally and exclusively used. Against the backdrop of this accepted rule for treaty interpretation, it is puzzling that both states and experts have been eager to declare that despite its wording, ILO 169 Article 14.1 does in fact not require states to recognize ownership rights over land of indigenous peoples. In fact, since the adoption of ILO 169 and until at least recently, there seems to have been more or less agreement that the first sentence of ILO 169 Article 14.1 merely expects states to acknowledge that indigenous peoples enjoy a right to secured continued use of land. Recognition of formal ownership rights is not, it has been asserted, necessary.[22] Even the ILO's Committee of Experts, which has been authorized to authoritatively oversee the implementation of ILO 169, has submitted that '[it] does not consider that the Convention requires title to be recognized in all cases in which indigenous . . . peoples have rights to lands traditionally occupied by them . . .'.[23] Irrespective of Article 14.1's unambiguous formulation, the preferred understanding of the provision has thus been that it enshrines a right more akin to a cultural right. Such an interpretation obligates states to ensure that indigenous communities can continuously pursue traditional livelihoods and other culturally-based land uses.[24] But states need not recognize that an indigenous community hold an ownership right to any specific land area.

How is it that both states and legal scholars appear to have taken for granted that ILO 169 Article 14.1 does not set forth an ownership right, in direct violation of the wording of the provision and accepted norms for treaty interpretation? One

[22] Geir Ulfstein, 'Indigenous Peoples' Right to Land' [2004] *Max Planck UNYB* 8 19–21; Manuela Tomei and Lee Swepston, *Indigenous and Tribal Peoples: A Guide to ILO 169*, (ILO, 1996).

[23] CEACR 1995/65th Session. [24] Compare Section 5.5.2.

plausible explanation might be that at the time of the adoption of ILO 169 (in 1989), indigenous land rights were, as Section 5.5 briefly discusses, largely thought of in terms of cultural rights. Thus, despite the unambiguous wording of Article 14.1, it might have been far-fetched for many that the provision actually calls for recognition of property rights, and in particular property rights in the form of ownership rights. As further described, this reluctance can in turn probably partly be explained by lingering influences of the *terra nullius* doctrine. The fact that for centuries it had been taken for granted that indigenous land uses could not establish property rights to territories might have impacted on how states and others read ILO 169 Article 14 at the time.

However, whatever interpretations of ILO 169 Article 14.1 have been put forward in the past, these can hardly be substantiated today. As seen, contemporary international law is crystal clear that indigenous communities hold property rights to territories traditionally used, including ownership rights provided that the use has been and is sufficiently dominant. Against the backdrop of these developments, and bearing VCLT Article 31.1 in mind, the contemporary understanding of Article 14.1 must reasonably be the one which follows naturally from the wording of the provision as articulated above.[25]

8.6.2 Treaty body jurisprudence

As touched upon, the CERD Committee infers that to deprive indigenous peoples of their traditional lands constitutes a specific form of discrimination directed against them. The Committee calls on states to 'recognize and protect the rights of indigenous peoples to own . . . [and] control' their lands and natural resources. In other words, the CERD Committee underlines that the general right to property enshrined in CERD Convention Article 5(d)(v) applies to lands traditionally and collectively used by indigenous peoples. The Committee has reaffirmed this interpretation of Article 5(d)(v) in numerous country-specific observations.[26] As Section 9.2 elaborates, the CERD Committee has in addition indirectly confirmed that indigenous peoples hold property rights over territories traditionally used through repeatedly underscoring that they have the right to withhold or offer their consent to competing interests that seek access to their territories.

The CERD Committee's jurisprudence has been matched by similar conclusions by its sister expert body the Committee on Economic, Social and Cultural Rights (CESC). CESC also recognize the right of indigenous peoples to own and control lands and natural resources traditionally occupied and/or used. The Committee explicitly clarifies that the right that it acknowledges is a right to property by adding that natural resources need not be culturally significant for the right of the

[25] Compare Ulfstein, 'Indigenous Peoples' Right to Land' (n 23) 17–23; Gilbert, *Indigenous Peoples' Land Rights* (n 12) 103.

[26] See e.g. A/56/18(SUPP) (Sri Lanka) 335; CERD/C/64/CO/9 (Suriname) 11; Early Warning & Urgent Action Procedure initiated against New Zealand, Decision 1 (66), CERD/C/DEC/NZL/1.27/04/2005; the United States of America, DECISION 1 (68), CERD/USA/DEC/1.

people to offer or withhold consent to those that seek access to the territory to apply.[27]

In summary, the two UN treaty bodies that are in a position to authoritatively offer their opinion on indigenous property rights (as seen, the CERD Convention embraces the right to property in general, while the International Covenant on Economic, Social and Cultural Rights (CESCR) addresses property rights over creativity (Article 15)) have both inferred that such rights, including in the form of ownership rights, emerge as a result of indigenous communities' traditional use of a particular land area.[28]

8.6.3 The UN Declaration on the Rights of Indigenous Peoples (UNDRIP)

UNDRIP Article 26.1 proclaims that '[i]ndigenous peoples have the right to the lands, territories and resources which they have traditionally owned, occupied or otherwise used or acquired.' While Article 26.1 speaks about 'rights' in generic terms, Article 26.2 proceeds to explicitly confirm that the rights indigenous peoples have established over land through traditional use are property rights. The provision provides that '[i]ndigenous peoples have the right to own, use, develop and control the lands, territories and resources that they possess by reason of . . . traditional occupation or use . . . '. Hence, pursuant to Article 26.2, indigenous peoples hold ownership rights over lands and natural resources traditionally occupied or used, irrespective of whether the lands or resources are culturally important to the people in question. In addition, the right applies regardless of whether the state has officially acknowledged the existence of the right, as long as the people continuously 'possess' the territory.[29]

There is no universally applicable definition of 'possess' or 'possession'. Perhaps, however, *Black's Law Dictionary's* view is fairly representative. According to *Black's*, to 'possess' something is 'to have in one's actual control; to have possession of' a subject matter. 'Possession' then is: (i) the fact of having or holding property in one's power, the exercise of dominion over property; and (ii) the right under which one may exercise control over something to the exclusion of others.

Some may argue that indigenous land utilization has not been and is not sufficiently dominant and intense to qualify as 'possession'. This objection may in particular be raised against nomadic or semi-nomadic indigenous land uses, and against land uses that in other ways fluctuate in ways not common to

[27] CESC General Comment No 21 36.

[28] As Section 5.5 elaborates, the third of the most central treaty bodies, the HRC, examines indigenous land rights through the prism of cultural rights. The CCPR does not contain any property right provisions.

[29] In interpretative statements delivered in connection with the UN General Assembly's adoption of the UNDRIP, the United States, Canada, New Zealand, and Nigeria expressed dissatisfaction with the land and resource rights provisions in the Declaration. Still, as Section 5.7.4 explains, negative comments delivered by a few states in connection with its adoption cannot reasonably impact on the outlined understanding of the Declaration. For a similar opinion, see Wiessner, 'Indigenous Sovereignty' (n 19) 1162. Also, the aforementioned states have three of the aforementioned states have subsequently reversed their previous position and now officially endorse the UNDRIP.

non-indigenous cultures. A careful analysis suggests, however, that the reference 'possess' in UNDRIP Article 26.2 can hardly be ascribed to such a restrictive meaning. To do so would essentially take the indigenous land rights regime back to the *terra nullius* doctrine era.

The above describes how international law has recently reinterpreted the concept of property rights to avoid discrimination against land and natural resource uses common to indigenous cultures. The term 'possess' in UNDRIP Article 26.2 must reasonably be understood against the backdrop of this development. It seemingly makes little sense to first recognize that indigenous peoples' traditional use of land result in property rights, only to immediately thereafter make such rights contingent upon that indigenous peoples 'possess' land in the conventional understanding of the term. As indicated, such a reading of Article 26.2 would leave the provision largely without meaning. This is an implausible interpretation, in particular in light of the articulated recent developments within the equality and property discourses.

There is a clear proximity between the concepts 'property rights' and 'possession'. If comparing *Black's* definition of 'possession' with the definition of 'property right' discussed in Section 8.2, one notes a clear resemblance between the two. This is only natural. A property right, once established, is essentially a right to legal protection of what one possesses. As seen, the understanding of what is required for indigenous communities to establish property rights over territories traditionally used has recently evolved. Reasonably, therefore, the understanding of what is required of indigenous peoples to legally 'possess' land must have evolved in a corresponding manner. To the extent this conclusion is correct, UNDRIP Article 26.2's reference to 'possess' must be understood as refering to what amounts to possession in the culture of the relevant indigenous people. It follows that pursuant to UNDRIP Article 26.2, indigenous peoples possess, and hold property rights over, territories that they use and inhabit in manners common to their respective cultures, provided that they have done so for a sufficient time-period. It bears repeating that this is so irrespective of how disperse and irregular these land uses may appear to members of the majority population. This interpretation of UNDRIP Article 26.2 finds support in juriprudence and the legal doctrine.[30]

[30] Kent McNeil underlines that 'possession' in the context of indigenous peoples must be understood to mean 'possession in fact'. This results in a presumption that the community also has 'possession in law'. See Kent McNeil, 'Emerging Justice?', in *Essays on Indigenous Rights in Canada and Australia* (University of Saskatchawan Native Law Centre, 2001) 141. Similarly, in *Delgamuukw*, the Canadian Supreme Court affirmed that physical occupation (i.e. possession in fact) by an indigenous community evidences possession in law— see *Delgamuukw v British Columbia* [1997] 3 SCR 1010. Alexandra Xanthaki too, notes that indigenous peoples' own customary land tenure systems result in 'possession' under the UNDRIP—see Xanthaki, 'Indigenous Rights in International Law over the Last 10 Years and Future Developments' [2009] *Melbourne Journal of International Law* 10 (1). In a similar vein, Javaid Rehman posits that the UNDRIP's land rights provisions are reflective of customary international law—see Rehman 'Between the Devil and the Deep Blue Sea: Indigenous Peoples as the Pawns in the US "War on Terror" and the Jihad of Osama Bin Laden', in Stephen Allen and Alexandra Xanthaki (eds.), *Reflections on the UN Declaration on the Rights of Indigenous Peoples* (Hart Publishing, 2011) 561–62. James Anaya made an observation in a similar tone back in 2005 with regard to the then draft

UNDRIP Article 26.2 does not employ ILO 169 Article 14's explicit distinction between territories where the indigenous land use still dominate, to which as a consequence ownership rights apply, and territories today shared with the majority population, that are subject to usufruct rights. Still, the former provision does refer to both rights to own and use. One can thus perhaps read the distinction between lands exclusively used and lands today shared with the majority population into the UNDRIP as well. That is particularly so since such a conclusion is in line with the position taken by international legal sources in general.

In summary, it is inferred that pursuant to UNDRIP Article 26.2, indigenous peoples hold ownership rights over territories traditionally used, and where their land use is still dominating. As to lands traditionally and continuously used, but which indigenous peoples today share with the majority population, usufruct rights apply.[31]

8.6.4 Regional legal sources— the Inter-American human rights institutions

In the ground-breaking *Awas Tingni Case* (2001), the Inter-American Court on Human Rights (IACHR) parted with the previous practice to evaluate indigenous land rights solely in the light of the right to culture. Instead, the Court applied the general right to property contained in the Inter-American human rights instruments to indigenous traditional land uses. The IACHR held that against the backdrop of recent developments in international law, the right to property must be understood to protect indigenous communities' traditional communal occupation and use of lands and natural resources. The Court underlined that such property

Article 26—see S James Anaya, 'Indigenous Peoples' Participatory Rights in Relation to Decisions about Natural Resource Extraction' [2005] *Arizona Journal of International and Comparative Law* Vol 22, No 1 8.

[31] As with regard to the right to self-determination, it is pertinent also here to touch briefly upon potential implications of UNDRIP Article 46.2 for the conclusions drawn. Recall how this provision proclaims that the rights UNDRIP enshrines may be subject to limitations that are 'non-discriminatory and . . . necessary . . . for the purpose of securing due . . . respect for the rights . . . of others . . . and for meeting the just and most compelling requirements of a democratic society'. In addition, pursuant to UNDRIP Article 46.3, the rights contained in the UNDRIP shall be 'interpreted in accordance with the principles of justice, democracy, respect for human rights, equality, non-discrimination, good governance and good faith'. Some may argue that UNDRIP Articles 46.2 and 46.3 limit the scope and applicability of Article 26. A careful examination reveals, however, that this appears not to be the case. First, respect for property rights can hardly conflict with a 'need to meet the most compelling requirements of society as a whole', nor with the principles of justice, democracy, and good governance. As Section 8.2 explains, each state may freely determine to what extent its domestic legal system recognizes private rights over property. As a consequence, property rights can, by definition, not conflict with principles of democracy etc. Recognition of property rights over lands and natural resources of indigenous peoples can conflict with rights of third parties established under the domestic legal system during a time when this system relied on *terra nullius* or similar doctrines. But, as the above outlines, the right to property is essentially a particular aspect of the right to equality, which has evolved to require respect for land uses particular to indigenous cultures. As limitations to the scope and content of the right to property enshrined in the UNDRIP must be non-discriminatory, Articles 46.2 and 46.3 cannot be invoked to argue that the UNDRIP proclaims a more restrictive right to property than the above infers.

rights are not contingent upon formal deed, title, or other forms of official state recognition.[32] It is worth underlining that in reaching its conclusion, the IACHR opined that indigenous communities' property rights over territories traditionally used are not confined to the Americans. On the contrary, the Court inferred that such rights have been accepted by international law in general.[33] In other words, the IACHR held that international customary law has evolved to embrace a right to property of indigenous communities over territories traditionally used.

In the subsequent *Dann Sisters*, the Inter-American Commission on Human Rights (IACommHR) affirmed the IACHR's conclusions in *Awas Tingni*. The Commission elaborated that 'general international legal principles applicable to indigenous human rights encompass a right for indigenous peoples of recognition of their property and ownership right with respect to lands, territories and resources they have traditionally occupied.' The IACommHR highlighted that indigenous peoples must only be deprived of their ancestral lands with their consent.[34] It bears underlining that the IACommHR emphasized the connection between the right to equality and indigenous peoples' property rights over land. The Committee reaffirmed that indigenous property rights are worthy of a protection equal to that protection which applies to conventional property rights held by non-indigenous individuals.[35] The IACommHR further echoed the IACHR's observation in *Awas Tingni* that indigenous communities' property rights over land are not unique to the Inter-American human rights system. Rather, the Commission held, customary international law provides that indigenous peoples have the right to '. . . recognition of their property and ownership right with respect to lands, territories and resources they have historically occupied . . .'.[36] In the *Belize Case*, the IACommHR affirmed the basic findings in *Awas Tingni* and *Dann Sisters*, and found that Maya communities in Belize had established property rights to land through

[32] See *Awas Tingni Case, Mayagna (Sumo) Community of Awas Tingni v Nicaragua*, Judgement of 31 August, 2001, Inter-Am Ct HR, (Ser C) No 79 (2001) 149. Regarding *Awas Tingni*, see also Anaya, *Indigenous Peoples in International Law* (n 1) 145–46; Luis Rodríguez-Pinero, 'The Inter-American System and the UN Declaration on the Rights of Indigenous Peoples: Mutual Reinforcement', in Stephen Allen and Alexandra Xanthaki (eds.), *Reflections on the UN Declaration on the Rights of Indigenous Peoples* (Hart Publishing, 2011) 462; Siegfried Wiessner, 'The Cultural Rights of Indigenous Peoples: Achievments and Continuing Challenges' [2011] *The European Journal of International Law*, Vol 22, No 1 135–37; Christina Binder, 'The Case of the Atlantic Coast of Nicaragua: The Awas Tingni Case, or Realizing that a Good Legal System of Protection of Land Rights Is no Guarantee for Effective Implementation', in Joshua Castellino and Niamh Walsh (eds.), *International Law and Indigenous Peoples* (Martinus Nijhoff Publisher, 2005) 249–51.

[33] See *Awas Tingni* (n 33) 151; also Anaya, *Indigenous Peoples in International Law* (n 1) 146; Anaya, 'Indigenous Peoples' Participatory Rights in Relation to Decisions about Natural Resource Extraction' [2005] *Arizona Journal of International and Comparative Law* Vol 22, No 1 13–14.

[34] *Mary and Carrie Dann v United States*, Case No 11.140 (United States); Inter-Am CHR Report No 75/02 (merits decision of December 27 2002) 29–37.

[35] In this context, see also Anaya, *Indigenous Peoples in International Law* (n 1) 146.

[36] See *Mary and Carrie Dann v United States* (n 35) 130; also Anaya, *Indigenous Peoples in International Law* (n 1) 147–48; Rodríguez-Pinero, 'The Inter-American System and the UN Declaration on the Rights of Indigenous Peoples' (n 33) 463.

traditional use,[37] as did the IACHR in two parallel cases concerning the Enxet people in Paraguay—the *Yakey Axa*[38] and *Sawhoyamaxa Cases*. In the latter case, the Court elaborated that 'traditional possession of their lands by indigenous peoples has equivalent effect to those of state-granted full property title', and that 'traditional possession entitle indigenous peoples to demand official recognition and registration of property title.'[39]

The IACHR's and the IACommHR's application of the general right to property enshrined in the Inter-American human rights instruments represents another example of how treaty provisions, through subsequent rulings by international tribunals, can evolve to take on expanded understandings. In a similar fashion as UN treaty bodies, the Inter-American human rights institutions have inferred that the right to property the Inter-American human rights instruments set forth applies to indigenous communities' traditional territories. They have reached this conclusion mindful that such a protection was not envisioned at the time of the adoption of the Inter-American human rights instruments, and that such an understanding of the right cannot be read out of the wording of these instruments either.

The articulated conclusions find support in the legal doctrine. Maia Campbell and James Anaya concur that the Inter-American human rights system affirms that indigenous communities' land and resource rights are to be viewed through the prism of the right to equality.[40] Robert A Williams infers that the Inter-American human rights institutions have held that the Inter-American human rights instruments call for respect for indigenous communities' property rights, including ownership rights, over territories traditionally occupied or used for the pursuit of their traditional livelihoods.[41] Nigel Bankes notes that the Inter-American human rights system requires states to award the same degree of protection to indigenous communities' property rights over land as they do with regard to rights of members of the non-indigenous population. Indigenous communities' traditional possession of land thus has equivalent legal effect as state-granted title, he maintains.[42] In the same vein, Andrew Huff concludes that Inter-American human rights law obliges states to recognize indigenous peoples' property rights over lands and natural resources traditionally used, to the same extent as it acknowledges other forms of property rights over lands and resources.[43] Jo Pasqualucci concurs that jurisprudence emanating out of the Inter-American human rights institutions provides that

[37] *Maya Indigenous Communities of the Toledo District v Belize*, Case 12.053, Inter-Am CHR, Report No 40/04 (decision of October 12, 2004) 117–20, 127, 132–35.

[38] *Yakey Axa Indigenous Community v Paraguay*, IACHR judgement of 17 June 2005, Series C No 141 (2005).

[39] See *Sawhoyamaxa Indigenous Community v Paraguay*, IACHR judgment of 29 March 2006, Series C No 146 (2006) 128. *Yakey Axa* and *Sawhoyamaxa* are in addition highly relevant in the context of a right to restitution of lands that indigenous peoples have traditionally used but which have subsequently been taken without consent. See further Section 8.8.

[40] Maia Campbell and S James Anaya, 'The Case of the Maya Villages of Belize: Reversing the Trend of Government Neglect to Secure Indigenous Land Rights' [2008] *Human Rights Law Review* 8:2 394.

[41] Robert A Williams, *Like a Loaded Weapon* (University of Minnesota Press, 2005) 184–85.

[42] Nigel Bankes, 'Land Claims Agreements in Arctic Canada in Light of International Human Rights Norms' [2009] *Yearbook of Polar Law*,1 222, 226.

[43] Huff, 'Indigenous Land Rights and the New Self-Determination' (n 14) 329–30.

indigenous peoples hold property rights over territories traditionally used, with equivalent legal status as state granted title.[44]

8.6.5 Regional legal sources outside the Americas

The extensive jurisprudence on indigenous communities' property rights over territories traditionally used that has emanated out of the Inter-American human rights system has not been matched by other regions. This is only natural. The American Continent is unique in that the vast majority of the American states both host indigenous peoples and recognize these groups as such. Still, judicial bodies outside the Americas have reached conclusions that correspond to those of the Inter-American institutions, albeit admittedly to a lesser degree.

In *Endorois*, the African Commission on Human and Peoples' Rights (AfCommHPR) allowed itself to be heavily guided by the jurisprudence emanating out of the Inter-American human rights system in general and by *Saramaka* in particular. The African Commission thus inferred that the Endorois have established property rights over their traditional territory through traditional use.[45] It is worth adding that already prior to *Endorois*, the AfCommHPR's Working Group of Experts on Indigenous Populations/Communities had interpreted the AfCPHR to extend property rights protection to territories traditionally used by indigenous communities. The Working Group inferred that dispossession of indigenous communities from their traditional lands amounts to a violation of the African Charter's property rights provisions.[46]

In Europe, the European Commission on Human Rights (ECommHR) and the European Court of Human Rights (ECtHR) have held that, in principle, indigenous communities' traditional land use results in rights protected as property rights under Article 1 of Additional Protocol 1 to the ECHR.[47]

As mentioned, the Asian region has only recently commenced cooperating within the field of human rights. This may explain why no jurisprudence similar to that of Europe, Africa, and, in particular, the Americas, has emanated out of that region.

[44] Jo Pasqualucci, 'International Indigenous Land Rights; A Critique of the Jurisprudence of the Inter-American Court of Human Rights in Light of the United Nations Declaration on the Rights of Indigenous Peoples' [2009] 27 *Wisconsin International Law Journal* 51 58–61.

[45] *Endorois People v Kenya Case. Centre for Minority Rights Development (Kenya) and Minority Rights Group International on behalf of Endorois Welfare Council v Kenya*, Comm 276/2003 (2010) 214–15.

[46] Report of the African Commission's Working Group of Experts on Indigenous Populations/Communities, adopted by the AfCommHPR at its 28th ordinary session (2005) 20–22.

[47] See *Könkämä and 38 other Saami Villages v Sweden* App No 27033/95-ECOHR; and *Handölsdalen Sami Village AO v Sweden* App no 39013/04 (ECtHR, 30 March 2010). For an outline of the former case, see Timo Koivurova, 'Jurisprudence of the European Court of Human Rights Regarding Indigenous Peoples: Retrospects and Prospects' [2011] *International Journal on Minority and Group Rights* 18 17–18. See also Patrick Thornberry, *Indigenous Peoples and Human Rights* (Manchester University Press, 2002) 305–06, where he notes that the former case 'recognises that such specific indigenous rights fall within the ambit of [Additional Protocol 1 to the ECHR]'.

Oceania too, is in want of regional human rights institutions. Here, however, as in Europe, domestic jurisprudence confirms that indigenous communities hold property rights over territories traditionally used.[48]

8.6.6 Some domestic examples of application of the evolved understanding of the right to equality

Canada

In *Delgamuukw*, the Canadian Supreme Court held that 'aboriginal title . . . arises from the prior occupation of Canada by Aboriginal peoples'. As to the scope and content of such title, the Court elaborated that it 'encompasses the right to exclusive use and occupation of the land held pursuant to the title for a variety of purposes, which need not be aspects of those aboriginal practises . . . which are integral to distinctive aboriginal cultures; [but] those protected uses must not be irreconcilable with the nature of the group's attachment to that land'.[49] In other words, under Canadian law, in conformity with international law, Canadian aboriginal communities hold property rights over lands exclusively occupied. According to the Supreme Court, such rights embrace not only natural resources traditionally used, but also resources such as standing timber and oil and gas. But the right is limited in the sense that Aboriginal communities may not use non-traditional natural resources in manners that prevent communities' traditional land-based activities, such as hunting and fishing.[50] Aboriginal title does not entitle the community to sell its land to any other entity than the Canadian state.[51]

Aboriginal title is not the only form of Aboriginal land and resource rights in Canada. Under Canadian law, an Aboriginal community's traditional use of particular natural resources, such as fish and game, results in usufruct rights to such resources, irrespective of whether the use of the particular land area has been exclusive or not. Such usufruct rights are, however, contingent upon that the resources were integral to the culture of the Aboriginal community at the time of European arrival. The content and scope of these usufruct rights are determined by practices and customs integral to the community at the time of first contact with the Europeans.[52]

South Africa

In *Richtersveld*, the South African Supreme Court of Appeal stated that it is 'racially discriminatory' to fail to recognize that an indigenous community that has occupied its traditional territory since time immemorial has established ownership

[48] See e.g. *New Zealand Maori Council v Attorney-General* [1987] 1 NZLR 641; and *Te Runanga o Wharekauri Rekohu Inc v Attorney-General* [1993] 2 NZLR 301.
[49] *Delgamuukw* (n 31) 114, 117. [50] Compare Section 2.4.
[51] McNeil, 'Judicial Treatment' (n 18) 7–8, 13–15, 36.
[52] See e.g. *R v Vand der Peet* [1996] 2 SCR 507; and *R v Sappier and Gray* [2006] 2 SCR 686; and also McNeil, 'Judicial Treatment' (n 18) 8, 16.

rights over the land. The Court elaborated that 'the racial discrimination lay[s] in the failure to recognize . . . indigenous . . . ownership while, on the other hand, according protection to registered title[s]' of members of the non-indigenous population.' The Court elaborated that dispossession of indigenous communities of their traditional land is racially discriminatory since it is 'based upon the false . . . premise that because of the . . . communit[ies'] race and lack of civilization, they had lost all rights in the land upon annexation.' It added that 'a nomadic lifestyle is not inconsistent with the exclusive and effective right of occupation of land by indigenous peoples.' Based on these principal conclusions, the Court inferred that the Richtersveld community's traditional use of land had established a right of exclusive occupation and use, akin to an ownership right. The right acknowledged embraced property rights over natural resources on and under that land, including to minerals and precious stones.[53]

Richtersveld is particularly interesting since it explicitly links not only colonization of indigenous lands—but also the continued reliance on such past practices—to the right to equality. *Richtersveld* thus illustrates well what underpins indigenous communities' property rights over territories traditionally used under contemporary international law.[54]

Belize

One of the more interesting cases coming out of domestic courts reflecting the evolved understanding of the right to equality is the Belize Supreme Court's ruling in *Cal.* Upon colonization of Belize, the United Kingdom had declared essentially all land areas in the colony Crown land. Following independence, as other former colonies, the Belizian state sought to adopt the policy of the former colonial power vis-à-vis the traditional territories of the indigenous communities of the country,[55] claiming that the new state hold ownership rights to indigenous communities' traditional territories in Belize.[56]

The legal validity of the position taken by the Belizian state was tested when a number of Maya communities claimed rights over territories traditionally used by them. The Belize Supreme Court found in favour of the communities. The Court applied the rights to property and equality, and found that customary use and occupancy of land by the Maya communities had resulted in property rights over the territory. It elaborated that 'respect for and protection of the private property of indigenous peoples on their territories . . . is mandated by the fundamental principle of non-discrimination . . .'. The Court further observed that Maya customary

[53] See *Richtersveld Cmty & Others v Alexkor Ltd & Another* (CCT19/03) [2003] ZACC 18; 2004 (5) SA 460 (CC); 2003 (12) BCLR 1301 (CC) (14 October 2003) 8, 9, 23, 27, 62, 96, 99, 102, 103; also Gilbert, *Indigenous Peoples' Land Rights* (n 12) 67, 111–12.

[54] See also Gilbert, *Indigenous Peoples' Land Rights* (n 12) 168–69. In a similar vein as in *Richtersveld*, in *Kalahari Game Reserve* the High Court of Botswana inferred that indigenous communities in the Reserve hold property rights over lands traditionally used. See *Kalahari Game Reserve Case* Misca No 52 of 2002, of 13 December 2006.

[55] Compare Section 2.3.3.

[56] Campbell and Anaya, 'The Case of the Maya Villages of Belize' (n 41) 379.

rights over lands are by nature different from regular property rights and by not accommodating for that difference, Belize discriminated against the Maya communities.[57] One may note that these conclusions were in line with previous rulings by the Court (and international law), where it had underlined that 'true justice does not give the same to all but to each his due: it consists not only in treating like things alike, but unlike things as unlike.'[58] In other words, *Cal* explicitly affirms the principal conclusion of this Chapter, i.e. that the evolved understanding of the right to equality directly impacts on indigenous communities' property rights over territories traditionally used.

As to the material scope of the property right held by the Maya communities, the Belize Supreme Court inferred that the content of the right must be determined in light of traditional customs observed by the communities.[59] The Court underlined that the right are communal in nature. Thus, the holders of the right were the communities as such, while individual members of the communities is beneficiaries of derivative rights to the particular land patches they use within the larger community according to Mayan custom. The Court referred to the right awarded as 'usufructuary' in nature.[60] Still, Maia Campbell and James Anaya maintain that the ruling may be understood to award the communities inalienable communal title over land.[61]

As a final point, it is worth underlining that as the Inter-American human rights institutions in the cases referred to above, the Belize Supreme Court relied on international law in general when reaching its conclusion. The Court held that 'customary international law . . . require[s] that Belize respects the rights of its indigenous people to their lands and resources'. The Court in particular relied on the UNDRIP. The Belize Supreme Court declared that the 'Declaration import[s] . . . significant obligations for the State of Belize in so far as the indigenous Maya rights to their land and resources are concerned.' The Court also cited ILO 169, although Belize is not party to the Convention, thus lending support to the conclusion that the right ILO 169 Article 14.1 articulates forms part of customary international law.[62] Campbell and Anaya posit that by drawing from international law when reaching its conclusions, the Belize Supreme Court 'contributes to the consolidation of a global standard protecting the rights of indigenous peoples to their traditional lands and resources.' They note that *Cal* confirms that the UNDRIP's land rights provisions reflect customary international law. Campbell and Anaya infer that since property rights law and policy is similarly designed in most domestic jurisdictions, *Cal* sets an important precedent for how indigenous peoples' property rights over lands and natural resources shall be understood also in other jurisdictions.[63] In

[57] *Cal (on behalf of the Maya Village of Santa Cruz) and Others & Coy (on behalf of the Maya Village of Cenejo) and Others v Attorney General of Belize and Minister of Natural Resources and Environment*, Claims Nos 171 and 172 of 2007, Judgement of 18 October 2007 24, 114, 119.

[58] Campbell and Anaya, 'The Case of the Maya Villages of Belize' (n 41) 395.

[59] *Cal* (n 58) 101 and 136. [60] *Cal* (n 58) 68 and 136.

[61] Campbell and Anaya, 'The Case of the Maya Villages of Belize' (n 41) 392.

[62] *Cal* (n 58) 127, 130, 133.

[63] Campbell and Anaya, 'The Case of the Maya Villages of Belize' (n 41) 384 (quote from this page) and 398–99.

summary, *Cal* affirms that indigenous communities hold property rights over territories traditionally used under international law. In addition, it serves as an important precedent globally as to how such rights are to be understood by, and implemented in, domestic jurisdictions.

Sweden

In *Nordmaling*, the Swedish Supreme Court affirmed that Sami reindeer herding communities' hold property rights in the form of usufruct rights over land areas traditionally used, but which they today share with the majority population. It is worth underscoring that the Swedish Supreme Court, like its counterpart in Belize, reached this conclusion irrespective of that Sweden has not ratified ILO 169, thus further indicating that the norm enshrined in ILO 169 Article 14.1 (and other international legal sources) forms part of customary international law.

The Supreme Court elaborated that when determining whether reindeer herding rights in the form of property rights have been established, one must take the particularities of Sami reindeer herding culture into account. The Court held that the continuity and intensity criteria must be accustomed to the manner in which Sami reindeer herding is actually pursued. For instance, property rights to reserve pasture areas, i.e. pasture areas that are used only in years when regular pasture areas are not suitable for pasture, can be established through relatively infrequent and irregular use, the Court held. The Swedish Supreme Court further noted that Sami reindeer herding requires large areas and that varying weather conditions etc. may result in different pasture patterns from year to year. Therefore, the Court concluded, an intensity criteria accustomed to the particularities of Sami reindeer herding can be met even if the pasture area is not used on a regular basis, but rather to varying degrees from year to year, and with occasional longer periods of non-use.[64]

In conclusion, *Nordmaling* confirms that indigenous communities' traditional land and resource uses result in property rights. Moreover, *Nordmaling* underscores that when evaluating whether traditional land utilization has resulted in property rights, the intensity and continuity criteria must be accustomed to the cultural particularities of the indigenous community concerned, reflecting the evolved understanding of the right to equality as articulated above.

8.6.7 The compatibility between indigenous land rights and the practice of extinguishment

As indicated, some states have sought to rely on extinguishment or similar practices when asserting that indigenous communities hold no, or limited, proprietary rights over their traditional territories. A state that invokes the practice of extinguishment

[64] See the *Nordmaling Case*, NJA 2011 s 109, in particular paras. 5–10, 12, 56. The Swedish Supreme Court's ruling in *Nordmaling* resemblances its Norwegian counterpart's ruling in *Selbu*, a few years earlier. See the *Selbu Case*, Rt 2001 side 769.

acknowledges that indigenous communities did hold historic rights over their traditional lands and, more importantly, that these rights could potentially carry legal relevance still today. At the same time, however, the state maintains that be that as it may, any potential right has been extinguished through a subsequent decree, act of parliament, or other similar measure. That is so, the state may submit, irrespective of whether the indigenous community is still inhabiting the land area in dispute. Alternatively, a state may not rely on a past act of extinguishment, but wish to extinguish the indigenous community's right over its territory today through a unilateral act to that effect.[65] The question is then whether extinguishment or other similar practices are compatible with indigenous communities' property rights over lands and natural resources under international law.

When assessing the legal relevance of the practice of extinguishment, it is again important to be mindful of the distinction between sovereign and property rights over lands. Section 8.2 explains how, from a property rights perspective, a state is sovereign to determine to what extent private entities can establish title over lands and natural resources within its jurisdiction. A state is free to use its sovereignty to determine that no private rights apply to lands and natural resources. In such instances, indigenous communities too cannot claim rights over territories based on the right to property, given the close proximity between this right and the right to equality.[66] But almost no states have exercised their sovereignty in such a manner. Domestic jurisdictions generally recognize that private entities can acquire property rights over land. Under such circumstances, as underlined repeatedly above, states must recognize that this right applies equally to all segments of society including to indigenous peoples. To put it differently, a state must not exercise its sovereign rights over its territory to a larger degree vis-à-vis certain segments of society, compared with others. As Jeremy Webber points out, indigenous communities' rights over territories traditionally used are proprietary rights that 'survive the non -indigenous government's assertion of sovereignty'. Webber adds that under 'the general rule in international law . . . property rights are not erased by a change of sovereignty but should, in principle, be recognized by the new sovereign'.[67]

From these basic features of the right to property, it follows that attempts to extinguish indigenous communities' rights over their traditional territories violates

[65] This Section 8.6.7 on extinguishment should be understood in conjunction with Section 8.8 on restitution. This section addresses to what extent states can legally extinguish indigenous communities' property rights over lands and natural resources today, or, alternatively, whether past such acts are valid, *when the indigenous community continuously use the land area in dispute*. Section 8.8 then surveys the legality of past takings of indigenous lands, which may have occurred through the practice of extinguishment, but also through other means, *but when the land area is no longer in the indigenous community's possession*.

[66] Another matter is that from a *self-determination perspective*, indigenous peoples can still hold rights over lands and natural resources also in countries that do not acknowledge private title to land. In addition, as Section 5.5.2 briefly outlines, also in states that do not recognize private property rights over land, indigenous peoples, and communities (or formally speaking indigenous individuals) can hold rights over lands and natural resources based on the right to culture.

[67] Jeremy Webber, 'The Public-Law Dimension of Indigenous Property Rights', in Nigel Bankes and Timo Koivurova (eds.), *The Proposed Nordic Saami Convention; National and International Dimensions of Indigenous Property Rights* (Hart Publishing, 2013) 79, 83.

international law. True, human rights, including the right to property, are, as a general rule, not absolute.[68] A state is free to exercise its sovereignty in a manner that limits the right to property. In order for such a limitation to be legitimate—rather than to constitute an illegal infringement in the right—certain criteria must, however, be met. First, the limitation must fulfil a legitimate aim, i.e. it must meet a great social need.[69] Second, it must be prescribed by law, i.e. it must not be arbitrary but rather foreseeable to the property right holder.[70] Finally, the limitation must be proportionate, i.e. it must 'strike a fair balance between the demands of the general interest of [society as a whole] and the requirements of the protection of the individual's fundamental rights'. There must be 'a reasonable relation . . . between the means employed and the aim sought to be realized by any measures applied by the state'.[71] What is decisive is whether the property right holder is left with a disproportionate and excessive burden as a result of the limitation.[72] For a limitation to be deemed proportionate, it is further of cardinal importance that it is applied in a non-discriminatory manner. The state must not arbitrarily, without objective reason, infringe upon one property right while at the same time leaving a comparable property right untouched.[73]

Attempts to extinguish indigenous peoples' property rights over territories traditionally used fail to meet the outlined criteria. Some might claim that extinguishment under certain circumstances meet a legitimate aim. That may for instance be the case if the purpose is to promote development projects of substantial value to society as a whole. But one can hardly argue that extinguishment strikes a fair balance between the interest of society as a whole and the rights of indigenous communities. As Section 9.2.2 elaborates, expropriation of a *smaller and targeted part* of an indigenous community's territory for the purposes of e.g. development *might* strike such a balance. But extinguishment is not a targeting practice. On the contrary, it seeks to sweepingly nullify indigenous property rights in general. To make matters worse, the practice of extinguishment is explicitly directed at the property of a particular ethnic, cultural, and racial group. No similar practice is attempted at land rights held by members of the majority population. The practice is therefore clearly discriminatory, both in effect and intent. As a consequence, such a practice can hardly be said to represent a reasonable relation between the means employed and the aim sought to be realized. Rather, it leaves indigenous peoples with a disproportionate and excessive burden.[74]

[68] Exceptions are the most fundamental human rights such as the right to life and the rights to be free from slavery and torture.

[69] See e.g. Article 1 of the Additional Protocol 1 to the ECHR, and also the ECtHR's ruling in *James and others v. United Kingdom* (1986) 8 EHRR 123.

[70] See e.g. *Iatridis v Greece* (1999) 30 EHRR 97 62.

[71] See e.g. the ECtHR's ruling in *Draon v France* (2005) 42 EHRR 78; and in *Hutten-Czapska v Poland* (2006) 45 EHRR 52 167.

[72] *James* (n 70) 54–55.

[73] See e.g. the ECtHR's ruling in *Willis v The United Kingdom* (2002) 35 EHRR 547.

[74] Erica I Daes concurs. She points out that extinguishment is a practice that exclusively target indigenous peoples and is therefore discriminatory. Daes notes that '[a]boriginal title is normally subject to the complete extinguishment by the . . . State, without the legal protection and rights that in

Against the backdrop of the arguments outlined above, it is no surprise that international legal sources have repeatedly rejected state attempts to extinguish indigenous communities' property rights over territories, holding that such practices constitute extreme forms of discrimination. For instance, the CERD Committee has in two early warning and urgent action procedures directed against the United States and New Zealand, respectively, affirmed that attempts to extinguish indigenous communities' traditional territories is racially discriminatory.[75] In a similar vein, the UN Human Rights Committee (HRC) has expressed concern over that property rights of indigenous communities over 'lands held by reason of long possession and use . . . can be extinguished on the basis of plenary authority of [the United States] Congress . . .'. The Committee called on the State party to 'grant [the tribes] the same degree of judicial protection [over their property rights to land] that is available to the non-indigenous population.'[76] Thus, the CERD Committee has affirmed (i) that indigenous communities' traditional use of land results in property rights, (ii) that such property rights enjoy the same legal status as conventional property rights held by others, and finally (iii) that, as a consequence, acts that seek to specifically extinguish indigenous communities' property rights over lands and natural resources while leaving non-indigenous property rights intact are discriminatory. In this context, it is also worth referring to *Delgamuukw*, discussed in Section 8.6.6, above. Here, the Canadian Supreme Court ruled that the Canadian provinces lack authority to extinguish Aboriginal title. The Court underlined that if a province wish to limit Aboriginal communities' rights over land, the province must go through the same expropriation processes that applies to property rights in general.[77]

It thus appears clear that states are not allowed to extinguish indigenous communities' property rights over territories that have survived to the present day. But what about the legal relevance of past such practices? Rather than seeking to extinguish property rights of indigenous communities today, states may wish to rely on historic acts with such aspirations to claim that indigenous communities hold no, or limited, rights over territories traditionally used. The answer as to whether such historic acts are lawful might not be as clear cut as with regard to attempts to extinguish indigenous communities' property rights over land today. Still, a number of good reasons suggest that states may not be allowed to rely on past acts of extinguishment either.

most countries protect the land and property of citizens.' See Human Rights of Indigenous Peoples: Indigenous People and their Relationship with Land, Working Paper, UN Doc E/CN4/Sub2/1997/17 29.

[75] CERD/C/USA/DEC/1, 11 April 2006 6; and CERD/C/DEC/NZL/1, 27 April 2005 6.

[76] See Concluding Observations with regard to the United States, CCPR/C/USA/CO/3/Rev1 37. The Committee has raised similar concerns, albeit framed in a more general manner, with regard to Canada. See CCPR/C/CAN/CO/5 8.

[77] See *Delgamuukw* (n 31) 172–83; also McNeil, 'Judicial Treatment' (n 18) 33–34, 37; Nigel Bankes, 'Recognising the Property Interests of Indigenous Peoples within Settler Societies: Some Different Conceptual Approaches', in Nigel Bankes and Timo Koivurova (eds.), *The Proposed Nordic Saami Convention; National and International Dimensions of Indigenous Property Rights* (Hart Publishing, 2013) 37.

First, one must be mindful that if the extinguishment occurred temporally long ago, the indigenous community might have, by continuously using the land area irrespective of the act of extinguishment, re-established a property right through traditional use. Conversely, if an extinguishment attempt occurred recently, it might be reasonable to take the same position towards such an effort with regard to attempts to extinguishment attempts in the present day.

Second, as the above touches upon, one cannot consider the practice of extinguishment in isolation. It must be understood in light of the right to restitution. Section 8.8 infers that a right to restitution that provides that territories taken from indigenous communities in the past without their consent should be returned or that alternatively compensation be provided for the land lost is at least about to crystalize into an international customary norm. To the extent this conclusion is correct, and indigenous communities thus retain property rights interests in lands traditionally used but no longer in their possession, it would appear illogical to simultaneously conclude that indigenous communities hold no property rights interests in lands they have traditionally used *and still* possess.

The third argument is possibly the most compelling one. As seen, the practice of extinguishment has been widely recognized as blatantly discriminatory. The above has addressed another historical 'practice' directed at indigenous peoples with the purpose of denying them rights to land which has also been deemed inherently discriminatory, namely the invocation of the *terra nullius* and other similar doctrines. As seen, international law has firmly established that states may not rely on previous invocations of the *terra nullius* and similar doctrines to deny indigenous communities rights over land today. True, the *terra nullius* doctrine differs from the practice of extinguishment in that the former professes that indigenous communities never held rights over their traditional territories as they are incapable of doing so. In contrast, a state that engages in the practice of extinguishment has initially recognized indigenous communities as possessors of rights over land, but now wishes to 'change its mind'. Notwithstanding, from a discrimination point of view, it is difficult to argue that it is more morally just to first recognize a right only to subsequently unilaterally terminate it, than to never recognize the right in the first place. It therefore appears that relying on past practices of extinguishment is as discriminatory as relying on previous invocations of the *terra nullius* doctrine. If so, the conclusion should be that if international law prohibits states from relying on past invocations of the *terra nullius* doctrine, it should reasonably take the same position towards past practices of extinguishment.

International legal sources seem to concur with the just inferred. In *Dann Sisters*, the United States sought to rebut claims that the Western Shoshone holds property rights over its traditional territory by invoking a historic act intending to extinguish such rights. The IACommHR's response was that '[w]hile the State has suggested that the extinguishment of Western Shoshone title was justified by the need to encourage settlement and agricultural developments in the western United States, the Commission does not consider that this can justify the broad manner in which the State has purported to extinguish indigenous claims . . . ’.[78] The Commission underlined that any act of extinguishment must conform with the rights to equality and property.[79] The findings of the IACommHR in *Dann Sisters* conforms to the conclusions above. While expropriation of a specific, smaller, part of an indigenous community's territory might not amount to a violation of the right to property, attempts to sweepingly extinguish indigenous communities' property rights over land are discriminatory and, as a consequence, violate the right to property.

Similarly, in *Richtersveld*, discussed in Section 8.6.6, the South African Supreme Court of Appeal held that the indigenous community's right over land had survived, i.e. was not extinguished by, annexation by the British Crown. The Court inferred that the South African Restitution Act, which claimed differently, was discriminatory.[80] In the same vein, in *Cal* the Belize Supreme Court held that neither the British Crown's assertion of sovereignty over the area, nor present day unilateral governmental acts, had extinguished the Maya communities' right over land. The Court concluded that although the state of Belize holds ultimate sovereign title over the land, that title was ‘burdened by the pre-existing rights to and interest of the [Maya communities] in the land’.[81] The ruling in *Cal* reminds us how cardinal it is to distinguish between *sovereign* rights over territory on one hand, and *private rights* to the same subject matter, on the other, when analyzing what rights indigenous communities possess over lands and natural resources traditionally used under international law.

The conclusions above find further support in the legal doctrine. Jérémie Gilbert asserts that, generally speaking, extinguishment practices are too broadly designed to meet human rights standards. He notes that extinguishment constitutes total and absolute confiscation of land, in stark contrast to international law's increased recognition of indigenous land rights.[82] Former National Chief of the Assembly of First Nations in Canada, Matthew Coon Come, aptly points out that ‘[e]xtinguishment is simply terra nullius applied after the fact.’[83] Coon Come thus shares the opinion articulated above that there is little rationale to conclude that relying on past practices of extinguishment is more morally justifiable than resorting to invocations of the *terra nullius* doctrine. In a similar vein, Blake Watson notes that if international norms of the 19th century are no longer accepted, legal doctrines based on such norms must be reconsidered.[84] Kent McNeil observes that extinguishment specifically targets indigenous lands even in jurisdictions where the constitution protects property rights. He dryly concludes that such practices seemingly are driven by political, rather than legal, considerations.[85]

[78] *Dann Sisters* (n 35) 145. [79] Gilbert, *Indigenous Peoples' Land Rights* (n 12) 76–77.

[80] *Richtersveld Cmty & Others v Alexkor Ltd & Another* (CCT19/03) [2003] ZACC 18; 2004 (5) SA 460 (CC); 2003 (12) BCLR 1301 (CC) (14 October 2003) 109, 110.

[81] *Cal* (n 58) 69–93.

[82] Gilbert, *Indigenous Peoples' Land Rights* (n 12) 75, 80–82.

[83] Presentation to the Royal Commission on Aboriginal Peoples by the Grand Council of the Cree: Eeyou Astchee (Montreal, Nov 18, 1993).

[84] Blake A Watson, ‘The Impact of the American Doctrine of Discovery on Native Land Rights in Australia, Canada and New Zealand’ [2011] 34 *Seattle U L Rev* 507 549.

[85] McNeil, ‘Judicial Treatment’ (n 18) 32–33.

In summary, practices of extinguishment, both past and present, are incompatible with indigenous communities' property rights over territories traditionally used. That is so since property rights are a particular aspect of the right to equality, and the practice of extinguishment is discriminatory due to the fact that it specifically targets indigenous lands while leaving property rights held by members of the majority population untouched. Consequently, international law appears to consider extinguishment and similar practices unlawful. States are not allowed to extinguish indigenous lands today in attempts to rebut the conclusion that indigenous communities hold property rights over territories traditionally used. Neither are states, it seems, allowed to rely on past such acts or attempts.

8.7 Conclusions

During the last two decades or so, there has been a paradigm shift in how international law understands the right to equality. As conventionally understood, the right merely called for formal non-discrimination. It only required states to treat equal situations equally. In their laws, policies, and practices, states did not need to consider different ethnic and/or cultural backgrounds among the population of the state. The right to non-discrimination has, however, recently evolved to take on a second facet. Formal equality is no longer sufficient. There must also be equality in practice. This entails that it is no longer sufficient that the state treats equal cases equally. Individuals whose ethnic and/or cultural background is significantly different compared with the majority population are entitled to differential treatment. In other words, states' laws, policies, and practices must take cultural differences into account in order to be non-discriminatory. The state may no longer offer education, health care services etc., based only on the language, customs, and priorities of the majority population. Members of minority groups are entitled to social services accustomed to their particular cultural background.

The described development has resulted in the right to equality extending protection, if not formally at least indirectly, also to groups as such. When among others indigenous individuals' cultural background is respected in the educational systems etc., this also protects the cultural identity of the group as such.

Some decades ago, international law rejected the *terra nullius* and similar doctrines. It came to acknowledge that indigenous communities' historic use of their respective traditional territories result in property rights over such areas. Notwithstanding, indigenous communities have until very recently faced great difficulties when seeking recognition of such rights in practice. That has been so since domestic courts continued to apply understandings of what amounts to intense, continuous, and dominant use of land derived from land uses common to the majority cultures also in cases where indigenous communities were seeking acknowledgment of property rights over lands and natural resources traditionally used.

The right to property constitutes a particular aspect of the right to equality. The right to property known to international law is a right to acquire property on equal footing with others and not to be arbitrarily deprived of property thus acquired. As a result, when the right to equality evolves to require not only that equal cases be treated equally but also that different cases be treated differently, this development should directly impact on the understanding of the right to property. If this assumption is correct, the result is an amended understanding of to what extent indigenous communities have established property rights over their respective territories through traditional use. Under such circumstances, the evolved understanding of the right to equality requires domestic courts, when ruling on whether an indigenous community's traditional use of land has resulted in property rights, to evaluate whether the land utilization has been intense, continuous, and dominant, based on what is understood as intense, continuous, and dominant use in the indigenous community's, and not the majority people's, culture. In other words, if the community has traditionally used a land area and natural resources there in manners customary to its culture, it has established a property right to the area.

Property rights theory thus provides that the evolved understanding of the right to equality should result not only in formal recognition that indigenous communities hold property rights to territories traditionally used, but also in acknowledgement of such rights in practice. And legal sources have responded in the manner property rights theory predicts. International, regional, and domestic legal sources have in a coherent manner come to affirm that indigenous communities' historic use of land in accordance with their own customs establishes property rights. International law further provides that states may not avoid the conclusions articulated above by seeking to extinguish indigenous property rights over lands and natural resources. It further appears that neither may states rely on past such practices. To do so would violate the fundamental right to equality.

The outlined conclusions find support in the legal doctrine. Eric Dannenmaier infers that read in light of one another, contemporary international legal sources establish that indigenous communities hold property rights over territories traditionally used.[86] James Anaya draws the same conclusion, placing particular relevance on the jurisprudence emanating out of the Inter-American human rights system.[87] Andrew Huff underscores that this development does not represent a radical departure from previous international legal norms. Rather, he observes—thereby aligning himself with the line of argument this book pursues—it merely represents a logical application of the right to equality in an indigenous context.[88] Jérémie Gilbert sings from a similar hymn book. He notes that the recent general trend has been for national jurisdictions to recognize indigenous communities' property rights over territories traditionally used.[89] Recall also how the immediately above outlines how the legal doctrine in addition largely agrees that once established, such property rights of indigenous communities cannot be legally extinguished.

[86] Eric Dannenmaier, 'Beyond Indigenous Property Rights: Exploring the Emergence of a Distinctive Connection Doctrine' [2008] *Washington University Law Review*, Vol 86:53 71.

[87] Amnesty International, *Amicus Curiae*, Index number: AMR 20/001/2011 8.

[88] Huff, 'Indigenous Land Rights and the New Self-Determination' (n 14) 321, 330.

[89] Gilbert, *Indigenous Peoples' Land Rights* (n 12) 110.

As seen, the Inter-American and African human rights institutions' progressive interpretation of the right to property is a result of these bodies allowing themselves to be influenced by general developments in international law. In line with what Chapter 4 infers, the fact that the findings of these institutions mirrors conclusions drawn by UN treaty bodies, as well as UNDRIP Article 26[90] and other relevant international legal sources, affirms that customary international law provides that indigenous communities hold property rights over territories traditionally used.

To conclude, one can safely infer that under contemporary international law, indigenous communites hold property rights to lands and natural resources traditionally used. What remains to survey then is what is entailed in such a right. This is the topic of the next chapter. But before turning to what more precise rights indigenous communities possess over territories traditionally and *continuously* used, this chapter shall take a look at whether such communities may in addition retain at least some property rights interests also in territories traditionally used, *but which have subsequently been taken* from them without consent.

8.8 The Right to Restitution

8.8.1 Introduction

Territories that indigenous communities still possess only make up parts, not seldom minor parts, of the entire traditional territory of most indigenous peoples. Many indigenous peoples have over time been deprived of considerable parts of their respective traditional territories through colonization, industrialization (or 'development' if one wishes), and other similar processes and practices. This section surveys to what extent the evolved understanding of the right to equality has resulted in acknowledgment that indigenous communities hold proprietary rights interests also in territories that during the course of history have been taken from them without their consent.

The above explains how domestic legal systems are responding to the new conception of equality through recognizing that indigenous communities hold property rights over territories traditionally and continuously used. Domestic legal systems are, however, largely yet to accept that indigenous communities in addition retain rights in lands once traditionally used, but which were subsequently taken from them without consent. States may defend this position by resorting to formal legal positivism. A state might concede that the *terra nullius* and other similar doctrines are difficult to defend from a moral perspective. At the same time, however, the state can perhaps be expected to maintain that be that as it may, such doctrines nonetheless resulted in law. Such law is, irrespective of perhaps perceived as morally questionable if judged by today standards, valid until substituted by new law.

90 Luis Rodríguez-Pinero observes that the Inter-American human rights institutions' position on indigenous communities' property rights over land is fully consistent with, and elaborates on, the UNDRIP's land rights provisions. See Rodríguez-Pinero, 'The Inter-American System and the UN Declaration on the Rights of Indigenous Peoples' (n 33) 467.

Hence, states pursuing this line of argument conclude, whatever property rights indigenous communities may have possessed in the past, if these lands were taken through processes that were lawful at the time, such actions erased the community's property right interest in the land.[91]

This section surveys whether the outlined position can be validated under the present international legal order. In other words, it addresses whether historic acts of dispossession—irrespective of how immoral we consider these acts today—have permanently terminated all property rights interests of indigenous communities in their traditional territories.

8.8.2 Universally applicable legal sources

ILO 169 encompasses no provision that proclaims a right to restitution of indigenous peoples. Judging by their wordings, ILO 169 Articles 13–15 only address lands and natural resources that indigenous peoples continuously use. Still, the ILO Secretariat has—in its guide to the ILO 169—asserted that the Convention's land rights provisions do embrace a right to restitution, albeit a limited one. According to the ILO Guide, for the right to restitution to apply the present day indigenous society must maintain some form of connection to the land area in question. As an example, the ILO Guide mentions when an indigenous group has relatively recently been expelled from its traditional territory.[92] It is uncertain to what extent states have accepted the ILO Secretariat's interpretation of ILO 169.[93] In any event, the right to restitution the ILO Secretariat reads into ILO 169 is clearly marginal.

The CERD Committee has gone further than the ILO Guide when reading a right to restitution into the CERD Convention. The Committee calls on states 'where [indigenous peoples] have been deprived of their lands and territories traditionally owned or otherwise inhabited or used without their free and informed

[91] Compare Anaya, 'Divergent Discourses' (n 296) 244–45. This Section should be read in conjunction with Section 8.6.7, on the practice of extinguishment. Section 8.6.7 addresses to what extent states can legally extinguish indigenous communities' property rights over land at present, as well as whether states may rely on past attempts to do so, *when the indigenous people still uses the land area in dispute*. This section, on the other hand, surveys the legality of past takings of indigenous lands, e.g. through the practice of extinguishment, which have resulted in indigenous peoples being dispossessed of the land area in question and thus no longer use or occupy it.

[92] See Tomei and Swepston (n 23) 31; also Gilbert, *Indigenous Peoples' Land Rights* (n 12) 162–63. Gilbert maintains that ILO 169 seeks to establish a balance between historical wrongs and the present day situation, and submits that the Convention does not apply to land areas from which indigenous peoples were dispossessed a long time ago, and to which they lack a present day connection. In this context, James Anaya asserts that viewed in light of ILO 169 Article 13, 'a sufficient present connection with lost lands may be established by a continuing cultural attachment to them . . .'. See *Indigenous Peoples in International Law* (n 1) 144.

[93] ILO 169 Article 16.3 might at first glance seem to set forth a right to restitution, as the provision proclaims that indigenous peoples, as a general rule, have a right to have lands taken without consent returned. On a closer reading, however, it is clear that the applicability of Articles 16.3–4 is limited to situations where indigenous peoples have been forcefully removed from their traditional territories pursuant to Article 16.2, as an exception to the general prohibition of forceful reallocation set forth by Article 16.1. In other words, the right to restitution Articles 16.3–4 enshrine applies only to lands that have been taken in accordance with Article 16.2, subsequent to a state party's ratification of ILO 169. The provision lacks retroactive effect.

consent ... to take steps to return those lands and territories.' According to the CERD Committee, when restitution in the form of return of lands taken is not feasible, compensation should be awarded, whenever possible in the form of alternate lands.[94] The Committee hence asserts that the right to property, viewed through the lens of the right to equality, requires states not only to recognize that indigenous communities hold property rights over territories traditionally and continuously used. In addition, the right to property obliges states to address past injustices by acknowledging that indigenous communities retain property rights interests in lands taken from them in the past without consent. The CERD Committee has subsequently elaborated on this general observation, e.g. expressing concern that 'the absence of an effective system for ... restitution of land rights prevents indigenous communities from gaining access to their ancestral lands.' The Committee called on the State party to 'adopt the necessary reforms ... for bringing about restitution of [indigenous communities'] lands'.[95]

The CESC has echoed the observations of the CERD Committee. It has proclaimed that when indigenous territories have become settled or otherwise used by the non-indigenous population without consent, states shall 'take steps to return these lands and territories'.[96] In a similar vein, the HRC has, with reference to a state party, stated that 'it regrets that it has not been possible to adopt legislation designed to guarantee the full enjoyment of all [indigenous communities'] rights under the Covenant, including the restitution of communal lands ...'.[97] In sum, the three UN treaty bodies most relevant to the indigenous rights discourse have all inferred that indigenous communities' rights over territories embrace a right to restitution with regard to lands taken without consent.

When adopted, the UNDRIP reaffirmed the position taken by the UN treaty bodies. Pursuant to its Article 28.1, '[i]ndigenous peoples have the right to ... restitution or, when this is not possible, just, fair and equitable compensation, for the lands, territories and resources which they have traditionally ... occupied or used, and which have been ... taken ... without their free, prior and informed consent'. As with UNDRIP Article 26.2, the key criterion is traditional use and/or occupation, rather than formal state recognition of rights. The phrase 'traditional use and occupation' must reasonably have the same meaning in UNDRIP Article 28.1 as in 26.2.[98] Thus, the provision should be understood in the cultural context of the particular indigenous people. Consequently, pursuant to UNDRIP Article 28.1, a territory that an indigenous community has historically used and/or occupied in a manner common to its culture, but which has subsequently been taken without its

[94] CERD Committee General Recommendation No 23 5.

[95] See CERD/C/PRY/CO/1-3 15 and 16. As Section 8.8.3, immediately below, elaborates, the IACHR has in *Yakey Axa* (n 39) and *Sawhoyamaxa* (n 40) explicitly called on the state party to facilitate the restitution of these communities' traditional lands. In Concluding Observations, the CERD Committee expressed particular concern that these communities' lands had not been returned. See para. 17.

[96] CESC General Comment No 21 36.

[97] CCPR/CO/72/GTM 29. Article 27 is of course a cultural rights provision. Notwithstanding, it is noteworthy that the HRC has recognized the principle of a right to restitution of indigenous communities, although this right is normally framed as a property right.

[98] See Section 8.6.3.

consent, shall, as a general rule, be returned. When return of land is not a feasible option, other forms of compensation may suffice but should preferably take the form of lands equal in size and quality with the territory lost.

8.8.3 Regional legal sources

Recall in Section 8.6.4 the explanation of how the Inter-American human rights instruments do not explicitly recognize a property right of indigenous communities with regard to territories traditionally and continuously used, but also how the Inter-American human rights institutions have read such a right into these instruments nonetheless. The same is true with regard to territories that indigenous communities have traditionally used, but which have subsequently been taken without consent.

In *Sawhoyamaxa* the IACHR held that 'members of indigenous peoples who have unwillingly left their lands, or lost possession thereof, maintain property rights thereto, even though they lack legal title unless the lands have been lawfully transferred to third parties in good faith'. The Court thus distinguishes between two situations. If no third party right applies to the land taken without consent the indigenous community is entitled to full restitution. If, on the other hand, third party rights apply, the IACHR elaborates that when '[lands which an indigenous community has unwillingly lost possession of] have been lawfully transferred to innocent third parties, [the community is] entitled to . . . obtain other lands of equal extension and quality'.[99] In other words, with regard to land previously taken but which today is burdened with third party rights, compensation in other forms than the full return of the specific land lost might suffice.

Similarly, in *Yakye Axa* the IACHR noted that if indigenous communities should be able to preserve their cultural identity, it might be necessary to restrict private ownership over lands that conflict with their communal rights. The Court added, however, that this does not mean that indigenous communities have an absolute right to have land returned in every instance where there is a conflict between indigenous communal rights and third party rights. Rather, the Court declared that when restitution is not a feasible option, the state should provide indigenous communities with alternate land, chosen by them by means of consensus.[100]

Similar to ILO 169 Article 16, according to its wording, the right to restitution that AfCHPR Article 21 enshrines is limited to lands taken subsequent to the ratification of the Convention. Notwithstanding, in *Endorois* the AfCommHPR confirmed that indigenous communities' property rights over lands embrace a right to restitution. Echoing the words of the ACHR in *Sawhoyamaxa*, the African Commission held that indigenous peoples that have unwillingly left their traditional lands retain property rights interests unless the area has been 'lawfully' transferred to third parties in good faith. In such instances, the Commission inferred, and when full restitution is not feasible, indigenous communities have a right to be

[99] *Sawhoyamaxa* (n 40) 128.

[100] *Yakye Axa* (n 39) 148, 149, 217.

provided with alternate land, equal in size and quality with the land lost.[101] Clive Baldwin and Cynthia Morel, co-counsels to the Enderois, note that in reaching this conclusion, the AfCommHPR drew heavily from the then draft UNDRIP Article 28.[102] This final remark suggests that the legal sources on indigenous communities' right to restitution that emanate from regional human rights institution, have reached their conclusions at least partly based on an understanding that a right to restitution of indigenous communities' with regard to lands traditionally used, but subsequently taken without their consent, form part of a customary international norm, or at least an emerging such.

8.8.4 Conclusions

International legal sources on the right to restitution are relatively scarce, compared with legal sources pertaining to indigenous territories traditionally and continuously used. Still, the legal sources that exist paint a coherent picture. UN treaty bodies concur that indigenous communities retain property rights interests in territories traditionally used but which have subsequently been taken without their consent. States have supported this conclusion by adopting UNDRIP Article 28. Regional human rights institutions that have opined on the matter have concurred that a right to restitution of indigenous communities has crystalized into an international customary norm.

Lands traditionally used but subsequently taken do, however, from an international legal perspective differ from territories traditionally and continuously used in one significant manner. As mentioned, domestic courts have been quick to pick up the global trend that indigenous communities hold property rights over the latter category of land. By contrast, domestic jurisdictions and legal systems have been reluctant to accept that indigenous communities retain property rights interests in territories traditionally used but subsequently taken.

In line with the conclusions in Chapter 4, the lack of support in state practice strongly suggest that international law has yet to embrace a right to restitution of indigenous communities. On the other hand, international legal sources, albeit relatively limited in number, are coherent and clear. Moreover, states have lent their support to the norm these sources reflect when adopting the UNDRIP, including its Article 28. In addition, Section 8.6.7 explains how states appear not to be allowed to rely on past practices of extinguishment to maintain that indigenous communities hold no rights over territories traditionally and continuously used. It seems that in such instances, states are obliged to 're-establish' rights of indigenous communities over land. Restitution can also be said to be a form of re-establishment of rights. The major difference between the two situations seems to be that—beyond the fact that in the case of restitution the indigenous community is

[101] *Endorois* (n 46) 204, 209, 232.

[102] Clive Baldwin and Cynthia Morel, 'Using the United Nations Declaration on the Rights of Indigenous Peoples in Litigation', in Stephen Allen and Alexandra Xanthaki (eds.), *Reflections on the UN Declaration on the Rights of Indigenous Peoples* (Hart Publishing, 2011) 129–30.

no longer physically inhabiting or using the land—when restitution is being considered, third party rights may attach to the land. But as the legal sources articulated above explain, third party rights need not be incompatible with a right to restitution of indigenous communities. The implementation of the right to restitution can take forms that are respectful of third party rights.[103]

To the extent the right to restitution has not crystalized into an international customary norm, it would appear that such a right is emerging. As to the content and scope of this norm—irrespective of whether already existing or emerging—the legal sources outlined above do not call for full restitution in all instances. Restitution in the form of return of land is the general rule, and should occur whenever reasonably feasible. But the articulated legal sources do acknowledge that return of land is often simply not a realistic option, and as a consequence do not necessarily require the full return of land either. When full restitution is not an option, it is accepted that the state may offer compensation instead. In such instances, compensation should ideally take the form of alternate land equal in size and quality with the land taken. But when such territories are not available, monetary compensation is acceptable.

As a final observation, when full restitution is not an option states should arguably not be too quick to resort to pure monetary compensation. Rather, as indigenous rights in general, such compensation should reasonably to the largest extent possible take forms that promote indigenous communities' possibilities to preserve and develop their distinct cultures and traditional ways of life. For instance, rather than immediately resorting to monetary compensation, a state might serve the interests and needs of an indigenous community better if it enters into an constructive arrangement with the community that awards the community with a property right in the form of a usufruct right over the land taken, offering some legal protection, combined with monetary compensation. Such an arrangement may allow the community to continuously pursue its traditional livelihoods, at the same time as the solution does not carry too heavy a burden on society as a whole.

[103] Compare Bankes, 'Recognising the Property Rights Interests of Indigenous Peoples' (n 78) 42.

9

The Content and Scope of Indigenous Communities' Property Rights over Lands and Natural Resources Traditionally Used

9.1 Briefly on the Relevant Legal Subject with Regard to Indigenous Property Rights over Lands

Human rights instruments on indigenous peoples' rights—such as the United Nations (UN) Declaration on the Rights of Indigenous Peoples (UNDRIP) and the International Labour Organization's Convention No 169 on Indigenous and Tribal Peoples in Independent Countries (ILO 169)—normally refer to 'indigenous peoples' as beneficiaries of rights to among other things lands and natural resources. This practice may be taken to suggest that it is indigenous peoples as a whole, rather than segments within the people, that are the holders of property rights over territories. That is, however, not necessarily the case. In fact, it is probably rare that the relevant legal subject in the context of indigenous territorial rights are indigenous peoples as such.

As the above elaborates upon in depth, what results in, or in other words is the legal ground for, indigenous property rights over lands and natural resources is traditional use. In addition to establishing the right, the legal ground also identifies the relevant legal subject. If the legal ground is traditional use, the legal subject is—by definition—the traditional user.

As indicated, it is probably unusual that an indigenous people as such use all its traditional territory as a collective. It is presumably considerably more common that indigenous peoples' societies consists of communities within the people, where the indigenous people's own customary legal system provides that the various communities have particular rights to the respective land areas they have traditionally used within the indigenous people's aggregate territory. As Jeremy Webber notes, '[i]t is very rare that indigenous peoples, by indigenous law, hold their entire territory in equal and undivided co-ownership. On the contrary, land is generally held by individuals, families and kinship groups.' As a consequence, Webber elaborates, the kinship group, rather than the people as a whole, is most often the primary societal unit in indigenous peoples' societies.[1] Thus normally, property rights over lands and natural resources vest with local communities within the indigenous people, rather than with the people as such. As Webber further notes, within an indigenous people, '[t]he traditional owners cannot be determined unless one knows, by that [indigenous people's own customary law], who is entitled to exercise authority over the [respective] lands'. He infers that one must normally not conclude that land is owned collectively by an indigenous people as such. Much more often, it is local communities within an indigenous people that have established property rights over land based on traditional use.[2]

Irrespective of what term opted for in international legal instruments on indigenous rights as touched upon above, Jeremy Webber's conclusions do find support in the major bulk of international legal sources on indigenous rights. In essentially all jurisprudence discussed in Section 8.6, it is indigenous communities within an indigenous people—rather than the people as such—that have claimed and been awarded property rights over lands and natural resources through rulings and decisions by regional human rights courts and other institutions as well as by domestic courts. In other words, when indigenous property rights over land are being implemented on the local level, it is essentially always indigenous communities that receive recognition of such rights, irrespective of the terminology used in globally applicable human rights instruments.[3] As mentioned, this is a reflection of the fact that with few exceptions, it is indigenous communities, rather than peoples, that are the traditional users of their particular land areas. Respectful towards the position of international law, this book refers to indigenous communities as relevant legal subjects when discussing indigenous property rights over lands and natural resources.

9.2 Indigenous Communities' Right to Withhold or Offer their Consent to Third Parties that Seek Access to their Traditional Territories

9.2.1 The general rule; consent

One core element of the right to property is the right to determine who can access land. This is especially true with regard to indigenous communities. Indeed, this element of the right is probably most often the principal reason that motivates an indigenous community to seek recognition that it holds a property right over its traditional territory. Property rights over land are attractive to indigenous

[1] Jeremy Webber, 'The Public-Law Dimension of Indigenous Property Rights', in Nigel Bankes and Timo Koivurova (eds.), *The Proposed Nordic Saami Convention; National and International Dimensions of Indigenous Property Rights* (Hart Publishing, 2013) 85 and 87.

[2] Ibid., 83.

[3] Ibid., 85 for a concurring opinion. Jeremy Webber points out that domestic courts and states have acknowledged that the internal allocation of lands within an indigenous people should be governed by the indigenous people's own customary normative system.

communities precisely because they may allow them to prevent industrial and other competing activities from entering their territories. Alternatively, property rights may ensure that the competing activities enter the community's territory only on its own terms.

Section 8.6 describes how indigenous communities' property rights over territories traditionally used have the same legal status as state granted title. As a consequence, indigenous communities must have the same right as others to withhold or offer their consent to third parties that seek access to their lands. Anything else would be discriminatory. If someone holds a property right over a land area, as a general rule, she or he has the right to say no to third parties that wish to enter the land. She or he need not offer any justification for the denied access. The right to property encompasses a right to say no to access for no other reason than that the property right holder is entitled to determine over the property. This aspect of the right must assumingly apply also to indigenous communities that hold property rights over territories traditionally used. And indeed, international legal sources do affirm that indigenous communities' property rights over territories bestow them with a right to deny third parties access to such lands. In fact, when applied to an indigenous context, human rights courts and institutions have in particular focused on this element of the right to property, thereby signalling its importance to indigenous communities.

The UN Committee on the Elimination of Racial Discrimination (CERD Committee) has, in a rich jurisprudence, affirmed that states must ensure that indigenous communities' consent is not only sought but obtained before third parties enter their traditional territories. The Committee has in particular emphasized that natural resource extraction must not occur in indigenous communities' traditional territories absent consent. The CERD Committee has for instance, with reference to Canada, confirmed that states must '[i]mplement in good faith the right to ... free prior and informed consent of [indigenous] peoples whenever their rights may be affected by projects carried out on their lands ...'.[4] In the particular context of resource extraction, the Committee has called on Peru to 'obtain [indigenous peoples'] consent before plans to extract natural resources [on their lands] are implemented'[5] and on Chile to 'obtain [indigenous peoples'] consent prior to implementation of projects for the extraction of natural resources' and further to 'ensure that the protection of the rights of indigenous peoples prevails over commercial and economic interests'.[6] The CERD Committee has further requested Ecuador to 'obtain consent [of the indigenous people concerned] in advance of the implementation of projects for the extraction of natural resources',[7] and Guatemala—with an explicit reference to the UNDRIP, thereby confirming that the norm enshrined in UNDRIP Article 26 reflects customary international

[4] CERD/C/CAN/CO/19-20, 9 March 2012 20 (a). For examples of similar observations, see e.g. CERD Concluding observations on Suriname, UN Doc CERD/C/SUR/CO/12, 3 March 2009; Philippines, CERD/C/PHL/CO, 23 September 2009 22 and 24; Cambodia, CERD/C/KHM/CO/8–13, 1 April 2010 16; El Salvador, CERD/C/SLV//CO/14–15, 14 September 2010 19.

[5] CERD/C/PER/CO/14–17, 3 September 2009 14.

[6] CERD/C/CHL/CO/15–18, 7 September 2009 22, 23.

[7] CERD/C/ECU/CO/19, 22 September 2008 16.

law—to 'obtain [indigenous peoples] consent before executing projects involving the extraction of natural resources',[8] to mention just a few examples.

Patrick Thornberry, former member of the CERD Committee, observes that the consent formula is now 'standard' when implementing the UN Convention on the Elimination of Racial Discrimination (CERD Convention) in an indigenous context. He distinguishes between situations that (i) pertain to all citizens of the country, and (ii) that concern an indigenous community directly. Thornberry submits that in the former situation, indigenous peoples have a mere participatory right. But in the latter scenario, he maintains that under the CERD Convention, indigenous communities enjoy a veto right with regard to among other affairs industrial activities that seek access to the community's traditional territory.[9] Jérémie Gilbert concurs with Thornberry's conclusions.[10]

In a similar vein, the UN Committee on Economic, Social and Cultural Rights (CESC) has interpreted the UN Covenant on Economic, Social and Cultural Rights (CESCR) as embracing a right of indigenous communities to withhold their consent to access to natural resources situated within their traditional territories.[11] James Anaya, former UN Special Rapporteur on the Rights of Indigenous Peoples, has echoed the conclusions of the treaty bodies. According to the Special Rapporteur, legal sources of authority, including the UNDRIP, 'lead to the general rule that extractive activities should not take place within the territories of indigenous peoples without their free, prior and informed consent'.[12]

In line with the position taken in treaty body jurisprudence and by the Special Rapporteur, as touched upon, UNDRIP Article 26 must be understood to embrace a right of indigenous communities to withhold or offer their consent to competing activities that seek access to their territories. As mentioned, Article 26 explicitly affirms that indigenous communities hold property rights, including ownership rights, over lands and natural resources traditionally used. As further discussed, one core element of this right is a right of the property right holder to deny third parties access to the territory. UNDRIP Article 26 must reasonably embed this aspect of the right to property, as anything else would be discriminatory. This conclusion also finds certain support if one reads UNDRIP Article 26 in light of Article 32.2. Recall how pursuant to the latter provision, '[s]tates shall . . . obtain [indigenous peoples'] free and informed consent prior to the approval of any project affecting their lands and territories and other resources, particularly in connection with the development, utilization or exploitation of mineral, water or other resources'. Section 6.3

[8] CERD/C/GTM/CO/12–13, 19 May 2010 11 (a).

[9] Patrick Thornberry, 'The Convention on the Elimination of Racial Discrimination, Indigenous Peoples and Caste/Decent-based Discrimination', in Joshua Castellino and Niamh Walsh (eds.), *International Law and Indigenous Peoples* (Martinus Nijhoff Publisher, 2005) 33–34; Patrick Thornberry, 'Integrating the UN Declaration on the Rights of Indigenous Peoples into CERD Practice', in Stephen Allen and Alexandra Xanthaki (eds.), *Reflection on the UN Declaration on the Rights of Indigenous Peoples* (Hart Publishing, 2011).

[10] Jérémie Gilbert, 'Indigenous Rights in the Making: The United Nations Declaration on the Rights of Indigenous Peoples' [2007] *International Journal on Minority and Group Rights* 14 222.

[11] See e.g. Concluding Observations on Colombia, UN Doc E/C12/COL/CO/5 9.

[12] Report of the Special Rapporteur on the Rights of Indigenous Peoples, James Anaya; Extractive Industry and Indigenous Peoples, A/HRC/24/41 27.

explains how UNDRIP Article 32.2 is more of a self-determination than a property rights provision. Still it lends certain support to the general idea that third party access to indigenous territories presupposes approval.

Jérémie Gilbert concurs with this conclusion. He submits that the property right UNDRIP Article 26 enshrines envelopes a right of indigenous communities to say no to competing activities that directly impact on them. According to him, UNDRIP requires states to obtain the consent from an affected indigenous community prior to undertaking, or allowing, any development project that impacts on the community's right over its traditional territory.[13]

The position globally applicable international legal sources have taken has been matched on a regional level. In *Dann Sisters*, the Inter-American Commission on Human and Peoples Rights (IACommHR) inferred that indigenous communities' property rights over land entails that the land cannot be taken from them without consent,[14] a position the Commission repeated in the *Belize Case*. Here, the IACommHR confirmed that 'one of the most central elements to the protection of indigenous peoples' property rights is the requirement that states . . . ensure a process of fully informed consent on the part of the indigenous community as a whole'.[15] In addition, even though perhaps not explicitly addressed, that indigenous communities' property rights over territories traditionally used encompass a right to withhold consent to resource extraction in such territories appears to be implicit in most of the cases Section 8.6.4 addresses. James Anaya concurs. He infers that the Inter-American human rights bodies have concluded that states must obtain indigenous peoples' consent when contemplating actions that may affect such peoples' property rights over lands and natural resources, including when such rights have been established through historical use.[16]

In summary, indigenous communities' property rights over territories traditionally used award them with a right to withhold or offer their consent to competing activities that seek access to their territories. As a consequence, for instance resource extractors may only enter an indigenous community's territory if either (i) reaching an agreement with the community to that effect, or (ii) managing to convince the state to expropriate the area in question.

Given the ever accelerating interest in extracting natural resources in indigenous territories,[17] under what circumstances indigenous lands can be subject to expropriation should reasonably be at the forefront of the indigenous rights regime. Against this background, it is puzzling that this issue has been subject to such limited debate. The next section explores, based on the relatively limited sources available, to what extent territories traditionally used by indigenous communities can be subject to expropriation.

[13] See Gilbert, 'Indigenous Rights in the Making' (n 10).

[14] *Mary and Carrie Dann v United States*. Case No 11.140, Inter-Am CHR Report No 75/02 (merits decision of December 27, 2002) 131.

[15] *Maya Indigenous Communities of the Toledo District v Belize*. Case 12.053, decision on October 12, 2004.

[16] S James Anaya, 'Indigenous Peoples' Participatory Rights in Relation to Decisions about Natural Resource Extraction' [2005] *Arizona Journal of International and Comparative Law* Vol 22, No 113.

[17] Report of the Special Rapporteur on the Rights of Indigenous Peoples (n 12) 1.

As a final note, before turning to the issue of expropriation, it is worth underlining that the above illustrates how it is incorrect to, as is often done, refer to a *right* to free, prior, and informed consent, or FPIC. Contrary to what much writings seem to suggest, there is simply no free-standing such right. The 'right' to consent or not is always a result of the applicability of an underlying material right. As far as the right to property is concerned, the just stated is reflected in that, as the above explains, one must *first* determine whether an indigenous community has established a *material right* to property over a territory through traditional use. Only subsequently can one proceed to analyze what *practical elements* are included in that right, where, as seen, a community's right to offer or withhold its consent (or FPIC if one wants) is one such element. In a corresponding manner, Section 5.5 articulates how one must analyze the more precise content and scope of the material right to culture in order to determine under what circumstances it follows from this right that an indigenous community (or formally speaking individual) is entitled to refuse access to an activity that competes with the cultural practice. In a similar vein, if an activity threatens to cause considerable damage to the health of individuals, the material right to health may provide that the consent formula kicks in. And so on. Again the point here is simply that free, prior, and informed consent (or FPIC) is nothing more than a way to effectuate a certain element of an underlying material right; in this particular instance indigenous communities' property rights to territories traditionally used.[18]

9.2.2 The possible exception to the general rule; expropriation—introduction[19]

Section 8.6.7 touches upon how the right to property, as most human rights, is not absolute. It is generally accepted that should states be able to govern in a reasonable manner, any infringement in any human right cannot be considered an unlawful violation of that right. Rather, states are allowed to legitimately infringe on most human rights, including the right to property—to a certain degree. Such infringements must not, however, be made haphazardly or arbitrarily. Rather, clear criteria distinguish between a legitimate infringement in a human right and an unlawful violation thereof. Lawful infringement in the right to property on the domestic level is normally referred to as expropriation, and presupposes that certain

[18] For a concurring opinion, see Report of the Special Rapporteur on the Rights of Indigenous Peoples, A/HRC/21/47 (6 July 2012), 51, and, in particular 79. The Special Rapporteur aptly notes that the common narrow focus on the processes of consultation, on one hand, and on free, prior, and informed consent, on the other, tends to blur the understanding of the relevant material human rights that underpin these processes. In order to correctly grasp relevant international legal standards, one is well advised to first develop a proper understanding of the right to property. Only subsequently should one turn to the consultation and consent *processes* in order to properly implement the *material* right of property.

[19] Sections 9.2.2–9.2.6 draw from an article by this author; 'To What Extent Can Indigenous Territories be Expropriated?', in Christina Allard and Susann Funderud Skogvang (eds.), *Autonomous Sámi Law: Indigenous Rights in Scandinavia* (Ashgate, 2015).

expropriation criteria are fulfilled. For expropriation to be lawful, it must be (i) prescribed by law, i.e. foreseeable to the individual, (ii) motivated by a legitimate aim, and (iii) proportionate, i.e. it must not place a disproportionate and excessive burden on the property right holder.[20]

Section 8.6.7 touches upon that the prescribed by law criterion is normally unproblematic. It is usually met as long as the state has enacted an expropriation act or comparable legislation that is sufficiently precise and accessible, thus allowing the property right holder to foresee the instances when an expropriation may occur.[21] As further touched upon, of greater relevance are the legitimate aim and, perhaps in particular, proportionality criteria. It is normally those that require careful evaluation when analyzing whether an intrusion into an indigenous communities' territory amounts to a violation of the right to property.

9.2.3 Generally on the legitimate aim and proportionality criteria

As mentioned, for the legitimate aim criterion to be fulfilled, an infringement in a property right must be motivated by a legitimate aim, i.e. a substantial social need.[22] In non-indigenous contexts, this criterion has been relatively uncontroversial. If a state maintains that expropriation is motivated by a vital societal need, the state's position is normally accepted without much second guessing. Exceptions may be when it is apparent that the expropriation decision was taken arbitrarily, or when it is evident that expropriation is motivated by an aim other than the one officially stated.[23]

Turning to the proportionality criterion, according to the European Court of Human Rights (ECtHR), an infringement is proportionate if it 'strike[s] a fair balance between the demands of the general interest of [society as a whole] and the requirements of the protection of . . . fundamental rights'. There must further be 'a reasonable relation . . . between the means employed and the aim sought to be realized by any measures applied by the state.'[24] The infringement must not leave the property right holder with a 'disproportionate' and 'excessive burden'.[25] In other words, it is not sufficient that expropriation is motivated by a legitimate aim, i.e. that it greatly benefits society at large. There are limitations on the sacrifices a state can require that individuals make for the benefit of society as a whole. The proportionality test thus aims to strike a fair balance between the interests of the larger society, and the interest of the individual property right holder.

In non-indigenous contexts, whether the proportionality test is met normally largely boils down to whether market value compensation is provided for the property taken. For instance, in *James*, the ECtHR held that 'compensation terms are material to the assessment whether the contested legislation respects a fair balance

[20] See e.g. *Saramaka People v Suriname*. Judgement of November 28, 2007, Inter-Am Ct HR (Ser C) No 172 (2007) 127.
[21] See e.g. *James and others v United Kingdom* (1986) 8 EHRR 123.
[22] Additional Protocol 1 to the European Convention on Human Rights, Article 1.
[23] See e.g. *James* (n 21) 54–55.
[24] *Draon v France* (2005) 42 EHRR 78; and *Hutten-Czapska v Poland* (2006) 45 EHRR 52.
[25] *James* (n 21) 54–55.

between the various interests at stake and, notably, whether it does not impose a disproportionate burden on the [property rights holders] .... [T]he taking of property without payment of an amount reasonably related to its value would normally constitute a disproportionate interference which could not be considered justifiable ...'.[26]

9.2.4 On the legitimate aim criterion when applied in an indigenous context

As mentioned, it is normally left to states to identify what constitute legitimate societal needs within their respective jurisdictions, without exaggerated in-depth outside scrutiny. Relying on the general rule, states will likely claim that at least resource extraction of scale in indigenous territories meets the legitimate aim criterion. Large-scale extraction projects are, the argument may go, important to the welfare of society as a whole. But the former UN Special Rapporteur on the Rights of Indigenous Peoples James Anaya cautioned otherwise. The Special Rapporteur asserts 'that [a legitimate aim] is not found in mere commercial interests or revenue-raising objectives, and certainly not when benefits from the extractive activities are primarily for private gain.'[27] The Inter-American Court on Human Rights (IACHR) has also held that one cannot simply assume that resource extraction in indigenous territories meets the legitimate aim criterion, albeit perhaps in somewhat more lenient wording compared with the Special Rapporteur. The IACHR accepts that indigenous communities' property rights over territories can be restricted, provided that such restrictions are geared towards satisfying an imperative public interest. A mere useful or opportune purpose is not sufficient, according to the court.[28]

Beyond those just mentioned, as indicated, international legal sources offer limited guidance as to when the legitimate aim criterion is fulfilled in the context of resource extraction or other activities in territories traditionally used by indigenous communities. As a consequence, it is at this point difficult to establish with any certainty when such is the case. A case may, however, perhaps be made for the position articulated below.

Obviously, one must be mindful that states are normally given substantial leeway when it comes to identifying pressing societal needs within the state. Against this background, at least when a resource extraction or another type of industrial enterprise generates substantial proceeds to the state, either because the state is the extractor, or because it has secured itself a substantial cut of the proceeds from the extraction through a royalty or similar scheme, one may perhaps assume that the legitimate aim criterion is, including when the activity will occur in an indigenous territory. This conclusion seems to conform with the ruling by the IACHR, and is

[26] Ibid.

[27] 'Extractive Industries and Indigenous Peoples' (n 17) 35.

[28] *Yakey Axa Indigenous Community v Parguay*. Judgement of 17 June 2005, Inter-Am Ct HR (Ser C) No 141 (2005) 145.

also in line with the position taken by the UN Special Rapporteur on the Rights of Indigenous Peoples.

The situation may be more complex, however, when the resource extractor or other form of industrial operator is a private entity, and the state receives little or no income from the industrial project. As seen, the Special Rapporteur on the Rights of Indigenous Peoples takes the position that in such instances, the legitimate aim criterion is unlikely to be met. To this assertion states may retort, however, that large scale extraction projects may carry substantial benefits to society at large beyond monetary proceeds. For instance, such enterprises may generate a substantial number of work opportunities. States are likely to argue that job creation is a legitimate aim, in particular in areas riddled by high unemployment. Another legitimate aim that governments may put forward is that a large scale industrial plant—even if privately operated—may result in the construction of infrastructure in the form of, for instance, roads, railroads, and electric power grids that, if fully or partly privately financed, generate considerable benefits to society at large. Presumably, the list of potential legitimate aims can be made longer.

Based on the limited guidance existing legal sources offer, it is difficult to rule out that domestic courts and regional and international human rights institutions may find themselves persuaded that for instance large scale job creation constitutes such a legitimate aims that can justify expropriation of indigenous territories. That is particularly so in light of the leeway normally given to states when it comes to identifying pressing legitimate societal needs within their jurisdictions. Such a conclusion seems also to gain support from the ruling by the IACHR in *Yakey Axa*. Assumingly, however, and further in line with *Yakey Axa*, it is a prerequisite that the extraction project genuinely generates substantial benefits to society. A project for private gain that does not generate a large number of jobs or brings other substantial benefits to society as a whole, presumably fails to meet the legitimate aim criterion.

In instances when one can establish that a resource extraction enterprise or other industrial activity is of such a scale that it does serve a legitimate social need, the question becomes whether the infringement is proportionate.

9.2.5 On the proportionality criterion when applied in an indigenous context

As seen, in non-indigenous contexts, the proportionality test most often largely boils down to whether the state provides market value compensation for the property taken. A property right holder must normally accept expropriation if fully compensated in monetary terms. To some, this might come across as unfair. The rationale is, however, probably to be found in what some might argue is a somewhat stereotypical approach towards in what terms individuals value property.

Certainly, some individuals attach emotional value, surely sometimes considerable, to a particular land area, also outside an indigenous context. This might for instance be the case with regard to a property that has been in a family's possession for generations. Notwithstanding, the market value compensation formula the lawmaker has opted for is probably motivated by an assumption that property is most often not predominantly valued by the holder because of emotional attachment. It is seemingly assumed that if an individual receives market value compensation for her or his property, expropriation should essentially be acceptable to her or him. After all, the compensation received allows the property right holder to purchase alternate land, equal in quality and value, to the land expropriated (at least if one presumes that the market forces work properly and that the compensation is calculated correctly). As mentioned, some may take issue with this reasoning, but it is the position the law has taken nonetheless.

Thus, with regard to property right holders who largely value their property in monetary terms—or at least are assumed to do so—it has been held reasonable to conclude that the proportionality criterion is met if market value compensation is provided. If such property right holders are awarded something (money) in return for their property that they value (or are assumed to value) to the same, or almost same, extent as the property taken, a fair balance between the interest of the property right holder and society as a whole is, it is considered, struck.

One can thus see the rationale behind the market value formula being applied in non-indigenous contexts, even if some may perceive it unfair. But can the same formula reasonably be applied to indigenous territories? Indigenous communities may not at all value their lands in monetary terms. Rather, assumingly, indigenous communities often value lands and natural resources traditionally used predominantly, or perhaps sometimes exclusively, because continued access to and control over such territories is fundamental to the continued existence of their cultures, identities, livelihoods, and ways of life. For an indigenous community whose cultural identity is deeply rooted in its traditional livelihoods, subsistence economies, and other forms of traditional land uses, every deprivation of land implies a blow to the very basis of its cultural identity. Loss of substantial parts of land can significantly threaten the existence of the community's society, culture, and way of life. In addition, contrary to the situation of non-indigenous property rights holders, an indigenous community that is deprived of parts of lands traditionally used will normally not be in a position to find alternate land elsewhere. The community may harbour a spiritual and cultural connection to its particular territory, for which there is no substitute. But even if the community is open to compensation in the form of alternate lands suitable for continued pursuit of its traditional livelihoods, other culturally-based land activities, and spiritual and cultural practices, such lands will probably often not be available.

The different ways in which non-indigenous peoples and indigenous communities value land, at least if generalizing, is a result of cultural differences. Section 7.4 explains how a contemporary understanding of the right to equality requires states to recognize cultural differences when designing domestic property laws and policies. This obligation must reasonably extend to legislation that regulates under what circumstances property can be subject to expropriation. After all, expropriation regulation is one factor that determines the scope and content of property rights and thus forms an integral part of the property rights regime. Further highlighting the dynamic of differences, one may add that indigenous communities opposed to resource extraction, generally speaking, have a much larger stake in the outcome of such expropriation processes compared with the extractor and the state, given the fundamental importance of land to them.[29] In this context, it is worth recalling that for an infringement in the right to property to be proportionate, it must be applied in a non-discriminatory manner. A state must not arbitrarily, without objective justification, limit one property right while at the same time leave a comparable property right untouched.[30]

To sum up, while in non-indigenous contexts the assumption that market value compensation fulfils the proportionality test may conform to international law, the same appears not to be true with regard to indigenous communities. On the contrary, given how significantly different many indigenous communities value land, compared with non-indigenous peoples, the right to equality seemingly requires that the market value formula is not employed when it comes to expropriation of indigenous territories. As Michael Walzer, among others, notes, justice criteria vary depending on the different values peoples assign to various things.[31] Similarly, Isabelle Anguelovski observes, with reference to Schlosberg, that to provide indigenous communities with market value compensation for their traditional lands is akin to not recognizing the unique values of their respective cultures.[32] In this context, one must be mindful that 'market value' compensation is always understood to be a value set by a market based on preferences within the majority, and not the indigenous, society. In line with the argument above, to impose foreign understandings as to how various properties should be valued on indigenous peoples violates the evolved understanding of equality.

In summary, a case has been built that since indigenous communities, generally speaking, do not value land predominantly in monetary terms, but rather because of its cultural and spiritual value, it is unreasonable, indeed seemingly discriminatory, to infer that market value compensation necessarily renders expropriation of indigenous territories proportionate. Rather, when an indigenous community withholds its consent to resource extraction, and the state, or a resource extractor with the assistance of the state, still want to pursue the project through expropriation, one must find alternative ways to measure whether the proportionality test is met. If pursuing this line of thought, to the extent the territory in question is predominantly of cultural and spiritual value to the indigenous community, it seemingly makes sense to consider the impact the resource extraction project or other forms of intrusions would have on the community's culture and spiritual values, including on traditional livelihoods and other culturally based land uses.

[29] Emily McAteer, Jamie Caretti, and Saleem Ali, 'Shareholder Activism and Corporate Behaviour in Ecuador—A Comparative Study of Two Oil Ventures', in Ciaran O'Faircheallaigh and Saleem Ali (eds.), *Earth Matters* (Greenleaf Publishing 2008) 195.

[30] *Willis v The United Kingdom* (2002) 35 EHRR 547.

[31] Michael Walzer, *Spheres of Justice: A Defence of Pluralism and Equality* (Blackwell, 1983).

[32] Isabelle Anguelovski, 'Environmental Justice Concerns with Transnational Mining Operations—Exploring the Limitations of Post-Crisis Community Dialogues in Peru', in Ciaran O'Farcheallaigh and Saleem Ali (eds.), *Earth Matters* (Greenleaf Publishing 2008) 206.

Former UN Special Rapporteur on the Rights of Indigenous Peoples James Anaya concurs with this line of argument. He infers that '[the proportionality criterion] will generally be difficult to meet for extractive industries that are carried out within the territories of indigenous peoples without their consent.'[33] In a similar vein, the CERD Committee calls on states to 'ensure that the protection of the rights of indigenous peoples prevails over commercial and economic interests'.[34] The IACHR takes a somewhat more cautious approach, holding that the proportionality criterion is not met in instances when expropriation would result in denial of indigenous traditions and customs that endangers the cultural survival of the community. The Court elaborates, however, that indigenous communities always have the right to preserve and protect their special relationship with their traditional territories and to continue to lead their traditional way of life.[35]

In summary, indigenous communities' property rights over territories traditionally used differ from property rights held by others in that when seeking to expropriate indigenous territories, the proportionality criterion is not necessarily met simply because market value compensation is provided. Rather, both reason and existing international legal sources suggest that in such instances, due consideration should be given to how profoundly important lands and natural resources traditionally used are to indigenous communities' cultures, ways of life, traditional livelihoods, other culturally-based land uses, and spiritual and cultural practices. When the negative impact a resource extraction project or other industrial activity would cause to an indigenous community reaches a certain scale, the fair balance test is no longer met, as the industrial activity would place a disproportionate and excessive burden on the community. The relatively few existing legal sources do not allow one to firmly establish precisely where the threshold is. But some conclusions may perhaps be drawn.

9.2.6 Conclusions

As seen, to lawfully expropriate an indigenous community's traditional territory, the resource extraction project must simultaneously meet the legitimate aim and proportionality criteria. To do so might prove to be a challenge.

Even large-scale resource extraction projects may fail to meet the legitimate aim criterion, if motivated by private gain. Publicly operated large scale resource extraction will, however, presumably normally fulfil a legitimate and pressing societal need. And based on existing legal sources, one cannot rule out that also projects motivated by private gain may be considered to meet the legitimate aim criterion, to the extent they deliver substantial benefits of other sorts to society at large, such as mass employment. But in any event, in all likelihood only natural resource extraction projects of considerable scale will be held to fulfil a substantial and therefore legitimate societal need. Resource extraction projects of lesser scale, and hence of lesser importance, will presumably find it difficult to pass the legitimate aim test.

[33] 'Extractive Industries and Indigenous Peoples' (n 17) 35–36.

[34] CERD/C/CHL/CO/15-18, 22-23.

[35] *Saramaka* (n 20) 37.

If large scale resource extraction projects can at times meet the legitimate aim criterion, they may find it harder to pass the proportionality test. Large scale resource extraction is likely to consume significant parts of, and inflict considerable damage to, the affected indigenous community's territory. If so, there is an apparent risk that the project fails to meet the proportionality criterion, given the fundamental importance of lands and natural resources traditionally used to indigenous communities' cultures, livelihoods, and ways of life, in other words to their very identities as indigenous communities. Irrespective of whether the extraction project would generate great wealth to society as a whole, it can hardly be considered proportionate if it leaves a great scar on the society and culture of the indigenous community. If examining the relative importance, the very basis of indigenous communities' societies cannot reasonably be outweighed by monetary gain and job creation. To do so would seem to constitute a typical example of sacrificing a few for the benefit of society at large, to an extent that appears to go beyond what the proportionality test allows.

To sum up, as far as resource extraction in and other forms of intrusion into indigenous territories are concerned, projects that do not consume significant parts of an indigenous community's traditional territory, and do not in other ways substantially negatively impact on the community, at the same time as it genuinely generate considerable benefits to society as a whole, seems to have the best shot at meeting the legitimate aim and proportionality criteria simultaneously. Any other combination might find it harder to meet both the legitimate aim and the proportionality tests at the same time.

9.3 Natural Resources Traditionally Used

To the extent an indigenous community has traditionally used natural resources situated on or within its traditional territory, the community must reasonably hold the same right over such resources as it does with regard to the land area as such. As the IACHR affirmed in *Saramaka*, indigenous communities' 'right to use and enjoy their territories would be meaningless . . . if said right were not connected to the natural resources that lie on and within that land . . . it follows that the natural resources found on and within indigenous and tribal peoples' that are protected . . . are those natural resources traditionally used . . .'[36] Stefania Errico concurs. She concludes, again highlighting the intrinsic connection between the rights to property and equality, that indigenous communities' property rights over territories traditionally used embrace the same right over natural resources as any other property rights holder would have.[37]

36 *Saramaka* (n 20) 122.

37 See Stefania Errico, 'The Controversial Issue of Natural Resources: Balancing States' Sovereignty with Indigenous Peoples' Rights', in Stephen Allen and Alexandra Xanthaki (eds.), *Reflections on the UN Declaration on the Rights of Indigenous Peoples* (Hart Publishing, 2011) 334. Some may, based on an *e contrario* interpretation, argue that ILO 169 Article 15.1's second sentence implies that indigenous

9.4 Natural Resources not Traditionally Used by Indigenous Communities

9.4.1 International legal sources and the legal doctrine

As this book underlines throughout, natural resources traditionally used by indigenous peoples are integral to their cultures. To secure rights over such resources are therefore normally of the greatest concern to, and a priority of, indigenous communities. As a consequence, the natural resource rights regime's main focus has conventionally been, and continues to be, on natural resources traditionally used by indigenous communities.

Irrespective of the predominant importance of natural resources traditionally used to indigenous communities, more recently increased attention has in addition been directed at what rights may attach to sub-soil and sub-surface resources situated under indigenous communities' traditional territories which they have traditionally not used and which therefore do not form part of their culture in the traditional sense. (Some indigenous peoples do have a long tradition using sub-surface, and perhaps in particular sub-soil, resources. If so, such natural resources do not belong to this category of resources, but rather to the category 'natural resources traditionally used', which the section above addresses.) Typical examples of such resources are minerals, oil, and gas. These resources are normally of substantial commercial value. Therefore, states tend to take the position that minerals, oil, and gas situated within their territory are critical to the welfare of society as a whole, and, as a consequence, that such resources vest with the state. However, as indicated, more recently indigenous communities have increasingly challenged this position (at least partly), asserting that they hold certain proprietary rights interests also in sub-surface and sub-soil resources situated in their traditional territories.

Also in the context of natural resources not traditionally used by indigenous communities, one must distinguish between sovereign and property rights. As mentioned, from a property rights perspective, in the outset states hold sovereign rights over their respective territories, including over natural resources situated in and under that territory. The principle of state sovereignty leaves the state free to determine that no private entity can hold property rights over any natural resources. But, as further mentioned, almost no state has exercised its sovereignty in such a manner. In almost all jurisdictions, states have exercised their *sovereign rights* to determine that private entities indeed can establish private, i.e. *property rights*, over

communities' hold mere participatory rights with regard to natural resources traditionally used. Pursuant to this provision, indigenous peoples have a right to participate in the use, management, and conservation of natural resources. Such an interpretation makes little sense, however, if one views (as one must) the right to property through the lens of the right to equality. Doing so leads to the conclusion that Article 15.1 clarifies that in addition to the rights that follow from the right to property, indigenous communities are entitled to be involved in decision-making processes that establish general norms for the use of natural resources within their traditional territories, such as hunting licences, fishing quotas etc. In addition, participatory rights can be relevant to natural resources situated within an indigenous community's territory, but which the community has not traditionally used. See further Section 9.4, immediately below.

natural resources. In such instances—as this Part III underlines throughout—the state must award all segments of the state, including indigenous communities, equal opportunity to establish such property rights. The fact that the right to property must apply without discrimination implies that the state may not exercise its sovereign right over natural resources to a larger degree vis-à-vis certain segments of society compared with other segments. The cardinal norm of equality applies to sub-surface and sub-soil resources as well.

It follows from the above that whether indigenous communities that have not traditionally used sub-soil or sub-surface resources can claim rights over such resources is largely contingent upon whether the state in question recognizes private property rights over such sub-soil and/or sub-surface resources in general. If domestic law does not acknowledge private property rights over sub-soil and sub-surface resources, indigenous communities that have not traditionally used such resources cannot invoke the equality argument to claim extensive property rights over such. The principle of state sovereignty leave states free to determine that no private rights, including of indigenous communities, attach to sub-soil and sub-surface resources, as indeed a substantial majority of states have also done.[38] Conversely, to the extent domestic law does recognize that private entities can establish property rights over sub-surface and sub-soil resources, that right must apply equally to indigenous communities, meaning that they hold property rights over natural resources situated under their respective traditional territories irrespective of whether they have used the resource or not. When domestic law does not acknowledge private rights over sub-soil and sub-surface resources, indigenous communities are, under the right to property, entitled to benefit-sharing.

International law's position towards sub-soil and sub-surface resources is also reflected in ILO 169. ILO 169 Article 15.2 accepts that states retain rights over sub-surface and sub-soil resources situated under indigenous peoples' territories.[39] But the provision does not leave the right unconditioned. Having confirmed the general rule, Article 15.2 proceeds to proclaim that the indigenous peoples concerned shall whenever 'possible participate in the benefits of such activities'.[40] In line with ILO 169 Article 15.2, the CERD Committee has held that the right to property enshrined in the CERD Convention embraces a right of indigenous communities to participate in the exploitation of natural resources situated under their traditional territories.[41] The Inter-American human rights institutions have taken a similar position. In *Saramaka*, the IACHR held that indigenous communities have a right to share in benefits resulting from resource extraction on lands traditionally

[38] Again, another matter is that indigenous *peoples* can hold *self-determining rights* over sub-soil and sub-surface resources irrespective of what position domestic law takes towards *private rights* over such resources. See further Chapter 6.

[39] The provision actually employs the term 'ownership' right, something that comes across as odd or even as a fallacy since what states retain are sovereign, not property, rights over sub-soil and sub-surface resources.

[40] According to Jérémie Gilbert, ILO 169 Article 15.2 awards indigenous peoples (or rather indigenous communities, since the right in question is a property right) with a limited property right over sub-surface and sub-soil resources. See Jérémie Gilbert, *Indigenous Peoples' Land Rights Under International Law: From Victims to Actors* (Transnational Publishers, 2006) 105.

[41] See e.g. Concluding Observations with Regard to Suriname, UN Doc CERD/C/SUR/CO/12.

used by them. In *Endorois*, the African Commission on Human and Peoples' Rights (AfCommHPR) essentially echoed the position taken by the IACHR in *Saramaka*. The AfCommHPR affirmed that indigenous communities have a right to benefit-sharing when natural resources situated under their lands are being extracted.[42] Similarly, the World Bank's Operation Policy on Indigenous Peoples requires that benefits are shared with indigenous peoples when natural resource extraction occurs on their traditional territories. Such benefit-sharing shall, according to the World Bank, be provided in a culturally appropriate manner and shall be at least as extensive as benefits shared with any title holder.[43] The Asian Development Bank's Policy on Indigenous Peoples contains a similar provision, as does the Inter-American Development Bank's Operational Policy on Indigenous Peoples.[44]

State practice largely supports the conclusion above. Generally speaking, industrialized countries that are host to indigenous peoples and recognize the existence of such within their borders have established, or in some instances are about to establish, practices that entitle indigenous communities to share in benefits when natural resources situated within their territories are extracted for industrial purposes.[45]

The position that indigenous communities are entitled to benefit-sharing when states retain sovereign rights over sub-soil and sub-surface resources finds further support in the legal doctrine. For instance, Andrew Huff submits that the fact that ILO 169 Article 15.2 allows states to maintain control over sub-soil and sub-surface resources situated under indigenous communities' traditional territories is a legacy of the doctrine of discovery. He asserts that under contemporary international property rights law, policies that seek to cement state control over natural resources in indigenous communities' territories are discriminatory. Huff concludes that recent developments within international law should prompt states to adopt policies that require that natural resources situated in indigenous communities' territories be obtained only through agreements with them.[46] For his part, Nigel Bankes interprets the jurisprudence emanating out of the Inter-American human rights system as implying that indigenous communities must have at least the same right to sub-surface resources situated under their traditional territories as conventional title holders.[47] In the same vein, James Anaya observes that ILO 169 Article 15.2 is to be understood in light of the right to equality. He concludes that states must not deny indigenous communities rights over sub-surface and sub-soil resources to any larger extent than other segments of society. He infers that at a minimum, ILO 169 Article 15 awards indigenous communities a right to

[42] *Endorois People v Kenya Case. Centre for Minority Rights Development (Kenya) and Minority Rights Group International on behalf of Endorois Welfare Council v Kenya*, Comm 276/2003 (2010) 294.

[43] The World Bank Operational Policies on Indigenous Peoples (OP 4.10) 18.

[44] OM Section F3/BP, 25, September 2006 8 and OP-765, 22 February 2006 4.4 (b).

[45] See e.g. Arctic Human Development Report 2004, Akureyri: Stefansson Arctic Institute 132–34; *Apirana Mahuika et al v New Zealand*, Comm No 547/1993, views adopted 27 October 2000.

[46] Andrew Huff, 'Indigenous Land Rights and the New Self-Determination' [2005] 16 Colo J Int'l Envtil L Pol'y 295 305, 331.

[47] Nigel Bankes, 'Land Claims Agreements in Arctic Canada in Light of International Human Rights Norms' [2009] Yearbook of Polar Law, 1 227.

benefit-sharing when natural resources situated under their land are being exploited.[48] Jérémie Gilbert and Cathal Doyle infer that UNDRIP Article 26 affirms that indigenous peoples' land rights embrace rights over natural resources situated on, as well as under, their respective territories.[49] Stefania Errico joins the choir. She observes that at present, international law allows states to retain rights over sub-soil resources. She maintains, however, that this fact does not deprive indigenous communities of all property rights interests in such resources. Errico posits that indigenous communities' property right interest in sub-soil and sub-surface resources entitle them to a share in the profits generated by resource extraction.[50] Finally, Jo Pasqualucci, somewhat more cautiously, concurs that evolving standards of international law entitles indigenous peoples to benefit-sharing when natural resources are extracted from their territories.[51]

9.4.2 The underlying rationale behind indigenous communities' right to benefit-sharing

If considering the general principles that underpin indigenous communities' property rights over territories traditionally used, it should come as no surprise that international law provides that indigenous communities are entitled to benefit-sharing when resource extraction occurs within their territories. In order to access and extract sub-soil and sub-surface resources, the extractor necessarily also needs access to the surface area under which the resources are situated. But Section 9.2 explains how, as a general rule, the right to property provides that a resource extractor cannot legally gain access to such a territory without obtaining the consent of the relevant indigenous community. Reasonably, an indigenous community has little incentive to grant its consent unless the resource extractor offers something in return.

As Section 9.2 explains, the alternative to a negotiated agreement is if the resource extractor can convince the state to expropriate the part of the indigenous community's traditional territory under which the sub-soil or sub-surface resources are situated. But as Section 9.2 further concludes, expropriation might often not be a viable option, due to difficulties associated with simultaneously meeting the legitimate aim and the proportionality criteria.

Thus, in most instances the only option available to a resource extractor that seek access to an indigenous community's territory is presumably to reach an agreement with the community, an agreement that will then assumingly normally include

48 Anaya, 'Indigenous Peoples' Participatory Rights' (n 16) 10.

49 Jérémie Gilbert and Cathal Doyle, 'A New Dawn over the Land: Shedding Light on Collective Ownership and Consent', in Stephen Allen and Alexandra Xanthaki (eds.), *Reflections on the UN Declaration on the Rights of Indigenous Peoples* (Hart Publishing, 2011) 302.

50 Stefania Errico, 'The Controversial Issue of Natural Resources: Balancing States' Sovereignty with Indigenous Peoples' Rights', in Stephen Allen and Alexandra Xanthaki (eds.), *Reflections on the UN Declaration on the Rights of Indigenous Peoples* (Hart Publishing, 2011) 337, 340–41, 356.

51 Jo Pasqualucci, 'International Indigenous Land Rights; A Critique of the Jurisprudence of the Inter-American Court of Human Rights in Light of the United Nations Declaration on the Rights of Indigenous Peoples' [2009] 27 *Wisconsin International Law Journal* 51 91.

benefit-sharing arrangements. Importantly, however, even when expropriation may be an option, that does not necessarily mean that benefit-sharing is excluded.

In the presumably rare instances when there might be an opening for expropriation, it is reasonably still a prerequisite for meeting the proportionality test that the resource extractor provides benefit-sharing to the community. As Section 9.2 elaborates, to be lawful, an expropriation must not result in a disproportionate and excessive burden being placed on the community. If the corporation refuses to share benefits with the community (and the state fails to compel the corporation to do so), this will surely in most, if not all, instances result in the conclusion that the limitation in the community's property right places a disproportionate burden on it. Seemingly, it constitutes a prime example of a few having to carry a disproportionate and excessive burden for the benefit of all if resource extraction benefits only the majority society, and gives nothing back to the indigenous community that is forced to make its land available for the enterprise. It can hardly be called proportionate if one segment of society is left with all the burdens that follow with resource extraction, while other segments reap the benefits. To address this discrepancy, benefit-sharing must be provided. In conclusion, as a general rule, a resource extractor should as a first step seek to enter into an agreement with the affected indigenous community that includes benefit-sharing arrangements prior to embarking on resource extraction on the traditional territory of the community. But even when no such agreement has been reached, expropriation—if at all allowed—would normally presuppose that benefits are shared with the community, for the expropriation to be considered proportionate. (To avoid any risks of misunderstandings, it is underlined that benefit-sharing will only take place when the resource extractor either manage to reach an agreement with the community or the expropriation criteria are fulfilled. If neither of these conditions are present, no resource extraction can legally occur.)

In summary, international law does not award indigenous communities extensive property rights over sub-soil and sub-surface resources situated under their traditional territories in states that retain sovereign rights over such resources. But indigenous communities' property rights over territories traditionally used provide that also in such instances, communities retain some proprietary interests in sub-soil and sub-surface resources, which in turn entitle them to benefit-sharing when such resources are extracted.

9.5 Genetic Resources

It may appear unwarranted to treat genetic resources as a separate category of natural resources. After all, from a rights perspective it might be difficult to find a rationale to distinguish between genetic resources and other natural resources. But since a different position is not uncommonly put forward in various United Nations (UN) forums, for instance in meetings held under the auspices of the Convention on Biological Diversity (CBD) it might nonetheless be pertinent to devote a few sentences specifically to genetic resources, in order to straighten out some potential misunderstandings.

It is common for national jurisdictions to take the same position towards genetic resources as with regard to sub-soil and sub-surface resources. Domestic law often provides that the state retains sovereign rights over genetic resources situated within its territory.[52] If an indigenous community has not traditionally used a genetic resource found within its traditional territory, the same situation materializes itself as with regard to sub-soil and sub-surface resources, as Section 9.4 immediately above discusses. In other words, the state is free to retain rights to such genetic resources in accordance with the principle of state sovereignty, but the right might be burdened by some proprietary interests of the indigenous community, which, if so, entitles the community to benefit-sharing.

Thus, the law treats genetic resources in the same manner as sub-soil and sub-surface resources. That is, however, not necessarily the same thing as saying that states may retain rights over genetic resources to the same extent compared with the latter category of resources. While *the content of the norms* that govern rights over genetic resources, on one hand, and sub-surface and sub-soil resources, on the other, may be the same, there is a significant *factual difference* between the two categories of resources as they relate to indigenous communities. Sub-soil and sub-surface resources are of course often not readily accessible. This is also probably the reason why many indigenous peoples have not traditionally used such resources, although there are, as mentioned, certainly exceptions. By contrast, genetic material is most often found above, or at least very close to, ground. As a consequence, indigenous communities have often traditionally used genetic material situated within their traditional territories, at least if the genetic material carries properties of use to the community. Indeed, it is often the very use of a genetic material by an indigenous community through which the community has learnt about the genetic material's properties (traditional knowledge), that has transformed the genetic material into something that has value, i.e. a genetic resource.[53]

Genetic materials/resources traditionally used by an indigenous community lack the legal affinity to sub-soil and sub-surface resources the above discussed. Instead, such genetic materials/resources are from a legal perspective to be compared with other sorts of natural resources traditionally used by indigenous communities. To the extent an indigenous community has traditionally used a genetic resource, it has established property rights over that resource to the same extent as with regard to natural resources in general. The state's claim of sovereignty over its territory does not impact on such property rights anymore than it does with regard to other private property rights duly established through traditional use. In other words, from an international property rights perspective, it is not so much the nature of a natural resource that determine whether private rights attach to it. More important is whether it has been traditionally used by an indigenous community or not.

[52] See e.g. CBD Articles 3 and 15 and the Nagoya Protocol on Access to Genetic Resources and the Fair and Equitable Sharing of Benefits Arising From their Utilization to the Convention on Biological Resources Article 6.

[53] CBD Article 2 defines genetic resources as 'genetic material of actual and potential value'.

10
Summary

10.1 Introduction

The previous chapters have sought to explain how, in order to properly understand the indigenous rights discourse, one essentially only needs to know the answer to two questions; what is the understanding of (i) peoples, and (ii) equality, for international legal purposes?

The book describes how these two questions are answered fundamentally differently today compared with only a couple of decades or so ago. The two interrelated and recent developments within international law this book discusses and analyzes are of such fundamental character that they can hardly be described as anything less than two interrelated paradigm shifts. These have resulted in cardinal differences as to how we understand indigenous rights. To label these developments paradigm shifts is particularly pertinent if one (i) considers how the recognition of indigenous peoples as peoples for international legal purposes results in substantial transfers of jurisdiction from state institutions to indigenous peoples' decision-making bodies, and (ii) recognizes the impact the evolved understanding of the right to equality has on indigenous communities' possibilities to have property rights over territories traditionally used recognized.

The sections below recapitulate the main arguments of this book, and highlight the main conclusions.

10.2 Indigenous Peoples as Subjects of International Law

10.2.1 International law's understanding of 'peoples'

Sovereign states as we know them today and the international legal system emerged in tandem in Europe in the wake of the Peace of Westphalia in the mid-1600s. Following the end of the Thirties' Years War (1618–48), national borders in Europe were gradually drawn as a result of wars and power politics. The relative might of the European realms thus determined the stretch of these borders and, as a consequence, the shape of the emerging states. The 'nation-state', the first international legal subject, had emerged.

As to the other potential international legal subject 'peoples' there are essentially two basic options. One can, from an international legal perspective, define a people as a group of men with shared cultural and/or ethnic background. However, classical international law quickly dismissed, or perhaps more correctly did not even consider, this option. Instead, classical international law opted for defining 'peoples' in terms of aggregate groups of individuals that happened to find themselves residing within the borders of the newly formed 'nation-states'. As a result rarely, if ever, were these populations ethnically and culturally homogenous. Rather, the 'people' of the state came to consist of several nations. In other words, the 'nation-state' was no nation-state at all, but rather a nation*s*-state. Clearly, in such a legal order, there was no room for indigenous populations. As these were not state-forming peoples, they were deemed to lack international legal personality.

The position that for international legal purposes, 'peoples' are to be understood in terms of aggregate populations of states (or territories), and not in terms of common culture/ethnicity, became entrenched during the centuries that followed, and was eventually uncritically incorporated into the contemporary legal system that the young United Nations (UN) set out to craft in the aftermaths of World War II. As a consequence, the decolonization movement of the second part of the 1900s by-passed indigenous peoples' societies. Albeit of critical importance in many ways, from an indigenous perspective, decolonization only resulted in indigenous peoples having to relate to another colonizer, i.e. the colony now turned state. The decolonization movement resulted in territories, not peoples, gaining independence.

During the decolonization era, self-determination transcended from a principle into a right. This development was most visibly manifested by the inclusion of the right to self-determination in the common Article 1 of the Covenant on Civil and Political Rights (CCPR), and the Covenant on Civil and Political Rights (CESCR). But again, this development had little impact on indigenous peoples' rights. Records show that at the time when the right to self-determination was incorporated into the international legal system, the right clearly was understood to apply only to peoples in the meaning aggregate populations of states (or territories).

The outlined legal definition of peoples remained largely unchallenged into the 1980s. At this time, the UN started to address indigenous peoples' rights in earnest. In so doing, the world community recognized essentially from the outset that the situation of indigenous peoples differs considerably compared with that of minority groups.

Generally speaking, and although there are of course shades of grey, in contrast to minority groups, indigenous peoples have, despite colonization, integration attempts, and other forms of wrongs directed at them, managed to preserve their distinct societies to a significant degree. By and large, indigenous societies continue to exist side by side with the majority societies. As a consequence, from the outset the indigenous rights discourse came to focus on allowing indigenous peoples to maintain and develop these distinct societies. In this regard, particular attention was directed at territories and natural resources traditionally used by indigenous peoples, due to a recognition that such territories and resources constitute the very foundation upon which indigenous societies and cultures rest. Without continued access to their traditional lands, waters, and natural resources indigenous peoples can simply not exist.

From the above it further follows that from essentially its inception, the indigenous rights discourse came to focus on the collective dimension of indigenous rights. Rights of indigenous peoples and communities within the peoples early on propelled to the core of the regime, rather than rights of the individual members of the group. In that way, indigenous rights came to differ fundamentally from minority rights. The latter category of rights embraces only individual rights. Where the main aim of indigenous rights is to allow *indigenous peoples* to maintain and develop their distinct societies *side by side with that of the majority society*, minority rights aim to promote respect for *members of* minority groups' cultural identity *within the larger majority society*.

Given the immediate and lasting focus on the collective aspect of indigenous rights, it was only natural that soon the question of whether indigenous groups constitute peoples for international legal purposes became a key issue in the indigenous rights discourse. From the late 1990s and onwards, international legal sources increasingly proclaimed that indigenous peoples are indeed 'peoples' under international law, with rights as such, including the most central of peoples' rights, the right to self-determination. This development culminated with the adoption of the UN Declaration on the Rights of Indigenous Peoples (UNDRIP) in 2007. The Declaration explicitly confirms that indigenous peoples are peoples under international law, and that as peoples, indigenous peoples are beneficiaries of peoples' rights, including the right to self-determination.

As mentioned, the developments that led up to recognition of indigenous peoples as peoples for international legal purposes can hardly be described as anything less than a paradigm shift. Since it surfaced in the mid-1600s and almost to the present day, international law understood 'peoples' solely in terms of aggregate populations of states or (territories). During this entire time-period, groups defined by common ethnicity and/or culture could not constitute peoples under international law. The described conventional understanding of peoples rendered the notion of peoples' rights largely irrelevant. When peoples are defined as aggregate populations of states, peoples' rights essentially lack meaning. What matters then is, for all practical purposes, the relationship between states. When peoples are defined as the populations of states, one cannot talk about state-people relationships in any meaningful understanding of the term. Rather, under such circumstances it is states that, if not formally so at least in practice, exercise 'peoples' rights' through its 'proxy', the people, i.e. the aggregate population of the state.

The situation changes completely when indigenous peoples are recognized as peoples for international legal purposes and, as a consequence, a state can host more than one people. This development can potentially fundamentally change the political map of states that host indigenous peoples. Within such states, the indigenous peoples and the majority peoples—through their 'agents' the state's governing bodies—now will compete for, or, if one prefers a less confrontational expression, share jurisdiction. International law must now learn how to define the people-state relationship in a manner that was unnecessary when peoples were only understood in terms of aggregate populations of states (or territories).

10.2.2 The content and scope of the right to self-determination when applied to indigenous peoples

The right to self-determination is generally described as consisting of an external and an internal aspect. When international law understands 'peoples' only in terms of aggregate populations of states (or territories), the content and scope of both aspects are relatively straightforward. Put simply, with such an understanding of peoples, the external aspect of the right implies a right of the state (again as a proxy of the formal right holder, the 'people') to determine its relationship with other states, and to be free from outside interference in its internal affairs. For a colony, the external aspect includes the option to secede from it colonizer and to form its own state, or, alternatively, to form other political arrangements with it. The internal aspect then is a right of all citizens of the state, regardless of ethnic and cultural background, to participate in the political life of the state on an equal basis. In a democracy, the internal aspect of the right to self-determination thus largely boils down to an equal right of all citizens to vote and run for election.

The outlined content and scope of the right to self-determination can, however, no longer be relevant when the right is applied to indigenous peoples. When the right to self-determination is implemented in the context of a segment of the entire population of a state, the right must necessarily materialize itself in different manners compared with how the right has been conventionally understood.

When applied to an indigenous population that shares the territory of the state with the majority people, the external aspect of the right to self-determination does not embrace a unilateral right to secession of the indigenous people. Save in extreme circumstances, indigenous peoples must exercise their right to self-determination within existing state borders. The external aspect of the right does, however, bestow indigenous peoples with a right to represent themselves internationally and to determine their relationship with other peoples, at UN meetings and beyond.

As touched upon, the greatest impact of the recognition that indigenous peoples are beneficiaries of the right to self-determination is on the domestic level, since this development carries the potential to substantially reshape the political map in such states in which indigenous peoples today find themselves residing. That is so since the internal aspect of the right to self-determination—when applied to indigenous peoples—is no longer a mere right of indigenous individuals to participate in the political life of the state on par with other citizens. Rather, the internal aspect of indigenous peoples' right to self-determination is first and foremost to be exercised through indigenous peoples' own decision-making institutions (which might be traditional but also created more recently). The more precise powers of such indigenous decision-making bodies must be worked out through self-governance and autonomy arrangements within the state. That is far from saying, however, that states are free to formulate such political arrangements as they see fit. In fact, quite the opposite is true. International law demands that indigenous peoples' autonomy and self-governance arrangements are formulated in a manner so as to allow them to genuinely influence the outcome of decision-making processes of relevance to them.

From the just stated also follows that indigenous peoples' right to self-determination must not be confused with the right to consultation. The latter right is a *right to a process*—a right to be involved in decision-making. The right to self-determination encompasses process elements as well. But this right is still first and foremost a *material right*, i.e. a right to exercise genuine influence over the outcome of decision-making processes. The right to consultation does oblige states in good faith to engage indigenous peoples in decision-making processes and to do their utmost to find consensus solutions. Notwithstanding, if, despite efforts, a consensus solution is not to be found, under the right to consultation, the will of the state always prevails.

By contrast the right to self-determination provides that if a negotiation between an indigenous people and the state fails to generate common ground, the will of the state does not necessarily prevail in all instances. Rather, under the right to self-determination, there must—by definition—be examples when the will of the state has to yield to that of the indigenous people in cases of conflict. That is why the above refers to self-determination as a material right, albeit with processes elements embedded in it. But if the principal understanding of the right to self-determination is clear, another matter is to identify those situations when an indigenous people's position takes precedent over that of the state. As indicated, that such instances do exist can be digested from a careful analysis of the general nature of the right to self-determination, coupled with a survey of existing international legal sources. These sources do, however, offer limited guidance beyond that point. At present, existing international legal sources largely stop short of elaborating on the more precise content and scope of the internal aspect of the right to self-determination, when applied to indigenous peoples.

A clearer picture as to when, more precisely, an indigenous people's position takes precedent over that of the state will emerge only as states and indigenous peoples around the world move towards operationalizing indigenous peoples' autonomy and self-government arrangements, and as UN bodies etc. start to offer their view on how well those arrangements correspond with international law. But arguably, the relative importance of the issue that the decision-making process addresses to the indigenous people, on one hand, and to the state/majority population, on the other, should be a critical factor when establishing the scope and content of indigenous peoples' right to self-determination. If accepting this line of argument, one can illustrate the principle with a couple of examples that pertain to the right to self-determination's resource dimension.[1]

Lands and natural resources that indigenous peoples use as the basis for their traditional livelihoods and other culturally important activities constitute the backbone of their respective cultures. The argument therefore follows that with regard to decisions that relate to indigenous peoples' traditional lands, natural resources, and traditional livelihoods, the internal aspect of the right to self-determination should be far-reaching. In particular if the outcome of the decision-making process carries the

[1] It is underlined that this is only an argument by the author at this point, where the only authority is reason. As mentioned, there are at present no legal sources that back up this line of thought.

potential of a substantially negative impact on core elements of an indigenous people's culture, there might be a case that the will of the indigenous people should prevail over that of the state. If the right to self-determination cannot produce an outcome acceptable to indigenous peoples on matters that have the greatest importance to them, the right would appear to have limited meaning to them.

With regard to non-traditional natural resources, i.e. natural resources situated in (or probably more often under) indigenous peoples' traditional territories, but which they have not historically used, the situation must reasonably be different. Examples of such sub-soil and sub-surface resources may be oil, gas, and minerals. If not traditionally used by them, such natural resources are not integral to, or not even a part of, the people's culture, at least not from a historical perspective. Against this backdrop, it would appear difficult to convincingly argue that indigenous peoples have a greater interest in such resources compared with society at large. True, the sub-soil and/or sub-surface resources are situated in (or rather under) indigenous peoples territories. This justifies that indigenous peoples are allowed to participate in the management of such natural resources. In addition, they should arguably be allowed a cut of the benefits generated as a result of extraction of such resources. But this is probably the maximum amount of influence the right to self-determination should offer indigenous peoples when it comes to non-traditional natural resources. Indigenous people can hardly claim a decisive say in decision-making processes that pertain to such resources, again because their attachment to non-traditional natural resources is merely one of geography, and not culture. Thus, when the will of the state and that of the indigenous people cannot be reconciled when it comes to management of non-traditional natural resources, the will of the state prevails (unless, of course, extraction of the non-traditional resources substantially negatively impacts on the indigenous people's traditional livelihoods, lands, and natural resources, in which instances what has been articulated above applies).

10.3 The Right to Equality

10.3.1 The two facets of the right to equality

The conventional understanding of the right to equality did not require states to take cultural differences among its population into account when designing their laws and policies. It did not oblige states to adjust education, social services etc. to the cultural background of the recipient. To comply with this understanding of the right to non-discrimination, states needed only to provide services etc. based on standards derived from the culture of the majority population. The right merely required that all citizens of the state, regardless of ethnic and cultural background, had equal access to such services. In summary, the right to non-discrimination, thus understood, required only formal equality, or equality in law if one wants—that equal cases were treated equally. The meaning of the conventional understanding of the right to equality can be illustrated with the following example. It is sufficient that the state provides one educational system that offers education in and on the majority language, as long as all children in the state, irrespective of their cultural and lingual background, have the same right to access that educational system.

More recently, the right to non-discrimination has evolved to take on a second facet, which calls not only for formal equality, but also for practical equality (equality in fact). The right to non-discrimination no longer merely obliges states to treat equal cases equally. In addition, they must treat different cases differently. In other words, the evolved understanding of the right to equality requires states to adjust educational systems, social services etc. to the cultural background of members of minority cultures. If, returning to the example above derived from the sphere of education, it is no longer non-discrimination that the state cater for all children within the state receiving education in and on the majority language. Now it constitutes equality if indigenous children have the same right to access education in and on their mother tongue, as do children from the majority population and also in other ways have the education accustomed to their cultural background.

As with the recognition of indigenous peoples as peoples, the emergence of the evolved understanding of equality cannot be described as anything less than a paradigm shift. For more than 350 years, conventional individual liberalism's definition of non-discrimination had prevailed, first as a principle and subsequently also as a right under international law. This understanding of equality did not serve to protect the cultural distinctiveness of ethnically distinct groups such as indigenous peoples. It is not a concern to the conventional individual liberal if the application of the right to non-discrimination results in integration or even assimilation. On the contrary, many conventional liberals view universal individual human rights in general and the right to equality (as conventionally understood) in particular as tools for downplaying the importance of cultural identity to the individual, which they perceive might be necessary to protect the freedom of individual members of minority groups.

The evolved understanding of the right to equality implies that the right takes on a completely new meaning to indigenous peoples. Now, the right can serve essentially the opposite purpose compared with the conventional understanding. This version of the right to non-discrimination protects the cultural identity of groups, such as indigenous peoples, if not formally so at least indirectly. The contemporary understanding of the right to equality requires states to protect and promote the cultural and ethnic identity of indigenous individuals. As an indirect result, the right thus understood also serves to protect the cultural identity of the indigenous group to which the individual belongs.

10.3.2 The evolved understanding of the right to equality—implications for the rights of indigenous individuals in general

From what has been outlined above, one easily sees how the evolved understanding of the right to equality fundamentally impacts on indigenous individuals' rights within essentially all spheres of society and life. The principle that the above illustrates through the example taken from indigenous children's right to education can be applied to more or less all spheres of human activity within a society. To mention just a few additional examples, which can hopefully serve to further explain the general principle, according to the evolved understanding of the right to equality, indigenous elderly are entitled to social services accustomed to their cultural background. In the same vein, states must ensure that health care services are in tune with the particular culture of indigenous patients. And so on. In sum, essentially all human rights enjoyed by indigenous individuals—including cultural rights—can in fact be derived from the evolved understanding of the right to equality.

10.3.3 The evolved understanding of equality—particularly on its relevance to indigenous community's property rights over lands and natural resources traditionally used

Although the evolved understanding of the right to equality is, as just mentioned, highly significant in the context of cultural and other (formally) individual rights, the right's most significant impact is arguably within the sphere of indigenous communities' property rights over lands, waters, and natural resources traditionally used. That is so, since the right to property is at its core a particular aspect of the right to equality. International law does not know a positive right to be provided with property. Rather, the right to property is a right to have the same opportunity as others to acquire property and, once acquired, a right not to be arbitrarily deprived of the same. In other words, the right to property does not require a state to recognize private rights over property. But to the extent the state does so (as almost all states do), the possibility to acquire or otherwise establish rights over territories must apply without discrimination.

To properly understand the significance of the intrinsic connection between the rights to equality and property to indigenous communities' opportunities to have property rights over territories traditionally used recognized, it is pertinent to contrast international law's contemporary position on indigenous land rights with the historic ones. When doing so, it is relevant to schematically divide the position international law has taken towards indigenous communities' right over territories traditionally used into three time-periods.

The first period spans from the time of colonization of indigenous peoples' territories until the time when the right to equality was incorporated into the contemporary international human rights system following the establishment of the UN in the wake of World War II. In their aspirations to place indigenous peoples' territories and natural resources under their hegemony and control, European colonizers collaborated with liberal scholars of the era. Serving the interests of the European states, a doctrine was construed that provided that indigenous peoples could hold neither sovereign nor proprietary rights over their territories. In both instances, the weapon directed against indigenous peoples was one of distinction. It was held that only cultivation of land in manners sufficiently similar to the agrarian practices of the European 'civilized' cultures could establish private rights over lands and natural resources. In addition, liberal scholars professed, only European style 'civilized' societies can qualify for political—i.e. sovereign—rights over a territory.

In other words, in their capacity as ultimate creators of international law as professed by the principle of state sovereignty, the European powers determined that (i) indigenous peoples' societies were not sufficiently organized to hold sovereign rights over territories, and (ii) that indigenous communities' more fluctuating land uses could not result in private rights over lands and natural resources. As a consequence, international law of the era held that the European sovereign states were legally entitled to deprive among others indigenous peoples and communities of their territories, lands, and natural resources.

The outlined theory, which is most often referred to as the *terra nullius* doctrine, remained a valid international norm well into the 1900s.[2]

As noted above, in the second half of the 1900s the right to equality became firmly established as one of the core rights in the contemporary human rights system. This marks the start of the second era of international law's position towards indigenous communities' property rights over territories traditionally used. A coherent international legal system cannot reasonably at the same time hold as valid (i) *terra nullius* and other doctrines that profess that indigenous communities—simply by the very nature of their societies and cultures—are incapable of holding property rights over land, or that they can possess only limted such rights, and (ii) the right to equality. As a consequence, towards the end of the 1900s, international law took the position that states may no longer rely on *terra nullius* and similar doctrines to claim that indigenous communities' traditional use of land can per se not result in property rights. Now, international law came to formally require that national jurisdictions, to the extent they acknowledge private title over land in general, must also recognize that title can be established through indigenous communities' customary land uses, thereby ending the first stage of international law's position towards indigenous property rights over land.

But despite *formal* recognition, it remained *practically* difficult for indigenous communities to receive recognition that historical use of their traditional territories had resulted in property rights. That was so since the conventional understanding of the right to equality did not require domestic law to consider the cultural particularities of indigenous communities' land use when deciding what criteria more precisely must be fulfilled to establish property rights over land. As seen, by now international law had come to provide that indigenous communities 'traditional' land uses establish property rights. What, more precisely, amounts to 'traditional' use must, however, necessarily be specified in domestic jurisdictions, although subject to scrutiny by international human rights institutions. Naturally there are variations, but generally speaking domestic jurisdictions tend to require that a community's land use has been sufficiently continuous and intense in order to establish a property right in the form of usufruct right. For an ownership right to emerge, the

[2] That said, not all domestic jurisdictions applied the *terra nullius* doctrine in full. Other doctrines were also applied which did not take such an absolute position towards indigenous communities' proprietary rights over territories traditionally used. According to various forms of discovery doctrines, indigenous communities retain certain, albeit to varying extent limited, rights over their traditional territories.

use must in addition have been sufficiently dominating, or exclusive. But 'continuous', 'intensive', and 'exclusive' are not terms of art. They acquire their more precise meanings from a cultural context. For instance, one can expect a Sami nomadic reindeer herder to have a very different understanding of what amounts to continuous, intensive, and dominating use of land compared with a Scandinavian stationary farmer.

The conventional understanding of the right to equality did not require domestic property right law to take into account that what qualifies as continuous, intensive, and dominating use varies from culture to culture. The conventional understanding of the right to equality accepts that domestic property right law employs definitions of continuous, intensive, and exclusive land uses solely derived from the majority culture, even in situations whether an indigenous community's use of land has resulted in a property right. If returning to the Sami example, with such an understanding of equality, it is non-discrimination and sufficient if all persons in Scandinavia, Sami and Scandinavian individuals alike, have the same opportunity to establish property rights over land through Scandinavian style agriculture. Nomadic style reindeer herding need not result in rights.

But as seen, the right to non-discrimination has more recently evolved to take on an expanded understanding. The right no longer merely requires that equal cases be treated equally. In addition, it demands that states treat those differently that are culturally different. This shift in our understanding of equality marked the progression into the third stage of international law's position towards indigenous communities' property rights over territories traditionally used. When the right to equality requires that different cases be treated differently, i.e. that states take cultural differences into account in all its property laws and policies, domestic courts etc. may no longer rely on definitions of what amounts to continuous, intensive, and exclusive land uses derived from the majority culture when evaluating whether an indigenous community' traditional use of land has resulted in a property right. The applicability of the evolved understanding of the right to equality is not confined to spheres of education, social services etc. As the right to property constitutes a particular aspect of the right to equality, when the latter right evolves and takes on new meanings this inevitably impacts on the content and scope of the former.

The evolved understanding of the right to equality thus demands that states culturally adjust the continuity, intensity, and exclusivity criteria in cases concerning whether an indigenous community has established a property right to a territory through traditional use. In such cases, what matters is whether the use has been continuous, intensive, and dominating *based on standards derived from that indigenous culture*, and *not* from standards common to the majority culture. If returning to the Sami example, the right to equality requires more than that Sami individuals have equal opportunities compared with members of the Scandinavian population to establish property rights over land through engaging in agriculture common to the Scandinavian culture. For there to be equality, it is further required that a Sami reindeer herding community has the same possibility to establish property rights over land through migrating with its reindeer across mountains and through forests, as do Scandinavian farmers through agriculture. When evaluating whether a Sami reindeer herding community has established property rights over land, one must consider whether it has used the land continuously, intensely, and exclusively *based on what is common to Sami reindeer herding*. In other words, if the community has pursued reindeer herding in an area in a manner common to the Sami reindeer herding culture during a sufficient period of time, a property right has been established.

The impact of the evolved understanding of the right to equality on indigenous communities' possibilities to have property rights over territories traditionally used acknowledged has been reflected in numerous legal sources at the international, regional, and national level. Today, international law firmly establishes that indigenous communities' traditional use of lands, waters, and natural resources results in property rights.

As to the content and scope of the right, indigenous communities' property rights over territories envelopes not only lands and waters as such, but also all natural resources within traditionally used. To the extent domestic jurisdictions recognize private property rights to sub-soil and sub-surface resources, indigenous communities' property rights embrace such natural resources as well. In jurisdictions where states retain sovereign rights over sub-soil and/or sub-surface resources, indigenous communities are entitled to benefit-sharing when these are being extracted from their territories. But that is not to say that an indigenous community necessarily has to accept monetary compensation in return for land. On the contrary, as a general rule, indigenous communities' property rights over territories traditionally used award them with a right to withhold or offer their consent to competing activities, including industrial, that wish to access their territories.

10.4 The Right to Restitution

Recent progressive developments within the sphere of indigenous communities' property rights over territories traditionally used have not been confined to territories traditionally and *continuously* used. Current international legal sources further suggest that indigenous communities also retain property right interests in territories traditionally used by them, but which have subsequently been taken without consent through colonization, industrialization, or other wrongs directed at them.

True, international legal sources on the right to restitution are scarce compared with sources pertaining to territories that indigenous communities continuously use. Moreover, there is limited evidence of state practice that backs up the international legal sources that suggest that indigenous communities are entitled to restitution with regard to territories involuntarily lost in a distant or more recent past, beyond states' voting on the UNDRIP, including on Article 28 of the Declaration. Notwithstanding, existing legal sources at least suggest that a right to restitution of indigenous communities is about to crystalize into a customary international norm. This conclusion finds further support if one approaches the right to restitution in light of the position international law has taken towards the practice of extinguishment. Today, international law seemingly affirms that states are not allowed to rely on past practices of extinguishment to maintain that indigenous communities lack rights over territories that they still inhabit and use.[3] In such instances, states are obliged to 're-acknowledge' rights of indigenous communities. Restitution can also be said to be a form of re-acknowledgment of rights. The major difference between the two situations appears to be that in the case of restitution, third parties may, indeed normally have, established rights over the area subject to restitution in the absence of the indigenous community. One must of course not ignore such third party rights. Still, such rights and other third party interests can be managed through how the right to restitution is more precisely formulated and implemented. Third party rights need therefore not be incompatible with a right to restitution of indigenous communities. Neither do they, as a consequence, motivate a sharp distinction in attitude towards this right and the practice of extinguishment, respectively.

International legal sources on the right to restitution suggest that complete restitution, i.e. full return of all lands historically taken from an indigenous community, is not always necessary. Rather, the international norm appears to be that states shall return lands taken from indigenous peoples without their consent whenever feasible. This is thus the general rule. Still, the international norm further provides that when full restitution is not a practical option, other forms of compensations may suffice. Such compensation should ideally take the form of alternate lands, equal in size and quality with the land lost. But if no such lands are available, monetary compensation is acceptable.

10.5 Concluding Remarks

10.5.1 Recapture

The main aim of this book is to describe how an international legal system that for three and a half centuries was completely inhospitable towards the notion of both sovereign and private rights of indigenous peoples and communities has recently undergone two, to some extent interrelated, paradigm shifts of paramount importance to the indigenous rights discourse. This work has explained how these paradigm shifts must fundamentally change our understanding of what are indigenous rights under international law. It has articulated how, in only a few decades, international law has gone from being an enemy of indigenous peoples to becoming one of its closest allies, if properly understood.

From the inception of the classical international legal system in the wake of the Peace of Westphalia in 1648 until very recently, peoplehood was reserved for aggregate populations of states (or territories), irrespective of the cultural and ethnic composition of the state. However, in the late 1970s and early 1980s, the UN took tentative first steps towards addressing the particular situation of indigenous peoples in earnest. The indigenous rights discourse that subsequently gradually emerged increasingly challenged the conventional understanding of peoples, and

[3] Neither does international law allow states to unilateraly extinguish property rights today.

eventually successfully so. This resulted in indigenous peoples emerging as international legal subjects. They became recognized as 'peoples', with rights as such. This means, among other things, that indigenous peoples today are beneficiaries of the most prominent of peoples' rights—the right to self-determination. International legal sources are yet to elaborate on the more precise content and scope of this right when applied to indigenous peoples. Still, one can already at this point conclude that the right to self-determination, also when applied to indigenous peoples, is not a mere right to be involved in decision-making processes (i.e. a right to consultation), but first and foremost a right to exercise genuine influence over the outcome of such processes. This implies that the implementation of the right to self-determination will require transfer of some decision-making power—or sovereignty if one wants—today associated with state institutions to indigenous peoples' decision-making bodies. Such processes will reshape the political maps in states where indigenous peoples today reside in manners hitherto unknown and to extents that are not easily foreseen at present.

International law was largely created to legitimize the colonization of among others indigenous peoples' territories. Invoking the principle of state sovereignty, the European realms proclaimed that, by the very nature of their societies, indigenous peoples lacked the capacity to establish private rights over territories, lands, waters, and natural resources. With the emergence of the contemporary international legal system in the second half of the 20th century, however, the right to equality became an integral part of international law as it emerged as one of the fundamental human rights. This development rendered it impossible to uphold as valid a norm that provides that indigenous peoples—simply because of being 'too different' compared with western societies—lack capacity to hold rights over land. When more recently the right to non-discrimination took on a second facet that requires that states not only treat equally those in equal situations, but also those differently that are culturally different compared with the majority population, the door truly opened for indigenous communities to have property rights over territories traditionally used recognized also in practice.

As the right to property is essentially a particular aspect of the right to equality, the evolved understanding of the latter right requires domestic property laws to recognize that indigenous communities' traditional land uses establish property rights to the same extent as land uses common to the majority culture. This acknowledgement has resulted in a wave of rulings and decisions by regional human rights institutions and domestic courts where indigenous communities receive recognition that they indeed hold property rights over territories traditionally used. As the implementation of the right to self-determination of indigenous peoples, this development will have fundamental implications on the domestic level. Invoking the right to property, indigenous communities should be able to establish control over large areas in the states which they inhabit, and among other things require resource extractors to obtain their consent before entering their traditional territory.

The evolved understanding of equality is thus of paramount importance in the context of indigenous communities' rights over territories, lands, and natural resources, but it also underpins a large number of rights of indigenous individuals.

As mentioned, the second facet of the right to non-discrimination requires that states treat differently those that are culturally different. This implies that the right to equality provides that it is no longer sufficient that states cater for one educational system, one health care system etc. based on standards set by the majority culture. On the contrary, states must now provide societal services accustomed to indigenous individuals' cultural background. This implies that essentially all indigenous individual rights, such as the right to education in and on their own mother tongue, the right to otherwise effectively use that language in all aspects of daily life, the right to be provided with health care and social service accustomed to their cultural background, to mention just a few, can be traced back to a correct understanding of the right to equality.

The right to self-determination, rights over lands and natural resources, and individual cultural rights such as language rights essentially make up the entire indigenous rights regime. This book has demonstrated that all these rights—and thereby the indigenous rights discourse—can be explained by a proper knowledge of what are 'peoples' and what is 'equality', for international legal purposes.

10.5.2 Final reflections

More than three hundred years ago, European nations self-proclaimed themselves as 'civilized' in relation to 'uncivilized' peoples, mostly found in other continents.[4] Among those defined as uncivilized, indigenous peoples constituted prime examples.

The self-proclaimed civilized nations unilaterally decided that only they could be subjects of the international normative system they had embarked on creating. In that way, international law became yet another weapon in the arsenal of those 'civilized', complementing guns, swords, and the bible. As the other weapons before it, international law was directed at indigenous peoples, and contributed to place indigenous territories and natural resources under the European's hegemony and control. As Carlos Calvo puts it, '[i]nternational law is one of the most precious fruits of civilization.'[5]

For centuries, international law—resting steadily on its constitutional principle, i.e. that of state sovereignty—was used to proclaim the colonization of among others indigenous peoples' territories and natural resources legal. Against the international law argument, indigenous peoples had no defence. As the 'civilized' sovereign European nations unilaterally decided what the law was, their behaviour was always on the right side of the law, irrespective of how detrimental to indigenous peoples.

But to distinguish between 'civilized' and 'uncivilized' is obviously a fiction. 'Civilization' is a subjective opinion, not a term of art. When questioned about his

[4] On the concepts of 'civilized' and 'uncivilized', see generally Liliana Obregón Tarazona, 'The Civilized and the Uncivilized', in Bardo Fassbender and Anne Peters (eds.), *The Oxford Handbook of the History of International Law* (2012).

[5] Carlos Calvo, *Dictionnaire de Droit International Public et Privé* (Puttkammer & Muhlbrecht, 1885), cited from Obregón Tarazona, 'The Civilized and the Uncivilized' (n 4) 4.

opinion on European civilization, Mahatma Gandhi is said to have answered something in line with: 'European civilization? I think it would be a good idea.' As most fictions, the practice of labelling certain cultures civilized and others not was eventually exposed. Decolonization followed. When there are no civilized or uncivilized nations, just nations, an argument that it is just that one nation should be a colony of another is difficult to sustain. Because what legal norm could give one nation a legal right to rule over another that is its equal? As already Roman law established: '*par in parem non habet imperium*'.

The 'revelation' that there are no 'civilized' or 'uncivilized' peoples, only peoples, and the decolonization movement this recognition brought with it, reshaped the political map of the world in a manner never seen before or after. But the effects of this recognition did not end with decolonization and the creation of a large number of new states. The dismissal of the civilized/uncivilized dichotomy necessarily impacted on the international normative system. It required acknowledgment of the right to equality as a keystone right in the human rights regime. Similarly, when indigenous peoples could no longer be labelled 'uncivilized', the notion that had been valid since a unilateral decision to that effect was taken more than 300 years earlier—that indigenous peoples, by the very nature of their cultures and societies—cannot be subjects of international law necessarily had to yield as well.

With the 'uncivilized' stamp washed away, indigenous peoples have emerged as subjects of international law, resulting in a paradox. As seen, throughout history indigenous peoples have experienced how the international legal system has been invoked against them when seeking to retain control over their societies, lands, territories, and natural resources. However, with the emergence of the contemporary human rights regime—heavily rooted in the principle of equality rather in a categorization of peoples as civilized or uncivilized—international law is suddenly a weapon found in new hands. A new understanding of justice has emerged. With it has followed an increasing practice among indigenous peoples to invoke international law against states in support of their claims for equity, rather than the other way around.

Many centuries ago, international law was created largely for the purposes of legally depriving indigenous peoples of both their sovereignty and their private rights to territories and natural resources. It is rather ironic, therefore, that today international law has emerged as indigenous peoples' principal and preferred tool when arguing that justice require that those things are returned.

Epilogue

On 22 September 2014, after I had finished writing this book, the United Nations (UN) General Assembly (UNGA) adopted, by consensus, the outcome document of the High-level Plenary Meeting of the General Assembly on indigenous peoples, known as the World Conference on Indigenous Peoples (World Conference).[1] The main focus of the World Conference was on creating mechanisms for the effective implementation of the human rights of indigenous peoples, and in particular those enshrined in the UN Declaration on the Rights of Indigenous Peoples (UNDRIP). The aim of the World Conference was thus not to create new rights, nor to elaborate on or authoritatively interpret existing rights. Notwithstanding, the outcome document of the World Conference contains a number of recommendations that offer further guidance as to what rights indigenous peoples and communities possess under international law. Generally speaking, the recommendations included in the outcome document draw heavily from the language contained in the UNDRIP, and largely support the conclusions made in this book.

Before turning to the material outcome of the World Conference, it is pertinent to register the significance of indigenous peoples' participation in the process. True, towards the very end of the perparatory process for the World Conference, the deliberations on the outcome document were conducted, at least formally, in a purely intergovernmental setting. Nevertheless, the outcome document was largely negotiated in cooperation between state and indigenous peoples' representatives. For the present purposes, the format of the deliberations are noteworthy first and foremost because indigenous peoples participating in the formulation of the World Conference outcome document essentially on par with states underlines the particular legal status indigenous peoples have recently achieved within the UN system and on the international arena in general.[2]

Turning to the material recommendations contained in the World Conference outcome document, one can, as touched upon, first note that the outcome document underscores throughout the relevance of the UNDRIP as an indicator of what rights indigenous peoples and communities possess under international customary law. As mentioned, many recommendations borrow language from the Declaration and several others make explicit references to the UNDRIP.[3] But most noteworthy, some of the recommendations speak explicitly to the legal relevance of the Declaration. For instance, in para. 3 states reaffirm their support for the UNDRIP and commit to adhere to one of the key principles contained therein, the right of indigenous peoples to consent before states adopt legislative and administrative measures impacting on them.[4] This right in turn is derived from the right to self-determination as enshrined in UNDRIP Article 3. In the World Conference

[1] General Assembly Resolution A/69/L1. [2] Compare Section 5.7.7.
[3] See paras. 3, 4, 5, 7, 8, 20, 21, 27, 29, 30, 32, 40.
[4] Compare UNDRIP para. 19.

outcome document para. 4, states subsequently reaffirm their commitment to respect, promote, and advance the rights of indigenous peoples and to uphold the principles of the UNDRIP. World Conference outcome document paras. 7 and 8 then contain the most concrete and action-oriented recommendations in the outcome document, as far as implementation of the rights enshrined in the UNDRIP is concerned. In World Conference outcome document, para. 7, states commit to take measures, including legislative, to implement the Declaration, and in para. 8 states undertake to develop and implement national action plans in order to realize the rights contained in the UNDRIP. That states commit to implement the Declaration, through means such as legislation and national action plans, seemingly acknowledges that irrespective of that the UNDRIP as such is formally speaking not legally binding, many of the articles contained in the Declaration are nonetheless reflective of customary international law.[5] The legal relevance of the UNDRIP is further underlined by the invitation by the World Conference outcome document, para. 29 to the human rights treaty bodies to consider the Declaration in accordance with their respective mandates.

As mentioned, para. 3 contains a recommendation on indigenous peoples' right to consent in the context of legislative and administrative measures. World Conference outcome document, para. 20 subsequently sets forth a recommendation on indigenous peoples', or in practice rather 'indigenous communities'[6], right to offer or withhold their consent in the context of natural resource extraction in territories traditionally used by them. Here, states commit to consult with indigenous peoples in order to obtain their consent prior to approving any project that affects the relevant indigenous people's territories and/or natural resources. In this context, it is also worth mentioning World Conference outcome document, para. 21, where states reaffirm their commitment to establish, at the national level, impartial and transparent processes for the advancement and adjudication of indigenous peoples' rights over lands, territories, and resources.

Finally, of interest in this context is para. 33 of the World Conference outcome document, a provision that should be read in conjunction with para. 40. Pursuant to para. 33, the UN Secretary-General shall present to the UNGA proposals that aim to enhance the participation of indigenous peoples in UN meetings of relevance to them. Para. 40 provides that such recommendations shall build on a report that the Secretary-General has already prepared on the topic. The general idea behind the proposal is that indigenous peoples should be allowed to appear before the UN not only as NGOs, as they presently do, but in their capacity as peoples, through their own representative institutions. In addition to furthering the more effective participation of indigenous peoples at UN meetings etc., such a decision, if adopted, would also underscore that indigenous peoples have emerged as

[5] Compare Section 5.7.4. That said, one should note that the World Conference outcome document is itself, as the UNDRIP, a UNGA resolution and thus not formally speaking binding upon states. Notwithstanding, being adopted at the UNGA High Level Segment, with many heads of states present, it carries significant weight.

[6] See Section 9.1.

international legal subjects, thus achieving a particular legal status within the international legal system.

Ultimately, the World Conference outcome document confirms and entrenches the paradigm shifts in international law that this book has discussed in depth. It bears witness to how indigenous peoples have emerged as relevant players and subjects on the international arena, and that they are now potently competing with state institutions for jurisdiction domestically. The World Conference outcome document further reaffirms that indigenous communities have established and have the right to recognition of substantial property rights over territories traditionally used.

Bibliography

Addis, Adeno; 'Individualism, Communitarianism, and the Rights of Ethnic Minorities' [1992] *Notre Dame Law Review*, Vol 67, Issue 3

Åhrén, Mattias; 'Can Indigenous Territories be Expropriated', in Christina Allard and Susann Funderud Skogvang (eds.), *Autonomous Sámi Law: Indigenous Rights in Scandinavia* (Ashgate, 2015, forthcoming)

Åhrén, Mattias; *The Saami Traditional Dress and Beauty Pageants: Indigenous Peoples' Rights of Ownership and Self-determination over their Cultures; (Doctoral Dissertation delivered at Tromsö University*, November 2010)

Åhrén, Mattias; 'The UN Declaration on the Rights of Indigenous Peoples—How Was it Adopted and Why is it Significant?'[2007] *Gáldu Cála, Journal of Indigenous Peoples Rights*, No 4

Åhrén, Mattias; 'Indigenous Peoples' Culture, Custom, and Traditions and Customary Law—The Saami People's Perspective' [2004] *Arizona Journal of International and Comparative Law*, Vol 21:1

Åhrén, Mattias, Scheinin, Martin, and Henriksen, John B; 'The Nordic Sami Convention: International Human Rights, Self-Determination and other Central Provisions' [2007] *Gáldu Cála, Journal of Indigenous Peoples Rights*, No 3

Al Attar, Mohsen, Aylwin, Nicole and Coombe, Rosemary J; 'Indigenous Cultural Heritage Rights in International Human Rights Law', in Catherine Bell and Robert K Paterson (eds.), *Protection of First Nations Cultural Heritage, Laws, Policy, and Reform* (UBS Press, 2009)

Alfredsson, Gudmundur; 'The Right to Self-Determination and Indigenous Peoples', in Christian Tomuschat (ed.), *Modern Law of Self-Determination* (Nijhoff, 1993)

Allen, Stephen; 'The UN Declaration on the Rights of Indigenous Peoples and the Limits of the International Legal Project', in Stephen Allen and Alexandra Xanthaki (eds.), *Reflections on the UN Declaration on the Rights of Indigenous Peoples* (Hart Publishing, 2011)

Alston, Philip; *Peoples' Rights* (Oxford University Press, 2005)

Alston, Philip; 'Peoples' Rights: Their Rise and Fall', in Philip Alston (ed.), *Peoples' Rights* (Oxford University Press, 2005)

Anaya, S James; 'The Right of Indigenous Peoples to Self-Determination in the Post-Declaration Era', in Claire Charters and Rodolfo Stavenhagen (eds.), *Making the Declaration Work: The United Nations Declaration on the Rights of Indigenous Peoples* (IWGIA, 2009)

Anaya, S James; 'Divergent Discourses, About International Law, Indigenous Peoples, and Rights over Lands and Natural Resources: Toward a Realist Trend' [2005] *Colorado Journal on International and Environmental Law and Policy*, Vol 16.2

Anaya, S James; 'Indigenous Peoples' Participatory Rights in Relation to Decisions about Natural Resource Extraction' [2005] *Arizona Journal of International and Comparative Law* Vol 22, No 1

Anaya, S James; *Indigenous Peoples in International Law* (2nd edn., Oxford University Press, 2004)

Anaya, S James; 'On Justifying Special Ethnic Group Rights: Comments on Pogge', in Ian Shapiro and Will Kymlicka (eds.), *Ethnicity and Group Rights* (New York University Press, 1997)

Anaya, S James; 'The Capacity of International Law to Advance Ethnic or Nationality Rights Claims', in Will Kymlicka (ed.), *The Rights of Minority Cultures* (Oxford University Press, 1995)

Anghie, Antony; *Imperialism, Sovereignty and the Making of International Law* (Cambridge University Press, 2004)

Anghie, Antony; 'Finding the Peripheries: Sovereignty and Colonialism in Nineteenth-Century International Law' [1999] *Harvard International Law Journal* 40

Anguelovski, Isabelle; 'Environmental Justice Concerns with Transnational Mining Operations—Exploring the Limitations of Post-Crisis Community Dialogues in Peru', in Ciaran O'Farcheallaigh and Saleem Ali (eds.), *Earth Matters* (Greenleaf Publishing, 2008)

Appiah, Kwame A; *Cosmopolitanism: Ethics in a World of Strangers* (Penguin Books, 2007)

Arel, Dominique; 'Political Stability in Multinational Democracies: Comparing Language Dynamics in Brussels, Montreal and Barcelona', in Alain G Gagnon and James Tully (eds.), *Multinational Democracies* (Cambridge University Press, 2001)

Arnardóttir, Oddný; *Equality and Non-Discrimination under the European Convention on Human Rights* (Kluwer Law International, 2003)

Aust, Anthony; *Modern Treaty Law and Practice* (Cambridge University Press, 2007)

Baldwin, Clive and Morel, Cynthia; 'Using the United Nations Declaration on the Rights of Indigenous Peoples in Litigation', in Stephen Allen and Alexandra Xanthaki (eds.), *Reflections on the UN Declaration on the Rights of Indigenous Peoples* (Hart Publishing, 2011)

Bankes, Nigel; 'Recognising the Property Interests of Indigenous Peoples within Settler Societies: Some Different Conceptual Approaches', in Nigel Bankes and Timo Koivurova (eds.), *The Proposed Nordic Saami Convention; National and International Dimensions of Indigenous Property Rights* (Hart Publishing, 2013)

Bankes, Nigel; 'Land Claims Agreements in Arctic Canada in Light of International Human Rights Norms' [2009] *Yearbook of Polar Law*, 1

Barelli, Mauro; 'The Role of Soft Law in the International Legal System: The Case of the United Nations Declaration on the Rights of Indigenous Peoples' [2009] *International and Comparative Law Quarterly*, Vol 58

Barth, William Kurt; 'Cultural Rights: A Necessary Corrective to the Nation State', in Francesco Francioni and Martin Scheinin (eds.), *Cultural Human Rights* (Martinus Nijhoff Publishers, 2008)

Bianchi, Andrea; 'Immunity versus Human Rights: The Pinochet Case' [1999] *European Journal of International Law*, 10, reprinted in Malcolm Evans and Patrick Capps (eds.), *International Law* (Vol II) (Ashgate Publishing, 2009)

Bilder, Richard; 'Beyond Compliance: Helping Nations Cooperate', in Dinah Shelton (ed.), *Commitment and Compliance: The Role of Non-Binding Norms in the International Legal System* (Oxford University Press, 2007)

Binder, Christina; 'The Case of the Atlantic Coast of Nicaragua: The Awas Tingni Case, or Realizing that a Good Legal System of Protection of Land Rights is no Guarantee for Effective Implementation', in Joshua Castellino and Niamh Walsh (eds.), *International Law and Indigenous Peoples* (Martinus Nijhoff Publisher, 2005)

Bloch, Anne-Christine; 'Minorities and Indigenous Peoples', in Asbjørn Eide, Catarina Krause, and Allan Rosas (eds.), *Economic, Social and Cultural Rights—A Textbook* (2nd edn., Martinus Nijhoff Publishers, 2001)

Blumm, Michael C; 'Why Aboriginal Title Is a Fee Simple Absolute' [2011] *Lewis & Clark Law School Legal Studies Research Paper*, No 24

Boyle, Alan and Chinkin, Christine; *The Making of International Law* (Oxford University Press, 2007)

Brownlie, Ian; *Principles of Public International Law* (6th edn., Oxford University Press, 2003)

Brownlie, Ian; 'The Rights of Peoples in Modern International Law', in James Crawford (ed.), *The Rights of Peoples* (Clarendon Press, 1988)

Brownlie, Ian; *African Boundaries: A Legal and Diplomatic Encyclopedia* (Hurst & Co Publishers, 1979)

Brown Weiss, Edith; 'Understanding Compliance with Soft Law', in Dinah Shelton (ed.), *Commitment and Compliance: The Role of Non-Binding Norms in the International Legal System* (Oxford University Press, 2007)

Buchanan, Allan; 'The Morality of Secession', in Will Kymlicka (ed.), *The Rights of Minority Cultures* (Oxford University Press, 1995)

Burger, Julian; 'The UN Declaration on the Rights of Indigenous Peoples: From Advocacy to Implementation', in Stephen Allen and Alexandra Xanthaki (eds.), *Reflections on the UN Declaration on the Rights of Indigenous Peoples* (Hart Publishing, 2011)

Calvo, Carlos; *Dictionnaire de Droit International Public et Privé* (Puttkammer & Muhlbrecht, 1885)

Campbell, Maia, and Anaya, James; 'The Case of the Maya Villages of Belize: Reversing the Trend of Government Neglect to Secure Indigenous Land Rights' [2008] *Human Rights Law Review*, 8:2

Carens, Joseph; 'Aliens and Citizens: The Case for Open Borders', in Will Kymlicka (ed.), *The Rights of Minority Cultures* (Oxford University Press, 1995)

Cassese, Antonio; *International Law* (2nd edn., Oxford University Press, 2005)

Cassese, Antonio; *Self-Determination of Peoples: A Legal Reappraisal* (Cambridge University Press, 1995)

Castellino, Joshua; 'The Protection of Minorities and Indigenous Peoples in International Law: A Comparative Temporal Analysis' [2010] *International Journal on Minority and Group Rights*, 17

Castellino, Joshua; 'Territorial Integrity and the "Right" to Self-Determination: An Examination of the Conceptual Tools' [2008] *Brooks Law Journal of International Law*, Vol 33:2

Castellino, Joshua; 'Conceptual Difficulties and the Right to Indigenous Self-Determination', in Nazila Ghanea and Alexandra Xanthaki (eds.), *Minorities, Peoples and Self-Determination—Essays in Honour of Patrick Thornberry* (Martinus Nijhoff Publishers, 2005)

Castellino, Joshua; 'The Right to Land, International Law & Indigenous Peoples', in Joshua Castellino and Niamh Walsh (eds.), *International Law and Indigenous Peoples* (Martinus Nijhoff Publisher, 2005)

Charlesworth, Hillary; 'Law-Making and Sources', in James Crawford and Martti Koskenniemi (eds.), *International Law* (Cambridge University Press, 2012)

Charney, Jonathan; 'Universal International Law' [1993] *American Journal of International Law* 87 (1993), reprinted in Malcolm Evans and Patrick Capps (eds.), *International Law* (Vol I) (Ashgate Publishing, 2009)

Charney, Jonathan; 'Compliance with International Soft Law', in Dinah Shelton (ed.), *Commitment and Compliance: The Role of Non-Binding Norms in the International Legal System* (Oxford University Press, 2007)

Cheng, Bin; 'Introduction to Subjects of International Law', in Mohammed Bedjaoui (ed.), *International Law: Achievements and Prospects* (UNESCO, 1991)

Chinkin, Christine; 'Normative Development in the International Legal System', in Dinah Shelton (ed.), *Commitment and Compliance: The Role of Non-Binding Norms in the International Legal System* (Oxford University Press, 2007)

Craven, Matthew; 'The UN Committee on Economic, Social and Cultural Rights', in Asbjørn Eide, Catarina Krause and Allan Rosas (eds.), *Economic, Social and Cultural Rights—A Textbook* (2nd edn., Martinus Nijhoff Publishers, 2001)

Crawford, James; *The Creation of States in International Law* (2nd edn., Clarendon Press, 2006)

Crawford, James; 'The Right of Self-Determination in International Law: Its Development and Future', in Philip Alston (ed.), *Peoples' Rights* (Oxford University Press, 2005)

Crawford, James; 'The Rights of Peoples: "Peoples" or "Governments"?', in James Crawford (ed.), *The Rights of Peoples* (Clarendon Press, 1988)

Crawford, James; 'The Criteria for Statehood in International Law' [1976] *British Yearbook of International Law*, 48 (1), reprinted in Malcolm Evans and Patrick Capps (eds.), *International Law* (Vol II) (Ashgate Publishing, 2009)

Crawford, James and Koskenniemi, Martti; *International Law* (Cambridge University Press, 2012)

Dannenmaier, Eric; 'Beyond Indigenous Property Rights: Exploring the Emergence of a Distinctive Connection Doctrine' [2008] *Washington University Law Review*, Vol 86:53

De Shutter, Olivier; *International Human Rights Law* (Cambridge University Press, 2010)

Donders, Yvonne; *Towards a Right to Cultural Identity?* (Intersentia, 2002)

Dugard, John and Raic, David; 'The Role of Recognition in the Law and Practice of Secession', in Marcelo G Cohen (ed.), *Secession: International Law Perspectives* (Cambridge University Press, 2006)

Dumberry, Patrick; 'Lessons Learned from the Quebec Secession Reference before the Supreme Court of Canada', in Marcelo G Kohen (ed.), *Secession: International Law Perspectives* (Cambridge University Press, 2006)

Dworkin, Ronald; *A Matter of Principle* (Harvard University Press, 1985)

Eide, Asbjørn; 'Economic, Social and Cultural Rights as Human Rights', in Asbjørn Eide, Catarina Krause, and Allan Rosas (eds.), *Economic, Social and Cultural Rights—A Textbook* (2nd edn., Martinus Nijhoff Publishers, 2001)

Eide, Asbjørn; 'The Use of Indicators in the Practice of the Committee on Economic, Social and Cultural Rights', in Asbjørn Eide, Catarina Krause, and Allan Rosas (eds), *Economic, Social and Cultural Rights—A Textbook* (2nd edn., Martinus Nijhoff Publishers, 2001)

Emerson, Rupert; 'Self-Determination' [1971] *American Journal of International Law*, Vol 65

Errico, Stefania; 'The Controversial Issue of Natural Resources: Balancing States' Sovereignty with Indigenous Peoples' Rights', in Stephen Allen and Alexandra Xanthaki (eds.), *Reflections on the UN Declaration on the Rights of Indigenous Peoples* (Hart Publishing, 2011)

Errico, Stefania; 'The UN Declaration on the Rights of Indigenous Peoples is Adopted: An Overview' [2007] *Human Rights Law Review* 7:4

Estébanez; María Amor Martín; 'Council of Europe Policies Concerning the Protection of Linguistic Minorities and the Justiciability', in Nazila Ghanea and Alexandra Xanthaki (eds.), *Minorities, Peoples and Self-Determination—Essays in Honour of Patrick Thornberry* (Martinus Nijhoff Publishers, 2005)

Evans, Malcolm and Capps, Patrick (eds.); *International Law* (Vol I) (Ashgate Publishing, 2009)

Falk, Richard; 'The Rights of Peoples (In Particular Indigenous Peoples)', in James Crawford (ed.), *The Rights of Peoples* (Clarendon Press, 1988)

Fassbender, Bardo; 'The United Nations Charter As Constitution of the International Community' [1998] *Columbia Journal of Transnational Law* 36, reprinted in Malcom Evans and Patrick Capps (eds.), *International Law* (Vol I) (Ashgate Publishing, 2009)

Fitzmaurice, Andrew; 'Discovery, Conquest, and Occupation of Territory', in Bardo Fassbender and Anne Peters (eds.), *The Oxford Handbook of the History of International Law* (2012)

Fitzpatrick, Peter; 'Terminal Legality: Imperialism and the (De)composition of Law', in Diane Elisabeth Kirkby and Catharine Coleborne (eds.), *Law, History, Colonialism; The Reach of Empire* (Manchester University Press, 2001)

Franck, Thomas M; 'The Emerging Right to Democratic Governance' [1992] *American Journal of International Law* 86, reprinted in Patrick Evans and Malcolm Capps (eds.), *International Law* (Vol II) (Ashgate Publishing, 2009)

Fredman, Sandra; 'Providing Equality: Substantive Equality and the Positive Duty to Provide' [2005] *South African Journal on Human Rights* 21

Fredman, Sandra; 'Combating Racism with Human Rights: The Right to Equality', in Sandra Fredman (ed.), *Discrimination and Human Rights: The Case of Racism* (Oxford University Press, 2001)

Freeman, Michael; 'Are there Collective Human Rights?' [1995] *Political Studies* XLIII

Friedmann, Wolfgang; *The Changing Structure of International Law* (Columbia University Press, 1964)

Fromherz, Christopher J; 'Indigenous Peoples Courts: Egalitarian Juridical Pluralism, Self-Determination, and the United Nations Declaration on the Rights of Indigenous Peoples' [2008] *University of Pennsylvania Law Review*, Vol 156

Gagnon, Alain G; 'The Moral Foundations of Asymmetrical Federalism: A Normative Exploration of the Case of Quebec and Canada', in Alain G Gagnon and James Tully (eds.), *Multinational Democracies* (Cambridge University Press, 2001)

Garcia Alix, Lola; *The Permanent Forum on Indigenous Issues* (IWGIA Handbook, 2003)

Gellner, Ernest; *Nations and Nationalism* (Blackwell, 1983)

Ghanea, Nazila and Xanthaki, Alexandra; (eds.), *Minorities, Peoples and Self-Determination—Essays in Honour of Patrick Thornberry* (Martinus Nijhoff Publishers, 2005)

Gilbert, Jérémie; 'Indigenous Rights in the Making: The United Nations Declaration on the Rights of Indigenous Peoples' [2007] *International Journal on Minority and Group Rights* 14

Gilbert, Jérémie; *Indigenous Peoples' Land Rights Under International Law: From Victims to Actors* (Transnational Publishers, 2006)

Gilbert, Jérémie and Doyle, Cathal; 'A New Dawn over the Land: Shedding Light on Collective Ownership and Consent', in Stephen Allen and Alexandra Xanthaki (eds.), *Reflections on the UN Declaration on the Rights of Indigenous Peoples* (Hart Publishing, 2011)

Glazer, Nathan; 'Individual Rights against Group Rights', in Will Kymlicka (ed.), *The Rights of Minority Cultures* (Oxford University Press, 1995)

Gould, Carol C; 'Diversity and Democracy: Representing Differences', in Seyla Benhabib (ed.), *Democracy and Difference: Contesting the Boundaries of the Political* (Princeton University Press, 1996)

Gray, Andrew; 'The Indigenous Movement in Asia', in R H Barnes, Andrew Gray, and Benedict Kingsbury (eds.), *Indigenous Peoples of Asia* (Association for Asian Studies, 1995)

Haas, Peter; 'Choosing to Comply: Theorizing from International Relations and Comparative Politics', in Dinah Shelton (ed.), *Commitment and Compliance: The Role of Non-Binding Norms in the International Legal System* (Oxford University Press, 2007)

Habermas, Jürgen; 'Three Normative Models of Democracy', in Seyla Benhabib (ed.), *Democracy and Difference: Contesting the Boundaries of the Political* (Princeton University Press, 1996)

Hannum, Hurst; *Autonomy, Sovereignty, and Self-Determination: The Accommodation of Conflicting Rights* (Revised edn., University of Pennsylvania Press, 1996)

Hannum, Hurst and Lillich, Richard B; 'The Concept of Autonomy in International Law' [1980] *American Journal of International Law*, Vol 74, No 4

Hartney, Michael; 'Some Confusion Concerning Collective Rights', in Will Kymlicka (ed.), *The Rights of Minority Cultures* (Oxford University Press, 1995)

Hickford, Mark; 'Settling Some Very Important Principles of Colonial Law, Three "Forgotten" Cases of the 1840s' [2004] *Victoria University of Wellington Law Review* 35, 1

Hindess, Barry; 'Sovereignty as an Indirect Rule', in Trudy Jacobsen, Charles Sampford, and Ramesh Thakur (eds.), *Re-envisioning Sovereignty—The End of Westphalia?* (Ashgate Publishing, 2008)

Hinsley, Francis; *Sovereignty* (Basic Books, 1966)

Hudson, Wayne; 'Fables of Sovereignty', in Trudy Jacobsen, Charles Sampford, and Ramesh Thakur (eds.), *Re-envisioning Sovereignty—The End of Westphalia?* (Ashgate Publishing, 2008)

Huff, Andrew; 'Indigenous Land Rights and the New Self-Determination' [2005] 16 *Colo J Int'l Envtil L Pol'y* 295

Hylland Eriksen, Thomas; 'Ethnicity, class, and the 1999 Mauritian riots', in Stephen May, Tariq Modood, and Judith Squires (eds.), *Ethnicity, Nationalism and Minority Rights* (Cambridge University Press, 2004)

Idleman, Scott; 'Multiculturalism and the Future of Tribal Sovereignty' [2004] *Columbia Human Rights Law Review*, Vol 35

Ivison, Duncan, Patton, Paul, and Sanders, Will (eds.); *Political Theory and the Rights of Indigenous Peoples* (Cambridge University Press, 2000)

Jennings, Ivor; *The Approach to Self-Government* (Cambridge University Press, 1956)

Johnston, Darlene M; 'Native Rights as Collective Rights: A Question of Group Self-Preservation', in Will Kymlicka (ed.), *The Rights of Minority Cultures* (Oxford University Press, 1995)

Karmis, Dimitrios and Gagnon, Alain G; 'Federalism, federation and collective identities in Canada and Belgium: different routes, similar fragmentation', in Alain G Gagnon and James Tully (eds.), *Multinational Democracies* (Cambridge University Press, 2001)

Keal, Paul; 'Indigenous Sovereignty', in Trude Jacobsen, Charles Sampford, and Ramesh Thakur (eds.), *Re-Envisioning Sovereignty—The End of Westphalia?* (Ashgate Publishing, 2008)

Keating, Michael; 'So Many Nations, So Few States; Territory and Nationalism in the Global Era', in Alain G Gagnon and James Tully (eds.), *Multinational Democracies* (Cambridge University Press, 2001)

Kingsbury, Benedict; 'Legal Positivism as Normative Politics: International Society, Balance of Power, and Lassa Oppenheim's Positive International Law' [2002] *European Journal of International Law* 13, reprinted in Malcolm Evans and Patrick Capps (eds.), *International Law* (Vol I) (Ashgate Publishing, 2009)

Kingsbury, Benedict; 'Reconciling Five Competing Conceptual Structures of Indigenous Peoples' Claims in International and Comparative Law', in Philip Alston (ed.), *Peoples' Rights* (Oxford University Press, 2005)

Kingsbury, Benedict; '"Indigenous Peoples" as an International Legal Concept', in R H Barnes, Andrew Gray, and Benedict Kingsbury (eds.), *Indigenous Peoples of Asia* (Association for Asian Studies, 1995)

Kinnane, Steve; 'Indigenous Sustainability: Rights, Obligations, and a Collective Commitment to Country', in Joshua Castellino and Nimah Walsh (eds.), *International Law and Indigenous Peoples* (Martinus Nijhoff Publisher, 2005)

Kirgis, Frederic L; 'Custom on a Sliding Scale' [1987] *American Journal of International Law* 81

Kiwanuka, Richard N; 'The Meaning of "People" in the African Charter on Human and Peoples' Rights' [1988] *American Journal of International Law*, Vol 82

Kohen, Marcelo G (ed.); *Secession: International Law Perspectives* (Cambridge University Press, 2006)

Kontos, Alexis P; 'Aboriginal Self-Government in Canada: Reconciling Rights to Political Participation and Indigenous Cultural Integrity', in Joshua Castellino and Liamh Walsh (eds.), *International Law and Indigenous Peoples* (Martinus Nijhoff Publisher, 2005)

Koivurova, Timo; 'Jurisprudence of the European Court of Human Rights Regarding Indigenous Peoples: Retrospects and Prospects' [2011] *International Journal on Minority and Group Rights* 18

Koskenniemi, Martti; 'International Law in the World of Ideas', in James Crawford and Martti Koskenniem (eds.), *International Law* (Cambridge University Press, 2012)

Koskenniemi, Martti; 'The Politics of International Law—20 Years Later' [2009] *The European Journal of International Law*, Vol 20, No 1

Koskenniemi, Martti; *From Apology to Utopia—The Structure of International Legal Argument* (Cambridge University Press, 2005)

Koskenniemi, Martti; *The Gentle Civilizer of Nations—The Rise and Fall of International Law 1870–1960* (Cambridge University Press, 2002)

Koskenniemi, Martti; 'National Self-Determination Today: Problems of Legal Theory and Practice' [1994] *International & Comparative Law Quarterly*, Vol 43

Krause, Catarina; 'The Right to Property', in Asbjørn Eide, Catarina Krause, and Allan Rosas (eds.), *Economic, Social and Cultural Rights—A Textbook* (2nd edn., Martinus Nijhoff Publishers, 2001)

Kukathas, Chandran; 'Are There Any Cultural Rights?', in Will Kymlicka (ed.), *The Rights of Minority Cultures* (Oxford University Press, 1995)

Kunz, Josef; 'The Present Status of the International Law for the Protection of Minorities' [1954] *American Journal of International Law*, Vol 48, No 2

Kymlicka, Will; 'Beyond the Indigenous/Minority Dichotomy?', in Stephen Allen and Alexandra Xanthaki (eds.), *Reflections on the UN Declaration on the Rights of Indigenous Peoples* (Hart Publishing, 2011)

Kymlicka, Will; *Multicultural Odysseys—Navigating the New International Politics of Diversity* (Oxford University Press, 2007)

Kymlicka, Will; *Contemporary Political Philosophy: An Introduction* (Oxford University Press, 2002)

Kymlicka, Will; 'American Multiculturalism and the "Nations Within"', in Duncan Ivison, Paul Patton, and Will Sanders (eds.), *Political Theory and the Rights of Indigenous Peoples* (Cambridge University Press, 2000)

Kymlicka, Will; *Multicultural Citizenship: A Liberal Theory of Minority Rights* (Clarendon Press, 1995)

Kymlicka, Will (ed.); *The Rights of Minority Cultures* (Oxford University Press, 1995)

Lauterpacht, Hersch; 'The Problem of Jurisdictional Immunities of Foreign States' [1951] *British Yearbook of International Law* 28, reprinted in Malcolm Evans and Patrick Capps (eds.), *International Law* (Vol II) (Ashgate Publishing, 2009)

Lauterpacht, Hersch; *The Subjects of the Law of Nations* (LQR, 1947)

Lauterpacht, Hersch; 'The Grotian Tradition in International Law' [1946] *British Year Book of International Law* 23, reprinted in Malcolm Evans and Patrick Capps (eds.), *International Law* (Vol I) (Ashgate Publishing, 2009)

Lea, David; *Property Rights, Indigenous People and the Developing World: Issues from Aboriginal Entitlement to Intellectual Ownership Rights* (Martinus Nijhoff Publishers, 2008)

Lenzerini, Federico; 'Indigenous Peoples' Cultural Rights and the Controversy over Commercial Use of Their Traditional Knowledge', in Francesco Francioni and Martin Scheinin (eds.), *Cultural Human Rights* (Martinus Nijhoff Publishers, 2008)

Lenzerini, Federico; 'Sovereignty Revisited: International Law and Parallel Sovereignty of Indigenous Peoples' [2006] *Texas International Law Journal*, Vol 42

Lerner, Nathan; *Group Rights and Discrimination in International Law* (2nd edn., Martinus Nijhoff Publishers, 2003)

Lillich, Richard; 'Global Protection of Human Rights', in Theodor Meron (ed.), *Human Rights in International law: Legal and Policy Issues* (Clarendon Press, 1984 (reprint 1992))

Locke, John; *Two Treatises of Government* (1689)

Loukacheva, Natalia; 'On Autonomy and Law', at <https://www.ciaonet.org/wps/ighc/0007546/f_0007456_6419.pdf> accessed 2 February 2010)

Macklem, Patrick; 'Indigenous Recognition in International Law: Theoretical Observations' [2008] *Michigan Journal of International Law*, Vol 30 (1)

Makkonen, Timo; *Equal in Law, Unequal in Fact: Racial and Ethnic Discrimination and the Legal Response thereto in Europe* (Doctoral Dissertation presented at the Faculty of Law at the University of Helsinki, 5 March 2010)

Makkonen, Timo; 'Minorities' Right to Maintain and Develop Their Cultures: Legal Implications of Social Science Research', in Francesco Francioni and Martin Scheinin (eds.), *Cultural Human Rights* (Martinus Nijhoff Publishers, 2008)

Mancini, Susanna and De Witte, Bruno; 'Language Rights and Cultural Rights: A European Perspective', in Francesco Francioni and Martin Scheinin (eds.), *Cultural Human Rights* (Martinus Nijhoff Publishers, 2008)

Margalit, Avishai and Raz, Joseph; 'National Self-Determination', in Will Kymlicka (ed.), *The Rights of Minority Cultures* (Oxford University Press, 1995)

May, Stephen, Modood, Tariq, and Squires, Judith; 'Ethnicity, nationalism and minority rights: charting the disciplinary debates', in Stephen May, Tariq Modood, and Judith Squires (eds.), *Ethnicity, Nationalism and Minority Rights* (Cambridge University Press, 2004)

McAteer, Emily, Caretti, Jamie, and Ali, Saleem; 'Shareholder Activism and Corporate Behaviour in Ecuador—A Comparative Study of Two Oil Ventures', in Ciaran O'Farcheallaigh and Saleem Ali (eds.), *Earth Matters* (Greenleaf Publishing 2008)

McCrudden, Christopher; 'The New Concept of Equality' [2003] *ERA Forum*, Vol 4, No 3

McDonald, Michael; 'Should Communities Have Rights? Reflections on Individual Liberalism' [1991] *Canadian Journal of Law and Jurisprudence*, Vol IV, No 2

McGoldrick, Dominic; 'Multiculturalism and its Discontents', in Nazila Ghanea and Alexandra Xanthaki (eds.), *Minorities, Peoples and Self-Determination—Essays in Honour of Patrick Thornberry* (Martinus Nijhoff Publishers, 2005)

McHugh, Paul; *Aboriginal Societies and the Common Law: A History of Sovereignty, Status and Self-Determination* (Oxford University Press, 2004)

McNeil, Kent; 'Judicial Treatment of Indigenous Land Rights in the Common Law World', in John V Cioffi and Peer Zumbansen (eds.), *Indigenous Peoples and the Law: Comparative and Critical Perspectives* (Hart Publishing, 2009)

McNeil, Kent; 'Emerging Justice?', in *Essays on Indigenous Rights in Canada and Australia* (University of Saskatchawan Native Law Centre, 2001)

Mégret, Frédéric; 'International Law as Law', in James Crawford and Martti Koskenniemi (eds.) *International Law* (Cambridge University Press, 2012)

Miller, David; 'Nationality in Divided Societies', in Alain G Gagnon and James Tully (eds.), *Multinational Democracies* (Cambridge University Press, 2001)

Minde; Henry; 'The Destination and the Journey—Indigenous Peoples and the United Nations from the 1960s through 1985' [2007] *Gáldu Čála, Journal of Indigenous Peoples Rights*, No 4

Moore, Margaret; 'Liberalism, Communitarianism, and the Politics of Identity', in Thomas Christiano and John Christman (eds.), *Contemporary Debates in Political Philosophy* (Blackwell Publishing, 2009)

Morrison, Fred L; 'Legal Issues in the Nicaragua Opinion' [1987] *American Journal of International Law* 81

Munzner, Stephen R; *A Theory of Property* (Cambridge University Press, 1990)

Myntti, Kristian; 'National Minorities, Indigenous Peoples and Various Modes of Political Participation', in Frank Horn (ed.), *Minorities and the Right to Political Participation* (Northern Institute for Environmental and Environment Law, 1996)

Nobel, Peter; 'The Concept of "Peoples" in the African Charter on Human and Peoples' Rights', in Peter Nobel (ed.), *Refugees and Development in Africa* (Scandinavian Institute on African Studies, 1987)

Norman, Wayne; 'Justice and Stability in Multinational Societies', in Alain G Gagnon and James Tully (eds.), *Multinational Democracies* (Cambridge University Press, 2001)

Nowak, Manfred; *Introduction to the International Human Rights Regime* (Brill, 2003)

Nozick, Robert; *Anarchy, State, and Utopia* (Basic Books, 1974)

Obregón Tarazona, Liliana; 'The Civilized and the Uncivilized', in Bardo Fassbender and Anne Peters (eds.), *The Oxford Handbook of the History of International Law* (Oxford University Press, 2012)

Okin, Susan M; 'Is Multiculturalism Bad for Women' [1997] *Boston Review 22*

O'Neil, Shane; 'Mutual Recognition and the Accommodation of National Diversity: Constitutional Justice in Northern Ireland', in Alain G Gagnon and James Tully (eds.), *Multi national Democracies* (Cambridge University Press, 2001)

Oommen, T K; 'New nationalisms and collective rights: the case of South Asia', in Stephhen May, Tariq Modood, and Judith Squires (eds.), *Ethnicity, Nationalism and Minority Rights* (Cambridge University Press, 2004)

Oppenheim, Lassa; 'The Science of International Law: Its Task and Method' [1908] *American Journal of International Law* 2, reprinted in Malcolm Evans and Patrick Capps (eds.) *International Law* (Vol I) (Ashgate Publishing, 2009)

Oppenheim; Lassa; *International Law: A Treatise* (2nd edn., Longmans, Green & Co, 1905)

Orakhelashvili, Alexander; *The Interpretation of Acts and Rules in Public International Law* (Oxford University Press, 2008)

Otto, Diane; 'Rethinking the "Universality" of Human Rights Law' [1997] *Columbia Human Rights Law Review* 29

Owen, David and Tully, James; 'Redistribution and Recognition: Two Approaches', in Simon Laden and David Owen (eds.), *Multiculturalism and Political Theory* (Cambridge University Press, 2007)

Packer, John; 'The OSCE High Commissioner on National Minorities: Pyrometer, Prophylactic Pyrosvestis', in Nazila Ghanea and Alexandra Xanthaki (eds.), *Minorities, Peoples and Self-Determination—Essays in Honour of Patrick Thornberry* (Martinus Nijhoff Publishers, 2005)

Parekh, Bhikhu; 'Redistribution or recognition? A misguided debate', in Stephen May, Tariq Modood, and Judth Squires (eds.), *Ethnicity, Nationalism and Minority Rights* (Cambridge University Press, 2004)

Parekh, Bhikhu; 'The Rushdie Affair: Research Agenda for Political Philosophy', in Will Kymlicka (ed.), *The Rights of Minority Cultures* (Oxford University Press, 1995)

Pasqualucci, Jo; 'International Indigenous Land Rights; A Critique of the Jurisprudence of the Inter-American Court of Human Rights in Light of the United Nations Declaration on the Rights of Indigenous Peoples' [2009] 27 *Wisconsin International Law Journal* 51

Patten, Allan; 'Liberal Citizenship in Multinational Societies', in Alain G Gagnon and James Tully (eds.), *Multinational Democracies* (Cambridge University Press, 2001)

Petit, Philip N; 'Minority Claims under Two Conceptions of Democracy', in Duncan Ivison, Paul Patton, and Will Sanders (eds.), *Political Theory and the Rights of Indigenous Peoples* (Cambridge University Press, 2000)

Petrova, Dimitrina; 'Racial Discrimination and the Rights of Minority Cultures', in Sandra Fredman (ed.), *Discrimination and Human Rights: The Case of Racism* (Oxford University Press, 2001)

Philips, Anne; 'Democracy and Difference: Some Problems for Feminist Theory' [1992] *Political Quarterly* (63) 1

Pieterse, Jan; 'Ethnicities and multiculturalism: politics of boundaries', in Stephen May, Tariq Modood, and Judith Squires (eds.), *Ethnicity, Nationalism and Minority Rights* (Cambridge University Press, 2004)

Pityana, N Barney; 'The Challenge of Culture for Human Rights in Africa: The African Charter in a Comparative Context', in Malcolm Evans and Rachel Murray (eds.), *The African Charter on Human and Peoples' Rights: The System in Practice, 1986–2000* (Cambridge University Press, 2002)

Pogge, Thomas; 'Group Rights and Ethnicity', in Ian Shapiro and Will Kymlicka (eds.), *Ethnicity and Group Rights* (New York University Press, 1997)

Quane, Helen; 'The UN Declaration on the Rights of Indigenous Peoples: New Directions for Self-Determination and Participatory Rights?', in Stephen Allen and Alexandra Xanthaki (eds.), *Reflections on the UN Declaration on the Rights of Indigenous Peoples* (Hart Publishing, 2011)

Raic, David; *Statehood and the Law of Self-Determination* (Kluwer Law International, 2002)

Rawls, John; *A Theory of Justice* (Oxford University Press, 1971)

Rehman, Javaid; 'Between the Devil and the Deep Blue Sea: Indigenous Peoples as the Pawns in the US "War on Terror" and the Jihad of Osama Bin Laden', in Stephen Allen and Alexandra Xanthaki (eds.), *Reflections on the UN Declaration on the Rights of Indigenous Peoples* (Hart Publishing, 2011)

Reisman, Michael; 'Protecting Indigenous Rights in International Adjudication' [1995] *American Journal of International Law* 89

Requejo, Ferran; 'Political Liberalism in Multinational States: The Legitimacy of Plural and Asymmetrical Federalism', in Alain G Gagnon and James Tully (eds.), *Multinational Democracies* (Cambridge University Press, 2001)

Reuter, Paul; *Introduction to the Law of Treaties* (Kegan Paul International, 1995)

Reynolds, Henry; 'Aborigines and the 1967 Referendum: Thirty Years On', in *Department of the Senate Occasional Lecture Series, Parliament House, Australia* (14 November 1997)

Robertson, Lindsay; *Conquest by Law: How the Discovery of America Dispossessed Indigenous Peoples of their Lands* (Oxford University Press, 2005)

Rodríguez-Piñero, Luis; 'The Inter-American System and the UN Declaration on the Rights of Indigenous Peoples: Mutual Reinforcement', in Stephen Allen and Alexandra Xanthaki (eds.), *Reflections on the UN Declaration on the Rights of Indigenous Peoples* (Hart Publishing, 2011)

Rodríguez-Piñero, Luis; *Indigenous Peoples, Postcolonialism, and International Law* (Oxford University Press, 2005)

Ross, Alf; *A Textbook of International Law* (London, 1947)

Sandel, Michael; 'The Procedural Republic and the Unencumbered Self', in Shlomo Avineri and Avner de-Shalit (eds.), *Communitarianism and Individualism* (Oxford University Press, 1992)

Scheinin, Martin; 'Impact on the Law of Treaties', in Menno T Kamminga and Martin Scheinin (eds.), *The Impact of Human Rights Law on General International Law* (Oxford University Press, 2009)

Scheinin, Martin; 'Characteristics of Human Rights Norms', in Catarina Krause and Martin Scheinin (eds.), *International Protection of Human Rights: A Textbook* (Institute for Human Rights, Åbo Academi University, 2009)

Scheinin, Martin; 'The Right of a People to Enjoy its Culture: Towards a Nordic Saami Rights Convention', in Francesco Francioni and Martin Scheinin (eds.), *Cultural Human Rights* (Martinus Nijhoff Publishers, 2008)

Scheinin, Martin; 'Indigenous Peoples' Rights under the International Covenant on Civil and Political Rights', in Joshua Castellino and Niamh Walsh (eds.), *International Law and Indigenous Peoples* (Martinus Nijhoff Publisher, 2005)

Scheinin, Martin; 'What are Indigenous Peoples?', in Nazila Ghanea and Alexandra Xanthaki (eds.), *Minorities, Peoples and Self-Determination—Essays in Honour of Patrick Thornberry* (Martinus Nijhoff Publishers, 2005)

Scheinin, Martin; 'How to Resolve Conflicts Between Individual and Collective Rights?', in Martin Scheinin and Reeta Toivanen (eds.), *Rethinking Non-Discrimination and Minority Rights* (Institute for Human Rights, Åbo Academy University, 2004)

Scheinin, Martin; 'The Right to Self-Determination under the Covenant on Civil and Political Rights', in Pekka Aikio and Martin Scheinin (eds.), *Operationalizing the Right of Indigenous Peoples to Self-Determination* (Åbo Akademi University, 2000)

Shachar, Ayelet; 'Feminism and Multiculturalism: Mapping the Terrain', in Anthony Laden and Simon Owen (eds.), *Multiculturalism and Political Theory* (Cambridge University Press, 2007)

Shachar, Ayelet; *Multicultural Jurisdictions—Cultural Differences and Women's Rights* (Cambridge University Press, 2001)

Shaw, Malcolm; 'Self-Determination and the Use of Force', in Nazila Ghanea and Alexandra Xanthaki (eds.), *Minorities, Peoples and Self-Determination—Essays in Honour of Patrick Thornberry* (Martinus Nijhoff Publishers, 2005)

Shaw, Malcolm; 'The Heritage of States: The Principle of Uti Possedetis Juris Today' [1996] *British Yearbook of International Law* 97

Shelton, Dinah; 'Normative Hierarchy in International Law' [2006] *American Journal of International Law* 100, reprinted in Malcolm Evans and Patrick Capps (eds.), *International Law* (Vol I) (Ashgate Publishing, 2009)

Shelton, Dinah; 'Commentary and Conclusions', in Dinah Shelton (ed.), *Commitment and Compliance: The Role of Non-Binding Norms in the International Legal System* (Oxford University Press, 2007)

Shelton, Dinah; 'Law, Non-Law and the Problem of "Soft Law"', in Dinah Shelton (ed.), *Commitment and Compliance: The Role of Non-Binding Norms in The International Legal System* (Oxford University Press, 2007)

Simma, Bruno and Alston, Philip; 'The Sources of Human Rights Law: Custom, Jus Cogens, and General Principles' [1992] *Australian Year Book of International Law* 12

Simpson, Audra; 'Paths Toward a Mohawk Nation: Narratives of Citizenship and Nationhood in Kahnawake', in Duncan Ivison, Paul Patton, and Will Sanders (eds.), *Political Theory and the Rights of Indigenous Peoples* (Cambridge University Press, 2000)

Simpson, Gerry; 'International Law in Diplomatic History', in James Crawford and Martti Koskenniemi (eds.), *International Law* (Cambridge University Press, 2012)

Simpson, Gerry; 'Two Liberalisms' [2001] *European Journal of International Law* 12, reprinted in Malcolm Evans and Patrick Capps (eds.), *International Law* (Vol I) (Ashgate Publishing, 2009)

Spinner-Halev, Jeff; 'Multiculturalism and its Critics', in John S Dryzek, Bonnie Honig, and Anne Phillips (eds.), *The Oxford Handbook of Political Theory* (Oxford University Press, 2006)

Stavenhagen, Rodolfo; 'Making the Declaration on the Rights of Indigenous Peoples Work: The Challenge Ahead', in Stephen Allen and Alexandra Xanthaki (eds.), *Reflections on the UN Declaration on the Rights of Indigenous Peoples* (Hart Publishing, 2011)

Stavenhagen, Rodolfo; 'Cultural Rights: A Social Science Perspective', in Asbjørn Eide, Catarina Krause, and Allan Rosas (eds.), *Economic, Social and Cultural Rights—A Textbook* (2nd edn., Martinus Nijhoff Publishers, 2001)

Swepston, Lee; 'Indigenous Peoples in International Law and Organizations', in Joshua Castellino and Niamh Walsh (eds.), *International Law and Indigenous Peoples* (Martinus Nijhoff Publisher, 2005)

Szyszczak, Erika; 'Protecting Social Rights in the European Union', in Asbjørn Eide, Catarina Krause and Allan Rosas (eds.), *Economic, Social and Cultural Rights—A Textbook* (2nd edn., Martinus Nijhoff Publishers, 2001)

Talmon, Stefan; 'The Constitutive Versus the Declaratory Theory of Recognition: *Tertium Non Datur?*' [2004] *British Yearbook of International Law*, 75, reprinted in Malcolm Evans and Patrick Capps (eds.), *International Law* (Vol II), (Ashgate Publishing, 2009)

Tancredi, Antonello; 'A Normative "Due Process" in the Creation of States through Secession', in Marcelo G Kohen (ed.), *Secession: International Law Perspectives* (Cambridge University Press, 2006)

Tasioulas, John; 'In Defence of Relative Normativity: Communitarian Values and the Nicaragua Case' [1996] *Oxford Journal of Legal Studies* 16, reprinted in Malcolm Evans and Patrick Capps (eds.), *International Law* (Vol I) (Ashgate Publishing, 2009)

Thio, Li-ann; 'International Law and Secession in the Asia and Pacific regions', in Marcelo G Kohen (ed.), *Secession: International Law Perspectives* (Cambridge University Press, 2006)

Thornberry, Patrick; 'Integrating the UN Declaration on the Rights of Indigenous Peoples into CERD Practice', in Stephen Allen and Alexandra Xanthaki (eds.), *Reflection on the UN Declaration on the Rights of Indigenous Peoples* (Hart Publishing, 2011)

Thornberry, Patrick; 'The Convention on the Elimination of Racial Discrimination, Indigenous Peoples and Caste/Decent-based Discrimination', in Joshua Castellino and Niamh Walsh (eds.), *International Law and Indigenous Peoples* (Martinus Nijhoff Publisher, 2005)

Thornberry, Patrick; *Indigenous Peoples and Human Rights* (Manchester University Press, 2002)

Thornberry, Patrick; 'Self-Determination and Indigenous Peoples: Objections and Responses', in Pekka Aikio and Martin Scheinin (eds.), *Operationalizing Self-Determination* (Institute for Human Rights, Åbo Akademi University, 2002)

Thornberry, Patrick; *International Law and the Rights of Minorities* (Oxford University Press, 1993)

Tomasevski, Katarina; 'Indicators', in Asbjørn Eide, Catarina Krause, and Allan Rosas (eds), *Economic, Social and Cultural Rights—A Textbook* (2nd edn., Martinus Nijhoff Publishers, 2001)

Tomei, Manuela and Swepston, Lee; *Indigenous and Tribal Peoples: A Guide to ILO 169*, (ILO, 1996)

Tomuschat, Christian; 'Secession and Self-Determination', in Marcelo G Kohen (ed.), *Secession: International Law Perspectives* (Cambridge University Press, 2006)

Tully, James; 'Identity Politics', in Terence Ball and Richard Bellamy (eds.), *The Cambridge History of Twentieth-Century Political Thought* (Cambridge University Press, 2003)

Tully, James; *Multinational Democracies*, Alain G Gagnon and James Tully (eds.) (Cambridge University Press, 2001)

Tully, James; 'The Struggles of Indigenous Peoples for and of Freedom', in Duncan Ivison, Paul Patton, and Will Sanders (eds.), *Political Theory and the Rights of Indigenous Peoples* (Cambridge University Press, 2000)

Tully, James; *Strange Multiplicity: Constitutionalism in an Age of Diversity* (Cambridge University Press, 1995)

Ulfstein, Geir; 'Indigenous Peoples' Right to Land' [2004] *Max Planck UNYB* 8

van Dijk, Pieter; 'The Implementation of the Final Act of Helsinki: The Creation of New Structures or the Involvement of Existing Ones?' [1989] *Michigan Journal of International Law*, Vol 10

Van Dyke, Vernon; 'The Individual, the State, and Ethnic Communities in Political Theory', in Will Kymlicka (ed.), *The Rights of Minority Cultures* (Oxford University Press, 1995)

Van Dyke, Vernon; 'Collective Entities and Moral Rights: Problems in Liberal-Democratic Thought' [1982] *The Journal of Politics*, Vol 44, 01

van Genugten, Willem; 'The African Move towards the Adoption of the 2007 Declaration on the Rights of Indigenous Peoples: The Substantive Arguments behind the Procedures', at <http://ssrn.com/abstract=1103862> accessed on 30 July 2012

Vattel, Emmerich de; *The Law of Nations* (1758)

Voyiakis, Emmanuel; 'Voting in the General Assembly as Evidence of Customary International Law', in Stephen Allen and Alexandra Xanthaki (eds.), *Reflections on the UN Declaration on the Rights of Indigenous Peoples* (Hart Publishing, 2011)

Vrdoljak, Ana Filipa; 'Self-Determination and Cultural Rights', in Francesco Francioni and Martin Scheinin (eds.), *Cultural Human Rights* (Martinus Nijhoff Publishers, 2008)

Waldron, Jeremy; *The Right to Private Property* (Clarendon Paperbacks, 1998)

Waldron, Jeremy; 'Minority Cultures and the Cosmopolitan Alternative', in Will Kymlicka (ed.), *The Rights of Minority Cultures* (Oxford University Press, 1995)

Walker, Brian; 'Plural Cultures, Contested Territories: A Critique of Kymlicka' [1997] *Canadian Journal of Political Science*, Vol 30, No 2

Walzer, Michael; *Spheres of Justice: A Defence of Pluralism and Equality* (Blackwell, 1983)

Watson, Blake A; 'The Impact of the American Doctrine of Discovery on Native Land Rights in Australia, Canada and New Zealand' [2011] 34 *Seattle U L Rev* 507

Webber, Jeremy; 'The Public-Law Dimension of Indigenous Property Rights', in Nigel Bankes and Timo Koivurova (eds.), *The Proposed Nordic Saami Convention; National and International Dimensions of Indigenous Property Rights* (Hart Publishing, 2013)

Weeks, Jeffrey; 'The Value of Difference', in Jonathan Rutherford (ed.), *Identity—Community, Culture, Difference* (Lawrence and Wishart, 1990)

Weil, Prosper; 'Towards Relative Normativity in International Law?' [1983] *American Journal of International Law* 77, reprinted in Malcolm Evans and Patrick Capps (eds.), *International Law* (Vol I) (Ashgate Publishing, 2009)

Weinstock, Daniel M; 'Liberalism, Multiculturalism, and the Problem of Internal Minorities', in Simon Laden and David Owen (eds.), *Multiculturalism and Political Theory* (Cambridge University Press, 2007)

Weller, Marc; 'Towards a General Comment on Self-Determination and Autonomy: Working Paper Submitted to the Sub-Commission on the Protection and Promotion of Human Rights', Working Group on Minorities, UN Document E/CN4/Sub2/AC5/2005/WP5

Weller, Marc; 'Settling Self-Determination Conflicts: Recent Developments' [2009] *European Journal of International Law*, Vol 20, No 1

Wheatley, Steven; *Democracy, Minorities and International Law* (Cambridge Studies in International and Comparative Law, 2005)

Williams, Robert A; *Like a Loaded Weapon* (University of Minnesota Press, 2005)

Wiessner, Siegfried; 'The Cultural Rights of Indigenous Peoples: Achievements and Continuing Challenges' [2011] *The European Journal of International Law*, Vol 22, No 1

Wiessner, Siegfried; 'Indigenous Sovereignty: A Reassessment in Light of the UN Declaration on the Rights of Indigenous Peoples' [2008] *Vanderbilt Journal of Transnational Law* 41

Xanthaki, Alexandra; 'Indigenous Rights in International Law over the Last 10 Years and Future Developments' [2009] *Melbourne Journal of International Law* 10 (1)

Xanthaki, Alexandra; *Indigenous Rights and United Nations Standards—Self-Determination, Culture and Land* (Cambridge University Press, 2007)

Xanthaki, Alexandra; 'The Right to Self-Determination: Meaning and Scope', in Nazila Ghanea and Alexandra Xanthaki (eds.), *Minorities, Peoples and Self-Determination—Essays in Honour of Patrick Thornberry* (Martinus Nijhoff Publishers, 2005)

Young, Iris M; 'Structural Injustice and the Politics of Difference', in T Christiano and J Christman (eds.), *Contemporary Debates in Political Philosophy* (Wiley-Blackwell, 2007)

Young, Iris M; 'Two concepts of self-determination', in Stephen May, Tariq Modood, and Judith Squires (eds.), *Ethnicity, Nationalism and Minority Rights* (Cambridge University Press, 2004)

Young, Iris M; 'Hybrid Democracy: Iroquois Federalism and the Postcolonial Project', in Duncan Ivison, Paul Patton, and Will Sanders (eds.), *Political Theory and the Rights of Indigenous Peoples* (Cambridge University Press, 2000)

Young, Iris M; 'Together in Difference: Transforming the Logic of Group Political Conflict', in Will Kymlicka (ed.), *The Rights of Minority Cultures* (Oxford University Press, 1995)
Yupsanis, Athanasios; 'ILO Convention No. 169 Concerning Indigenous and Tribal Peoples in Independent Countries 1989–2009: An Overview' [2010] *Nordic Journal of International Law* 79

Index